Earth Calling

Earth Calling

A Climate Change Handbook
for the 21st Century

Ellen Gunter and Ted Carter

FOREWORD BY Caroline Myss

North Atlantic Books
Berkeley, California

North Atlantic Books
P.O. Box 12327
Berkeley, California 94712

Cover photos: Nest © iStockphoto.com/malerapaso; Earth © iStockphoto.com
/jimmyjamesbond; Collage by Mary Ann Casler
Cover and book design by Mary Ann Casler
Printed in the United States of America

Earth Calling: A Climate Change Handbook for the 21st Century is sponsored by the Society for the Study of Native Arts and Sciences, a nonprofit educational corporation whose goals are to develop an educational and cross-cultural perspective linking various scientific, social, and artistic fields; to nurture a holistic view of arts, sciences, humanities, and healing; and to publish and distribute literature on the relationship of mind, body, and nature.

North Atlantic Books' publications are available through most bookstores. For further information, visit our website at www.northatlanticbooks.com or call 800–733–3000.

Library of Congress Cataloging-in-Publication Data
Gunter, Ellen, 1947-
Earth calling : a climate change handbook for the 21st century / Ellen Gunter and Ted Carter ; foreword by Caroline Myss.
     pages cm
Summary: "Nature - Environmental Conservation & Protection"—Provided by publisher. ISBN 978-1-58394-767-8 (pbk.) 1. Human ecology—Philosophy. 2. Environmental degradation. 3. Climate change—Social aspects. 4. Mind and body. I. Carter, Ted, 1956- II. Title.
GF21.G86 2014 304.2'5—dc23   2013034234

1 2 3 4 5 6 7 8 9 Malloy 18 17 16 15 14

Printed on 100% recycled paper

For Johnny,
called home first
—ELLEN GUNTER

For my life partner, Greg Bembry,
and my parents, Bob and Julie Carter
—TED CARTER

Contents

PART 2: WAKING UP

PART 3: YOUR EARTH CALLING

Foreword

If I could, I would make this book, *Earth Calling*, essential reading for every single person drawing a breath on this planet. There is not one living human being whose survival is not intimately woven into the exquisite ecological systems of this Earth, all of which are designed to support the whole of life. Let's face it, when it comes to the business of living, we human beings are takers. We have to learn how to be givers. We consider it a progression of our conscious awareness to come to the realization that we should not litter or pollute, though we are making meager progress on that front. We still think of recycling as an environmental advancement. Let's be honest—we are still living in a sort of haze about the environment crisis brewing in our atmosphere. It's sort of real, but not really real. A crisis that is represented through statistics and predictions can only inspire people to change so much, right?

Reports of melting ice sheets that will subsequently cause water levels in the oceans to rise—which, in turn, will cause the eventual disappearance of small islands and coastal cities—seem like the makings of a good Hollywood action film. Actually, Hollywood has made several films already capitalizing on the threat of ecological disasters, making them not more real for viewers but, sadly, more make believe. Meanwhile, as film watchers enjoy the fictitious presentation of the breakdown of Earth's ecological system, Al Gore continues to trumpet his powerful message, presenting some of the same scenarios being depicted in Hollywood films, only the possibilities and probabilities Gore speaks about are real. While Gore has acquired world-wide recognition and growing support for his relentless efforts to raise global awareness that the Earth's ecological system is in crisis now—right now—he is constantly derided by a largely skeptical public that still wants the facts delivered Hollywood style. And it has to be noted that among those skeptics are Earth's major power brokers—that is, those who would have to change their way of making wealth if they actually admitted that their "taker" lifestyle is contributing to the destruction of the life system of the planet. We've never had global crimes or global criminals before, but we do now.

The majority of the population, of course, still wants to simply believe that all this business about climate change and a multitude of environmental problems—from personal health to the destruction of our soil, our seeds, and our animals—is the stuff of good fiction and great films. I don't blame them. I'd love to live in that bubble, too. But I know far too much, and so does Ellen Gunter, who with great care and, I might add, with enormous personal anguish, devoted years of her life to writing a book with the intention of shattering personal bubbles.

I can't tell you how many times I called Ellen and asked, "How's the writing going today?" only to find her in a dark, sad place. Perhaps that day or that week she was organizing the data about air pollution in China, the latest oil industry scandal, a disappointing ruling from the EPA, or what GMOs are doing to our health. Every deep researcher of social, political, medical, or any truth experiences a particular type of exhaustion that comes from acquiring an overload of facts that so many people do not know, but should. With *Earth Calling*, Ellen has been able to pair that with an even deeper desire to find the right words that can inspire people to realize the significance of all that she has learned.

More importantly, Ellen understands that if enough readers actually "get" the urgency and power of her message, we can shift the direction of the Titanic. We don't have to hit the iceberg this time. We can each do our individual parts, and together we can weave an alternative to endless pollution, underwater water reserves being poisoned by fracked gas and oil, and corporations determining what vegetables you can plant or buy. The list is so long. And it's all in this book.

This book owes much to Ted Carter's understanding of how the Earth works and how it speaks to us in countless ways. He was a tireless source of wisdom, insight, and clarity, and his steady voice was a constant through this long birthing.

Ellen and Ted gave the book the title *Earth Calling*, and nothing could be more appropriate, as Earth is a living Being—granted, the largest living Being you will ever encounter—and it is calling each of us to fall back into alignment with the laws of nature. That call manifests through our intuition, through our organic knowing that something is not right with how the forces of life feel. We can all sense this in our bones and in our blood. We can feel the pain in the animal kingdom—admit it. We've grown more sensitive to the feelings of animals. We are all becoming "animal whisperers" now, whether we want to be that sensitive or not.

We are all awakening to the understanding that it's not okay to do nothing when you know something should be done. No more looking around like some sort of helpless ninny and saying, "Someone should do something!"

If someone said that to me now, I would hand that individual this book with these instructions: Read until you are fully inspired.

Don't worry; you will be.

Every one of us is living through a historic time, one of environmental and ecological transformation. Earth itself is a participant—indeed, the greatest participant of all. If she does not make it, none of us will. As human beings, as spiritual brothers and sisters, we have a calling to participate in this transformation of life that is unfolding before us—and within us. We have a calling to walk this beautiful

Earth together, to participate in our own and in the Earth's transition into a global human community. Perhaps none of us will live to see that, but we must all begin to walk together in that direction— it's where we are all being called.

Earth is calling. Of that I have no doubt.

Caroline Myss
Oak Park, Illinois
January 2014

Introduction

There is a Zen saying about becoming a pilgrim on a spiritual quest: "If you're not going to finish the journey, it's best you never start." Because there is no going back, no unscrambling of the egg. Making that commitment ignites a fire that alters the axis of your life's orbit. And when that axis shifts, it can begin as such a gentle touch that you don't have the slightest clue that your life has just taken a 180-degree turn.

Ted and I hatched the idea for this book during just such a gentle shift in the summer of 2007, when my husband and I were visiting him and other friends in Maine. We had often talked by phone well into the night about what was happening to the earth and what the two of us could possibly do in response. One day I joined him on a visit to some of the places he and his firm had done landscape design for. As I looked around at the stunning landscapes he had helped nurture, my understanding of how we can relate to the earth changed. I asked him to describe what he did in his work.

"I help create sacred spaces in people's homes and yards," he said, "and I teach clients how to see and hear how the earth speaks to them."

Ten years before that, such a declaration would have made me raise my eyebrows and roll my eyes; now it made perfect sense. My own lifelong spiritual questing had slowly shifted my "bandwidth," my capacity to see differently, and made room for a bigger truth. This, as Ted and I have learned, is the way the cosmos reveals itself, gently drawing you in one direction, then almost imperceptibly taking you someplace you had not imagined. That bigger truth became this book.

Until I met Ted, my idea of a landscaper was someone who threw plants into the ground in strategic places and sent you a bill. But what he did was profoundly different. Walking around some of the properties he had transformed just felt good. There was a magical sense to each space, a sort of aliveness in the air that turned up the senses. For him, working with the earth isn't a job, it's artistry, a calling—something he does with reverence and respect. To Ted, the earth is an extension of himself.

Here was common ground we shared. We had both grown up with a distinct reverence for the earth, a deep sense of wonder about its mystery and majesty. I had spent much of my childhood in Miami, Florida, in the mid-1950s. Violent weather patterns—particularly hurricanes—were a fact of life. A short time after a hurricane passed, the DDT trucks would drive through the neighborhoods, dousing them in thick clouds of insecticide to keep mosquitoes from hatching out of the pools that lay stagnant after a storm. All of us kids would go out and play in those foggy plumes, jumping on our bikes to follow along behind the spraying trucks. Nobody knew there was anything wrong with that then. In fact, old public service ads from those days show people sitting on the beach getting blasted with a cloud of DDT, and everyone acting as though it was as refreshing as bath powder. One ad showed a scientist demonstrating its benign nature by spraying it on his porridge—then eating it. No worries; that was the message.

The way we treat the earth did not seep into modern thinking until Rachel Carson began to educate us about pesticides like DDT in 1962 when her pivotal book *Silent Spring* was published. It forever altered my understanding of how the world worked. I was astounded, not only at the news it conveyed about the devastation being done to the planet and to all of the species that inhabit it, but also with how obvious it was, after the book's publication, that many of the people at the center of the controversy about pesticide use—government agencies, farmers, and particularly the chemical companies—wanted to keep things just as they were.

Nobody wanted to admit that anything was wrong, despite the overwhelming evidence Carson presented. I was stunned to find out that the government was doing such a poor job of protecting us, and I was appalled at the way Carson was subsequently demonized and characterized as unqualified, a scaremonger who wanted to erase all the progress made by American farmers since the end of the war. In fact, she was a highly esteemed biologist who had taught at Johns Hopkins and the University of Maryland and then became editor in chief of publications at the U.S. Department of Fish and Wildlife. Before *Silent Spring,* she had written two acclaimed best sellers about the biology of the sea.

She had criticized the regulatory agencies of the government for carrying water for corporations like Monsanto, the manufacturer of DDT, failing to warn the American public of the potential dangers and the unknown long-term effects that these chemicals would have on the earth and ultimately on us, our genes, and—as a result—our children. There was, she pointed out, no mechanism of accountability, no sense of responsibility, and seemingly no concern about the American public remaining out of the loop. She quoted French biologist and philosopher Jean Rostand, "The obligation to endure gives us the right to know." And she thought that we should do better than just endure.

As I was awakening to the horrors of the slow poisoning of our planet, Ted's parents were patiently ensuring that his education included an abiding respect for the earth. His mother fed the family from her extensive organic garden. She took turns with the neighbors working in co-ops, helping to unpack crates and wait on customers for a share of butter, eggs, and milk from local farms. Shared acts of community like this in the 1960s were nuances in the cracking open of the modern consciousness, the first whispers to us that the closer we stayed to our food sources, the better.

Eventually his mother's passion for good, safe, fresh food would inspire Ted's family to start a company that specialized in fresh fruit juices. Their line, called Fresh Samantha (named for Ted's niece), was a favorite on the U.S. East Coast in the 1990s. "Having parents who showed me how the earth works and how to work in the earth formed me. And it ignited my imagination. When I think of children today, I wonder how they learn to be at home outside in nature instead of inside the spaces that wall them off from those experiences."

In fact, the amount of time children spend outside the house in nature has steadily declined in the last thirty years. During that same time period, the number of hours children spend on a variety of high-tech devices has steadily risen in lockstep with the incidence of childhood obesity.

Richard Louv, whose pivotal book *Last Child in the Woods* looks squarely at a condition he calls "nature deficit disorder," says that this isn't good for the species as a whole, but it's especially harmful for children. Throughout human history and prehistory, he says, "children spent much if not most of their developing years either working or playing outside." In less than three decades, "we're seeing the diminishment and perhaps the disappearance of that."

According to Louv, there is a theory called the biophilia hypothesis that says that for all our modern technological savvy, at a biological level we are still hunters and gatherers. At some level we don't understand, he says, human beings need a direct connection to nature. "We need to see natural shapes in the horizon. And when we don't get that, we don't do so well."[1]

One of the goals of this book is to show the earth as something more than the raw materials we gather from it, to see it as the fount of life, what British research scientist James Lovelock called *Gaia*, a giant living organism. To be so disconnected from it as to have no sense of its presence everywhere in our lives is to lose one of the most primal balancing components of our bodies and spirits.

We live in an age of hyperconsumerism. The contents of our meals travel an average of 1,500 miles before reaching our plates. We take for granted the ability to make trips in an afternoon that would have required weeks of laborious, dangerous travel barely a century ago. We talk, play games, and text with people around the world on small, hyper-capable devices that didn't exist a decade ago. Some experts estimate that we consume more energy in five minutes than our cave-dwelling ancestors did in an entire year.

We used to be an agriculture-based culture. Now giant combines do the work our hands used to do. Technology has made the job of raising and transporting our food much more efficient. But this efficiency has come at a high cost: not only has it compromised and exhausted our soil and water resources, it has also polluted our air and land with staggering quantities of toxins and unknown change agents. Some experts believe it has disoriented, exhausted, and poisoned the very bees we count on to pollinate our food crops. The effect on our own bodies and DNA is, quite literally, unknown.

In an endless Möbius strip of cause and effect, this industrialization of farming has also made us lose touch with what we come from. We have become removed from the earth, blind and deaf to her cries. Today we live in a totally new paradigm, often many stories above the earth in a hermetically sealed room with no access to fresh air or any way to feel what is beneath our feet.

In 2005, the Dalai Lama spoke at a weekend conference on healing in Washington, DC. His topic was the growing convergence of science and spirituality, how practices like meditation naturally dovetail with healing. His Holiness referred to a graph that showed that as the U.S. Gross Domestic Product—the traditional way we measure our economic health—has risen in the last fifty years, it has been mirrored by a corresponding increase not only in depression but also in the use of the drugs that treat this ailment and the conditions related to it. In other words, as our consumption of goods has risen, our levels of contentment have headed in the other direction. As we devour more, we are not only *not* satisfied, we are more starved.

What the Dalai Lama talked about is rampant. We are in what

could be called a crisis of *un*consciousness. Today the United States, which manufactures most antidepressants, accounts for two-thirds of their prescriptions. Growing numbers of Americans find that smoothing the edges and staying unconscious—with one of the thirty different types of antidepressants on the market—is an ever-easier path. According to Charles Barber's book, *Comfortably Numb: How Psychiatry Is Medicating a Nation,* the number of prescriptions filled for antidepressants in the United States is rising steadily (from 227 million in 2006 to 264 million in 2011[2]), and although prescriptions for antidepressants used to be disseminated strictly by psychiatrists, it's increasingly true that family doctors, not mental health professionals, now routinely prescribe these drugs to patients.

That's not accidental. According to Barber, pharmaceutical companies spend roughly $25,000 per year *per doctor* tracking what each physician nationwide prescribes, a bit of data mining that helps Big Pharma maintain pinpoint precision on what the best markets are and how to better shape their messages.[3] Meanwhile, even though more and more of us are seeing just how dire the problems are, nobody seems to know how to get us out of the mess we have gotten ourselves into on our planet.

Rather than sleeping, it's time for us to awaken to the challenges, the promises, the responsibilities, and the exciting opportunities that await us. We not only have to wake up, we also have to open our eyes wide to what is happening to our planet, our country, our cities, our neighborhoods, and—inevitably—our bodies. One of the purposes of this book is to outline the steps to that awakening—through a somewhat different lens, one that not only acknowledges the problems we face as twenty-first century beings but also offers a new way of looking at the solutions they require.

Why? Because for all that's wrong, there is also much that's right. This companion truth—that we can undo this great harm we have all contributed to—is also part of our birthright as earthlings. Our real nature is to find a way to share and live in community, not just to compete. Andy Lipkis, president and founder of Tree People, a nonprofit that rescues and rebuilds decimated landscapes, says that research shows that T cell counts, the immune system boosters in our bodies, rise when people volunteer and help.

> *We are designed to reach out and lend a hand.*
> —ANDY LIPKIS

It is one of the legacies of being human. Helping is a creative act that creates a feedback loop. Creative energy is spiritual energy, and those energies feed the longing for connection to one another that plagues our hearts. It all goes back, as the Dalai Lama suggests, to our starving hearts.

Want proof? Point to yourself. Seriously, take a moment and do this physically. Did you point to your stomach? Your head? Probably not. Most people point to their chests, the homestead of the heart. We all know where we live. And *Earth Calling* is all about how to excavate your way back to that vital core of your being.

This distancing is not just physical, because we are more than mere bodies. We are also spiritual beings, energy beings, with aspects that are invisible but quite real. Anyone who has ever studied a martial art or been treated with acupuncture knows about the energy meridians in the body, how heat can be concentrated and drawn through the body, focused for healing or even combat.

Before Caroline Myss wrote the pivotal book *Sacred Contracts,* which drew Ted and me to her great body of work, she wrote about the body's energy systems, called *chakras,* in her book *Anatomy of the Spirit.* These seven energy centers were first identified and explained by the mystics of India; Myss describes them metaphorically as little revolving hard drives, loaded with memories and purpose. The chakras run along the spine to the top of the skull. The lower three are in the area from the tailbone to the solar plexus. They deal with our survival needs: acquiring food, drink, shelter, protection—material things—solidifying our connection with family and earthly roots. The upper three, from the throat to the crown of the head, regulate the needs of our minds and spirits: choice, speech, logic, reason, intuition, connection, meaning, destiny. The fourth, between the solar plexus and the throat, mediates the upper and lower chakras and is the seat of emotion. It is called the heart chakra.

Symbolically speaking, we could say that today, while our lower three chakras are devouring (obesity is at epidemic levels), our upper three are starving (ditto depression and a sense of hopelessness). Our heart's task is to find the happy medium so that our upper and lower energy systems can be congruent. It's a monumental task for our stressed-out, overworked hearts. Notice how many television commercials feature medications aimed at treating heart disease, high blood pressure, and high cholesterol. The pharmaceutical companies know what ails us, even if we don't.

The template of the body's seven chakras illustrates the wisdom of our own unraveling, how we have much to learn from what our own bodies are telling us—if we will only listen. There is healing in that listening and in that effort to reconnect ourselves to the global life force we are all a part of. Reestablishing a connection to the earth reunites us to our hearts. Working with the earth is intrinsically healing and heart based.

Earth is at the center of our existence; we are born from her and return to her at the end of our lives. She connects us as human beings—like one body with over seven billion movable but integrated parts. What happens to the earth happens to us—we are not separate from her, and we are not separate from one another. Once we begin to see that, the way we look at our own lives can shift, opening a whole new world of possibility to each of us.

Our first chakra is the one closest to the earth when we sit on the ground. Our seventh resides at the top of the skull. A break in the first chakra means that there can be no congruence for the whole, no feedback loop for the system. Because of the broken connection in our first chakra and the wounding and disconnection of our fourth, the heart chakra, people are starving for connection and for meaning.

Anyone who turns on the television for five minutes or scans the titles of books, magazine covers, or internet blogs knows the truth. Something has to change, and it has to happen quickly. It's time for us to awaken from our stupor and acknowledge that waiting for someone else to step up and make the first move isn't the answer. The people we've been waiting for are already here. It's us—concerned citizens, neighbors, fathers, mothers, siblings, professionals, the young, and the wisdom holders.

You know—earthlings.

Ted once reminded me of a trip he had made to visit a Yaqui shaman friend of ours named Lench Archuleta, with whom he had studied nature and earth spirituality in the Arizona desert. "One afternoon we sat on a bluff overlooking what appeared to be a distant dust storm. It wasn't. The bulldozers cutting deep swaths were making space for yet another new subdivision. As we watched, Lench told me his tribe has a name for us. They call us *termite people,* because we are eating the earth's flesh. And by doing that, we are literally eating our future, our world. It is, he said, a form of madness, of suicide."

We are guests on Planet Earth. Most of us learn as children to be respectful of the places we visit, to leave them clean, as we would hope others would do for us: a sort of golden rule of earthly manners. We have not been worthy of our host. In fact, we've been very poor stewards, misbehaving on a horrendous scale, so much so that we have changed the planet's very chemistry, altering its biosystems, its topography, even its geological structure.[4]

In an age when truth is at a premium and most members of the media are too frightened to offend their sponsors or owners, it is incumbent upon us as citizens to investigate and broadcast the truth. Just as most of the people who fought for our independence from Great Britain were citizen soldiers, today's leaders in the movement to save the earth for future generations take their authority from the right to breathe clean air and eat uncontaminated and available food. At an award ceremony in 2008 in which ordinary citizens were being acknowledged for their work in truth telling, the award-winning journalist Bill Moyers said that "the most important credential of all is a conscience that cannot be purchased or silenced."[5]

Understanding the depth and scope of the ecological crises

before us is not easy. If we are to understand the issues swirling around us—from global warming and climate change[6] to skyrocketing resource costs, to the state of our soil and seed, to disappearing water resources, to food riots around the world—we have to understand that they derive from one simple but telling truth. We have numbed ourselves to what is happening around us. On some level, we sense what we are losing—that most basic connection to the earth that is an ancestral birthright of our species. And it is a loss that must be healed.

In the many decades since Rachel Carson first shocked the world with the realities of the killing power of toxic pesticides like DDT, the environmental movement has been missing a key ingredient—a spiritual sensibility. As Rabbi Michael Lerner says, "The environmental movement can't just teach about the scientific facts; it has to also teach about a new spiritual vision."[7] It is not possible to see a complete picture of what is happening to us and the earth we all share without examining it through a lens of spiritual consciousness.

That vision Rabbi Lerner is talking about is creating what would have previously been seen as unlikely alliances. Nobel laureate and director of the Center for Health and the Global Environment at Harvard Medical School, Dr. Eric Chivian, met for lunch one day in 2005 with Rev. Richard Cizik, a leader of the National Association of Evangelicals, to discuss their shared concern for the growing human impact on the earth's resources. Together they formed the Scientists and Evangelicals Initiative. "Whether you believe God created life on earth, or that it evolved over billions of years, it doesn't matter. We all feel that life, however it came to be, is sacred," says Chivian, "And it is our shared duty to protect it."[8] In May 2008 the environmental movement's odd couple was named to *Time* magazine's list of the one hundred most influential people.

> *We have created a Star Wars civiliation, with Stone Age emotions, medieval institutions, and god-like technology.*
> —E. O. WILSON[9]

Earth Calling is not a diatribe against technology, nor is it a call to go back to the ways of eighteenth-century farmers. Rather, it is an examination of what is happening in our world and how we can fix it, collectively and individually, by reconnecting with the earth that nurtures us on a spiritual—not just a physical—level.

When *Silent Spring* exposed the widespread and growing use of chemical pesticides and fertilizers and its attendant dangers, Rachel Carson was describing an unfolding national health crisis. Now we face that crisis on a much grander, planetary scale, with a much larger cast of characters, part of a drama called "global warming" and "climate change," in which humanity has a starring role—a modern tale of our indifference and neglect—and the consequences of our separation from the earth. We stand, half a century after *Silent Spring*, in the future Carson warned us about, asking the same questions, wondering why the accountability is still lacking from the same institutions that went to such lengths to undermine her dire warnings—the government, the fossil fuel and chemical industries, and the conventional agriculture community—when the consequences of our inaction have never been more obvious or dispiriting.

But this time we know something we did not know then—that saving our planet and ourselves is up to us. *Earth Calling* was written to mark the moment in time between what we have been and what we are becoming. It is our hope it will awaken a sense of urgency in you and help point you toward meaningful action, not just as a consumer, but as an earthling with an open heart who can hear the call of your spirit. For Ted and me, writing this book became our earth calling. What are you being called to do?

Tread softly. All the earth is holy ground.
—Christina Rossetti

Part 1

We Snooze. We Lose.

The fault, dear Brutus, lies not in our stars, but in ourselves.
—*Julius Caesar*, Act 1, Scene 2

Chapter 1

Understanding What We're Made Of

Everything alive pulsates with energy and all of this energy contains information.

—CAROLINE MYSS, *Anatomy of the Spirit*

We are energy beings. If we trace our history from some of our most recognizable starting points—from the Big Bang theory and the Bible's description of the birth of light on earth to the age of nuclear energy and the silent power of the internet, it is clear that our epoch as humans has an energetic framework.

When it comes to analyzing and coping with our world, our brains defy description and understanding. Paired with our hearts, they are the dynamic duo—with often opposing agendas—that we rely on to resolve our most familiar dilemmas. Thinking and feeling, hearts and minds, the above and below of us: they are our sources of power and mystery. No one can really explain why a heart starts beating and goes on for decades or how a brain finds a cure for a disease, much less how it knows to warn us that someone is untrustworthy or why it finds solace in prayer. These are our mysteries. They are ideas that are too big to be described with words. That's why we resort to the symbolic language of literature and art to explain them to ourselves. As each generation passes into the next, we leave our best efforts in our wake, like a trail of breadcrumbs, hoping someone along time's path can decipher what we could not.

What is happening to our planet and to our selves—our external and internal worlds—cannot be explained or healed with data or warnings alone. So this book does not resort simply to statistics, pleadings for common sense, or threats of extinction. The scope and gravity of what is going on with our earth requires a deeper context, a more tender and three-dimensional picture, one that appeals not just to our hearts and minds but also to our very souls. It calls for a perspective that is not often combined with information on the environment.

Rather than looking at the crises we face as issues on a to-do list, we need to see beneath the words to the real messages trying to get through to us. We as a culture are unmatched at assembling facts and events into a mosaic of a condition-at-large and taking it on with hard work and a can-do attitude. We have giant hearts and giving and compassionate natures. Why isn't this enough to motivate us to look more deeply, to make sense of this, and to demand change of our leaders and ourselves?

To begin to answer this, we need to understand how different this challenge is from anything we have ever faced before. We need to see this as a call to our spirits to awaken and look at the earth and our relationship to her differently. And we need to understand where things have come apart, where we are broken, and why and how we can fix ourselves, each other, and the conditions that are harming our planet.

We must add a spiritual lens to our eyes and then look inside as well as outside—not just at the material, intellectual, and emotional worlds, but at our spiritual insides too. While the ability to reason got us out of the Dark Ages and into the Age of Enlightenment, the mere copious application of that genius to invention, technology, speed, wealth, and sheer determination cannot heal us. Reconnecting to the earth also reconnects us to our spirits and a fuller recognition of what life is meant to be about. And that is the beginning of how we determine what each of us is being called to do. Finding your own earth calling requires that you wake up your conscience as well as your consciousness, so you can begin to see and hear more deeply than you ever have before.

A Stroke of Good Fortune

It's common knowledge that we use our left brains to understand the data and sensations that come at us and the right brain to intuit their symbolic importance. The scientist James Lovelock likens our left-brain genius and the computers and modes of communication it created to the nervous system of the earth's body, connecting us as an energetic whole. As with a computer, sometimes your software needs updating, but if you're disconnected, as so many of us are these days, with our full schedules and stressed-out lives, no downloads can get through. When that happens, it occasionally requires a timely lightning bolt to bypass those disconnections.

That's what happened to neuroanatomist Dr. Jill Bolte Taylor when she had a stroke at the age of thirty-seven. Her stroke opened a window on life that she could not have seen any other way. Taylor had decided early on to devote her career to understanding her brother's schizophrenia, why his circuitry ended up in delusions while her brain is able to give her the life she wanted, so she studied brain circuitry at the Harvard Department of Psychiatry, learning how differently brains communicated at the cellular and chemical levels. She and her colleagues were, as she would later explain, "mapping the micro-circuitry of the brain." Her life was rolling along, seemingly full of meaning and direction.

On a December morning in 1996 she awoke with a pain behind her left eye. She ignored it and began her morning ritual of a workout and shower. Within minutes, she realized something was wrong. Her limbs did not look right to her and, as she walked to the shower, she realized her mental processes had slowed. She had the peculiar sensation that she was outside of herself watching what was going on inside. But still she ignored it. She was way too busy to admit what her instincts were trying to telegraph to her, as her left brain efficiently kept her locked into her morning routine. There were all those to-do lists to complete.

In the shower she lost her balance and, as she propped herself against the wall, she realized she could not tell where her hand ended and where the wall began. The whole thing was just one big field of molecules. Everything had melded into a single pulsating field of energy. At that moment, her left hemisphere went offline, and with the brain chatter off, she experienced what many have sought but few Westerners have achieved: a silent brain. Rather than finding herself listening to the usual inner prattle centered on job stresses, the endless lists of the tasks of everyday life, or the emotional baggage she had accumulated over her lifetime, she found something else: euphoria.

As she made her way out of the shower, her right arm became paralyzed, and in that instant, alarms went off: she was having a stroke in the left hemisphere of her brain. At the same time, the pragmatic, functioning scientist in her was delighted: "How many brain scientists get to follow the process of a stroke from the inside out?"

Just as a loose connection can make a light sputter and flicker, her left brain would periodically come back "on," and using these moments, she slowly made her way to her desk and devised a method for calling for help.

From the stroke's onset, it would be four hours before she could negotiate an SOS. During those hours, she was able to witness the slow disintegration of her ability to rely on reason for survival. Curled into a fetal position during the ambulance ride to the hospital, she thought she would die and said goodbye to her life. She remembered floating expansively in a space that was definitely outside of what she now saw was her very tiny body. She called it Nirvana. When she realized that she wasn't dead after all and became suddenly aware not only that was she still experiencing this Nirvana but that everyone could experience it, a clarity came over her. "I realized what a tremendous gift this experience could be, what a stroke of insight this could be to how we live our lives. And it motivated me to recover."

Surgery to remove the golf ball–sized blood clot from the left side of her brain would save her. It would take her eight years to fully recover. What she discovered in those first moments—standing in her shower, watching herself merge with all matter—was key: that if this was true for her, it could be true for anyone at any time. This is a place each of us can choose to visit. It's ready and waiting. Nobody has to have a stroke to get there.

Twelve years after her stroke, Taylor described what happened to her in a hugely popular TED lecture.[1] Holding a bisected brain in her hands, she talked about how the two sides of the brain think and care about very different things and how they process information differently.

"Our right hemisphere is all about this present moment. It's all about right here, right now. It thinks in pictures and learns kinesthetically through the movement of our bodies. Information in the form of energy streams in simultaneously through all of our sensory systems. And then it explodes into this enormous collage of what this present moment looks like, smells like, and tastes like, what it feels like and what it sounds like. . . . We are energy beings connected to one another through the consciousness of our right hemispheres as one human family. And right here, right now, we are all brothers and sisters on this planet, here to make the world a better place. And in this moment we are perfect. We are whole. And we are beautiful."

The left hemisphere, on the other hand, she said, is designed to think in language and take the right hemisphere's messy wisdom and organize it. "It's that ongoing brain chatter that connects me and my internal world to my external world. It's that calculating intelligence that reminds me when I have to do my laundry. But perhaps most important, as soon as my left hemisphere says to me 'I am, I am,' I become separate. I become a single, solid individual separate from the energy flow around me and separate from you.

"Right here, right now, I can step into the consciousness of my right hemisphere, where we are—I am—the life force power of the universe, and the life force power of the fifty trillion beautiful molecular geniuses that make up my form. At one with all that is. Or I can choose to step into the consciousness of my left hemisphere, where I become a single individual, a solid, separate from the flow, separate from you. These are the 'we' inside of me."

For Taylor, the slow stroke she endured enabled her to shut down her logical left brain to harvest the insights and soul-connectedness of her right side. In losing her balance in the shower and then seeing herself as an energy being, seamlessly connected to all other beings and to the source of life itself, she regained a much more important balance, and it changed her life.

This is so often the way the universe reveals its secrets. Using her brilliant left brain, Jill Taylor went looking for ways to understand how to connect with her brother's thinking process. What she found instead was how her equally brilliant right brain was waiting for her with the gift of a lifetime, a key to how we can all learn to connect with each other and see the magnificence of what we are all a part of.

We are living in times that are moving too fast for us to see clearly if our rational minds are all we rely on. In almost no time at all on the cosmic clock, we have spun out of a place we can understand in a meaningful physical or emotional context. "The Internet consists of a quintillion transistors, a trillion links and a million emails per second."[2] A quintillion is a one followed by twenty-four zeroes. (To put that in perspective, a billion has nine zeroes.) If it took you two seconds to read that last quoted sentence, just think how much transpired in that tiny space of time. Now add this: in a single second, our bodies have blown through ten times more processes than there are stars in the universe.[3]

The point is that, like Jill Taylor, we have to open ourselves to see everything differently. What our right brains are trying to tell us is that we can no longer live just as analytical thinkers. We have to see our own hands on the shower wall, how we and what's outside of us are one. We have to try seeing what our left brains would tell us is not there, because our right brains know otherwise.

Luckily, we are built to do just that.

Our Spiritual Skeleton

In 1996 Caroline Myss wrote a best-selling book called *Anatomy of the Spirit*, which explains that we not only have a physical skeleton but also a spiritual skeleton whose existence is easily confirmed by the basic tenets of Christian, Judaic, Hindu, and Buddhist thought. As a medical intuitive, Myss also speaks authoritatively about how our actions, thoughts, and belief systems not only impact our physical and emotional selves but also create a direct feedback loop with our spiritual lives.

"The universal jewel within the four major religions is that the Divine is locked into our biological system in seven stages of power that lead us to become more refined and transcendent in our personal power."[4] Presenting a modern reinterpretation of the ancient theories of the seven chakras, Myss describes these power centers as an "energy spinal cord through which the life force, or prana, flows into our physical body."[5] Together they make what could be called the framework of our spiritual anatomy.

Via those energy centers, our spines serve as conductors of energetic impulses and data. Learning the vocabulary of the chakras helps clarify that our physical, mental, and spiritual bodies not only are *not* separate entities but, together, actually speak a mutually reinforcing language.

If you have ever been treated with acupuncture or studied yoga, tai chi chuan, or chi gong, you have probably heard some of this vocabulary, and perhaps you felt the rush of heat, power, and even calm that coincides with your energy centers being lined up or cleared. Arranged vertically along our spines from our tailbones to the top of our heads, these centers, while they have no material form, carry very real packets of data about us. Myss encourages us to envision them as separate little whirring hard drives of energetic and biological information that work in tandem. What registers in one chakra registers in all, speaking to us in the language of the spirit, with a unique chakra-specific message.

Each chakra can be matched with specific body parts and emotional states of being. Each also honors a unique spiritual challenge. And each has emotional and spiritual lessons that are always connected to some version of waking up our consciousness. If we ignore those lessons, we can often see the results in our bodies, in the form of unrest, stress, or illness. Conversely, if we understand that illness can be a call to spiritual awakening, we can begin to heal ourselves by honoring the lessons the chakras lay out for us, whether they are about ridding ourselves of guilt, blame, or victimhood, standing up for ourselves; being honest about where we sabotage our relationships, opening up our creativity—or finding the calling that feeds our lives.

Understanding how the chakras work gives us a vast new set of tools that we can use to seek solutions to our problems. Because these teachings cross religious and cultural boundaries, they can work globally. Although this chapter deals primarily with the first chakra, what affects it affects the other six, so it helps to understand how all seven work as a whole. The following table explains where the chakra energy centers reside in the body and names each chakra's corresponding emotional and spiritual lessons.

Table 1. The chakras: their locations, issues, and lessons[6]

Chakra	Physical location	Body organs, related conditions	Emotional strengths and challenges	Spiritual lesson
7	Top of skull; the soft spot at birth	Skin, skeletal, and muscular systems. Energetic disorders, mystical depression (the dark night of the soul), heightened sensitivities to light; sound; pollutants in food, air, water, and soil; other environmental factors.	Intuition, doorway to divine, faith, spirituality. Ability to trust life and see larger pattern. Values, ethics, courage, selflessness, inspiration, devotion. Realm of visionaries and humanitarians. "Thy will be done." and "I have a dream."	Our connection to heaven. Transformative experiences; spontaneous healings, mystical compassion; development of a spiritual backbone, ability to surrender to Divine. Your container for grace.

Chakra	Physical location	Body organs, related conditions	Emotional strengths and challenges	Spiritual lesson
6	Area above and below eyes	Brain, eyes, nose, ears, pineal and pituitary glands, nervous system. Brain tumor, hemorrhage, stroke, blindness, deafness, spinal problems, learning disabilities, seizures.	Mind, intellect, intuition. Truth, self-evaluation, feelings of adequacy, attitudes, beliefs, openness to ideas of others, emotional intelligence. Realm of inventors and philosophers. "I think, therefore I am." and "Trust the force, Luke."	Spiritual wisdom and maturity. Comfortable with inner power.
5	Throat and mouth	Throat, thyroid, teeth, mouth, gums, trachea, neck vertebrae, esophagus, parathyroid, hypothalamus. Chronic sore or raspy throat, mouth ulcers, temporomandibular joint disorders, scoliosis, laryngitis, swollen glands, thyroid problems.	Choice, addiction, truth, will, regrets, passage of lies and deceit, judgment and criticism, faith and knowledge, following one's dream, capacity to make decisions. The place where desires of heart meet with wisdom of mind. "I swear to tell the truth, the whole truth, and nothing but the truth." and "My name is Bill and I'm an alcoholic."	Healing of addictions; standing in authentic self; truth. Choice through enlightened self-knowledge.

Chakra	Physical location	Body organs, related conditions	Emotional strengths and challenges	Spiritual lesson
4	Heart area	Heart and lungs, circulatory system, shoulders and arms, ribs, breasts, thymus gland. Congestive heart failure or heart attack, mitral valve prolapse, asthma or allergies, lung or breast cancer, upper back, shoulder issues, bronchial pneumonia, high blood pressure, depression.	Love, forgiveness, compassion, hatred, resentment, vengeance, grief, anger, loneliness, commitment, hope and trust. Realm of poets, mystical expression. "How do I love thee? Let me count the ways." and "I'll get even with you if it's the last thing I ever do."	Not compromising emotional well-being. Transcending self for others, doorway to soul.
3	Waist (gut)	Upper intestines, stomach, liver, gallbladder, kidney, pancreas, adrenal glands, spleen, middle spine. Arthritis, ulcers, colon or intestinal problems, indigestion, anorexia, bulimia, obesity, liver or adrenal dysfunction, diabetes, pancreatitis.	Ego, personality, self-esteem, need for applause, integrity, shame, pride, arrogance, dignity, fear of humiliation, gut instinct, personal power and identity, self-empowerment. Honor code formed here. "You'll never amount to anything." and "You're the best thing that ever happened to me."	Empowering others. Humility, liberated from arrogance. Not dependent on opinions of others.

Chakra	Physical location	Body organs, related conditions	Emotional strengths and challenges	Spiritual lesson
2	Genitalia, lower hips	Sex organs, large intestine, lower vertebrae, hip area, pelvis, appendix, bladder. Chronic pelvic or lower back pain, ob/gyn issues, sexual impotency, urinary problems.	Sexuality, job, physical desire, competition, power, creativity, money, seat of betrayal, partnerships, "weapons room." "Want to race to the corner?" and "I made him an offer he couldn't refuse."	Having creative, physical, financial resilience. Living in integrity and intentionality.
1	Tip of tailbone, root chakra	Legs, bones, base of spine, feet, rectum, physical body support, immune system, sense of smell, connection to earth. Chronic lower back pain, sciatica, varicose veins, rectal tumors or cancer, depression, immune system disorders.	Material world. Rootedness and feeling at home; family first, groups, tribes, gangs, organizations, religions, political parties, values, beliefs, superstitions, entitlement, genetic inheritance, sense of home, fight or flight. Filter of every transaction. "My country 'tis of thee." and "We're number one."	Honoring root connection to earth; leaving the tribe to individuate and expand and strengthen its wisdom; connecting to global consciousness. All is One.

Why the First Chakra Is Important

The first chakra, the seat of our rootedness, drives everything in our lives. It is the filter of every transaction, the gateway to the rest of the chakras. It tells us whether we fight, flee, or relax when someone approaches. It tells us whom to trust and when we're safe. It also tells us when we are in danger. It's no accident that the sense of smell is tied to this chakra. In the millennia before fire departments, civil defense warning horns, and the Weather Channel, we had to be more alert to smell approaching fires and to sense changes in weather.

Physically, the first chakra is our structure, foundation, and elimination system—bones, tendons, ligaments, skin, feet, and rectum. It's also home to our immune system, our social connections (tribe, family, home, country, the earth), and our emotional connections (personal and family security—knowing whether to flee or fight— and our mental health). At the first chakra, all of these connections merge with our primary connection to the earth itself. When that connection is broken, we are out of balance at a very basic level of survival, safety, and sanity. We do not know who we are as humans. We are unconscious. The truth of this chakra, says Myss, is "All is One." This is reflected in the Christian sacrament of baptism that blesses the newborn (Catholicism) or the one reborn into belief in Christ (Protestantism), and it is reflected in Shekinah in Judaism, which is "symbolic of the mystical community of humanity."[7]

Because it's part of our spiritual architecture, it's always there for us to connect to. It's part of our fiber and fabric. It's what Jill Taylor experienced—not just as a mental exercise, but as a physical fact—as she stood in her shower, watching it unfold before her eyes. For her soul, those precious moments of clarity were the equivalent of what Galileo saw that moment he first realized (like Copernicus before him) that the sun, not the earth, is at the center of the universe. It's not us at the center of the giant wheel of creation we all belong to, but God.

Our chakras always point the way for us, like signals to watch and listen for. Understanding how they work helps us make sense of the mysteries in our lives. Our first chakra ties us to the earth, to nature. As chapter 4 describes in more detail, we used to be closer to the land for all our needs. That passed with the coming of the Industrial Age, when our urban and suburban areas began to fill and sprawl, with much of our remaining rural areas put under the knife of giant corporate agrifarms. As we live increasingly busy and distracted lives, detached both from the source of the food we eat and the land that nourishes us, we have become numbed to the havoc being wreaked on our planet and the illness that is slowly suffocating her—and us.

This is how our broken first chakra affects us and plays out in the environmental crises we find ourselves surrounded by. The issue is not that we must race to fix the world to save it. If the world burns up in a global warming skillet and we all perish, the earth will recover quite nicely. It doesn't need us, as Alan Weisman points out so chillingly in *The World Without Us*. Rather, we need the earth. What must change is us and the way we view and honor the planet we live on. "It is the world view we are trying to heal, not the world."[8]

To heal that view, we have to heal our broken connection to the earth.

The Earth Is an Energy Being Too

Just as we have a two-sided brain, we have the capacity to speak to and listen to two worlds simultaneously. Our inner worlds are constantly receiving messages through all sorts of signs: synchronicities, chance meetings, coincidences—all the components leading up to the "aha" moments that finally illuminate us. As Wendell Berry said, "We receive more information from the environment than ever enters the limelight of our conscious awareness."[9]

Our lives break down when we try to give our outer worlds more authority over us than our inner worlds. We all know people who spend their lives in jobs they hate or in relationships that no longer work, because they cannot see past their fears of what might happen if they left.

Just as we have to look at our own physical and spiritual energy, we have to begin to look at the earth's energy in a different way too. This is where understanding a bit of how other people view the world can help us Westerners look at ourselves in a new way. In Ang Lee's first film, *Pushing Hands*, he gives Westerners insight into just how this energy can work. Retired tai chi master Chu leaves Taiwan to come to New York to live with his son and daughter-in-law. He ends up as a humble dishwasher at a Chinese restaurant, where, at the film's end, a cultural collision pits the small, seventy-year-old master against more than a dozen assailants whose goal is to remove him from the restaurant by force. Pushing, pulling, lifting, shoving, even throwing their bodies against him en masse cannot budge him; he is immovable. While this amounts to an entertaining scene, it depicts an absolute truth. A person who is rooted in his or her first chakra earth energy is immovable beyond rational explanation. Equally true, when you are *un*rooted, you are powerless. That's what it means to be disconnected, to be separate from the earth's energy.

We are living in an age when we have to acknowledge and embrace unseen power and wisdom such as this in order to retrain our minds to take in information we have sensed but never articulated before. Information about the chakras has been traced to Hindu writings from more than two thousand years ago. Today their names and locations are a common part of the vocabulary of exercise classes that stress the alignment of breath and movement. Understanding the way the human energy anatomy works is one way to see how our inner and outer worlds relate together as body, mind, and spirit, because the chakras have not only physical aspects but emotional and spiritual aspects as well.

They take the form of the powerful hits we feel when we lock onto something connected to our spirits and souls, those moments of clarity: when we jerk at an insight uncovered in a therapist's office, when a friend reveals a truth in anguished confidence, when we hear in our meditations or see in a film or read in a book something that speaks to us. It's that something that "hits a nerve," when an undeniable truth suddenly drops down into our consciousness and reveals itself. We react almost instinctively, physically jarred from the buzz. This too is part of our spiritual natures. It is through this vortex of energy, this swirling tunnel of light and storm, that we con-nect to our potential as humans, and these experiences are very real and tangible steps in our soul's journey. They are the often palpable little hits to our very conscious sixth-chakra selves, the exchange of information between the intuitive, spirit-connected right brain and the rational, linear left brain. This is where those thoughts and insights must invariably find purchase, fertile soil, where the left brain accepts them, rolls them over, and, using right-brain intel-ligence and imagination, transforms them into language.

This is another reason why connecting to the land is so critical. Sitting on the energy of the earth, we can receive healing signals too. Think of the way nature calms you. The next time you are able, go find a quiet place outside. Sit down and close your eyes. Sooner or later you will sigh. This is your rational side letting down the bridge to your interior by breathing in a surge of breath, what Hindus call *prana*. This is how we can plug in, become more whole, become one, in touch with our natures, with nature itself.

The energy of the earth has always called to people. There are rea-sons why sacred places like the pyramids, Stonehenge, the statues of Easter Island, the cathedral at Lourdes, Machu Picchu, Medjugorje, the Temple of Heaven in Beijing, Delphi, and countless others exist where they do, and why, as feng shui master Bob Longacre says, for millennia building projects began with a sacred ceremony to recog-nize and honor what was being birthed and given a home in this new construction. They possess a unique spiritual energy that called to their builders: this is the spot. And they still call to the pilgrims who visit them every day.

Our Common Immune System

The earth has an immune system every bit as real as our own. And we are connected to it by every element in our environment. That means, quite simply, that what happens to the earth happens to us.

As we toxify it, we are ourselves poisoned. The way we treat one another is also mirrored in the way we treat the earth.

What is happening to the earth is damaging its immune system in every aspect—air, water, soil, food, and beauty—from the ground beneath our feet to the polluted skies that block the stars above us. As chapter 2 shows, if we open our eyes, we can see the consequences of our disconnection from what is happening to all of us. As we sit in our heated and air-conditioned homes with stocked refrigerators and hundreds of television channels to keep our minds distracted, if we don't look too closely, the outside world may seem normal enough, but at a deeper level, we know better.

What an immune system does is usually described in the military language of invading viruses and medicines that can fight off and overwhelm any infection, but environmentalist and author Paul Hawken suggests that the earth's immune system is designed as a response to a need rather than a call to battle. "The ultimate purpose of a global immune system," he says, "is to identify what is not life affirming and to contain, neutralize, or eliminate it."[10]

Hawken says, "Because a lot of people know we are sick and want to treat the cause, not just the symptoms, the environmental movement can be seen as humanity's response to contagious policies killing the earth, while the social justice movement addresses economic and legislative pathogens that destroy families, bodies, cultures and communities. They are two sides of the same coin because when you harm one, you harm the other."[11]

In *The Botany of Desire,* Michael Pollan asks if we choose to admire the flower—or is it that the flower makes itself so irresistible that we are seduced into looking at it and perhaps eating it or planting it in our garden to help it perpetuate its species? Hawken asks the same question on a larger scale: are we motivating ourselves or are all the non-government organizations (NGOs) popping up all over the globe (he estimates there may be as many as two million of them worldwide) actually a part of the earth's attempt to get us moving before it's too late? If we are part of the earth, isn't it possible that we are behaving the same way we would if our brains were having a stroke, and, like Jill Taylor, we were getting a warning shot over the bow in time to save ourselves and, along the way, help us appreciate the universe we are a part of? If so, it is just as feasible that at this juncture we are sharing the earth's sense of danger and acting as cocreators of mutual healing of our common immune system.

Nature as the Cure to Our Disconnection

According to Paul Devereux, what's required is a reinstatement of an "ancient sense of our relationship with nature." He posits that in an ecopsychological sense, it's the mind that needs healing, and modern mentors and therapists use nature to accomplish that, reflecting a nod to old times. "Traditional and archaic peoples actually saw the world in animistic terms."[12]

Yaqui shaman Lench Archuleta, for example, takes clients into the Arizona desert to "get their spirits back," stressing quiet, contemplation, and time spent alone in nature. "One of the first things I do is make people take their shoes off and wiggle their toes in the earth. They've lost that connection to Mother Earth and they need to get it back. It usually takes them a day or two to detox from the stress they left behind. Once they get used to the quiet, things begin to open up in them. They become alert in ways they did not know they could be. That's because being in nature gently forces you to use your five senses."[13]

It's a simple thing—to take your shoes off—but it's also very powerful. It makes you keenly aware of how different the earth feels on your skin. We walk on the earth all the time without having any sense of its texture and temperature. As you walk around, he encourages you to name what you see. Naming things is another small but powerful act. When you name something, you have to look at it and acknowledge its existence. Naming objects is one of the first lessons we teach our children. It's how we connect them to their world, how they identify its component parts and grow familiar with their surroundings. It gives them a sense of home.

It's the same with nature. The problem is that our disconnection from nature is a manifestation of our blindness to what we are doing to it. As Rachel Carson said, humanity's war against nature "is inevitably a war against himself." When *Silent Spring* was published, in 1962, the chemical companies making the pesticides (mostly DDT) used a spokesman, a scientist named Dr. Robert White-Stevens, to destroy Carson's credibility. His main weapon was fear, saying that if we couldn't control pests in the fields, we would "return to the dark ages," and within a few years Americans would be spending most of their income on food.

"Miss Carson maintains that the balance of nature is a major force in the survival of man," White-Stevens said, "whereas the modern scientist believes that man is steadily controlling nature."[14] The hubris in that statement betrays how we got to this point in the first place—by believing that our intellects are the only worthy guides. But it was and is a point of view that works for the best interests of those who benefit most from an absence of dissent. C. S. Lewis once noted, "What we call Man's power over Nature turns out to be a power exercised by some men over other men with Nature as its instrument."

"We *are* nature," says Hawken. "We live in community, not alone, and any sense of separateness that we harbor is illusion."[15] Awakening to this lack of separateness offers us a chance to stretch ourselves, to expand beyond our egos. "Through nature, the species is introduced to transcendence, in the sense that there is something more going on than the individual. Most people are either awakened to or strengthened in their spiritual journey by experiences in the natural world."[16]

Sadly, many studies indicate that in the last fifty years, and especially the last twenty, the practice of encouraging children to spend time in nature has declined tremendously. One of the painful results is that children recognize the component parts of nature less and less. The discouragement of natural play stems from several sources. In *Last Child in the Woods*, Richard Louv explains that there are many causes: a marked increase in the amount of television children watch each day, the rise in personal computer and internet usage, the increase in organized play versus unsupervised play and the huge popularity of video games, tablets, and smart phones.

Shrinking green spaces and the preponderance of lawsuits now make playing outside a high-cost risk, but even the pervasive use of air-conditioning is part of the problem. The end result is the same. Children as well as adults have less and less of an understanding of what nature is all about. Not knowing nature's vocabulary limits our understanding of our place in it. It also limits its preciousness to us. You cannot value what you cannot name.

In 1972, when we saw pictures of our planet from space—the famous big blue marble shots sent back by the astronauts—it shocked and delighted the whole human race. The picture became so ubiquitous that psychologist Jean Houston reported seeing it pinned on the walls inside huts in remote tribal villages. "It went into our minds—we psychically internalized our planetary home."[17]

We believe what we see and hear, and nothing makes that as real to us as nature does. The stewardship we need to invest in is ultimately not for the earth's sake but for our own. We can never again risk the hubris of believing ourselves masters of nature, even if it's under the guise of healing it.

A Marriage Made in Heaven

A more earth-centric awareness began piercing the global mind decades ago. A 1995 report published by the Massachusetts Institute of Technology not only found an "increased environmental consciousness" over a twenty-year period (largely due, it surmised, to the clarity of Rachel Carson's message in *Silent Spring* and the corresponding outgrowth of proenvironment cultural messages), it also found that when respondents focused their concern for the environment on what was best for their children and subsequent descendants, environmental awareness took on a sacred cast. Nature was a sacred and spiritual connection, though not necessarily tied to religious teaching of a particular stripe. "The consideration of the right of future generations to God's creation—with its formative and restorative qualities—is a spiritual act, because it looks far beyond our own generation's needs. This spiritual argument, made on behalf of future children, is the most emotionally powerful weapon we can deploy in defense of the earth and our own species."[18]

Modern theologians could not agree more. Any attempt to envision solutions to what ails us and the earth must come not just from a scientific or economic set of needs but from one that speaks to our souls. Rabbi Michael Lerner says that this is what the environmental movement has been missing. "What they haven't been adequately sensitive to is the need to help people understand the spiritual crisis in the society that makes them feel so despairing about the possibility of changing the world. And basing it on love, on caring, on generosity, and on awe and wonder of the universe. The environmental movement can't just teach about the scientific facts, it has to also teach about a new spiritual vision."

Imam Feisal Abdul Rauf, founder and CEO of the American Society for Muslim Advancement, says the same is true in Islam.

> The Koran is very specific. We are custodians of the earth. Islamic law has some very specific things. We are prohibited, for example, under Islamic law from polluting bodies of water. We are prohibited from destroying trees. I can see in the context of the desert climate of Arabia where the prophet Muhammad was born, lived and died, polluting a well or destroying a tree was really destroying a resource which was the common property of not only all of humanity but all of the animal kingdom. Certain parts of the earth are the common property of not only all of humankind but all of the animal kingdom as well. And we have to be observant of not only our rights but the rights of other tenancies which exist on this earth.

By using a spiritual connection to the environmental crisis, Rabbi Lerner says that one key fear can be addressed that doesn't usually show up in most discussions: the fear of being first. The environmental movement also has to address this notion that "if they take the first steps towards love, caring, generosity and environmental sensitivity, that they will be the ridiculous ones, the fools, the adolescents, the people who have lost all touch with reality."

What we need, he says, are some Daniel Boones.

> It's so critical right now for there to be people who are willing to be the pathfinders, the first people out of the closet as spiritual people, saying "yeah, I really believe in the voice of hope. I'm not going to settle anymore for a politics that's a politics of compromise, I'm not going to go for the lesser evil anymore, I'm not going to settle for political candidates whose environmental sensitivity never leads to the dramatic steps that are necessary to save the planet. I'm going to stop all those compromises and go for my highest vision."

It is time, he says, for us to step out of the fears that have plagued us for so long and which the media have helped perpetuate, to get beyond the "I" consciousness of the isolated individual, "and actually form a group of people working for a higher purpose together.[19]

How We Start Healing

We begin by looking squarely at the problems in front of us. We must teach ourselves to take in the scope of what is happening, and we must understand it not only with our minds but also, perhaps more significantly, with our hearts. We must risk being the first ones, the pathfinders, the ones others may shake their heads at in disbelief, because it's worth it and it's the right thing to do. Once awake, you can no longer pretend you're still asleep. You must own what you know.

As Wendell Berry said, "One must begin in one's own life the private solutions that can only in turn become public solutions."[20] In other words, we become the leaders we've been waiting for.

Chapter 2

The Bed We Have Made

Out of the south cometh the whirlwind.

—Job 37:9

Around Thanksgiving of 2004, Beth LeBlanc, a resident of the Lakeview neighborhood of New Orleans, noticed water seeping into her front yard on Bellaire Drive. The seepage soon morphed into a pool eighty feet long, ten feet wide, and half a foot deep. As it grew, it poured into her next-door neighbor's yard. Despite her pleas to the city's Sewage and Water Board, it would be three months before someone showed up to determine the source of the leak: drinking water or sewage from a broken pipe—or even water from nearby Lake Pontchartrain. The investigator told LeBlanc that it looked like the water was leaking into her yard from the nearby Seventeenth Street Canal levee. City workers dug up sidewalks and driveways in an attempt to remedy the problem, but neither LeBlanc's or her neighbor's yards dried out. The seepage kept the area a mud pit.

The Microcosm of Us

LeBlanc's house sat in the levee's shadow, a hundred yards south of the spot that, six months later, would crumble under the winds and storm surge of Hurricane Katrina, drowning and destroying her block and helping to put 80 percent of New Orleans under water.[1]

J. David Rogers, a forensic engineer from the University of Missouri who specialized in levees and floodwalls, led the inspection that looked into what made the New Orleans levees fail. "The catastrophic nature of the floodwall failures indicate this was a systemic problem, something that had been building for some time," Rogers said of the Seventeenth Street Canal. "It tells us that, in all probability, these levees and the soil under the floodwall were already saturated before Katrina came along. This report of saturated yards only adds weight to that."[2]

The Army Corps of Engineers, whose work on the levees was widely blamed as the cause of the break in the storm's aftermath, claimed they had no record of being contacted about the Lakeview leaks. According to Jerry Colletti, operations manager in charge of completed projects at the Corps' New Orleans office, "If someone had told us there was lake water on the outside of that levee—or any levee—it would have been a red flag to us, and we would have been out there, without question."[3]

University of California–Berkeley engineering professor Bob Bea helped lead an investigation of the levee failures for the National Science Academy. He took calls from residents living along the Seventeenth Street and London Avenue canals who, before the storm, had reported sand boils but had never heard back from any city agencies. Sand boils result from water moving sand from the foundation aquifer through the soil to the surface. They indicate an advanced stage of seepage and weakness. The closer to a levee a sand boil is seen, the worse the prognosis for the levee.[4]

While seepage and sand boils indicate serious conditions, there are other things that weaken the understructure of levees by opening up spaces for water. Among the activities to avoid near levees are uprooting big trees and driving pilings for buildings, but a couple of months before Katrina hit, a neighbor of LeBlanc's, Gary Breedlove, noticed two old homes on his block being demolished, their large trees uprooted. "They pulled them right out of the ground, roots and all." He remembers work crews bringing in pile drivers, pounding what was to be foundation for the construction to replace the demolished homes. "They were pounding away and the ground really shook," he said. "I'm sure the levee shook too. It was right before Katrina. But I didn't really think about it then." The two lots were at the exact site of the levee breach that quickly became a hole spanning three hundred feet.[5]

The layers of bureaucracy that permeate the oversight and maintenance of the levee system in New Orleans are convoluted, and their inefficiency turned out to be deadly. "We had a diffusion of responsibilities, we had a confusion of those responsibilities and the system appeared benign when it was warning us it was ready to fail," said Bob Bea. "You often find things like this could only have happened because people were not looking for it."[6]

What happened before, during, and after Hurricane Katrina made landfall showcases much of what is at the heart of environmental issues that face our nation and world. No single factor can explain why the city of New Orleans was so brutally damaged on August 29, 2005, or account for the paralysis of the local, state, and national governments who, because of their incompetent response, shoulder much of the blame for the 1,300 deaths. In the years preceding the storm, eerily prophetic books and newspaper series—even a weeklong FEMA-based disaster scenario carried out a year before Katrina—spelled out in excruciating detail what the outcomes were likely to be. There was a generally held opinion that the Big One was inevitable. Despite all of that, no plan was implemented that looked squarely at the likely consequences of a storm hitting the city with such catastrophic power. The Big One *would* come to drown the Big Easy. The only question was when.

The people of New Orleans are not alone. They are the microcosm of us. We as a nation are not looking at what is staring us in the face. If we can take just one lesson away from Hurricane Katrina, perhaps it is that Ben Franklin's maxim is true: "a little neglect may breed great mischief." Not listening to the messages of Mother Earth is a path to disaster and heartache. This kind of willful blindness—this cooperative group unconsciousness—is a manifestation of our collective broken connection with the earth and, sadly, what its consequences look like.

New Orleans residents now commonly refer to their lives there as "PK" (pre-Katrina) and "AK" (after Katrina). They are living the consequences that so many of us cannot understand beyond scientific data and sound bites and bits of video on the nightly news. The story of New Orleans shows us what global warming can mean when mixed with the human capacity of denial. The victims of the Ninth Ward we saw atop their roofs—terrified, neglected, and dying—were not nameless faces from a war-torn country halfway around the world. They were us.

Every day, headlines and new stories are showing a clearer picture of the extent of the changes in our climate and the effects of the earth's warming: milder winters and hotter summers; prolonged and violent storms; and the early, false springs that weaken the grasses and other flora that provide the oxygen that keeps the air breathable. When many plants bloom too early and then are caught by a late frost, they may bloom again in that season, but they are weakened and, if this happens two or three years in a row, it can make them too weak to survive. Fruit trees, however, can't set more blossoms, and the crop is lost. And when many food crops emerge from the soil early and then freeze, whole harvests perish. The only recourse is replanting or waiting a full growth cycle. Our interactions with the sky above and the earth below have consequences.

When we talk about the effects of climate change and global warming, it's important to remember that they are systemic conditions that affect every aspect of our world and are caused by a number of factors, some immediately recognizable and others more subtle, but no less disturbing. They include a range of conditions that often affect one another: stronger storms and increased flooding, drought and longer wildfire seasons, heat waves and crop loss, spread of disease and loss of natural resources. All of these in turn affect human life; the cost of food, fuel, and commodities; our economic viability and quality of life—even, says the Pentagon, our ability to keep our nation secure.

It's not just that we burn too much gasoline in our inefficient cars or that we eat so much meat that we increase the amount of methane pumped into the atmosphere from animal waste, or even that we poison our streams and waterways and soil with the countless tons of chemicals we pour onto our fields to make them deliver bigger, faster harvests. It's also the unconsciousness of our intention and willfulness of our ignorance. Just as with New Orleans, the warnings have been out there for decades. The earth has been trying to tell us something, but we have been living in a buffer of grace, not yet ready or willing to pay the piper, hoping he'll end up being the stuff of fairy tales.

New Orleans PK

New Orleans isn't just the site of one of our greatest natural disaster to date. It has long played a key role in America's destiny and mirrors some of the brightest and darkest aspects of our national character. A French Canadian nobleman named Sieur de Bienville founded the town in 1718, simultaneously bestowing on it its polycultural roots and defiant attitude. He ignored those who urged him to move the town eighty miles up river, to the spot where Baton Rouge now stands. When a hurricane inundated the fledgling town in 1722 (one of many storms that year), Bienville was unmoved.

From the beginning, a sense of adventure trumped common sense. Hurricanes or no hurricanes, New Orleans stayed, defiant against the winds and water that nature regularly threw its way. Bienville saw New Orleans's potential as a port and ignored the fact that it was entirely surrounded by water. In fact, New Orleans is flanked and bisected by water—Lake Pontchartrain on the north, swamps on the west, the Gulf of Mexico on the near east and south, with the ribbon of the Mississippi rolling through it, creating the boomerang shape on its eastern side that gives it one of its nicknames, the Crescent City. Baton Rouge might have been drier, but sailing upriver against the Mississippi's mighty current in those days was problematic. Likewise, the shifting sandbars that appeared without warning and ran ships aground added a definite chill to the forward march of commerce.[7]

New Orleans did grow into a vital port. It was this fact that made Napoleon Bonaparte loathe to part with it, but by 1803 he needed an infusion of cash to support his bankrupt republic and to consolidate his power, recently challenged by his malaria-ridden army's failure to quell a slave revolt in the French territory of Haiti. He was able to do both by selling France's territorial possessions to the United States.

At a price of $15 million (less than three cents per acre), the Louisiana Purchase doubled the size of the continental United States, greatly increasing its president's cache, and making New Orleans its greatest southern port, freeing the entire length of the Mississippi to river traffic. The Mississippi, which had once been its western frontier, became the country's circulation system and the heart of its water commerce. Within a year, Thomas Jefferson would call on his assistant Meriwether Lewis to explore this mammoth addition of more than 820,000 square miles, which spanned an area from the Gulf of Mexico in the south to what now exceeds the northernmost border of North Dakota, and from the Mississippi River in the east to the Rocky Mountains in the west.

The Gulf Coast has long been the bull's-eye of storms. In September of 1900, one of New Orleans's neighbors, Galveston, Texas, which sat less than nine feet above sea level, suffered the deadliest natural disaster in U.S. history to date, when a fifteen-foot storm surge from a category 4 hurricane blew ashore, killing eight thousand to twelve thousand people—as much as one-fifth of its population—and destroying much of the defenseless city, including 3,600 homes. With its bridges washed out, its railroad link to Houston wrecked, and telegraph wires down, no one could know the predicament of the besieged Galvestonians. As mainland facilities for handling the dead were quickly exhausted, funeral pyres set up on the debris-strewn beaches burned for weeks. By 1904, the city had begun to build a seventeen-foot wall that eventually stretched along ten miles of Gulf beach, which has, in large measure, protected it from storms ever since.[8]

In 1935, hundreds of encamped World War I veterans, hired by the WPA to build U.S. Highway 1, were killed by the Labor Day hurricane, which destroyed everything it its path with its 200 mph winds, including the Florida East Coast Railway, the veterans' only means of escape.[9] Until the 2005 hurricane season, the Labor Day hurricane was regarded as the most vicious Atlantic hurricane ever recorded. (The 1948 film *Key Largo* immortalized the 1935 hurricane's fierce impact in a tension-filled scene set against the sound of a gale blowing outside.)

Hurricane Categories

Category	Wind speed (mph)
5	Above 156
4	131–155
3	111–130
2	96–110
1	74–95
Tropical Storm	39–73
Tropical Depression	0–38

The weather service did not start naming hurricanes until 1954. Today there are twenty-one names per year, and if the number of storms exceeds twenty-one, they are named after Greek letters. In 2005, the year Katrina hit, fifteen hurricanes and a dozen tropical storms exhausted the official list of names, requiring the addition of six Greek letters (from Alpha to Zeta) to finish the season. Five of the hurricanes became category 4, tying a record, and a record four become category 5, including Katrina (winds of 175 mph, 902 mbar), the most destructive, and Wilma, the most powerful ever recorded, with winds in the eye wall exceeding 200 miles per hour (882 mbar, the lowest ever recorded in the Atlantic).[10]

Hurricanes are simply a fact of life in communities on the Atlantic and Gulf coasts. Just as Galveston had tragic warnings from the 1900 hurricane, reinforced by a second storm fifteen years later, New Orleans has had plenty of practice preparing for and coping with storms. Besides the baptismal hurricane of 1722, only four years after its founding, New Orleans endured a couple of other big storms in the days before accurate weather forecasting gave residents enough time to leave. On an August night in 1856, a category 4 hurricane struck off the tip of Terrebonne parish. More than two hundred people, many of them summer vacationers, were drowned or crushed in the darkness by wreckage flying around in winds that exceeded 130 miles per hour. An eight-foot storm surge "raked the island and tore it in two." In 1909 a hurricane hit with a ten-foot wave, killing 350 people.[11]

For several years, Hurricane Betsy (1965) was the storm by which a generation measured severe weather. Betsy made landfall as a high category 3 storm and was costly, earning it the nickname Billion Dollar Betsy. After Betsy, New Orleans replaced existing floodwalls and levees with the current system that zigzagged 350 miles through the city and boosted the height of the walls to ten to fifteen feet. The system was geared to withstand category 3 storms. But just four years later, Hurricane Camille crashed into Bay St. Louis, just east of New Orleans, and roared across the Mississippi delta, its winds so powerful they destroyed the wind-recording equipment (the best estimates are 200 mph). It veered east, just south of Missouri, and chugged back toward the Atlantic, splitting the country, stalling when it reached the Appalachian mountains of Virginia, dumping twenty-eight inches of rain in eight hours and killing 150.[12] What no one could know was that Camille wasn't an aberration, but the beginning of a trend. Storms to follow would become much stronger, move more slowly, and take longer to blow themselves out.

The current process of calibrating hurricane categories was derived from a formula created by consulting engineer Herbert Saffir and the former director of the U.S. National Hurricane Center, Robert Simpson. Prior to the five-level scale, hurricanes had been described simply as major or minor. After Hurricane Camille's devastating ride along the Gulf Coast, the two men decided that there had to be a better way to gauge likely wind and storm damage so that cities could make realistic preparations for evacuations and aid to survivors.

As Hurricane George chugged toward New Orleans in 1998, the city opened the Superdome, using it for the first time as a shelter for those who could not leave town. In 2004, category 5 Hurricane Ivan made landfall near Gulf Shores, Alabama, close enough that Louisiana's governor, Kathleen Blanco, ordered an evacuation of the New Orleans. With all the traffic converging on the same single highway, many people were unable to leave town. Blanco implemented the contra-flow evacuation plan, which turned all highway lanes into exit lanes, basically doubling the amount of traffic that could leave the city. A year later, that evacuation plan enabled a fairly orderly exodus of those who could flee from Katrina, doubtless saving many lives. Testifying before a House committee in 2006, the governor said that Hurricane Katrina "would have been far worse if the initial evacuation had not been so efficient and safe."[13]

In 2005, Katrina's warning signs had been there since the storm formed, but in the hours preceding landfall, it was clear to everyone who still had some sort of access to weather bulletins that this would be a decidedly deadly storm. The now famous—and very graphic—warning issued by the U.S. National Weather Service minced no words. (To see the original bulletin, visit the NOAA site: http://www.noaanews.noaa.gov/stories2006/s2656.htm.)

The sad fact was that many of the people who could not get out did not know of the bulletin or what was about to blow their way. But there were other warnings. Before Katrina hit, several people reported feeling a dread about what was coming. On Monday night, even though the storm had veered easterly and the mayor was announcing to news cameras that they had "dodged the bullet," a sense began to permeate those who had stayed in town that something was very wrong. "Many of these non-evacuees felt vaguely ill that Monday evening. They sensed that something was horrifically wrong with their beloved city, something deeper than surface wounds."[14] Just blocks from downtown, the levees were rupturing, but the people who were no longer in danger had not yet gotten the news about the people who were.

*This was a systemic problem,
something that had been building for some time.*
—Forensic engineer J. DAVID ROGERS,
head of the team inspecting the failure of New Orleans levee system

Despite decades of warnings, New Orleans remained, because of its geography and lack of wetlands protection, as exposed as a saucer floating in a bowl of water. It was, from the moment Katrina first formed in the Atlantic, defenseless to what was about to come ashore. Afterward, in heartbreaking pockets of desperation and death, it would seem to have taken on the visage that adopted son and author James Lee Burke described: "an insane asylum built on a sponge."[15] The common refrain of people who watched the bedraggled survivors of Katrina begging for food and water on national television had departed was: "How could this be happening in the United States of America?" What *wasn't* wrong with this picture?

The Widening Impact of Global Warming

While the blame for any storm can't be placed on a single factor, scientists agree that global warming was certainly a factor. The offshore drilling for gas and oil didn't bring Katrina ashore, but the constant weakening of the marshlands by pipelines and toxic dumping took away much of the only land buffer between the storm and the cities.

Nassim Taleb calls an event such as Katrina a *black swan,* an occurrence so out of the realm of the expected that it shocks our senses—yet in hindsight was clearly inevitable. New Orleans is the great and tragic example that has much to teach us about inertia. Awareness is growing that environmental problems have reached a critical stage on the scale being described in reports like the one issued by the Intergovernmental Panel on Climate Change in 2007, Assessment Report 4 (AR4), which stated, "Warming of the climate system is unequivocal, as is now evident from observations of increases in global average air and ocean temperatures, widespread melting of snow and ice and rising global average sea level."[16] More than two thousand scientists from 154 countries participated in the writing of the report.[17] (The full update to this report, AR5, is scheduled to be released in 2014.)

The facts speak for themselves, and those facts are beginning to sink into our national consciousness. Each of us has a fair idea of what the rising cost of gasoline has on our bank accounts, and the cost of heating oil, natural gas, pasture land, food, and endless other items march in lockstep ever higher. But what is the cost to our spirits? We know something's going on. You can't use up a finite resource when there is accelerating need without sensing something is very wrong. As chapter 4 describes, we are on an eating binge, devouring our very seed, the stores of air, water, earth, plant, and animal species that we and future generations depend on. If there are to be future generations, it up to us to shepherd these resources into the future.

If we are to understand what we are facing as a nation, we have to consider how the effects of conditions like global warming and climate change all depend on and dance with each other. We have to acknowledge how our reluctance to confront the part of our national character that tells us we can straddle the fence that separates very different territories is already enabling the worst possible consequences. The effects of global warming are potentially monumental to our lives, its causes beyond our easy comprehension. But already the trail of evidence is available for us to put together like a jigsaw puzzle of seemingly disparate and unrelated pieces.

If it were possible to pluck an average American housewife from her 1942 victory garden and put a cell phone in her hands, it's entirely possible she would react like Ethiopian Me'en tribal members who, when shown a picture of an antelope in a coloring book, could detect nothing, because they had no "cognitive antecedent."[18] She might well look but, without a frame of reference, not see. Our conundrum is similar: we are being asked to understand the changes we are in the midst of and foresee solutions that can save us without having a frame of reference for either.

Katrina was not a stand-alone phenomenon but rather part of a tableau of interlocking effects. Likewise, the shifts in our climate and the warming of the globe are not just about the heat but also about the long-term and cascading relationships that make up the earth and the elements and how they relate to one another and affect our psyches. The truth and consequences of the warming of the globe revolve around the tripling of the world's population in the last half-century, the vast exploitation of resources that accompanied it, and the current effects of having so many consumers vying for the same finite resources to satisfy their needs and cravings, with more of the same on the horizon.

The real stresses to the globe include the drying up of the planet's water resources, crop destruction and the loss of food integrity and security, the melting of icecaps and glaciers and the attendant rise in ocean levels, more torrid heat waves and prolonged droughts, longer and more widespread wildfire seasons, depleted and arid topsoil, stronger storms and increased flooding, and the economic downturns that follow in the wake of such tragedies.

Unlike the victims of hurricanes from previous centuries, who could be drowned at night as they slept, we have the technological know-how to see the future—at least enough of it to decide what our choices are—using our climate-change models and our digital everythings. We need not settle for or resign ourselves to victimhood. Nor do we need to take the word of people whose vested interests profit most from no more than surface examination of complicated global issues. We must listen to the alarms going off inside us, which are trying to get our attention.

Drying Up—Our Dwindling Water Resources

Just as a hurricane swirls into life when given the right ingredients of heat, surface water temperature, and wind, the effects of the warming of the globe have their own independent and lethal stand-alone ingredients. During an interview with a *New York Times* reporter in the summer of 2007, Nobel laureate and director of the Lawrence Berkeley National Laboratory Steven Chu pondered the health of the fresh water supplies in the western United States, noting that the Sierra Nevada snowpack was at its lowest level in twenty years. Even the most optimistic climate models suggested a 30 percent to 70 percent loss of this water source by mid-century. "There's a two-thirds chance there will be a disaster," he said, "and that's in the best scenario."[19]

The fact is that it's not just the western United States that's drying up. The entire fresh water supply on earth is disappearing. In the 1960s, Lake Chad was Africa's third largest freshwater source, covering a surface area of 9,600 square miles. By 2001 the lake had all but disappeared, down to only 4 percent of its size forty years before (though its total area has improved since then). The lake basin has been drained not only by a decline in rainfall and an increasingly severe drought, but even more by the many irrigation projects undertaken by the countries that border it, Chad, Cameroon, Niger, and Nigeria, which count on it as their main water source. Water diverted from the lake quadrupled between 1983 and 1994 alone.[20]

The lake used to support a diverse ecosystem of birds, fish, crocodiles, and herds of grazing animals, as well as a population of fishermen. But with most of the lake evaporated, steadily encroached on during the prolonged drought by the nearby Sahara desert, most of the people who used to depend on the lake for their livelihood have turned to agriculture, which further strains the lake's resources. Communities that once ringed its shores can now find themselves dozens of miles away. While an ambitious project is planned to divert water from nearby rivers to revitalize the vast dried lake bed, experts doubt the plan can be funded and executed quickly enough to bring the lake back.[21]

Much the same fate is unfolding for Florida's Lake Okeechobee, which is, after Lake Michigan, the second largest freshwater lake completely contained within the United States. In the first decade of this century, portions of the lake had become so dried out that their exposed organic matter caught fire in May of 2007 (and has repeatedly since then). The drought that has dropped its water level and shrunken its shoreline was so severe that in that same year, state and wildlife workers took advantage of the situation and cleaned the exposed lake bed.

On the lake floor, they found boats, anchors, tires, motors, chains, and miscellaneous trash. Other items delighted them, including enough Native American artifacts to give archeologists and historians a much clearer picture of pre-historic native life in Florida. (One unearthed arrowhead was estimated to be eight thousand years old.) Other finds were not so welcome. As they began to excavate the mud on the lake floor, the South Florida Water Management District discovered that arsenic levels in the mud were four times the legal limit. The lake bottom was, in fact, so polluted from decades of fertilizer and pesticide use that it could not be disposed of on agricultural or commercial lands.[22] Over two million cubic feet of toxic sludge were removed.

In the spring of 2009, near the end of the yearly dry season, the water levels were so low that pumps were installed to keep water flowing to South Florida. The lake is the area's backup water supply.[23]

Other bodies of fresh water are also visibly declining, including the Colorado River, which feeds the ever-growing water needs of Nevada, California, Arizona, New Mexico, and Colorado. It now often ends in a trickle or even dries out before it can reach the northern edge of the Gulf of California. California's Owens Lake, which at the beginning of the twentieth century spanned two hundred square miles, lasted barely a decade after it was diverted as a water resource to Los Angeles in 1913. Mono Lake, also in California, has dropped thirty-five feet since 1941, when it too was diverted to water-hungry Los Angeles. (In an effort to decrease escalating water use, in 2009 the Los Angeles Department of Water and Power offered residential customers an incentive—one dollar for each square foot of turf that was replaced with drought-resistant plants, mulch, or "water permeable hardscapes.")[24]

In October of 2007, the southeastern United States reached

the most severe category of drought it had known in a hundred years, a condition so perilous that the city of Atlanta was only four months away from running out of water for its four million people. The drought, made worse by Atlanta's soaring population and nearly eighteen months of mostly rainless weather, had broken every one of the state's dry-weather records.[25] Georgia then tried to use the Army Corps of Engineers to siphon off more than their previous share of the water from Georgia's Lake Sidney Lanier to help alleviate their low supplies. The lake, which supplies much of northern Georgia's water, also supplies water and hydroelectric power to Alabama and Florida. An appeals court ruling in February 2008 voided the Georgia plan.[26]

> *Our analysis shows that it is no longer enough to say that global warming will increase the likelihood of extreme weather and to repeat the caveat that no individual weather event can be directly linked to climate change. To the contrary, our analysis shows that, for the extreme hot weather of the recent past, there is virtually no explanation other than climate change.*
> —JAMES HANSEN, chief climatologist, NASA, August 3, 2012[27]

Elsewhere in the world, Egypt's Nile, Pakistan's Indus, and India's Ganges now regularly recede to a trickle or stop altogether in the dry season. Many of their tributaries are completely gone. China's Yellow River, which once ran almost 2,500 miles before reaching the Yellow Sea, began running dry in 1972 and since 1985 regularly fails to reach the sea. Of the 1,052 lakes that were once in Hebei province, which surrounds Beijing, only eighty-three remain.[28] Mighty Anguli Lake, once 72 square miles in size, has become a dry lake bed in ten years. The temperatures in Hebei province have risen from 1.8°F–3.7°F (1.0°C–2.04°C) in the last fifty years. The annual average temperature of the region of Anguli Lake has risen 3.8°F (2.1°C) over that same time period, while average annual rainfall has dropped by almost 2.5 inches (62.1 mm).[29] As these once-mighty water sources dry up, the ecosystems and agricultural communities they supported for millennia are disappearing.

New Normal

Record-breaking hot weather in recent years has become less news than the new norm. By the spring of 2012, the United States had experienced its warmest twelve months since recordkeeping began in 1895. As parts of the United States experienced ninety-degree days in March, spring temperature averages were a full five degrees above the average set during *the entire twentieth century,* with some parts of the United States recording temperatures *20 degrees to 40 degrees* above average for March. According to NOAA, "Every state in the nation experienced a record warm daily temperature during March."[30] In all, fifteen thousand warm-temperature records were broken during March alone, with the average temperature in the lower forty-eight states *8.6 degrees higher* than the twentieth-century average.

By summer's end, drought conditions existed in 63 percent of the lower forty-eight states, and conditions were ripe for the dozens of raging wildfires that stalked the dry conditions across the west, from Oregon to Arizona. A map from NOAA showed a huge rust-colored swath snaking in a wide path from the west across the center of the United States, the so-called "orange states" of moderate to severe drought.

Jake Crouch, a climate analyst at NOAA's National Climatic Data Center in Asheville, NC, noted in 2012 that "the U.S. [had] had 15 straight months with above-average temperatures, which had never occurred since instrument records began in 1895. Also, summer was the third straight season to rank among the top five warmest, . . . which also had never previously occurred. All of this fits into the longer-term warming trend."[31]

These declines in water sources are exacerbated by widespread poor water management and lack of insight, and they are setting the stage for an inevitable tragedy as the reasons for the declines collide with the far-reaching consequences for ignoring them.

There are basically two types of fresh water available on the earth: surface water—lakes, rivers, and tributaries—and underground water. Water from underground aquifers can be shallow or deep. Shallow aquifers are mostly rechargeable and can be pumped until their levels no longer accommodate further pressure; then you must simply wait for them to recharge before pumping them again. Deep aquifers, also called fossil aquifers are, like oil, not replenishable. What is extracted from them is a one-time gift. Since the middle of the twentieth century, overpumping has become the norm, with countries like China, India, and the United States, the world's main grain producers, leading the way.

"The failure of governments to limit pumping to the sustainable yield of aquifers means that water tables are now falling in countries that contain more than half the world's people."[32] The long-term consequences are dire, because this is not just about drinking water. It's about the declining ability of countries to feed themselves and their people. The fact is that it takes an enormous amount of water to feed people. On average, each of us on the earth consumes about a gallon (four liters) of water in some form each day. Besides what we use daily for showers, watering our yards, and cleaning our clothes, consider that the food we consume each day requires another 528 gallons (2,000 liters) of water per day. Seventy percent of the world's water today is used to irrigate fields to produce food crops. The remaining 30 percent is divided between industrial and residential use.

The economies of growing food are unforgiving: it takes one thousand tons of water to grow a ton of wheat. As gallons of water are measured in dollars needed to irrigate the land to be able to grow the ever-increasing tons of wheat needed worldwide, it becomes abundantly clear that as water tables decline while populations in countries like India and China continue to climb, each country's ability to feed its population is going to be strained to the breaking point. Even with wheat fetching record prices, as water becomes harder to reach—and, therefore, a more precious commodity—countries are going to have to import more and more grain to cover their increasing domestic grain deficits. In fact, that is becoming the norm rather than the exception. Countries that don't have enough water to grow their own food are "using grain to balance their water books. Similarly, trading in grain futures is in a sense trading in water futures."[33]

Grain imports march in lockstep with water shortages. It is conceivable—some say inevitable—that the substance deemed most precious in this and succeeding centuries won't be oil, but water. Water deficits are already translating into grain deficits. The countries best suited to handle these changes are clearly the ones with the healthiest fiscal anatomies. The vast North China Plain, that country's breadbasket, producing more than half its wheat and a full third of its grain crops, is a case in point. As its water table continues to drop from overpumping, the country's grain production is becoming less and less sustainable. In 1998 grain production peaked at 392 million tons. By 2005, it had dropped to 358 million tons, while the country's population had increased by nearly sixty million.[34] China was able to avoid importing grain until 2004, when it used up its vast stores; in that year it imported seven million tons. Its wheat crop alone has continued to dwindle from a peak of 123 million tons in 1997 to a total of 105 million tons in 2007, a 15 percent drop in a decade that saw its population increase by eighty-five million. USDA reports, however, show totals rising modestly each year since.[35]

What complicates their ability to stay ahead of the food production curve is that China is already looking at losing more and more land to arid plains as hotter temperatures dry up surface water and turn once arable land into desert. In north central and western provinces, enormous deserts are shifting and merging to form even bigger deserts. "Highways running through the shrinking region between them are regularly inundated by sand dunes."[36] Dust storms are not unusual in northwestern China. On April 5, 2001, a huge dust storm that originated there and in Mongolia began a trip across the Pacific, blanketing the entire western half of the United States from

Arizona to Canada two weeks later. Swirling in that choking dust was a precious commodity: millions of tons of China's topsoil. A year later in Seoul, South Korea, a Chinese dust storm encased the city, closing down schools and filling clinics with people unable to catch their breath. Ten or so such dust storms now occur annually in China, providing "visual evidence of the ecological catastrophe unfolding in northern and western China." These occurrences have become commonplace enough in Korea to be known as the dread "fifth season." The principal cause: overgrazing.[37]

Desertification, the loss of once arable areas, is a process of land degradation that is often the result of a combination of factors including overgrazing; overuse and mismanagement of resources; and longer, drier summers. It's a serious problem affecting many countries, including India, the Mekong delta in southeast Asia, the Nile valley in Egypt, the Middle East, Mexico, Spain, South Korea, and several nations in Africa. Africa is particularly vulnerable, losing from two to three billion tons of topsoil annually. That loss of soil represents a loss of agricultural heritage and a critical part of that continent's capacity to feed its population, now and in the future. In Mauritania, the wind erosion is so severe that the number of dust storms has increased from two annually in the 1960s to eighty per year today.[38]

Even the United States, which once suffered a devastating loss of topsoil during the Dust Bowl of the 1930s, is not impervious to desertification. While only one-fifth of U.S. grain harvest depends on irrigated land (in India, it's three-fifths, and in China, a whopping four-fifths), and while the U.S. water supplies are much healthier than they are in many countries, three of our main grain-producing states, Texas, Nebraska, and Kansas, share a single fossil aquifer, the Ogallala, from which they glean 70 percent to 90 percent of their irrigation water. In the United States, a little more than a third (37 percent) of all irrigation water comes from underground sources, while the remaining nearly two-thirds comes from surface water— lakes, rivers, tributaries. Underground sources are popular because they can often be drilled at the site they are needed, maximizing water economy and limiting waste. Ground sources have the added attraction of being available even during droughts, when surface water often evaporates or is too far away from crop sites.

If there can be a bright side to surface waters disappearing, it is that they are visible. You know when their shorelines recede and water levels drop. With aquifers, you do not know the water is gone until nothing comes up. There is no ten-year warning. The pumps simply stop bringing up water.

One of the drawbacks to widespread dependence on fossil aquifers to support grain production is a lack of food security. In the northernmost of China's three river basins, the Hai River basin has a population of one hundred million people, and includes two of China's largest cities, Beijing (fifteen million) and Tianjin (eleven million). As populations migrate from the country into the city, where there is indoor plumbing, water consumption typically rises by as much as fourfold. A study done by the World Bank notes that wells drilled around Beijing have to go down half a mile to capture fresh water now, making the sheer acquisition of water prohibitively expensive. Chinese wheat farmers, who are having to drill a thousand feet for irrigation water, are being driven out of business by the cost of watering their crops. As the water shortfall in the Hai basin reaches nearly forty billion tons per year, once the aquifers are depleted, the loss to the country's grain harvest will be enormous, down by forty million tons, enough to feed 120 million Chinese.[29]

That would be the equivalent of the United States being unable to provide grain to a third of our people. But with much of our own grain growth dependent on the water from a single—though vast—fossil aquifer, the Ogallala, we have to ask, "How do we grow enough food now and in the future without destroying an essential, one-time source of water?" It doesn't take a rocket scientist to figure out that just as irrigation has helped triple grain harvests in the second half of the twentieth century, that kind of growth will be reversed when the water is gone.

What's Hot

It's seems that every year becomes either the hottest on re-
oord or at loaot among tho top ton. In 2012 two difforont ro
cords were broken: not only did the average annual temperature in the United States go up by a full degree for the first
time since record keeping began in 1880, but 2012 became
the latest hottest year ever. That means that the ten hottest
years on record have all occurred since 2000. (Monthly average temperature every year since 1985 have been above the
twentieth-century average.)[40]

The Heat Is On

While the hottest year on record in the United States seems to
change annually now, in Europe, the heat wave of 2003 marked the
hottest summer in five hundred years. Originally reported as total-
ing 35,000 fatalities, the number soared to more than 52,000 deaths
as updated reports trickled in over the next two years.[41] In France
alone, 14,802 people died, most of them elderly. Because summers
are usually moderate, most residents do not have air conditioning,
especially in the Auxerre section of France, where the temperature
in 2003 hit 104 degrees. Complicating the dogged heat during the
day was the fact that the evenings did not cool off.

Even more shocking were the 18,257 deaths in Italy (vastly
higher than the original estimate of 4,000), when August temperatures soared as much as 16 degrees warmer than the previous
August. Other countries also logged record-breaking temperatures
and deaths from heat: Germany: 7,000 deaths (105.4 degrees, hottest since recordkeeping began in 1901); 4,130 in Spain; 2,139 in
England and Wales; 2,099 in Portugal; 1,250 in Belgium; and 975
in Switzerland, which recorded its highest temperatures since 1540.
In London, where triple-digit temperatures were recorded for the
first time, 900 people died.

In total, the original estimates of the 2003 heat wave were fully 33 percent lower than the July 2006 totals. While deaths from heat waves don't usually get much press coverage, they reportedly kill more people annually than floods, tornadoes, and hurricanes combined.[42] Eight years earlier, during a hot week in mid-July, more than 700 people died during a fierce heat wave that blanketed Chicago. In the United States, heat waves don't just kill people, they also put an enormous strain on the country's antiquated power grid, much of which hasn't been significantly updated since the grid began getting pieced together in the late 1800s. In August 2003, as Europe was baking in record temperatures, the United States experienced a giant rolling blackout that affected fifty million people along the eastern United States and Canada, with an estimated $6 billion in damages resulting from the lost power.

The U.S. power grid is a problem in its own right, causing a full one-third of the emissions that contribute to global warming in this country. It is simultaneously inefficient, undependable, and vulnerable. Much of what tripped the safety switches during the 2003 blackout could have easily been prevented by trees in some of the service areas being trimmed so they didn't come into contact with the power lines and trip overload switches.[43]

Hotter weather also dries up water supplies and kills crops, depleting grain harvests and endangering food security across the globe. It creates a vicious cycle. As increased and prolonged heat evaporates surface water, the soil grows drier. Without water to evaporate into the atmosphere, there isn't enough moisture to form rain clouds. The ground grows more arid, and when rain does come, it is too brittle to absorb the water, and the runoff turns into floods. By the time autumn arrives, the warmer air causes more precipitation to fall as rain and less as snow. Farmers depend on the melting snowpacks for spring planting, and our forests need the snowpack and the spring melt to keep from drying out.

It gets worse. According to *Science* magazine, "Snowpacks are now melting 1 to 4 weeks earlier than they did fifty years ago, and streamflows thus also peak earlier."[44] Snowpacks are essential to water security in the western United States. In fact, 75 percent of what shows up in our streams in the spring comes from snowpack. This, in turn, affects our high-elevation forests, which used to be protected from wildfires by late snowpacks. Because of the earlier cycle of snowmelt, these forests are becoming more vulnerable to fire.[45]

No one can predict the long-range effects of earlier springs and earlier snowmelts, but every farmer knows how critical timing is to a growing season. During the life cycle of a crop, the most critical phase is pollination. Of the world's three staple grains—rice, wheat, and corn—corn is the most vulnerable to hotter temperatures during pollination. If the tassels burn before they can open and drop pollen on the silk strands of the cobs below—or if the silk itself burns before the endosperm can complete its job of traveling to each corn kernel—the corn cannot develop.

Rice is also vulnerable to high temperatures. In 2001, a paper presented by Pedro Sanchez, director of the International Centre for Research in Agriforestry, showed that at 93 degrees, rice can pollinate at almost 100 percent levels, but by the time it reaches 104 degrees, its ability to pollinate is near zero.[46]

Higher heat in general will also lower crop yields. A study by the International Rice Research Institute found that each rise of 1.8 degrees above the norm lowers wheat, rice, and corn yields by 10 percent. In India, where the population is expected to grow by another half billion people by midcentury, two scientists found that while a 1.8-degree increase in temperature did not meaningfully affect wheat yields, a 3.6-degree rise lowered yields at all test sites as much as 38 percent.[47]

These point to an additional corollary, the one with potentially the most catastrophic side effect of the heating of the globe: the world's fast melting glaciers and icecaps. In September 2005, scientists reported a worrisome fact: the Arctic icecaps were melting much faster than originally predicted—in leaps and bounds, in fact. The *New York Times* posted a graphic that lets you drag a slider to see the startling retreat from a single year—from 2006 to

2007—demonstrating how severely and quickly the planet is heating up.[48]

In September of 2007, Arctic ice specialists were stunned to see an area of ice twice the size of Great Britain melt away in a single week.[49] Two years later, in September of 2009, after examining the results of 50 million laser readings from its satellites, NASA coined a new term for the alarming rate of disappearing ice in both the Greenland and Antarctic masses: runaway melt.

Only five summers after the dramatic 2007 melt, the Arctic sea ice retreat broke another record. In September 2012, the ice minimum (the measurable amount of ice mass remaining after the summer thaw) broke 2007's record by a stunning 18 percent. This record melting represents the disappearance of the older, thicker ice accompanied by record shrinking of the Arctic ice mass at each summer's end. What replaces the older ice is less viable ice that, in the spring melt of 2013, evidenced visible and widespread cracking. "As Arctic sea ice extent has plummeted since 1979, down to a record low in September 2012, first-year ice has become much more common across the Arctic, as thick, multiyear ice has declined."[50] (This video shows the stunning difference of the 2012 ice melt.[51])

There are three main reasons why this is a tragic planetary change. First, the climate of the globe depends heavily on the health of its poles. When the ice melts, the planet loses the white expanse that reflects the heat of the sun, exposing darker, heat-absorbing ocean water. This, in turn, can melt and release previously frozen methane from the ocean floor, which adds more greenhouse gases to the atmosphere. Worse, methane is twenty-three times more potent a greenhouse gas than CO_2. An unchangeable feedback loop is set in motion: as more ice melts, more ocean is exposed, the planet absorbs more heat, and more ice melts, and so it goes.

Second, glaciers and ice caps provide snowmelt in the spring that feeds the rivers, springs, lakes, and tributaries that are the water sources for much of the earth. With more heat, there is less snow. With less snow, there is less water available for irrigation. "Every major river in Asia, where half the world's people live, originates in the Himalayas, including the Indus, the Ganges, the Mekong, the Yangtze, and the Yellow."[52] With glaciers melting in every highly populous part of the globe, the outlook for fresh water is fundamentally grim.

In the United States, the southwestern states depend on the Colorado River, which depends on snowmelt from the Rockies. California counts on snowmelt from the Sierra Nevada, as well as on the overly stressed Colorado River. Unless our national energy policy changes significantly and quickly, it's estimated that by mid-century, we will experience a 70-percent reduction in snowpack in the western states.

Third, the melting of the glaciers and ice caps has large-scale consequences. While most of what is melting in the Arctic each summer does not add to sea levels, because the weight of the water is already displaced by the existing ice, scientists estimate that the melting of the West Antarctic ice sheet or the Greenland ice sheet would raise sea levels worldwide anywhere from several inches to as much as twenty-three feet.[53] "When you warm the ocean, you also increase it, because it expands thermally," says David Barber, chairman of the Arctic System Science at University of Manitoba. What accompanies that is a quick and considerable rise in sea level—and for every one-foot rise in sea levels, the shoreline recedes twenty feet, on average. "If you live on a planet where most people live within a couple meters of the ocean level, the potential for problems [is] enormous. The poles of the planet are the early sentinels of global-scale climate change."[54]

The connectivity issue is extremely important for people to
understand. The Arctic is the early warning for the world.
It is the health barometer for the world.
We Inuit are in fact the mercury in that barometer.[55]
—Canadian Inuit activist SHEILA WATT-CLOUTIER,
Chair, Inuit Circumpolar Conference

Saving the Oceans: Earth's Blue Heart

Because we live on land, we can see the effects of our planet's warming in terms of wildfires, floods, and droughts, and shoreline-altering storms. Satellite photography archives the scars on the earth's skin from mountaintop removal, from tar sands tailing ponds, from burned out and clear-cut forestlands, and from encroaching deserts and disappearing glaciers. What we can't see so easily is what's happening to our oceans. So vast and mysterious to most of us, they have largely escaped our notice and concern. For all time, the seas have been archetypal symbols of power and constancy. To be on the ocean is to respect its caprice and to know how mortal and small you are in the midst of its vastness. Considering its encompassing mystery and unknowable depths, it's no wonder that its vulnerabilities come as a shock. Because, as it turns out, there are limits to even what the ocean can tolerate.

As oceanographer, author, explorer, and conservationist Sylvia Earle observes, "In Rachel Carson's lifetime [she died in 1964] she did not, could not, know about the most significant discovery concerning the ocean: It is not too big to fail. Fifty years ago, we could not see limits to what we could put into the ocean, or what we could take out. Fifty years into the future, it will be too late to do what is possible right now."

Probably no one on earth knows this better than Earle, a legendary advocate of the marine world. Earle probably has more firsthand scientific experience with the ocean than anyone else on earth. She was the first woman aquanaut, has led more than a hundred ocean expeditions, and holds numerous records for deepest solo dives and time spent underwater (seven thousand hours, much of that actually living on the floor of the ocean in submersibles). The National Geographic Society named her Explorer-in-Residence in 1998 and *Time* magazine declared her the first "Hero for the Planet." The Library of Congress calls her a "Living Legend." The *New Yorker* and *New York Times* refer to her as "Her Deepness." She once served as NOAA's chief scientist. (The list of her national and international honors goes on and on.)

She calls the ocean "the cornerstone of earth's life support system," because it is at the center of everything that gives us life. "It shapes climate and weather. It holds most of life on earth." And it's also where 97% of the earth's water resides. The earth is, after all, a system, like each of our bodies. What happens to one part affects every part. "Every drop of water you drink, every breath you take, no matter where on earth you live, comes from the sea."[56]

Although much of what's covered in this book deals with land-based consequence, every issue and idea affects the oceans, and in turn the oceans affect us. We are closely linked. Life began in the oceans. Our bodies are mostly composed of water. It provides most of our oxygen. It creates our weather. Its surface currents are critical redistributors of some of the heat it absorbs. More than half the people in the world live within fifty miles of a coastline and more than 70 percent depend on the ocean's bounty for their protein.

Our oceans are by far our greatest carbon sinks. They absorb about a third of all CO_2 generated. Because we have dumped so much CO_2 into the air (90 million tons daily), we have overwhelmed the ocean's ability to absorb it. And that has triggered a series of cascading consequences. When CO_2 dissolves in the ocean, it produces carbonic acid. Too much carbonic acid reduces coral's ability to calcify and form skeletons. In addition, the amount of carbonic acid has actually changed the ocean's pH. Just a 0.1 decline in surface pH represents a 30 percent rise in the ocean's acidity.

At the dawn of the Industrial Age there were about 280 parts per million of CO_2 is in the atmosphere; in 2013, that number hit 400 parts per million—and it's still going up. The more CO_2 in the atmosphere, the more heat and acidity in the oceans. Because of this heat and acidity, there are now patches in oceans where no plankton can grow at all—and we get 70 percent of our oxygen from plankton. When ocean temperatures rise too high, the algae that nourish coral (and give it its color) leave. This loss of color is called "bleaching." Bleaching kills the coral. Today half the coral reefs around the world are in this condition or past it. The acidification of the ocean stresses them and prevents them from recovering. Corals cover less than one tenth of one percent of the ocean floor but are home to 25 percent of the ocean's species. This has earned them the title "Rainforests of the Sea." And, like rainforests on land, they teem with life and almost inestimable diversity. While scientists' estimates of the number of their species vary wildly—from fewer than 250,000 to as many as several million—only a small percent of them have even been identified.[57] And we're losing them at an alarming rate. The current conditions in the oceans are at or near the upper temperatures that coral can survive in.

Coral reefs are ecosystems that deliver nutrients for larvae and in turn feed countless other species. When one form of marine life dies, the chain of interdependency that makes up the ecosystem loses links and weakens. This also affects life outside the sea, especially for anyone who fishes the sea as a livelihood.

Since Teddy Roosevelt started putting aside natural areas under the protection of the National Park System more than a century ago, about 14 percent of the total acreage worldwide has come under protection. Earle thinks we need to think that way about the oceans too. In 2003, at the World Parks Congress in Durban, South Africa, a goal was set for 2012: protection for 30 percent of the world's oceans. That goal wasn't met. Currently around 2 percent are protected. It needs to increase by a lot—and quickly.

Earle's Mission Blue initiative wants to change all that by igniting the public's awareness and support of the ocean's plight by demonstrating how interconnected the ocean's needs are with our own. She hopes to get much more of it protected, creating what she calls a network of "Hope Spots" all around the world to restore the ocean to health while we still can. We are land-based creatures, and it's understandable why most of the discussion of the planet's issues focus on terra firma, but there's a terra incognita off our shores that beckons us too. "We've got to somehow stabilize our connection to nature so that 50 years from now, 500 years, 5,000 years from now there will still be a wild system and respect for what it takes to sustain us."

We are at a critical juncture, she says, "in a *sweet spot* in time. Never again will there be a better time to take actions that can insure an enduring place for ourselves within the living systems that sustain us. We are at an unprecedented, pivotal point in history when the decisions we make in the next ten years will determine the direction of the next 10,000."

And restoring the ocean is a real possibility. There's still enough to work with. "There are plenty of reasons for despair," she says, "but I see it another way: Half the planet's coral reefs are still in good shape. Ten percent of the sharks, swordfish, bluefin tuna, groupers, snappers, halibut and wild salmon are still swimming. Best of all, there is widespread awareness that protection of nature is not a luxury. Rather, it is the key to all past, present and future prosperity. We may be the planet's worst nightmare, but we are also its best hope."[58]

The oceans are, after all, Earles says, "the blue heart of the planet; we should take care of our heart. It's what makes life possible for us."

A CO$_2$ Primer

- Carbon dioxide is the greenhouse gas most responsible for making earth temperatures rise.
- Excess carbon dioxide in the atmosphere results from the emissions of burning fossil fuels from industry, transportation, and agriculture, as well as from the loss of the carbon sinks that occur from deforestation and oversaturation of the oceans.
- Atmospheric levels have risen substantially:
  - 277 parts per million (ppm) before the Industrial Revolution.
  - 400 ppm globally in 2013 (this pivotal level began began showing in Arctic monitoring stations in the spring of 2012).[59]
  - James Hansen, the head of NASA's Goddard Institute for Space Studies, says efforts to reduce CO$_2$ levels to 350 ppm should be our immediate focus.
- Today, because of increased emissions, levels are rising four times the rate they rose in the 1950s.
- No one can know the effect on the parts-per-million levels as warming temperatures melt permafrost in northern areas, especially Siberia, which has the most potential CO$_2$ and methane locked away in its permafrost. As the permafrost thaws and dries out, it becomes a huge fire risk. A state of emergency was declared in 2012 as hundreds of fires raged out of control across the Siberian front near Mongolia. In 2007 alone, the average temperature in the once iconic frozen wasteland rose two full degrees centigrade.

Source: Environmental Defense Fund (www.edf.org)

The Age of Wildfires

In early June 2008, after the driest spring ever recorded had followed two years of low precipitation, governor Arnold Schwarzenegger proclaimed a statewide drought in California. That same week, farmers in some of the state's Central Valley, where $1.3 billion in cotton, tomatoes, garlic, and onions is grown annually, were already dealing with an edict from the U.S. Bureau of Reclamation, which had reduced the district's water share by 40 percent, forcing many farmers to make a Sophie's Choice on their upcoming season's harvests.[60]

Just two weeks later, on June 20, a dry lightning storm—lightning without rain—moved through central and northern California, peppering more than two dozen counties with six thousand lightning strikes. The 2,096 fires that resulted burned throughout much of the summer and would eventually require the services of more than twenty thousand firefighters from all over North America and from as far away as Australia and New Zealand.[61]

Drought causes tinderbox conditions that, ironically, are often ignited with the coming of rain or in the case of the California conflagration—collectively called the North California Lightning Series—dry lightning. The effects of wildfires, as with other natural disasters, aren't limited to the events they bring. Just as with floods and severe storms, crops, homes, businesses, natural resources, and lives can be lost. The air can become contaminated and toxic. In the aftermath of Hurricane Katrina, a chemical plant near New Orleans exploded, sending benzene fumes into the air. Even from a helicopter exploring the scene two thousand feet above the plume, people on board could not breathe.[62]

According to a report prepared in August 2004 by researchers with the U.S. Department of Agriculture, even a rise in summer temperatures of 2.8 degrees could double the number of wildfires in eleven western states. Along with that goes the estimate from a 2007 report by the Intergovernmental Panel on Climate Change that the annual wildfire season in the western states had already been extended by 78 days because of longer and warmer springs and summers.[63] Here again, the timing of the annual snowmelt is critical. In one thirty-four-year study, the years that had an earlier snowmelt (setting up longer, drier summertimes), there were five times as many wildfires as in years when the snowmelt was late.[64] Statistics show that since 1986, "longer, warmer summers have resulted in a fourfold increase of major wildfires and a sixfold increase in the area of forest burned" compared to the period of 1970 to 1986.[65]

Heat waves, drought, and wildfires are all first cousins in the global warming family. They exacerbate and feed off one another. Each is made worse by warming temperatures. Just as heat waves and drought threaten crop yields, wildfires threaten homes and businesses and vast natural resources, drying up stream and river beds, contaminating the air with smoke, causing respiratory difficulties downwind and altering the landscape of many of the parks and habitats we count as natural treasures.

As we've seen in the summers since the 2008 California wildfires, longer and more destructive wildfire seasons are turning out to be a trend. In a speech about global warming given on July 17, 2008, in the midst of the California wildfire's onslaught, Al Gore stated that scientists at Tel Aviv University had determined that "for every one degree increase in temperature, lightning strikes will go up another 10 percent."[66] According to the EPA, the temperatures in the lower forty-eight states have risen 1.4 degrees Fahrenheit since 1901, with the average temperatures rising faster since the late 1970s (from about a third to a half a degree each decade).[67]

The year 2005 was not only the first year that saw four category 5 hurricanes, it was also one of the warmest year recorded since recordkeeping began in the 1850s. With the scorching, drought-ridden summer of 2012 breaking all previous records, the world's ten warmest years have all occurred since 2000.[68] With scientists predicting anywhere from a 3- to 10-degree warming during this century, higher temperatures would clearly make wildfires an ever growing risk to the world's ecosystems.

Stormy Weather

Hurricane Katrina is the poster child for one of global warming's worst consequences, stronger storm systems. While there's no real indication that there are more hurricanes in the Atlantic or Pacific each summer and fall, it is clear that the trend is toward stronger and more devastating systems. With stronger storms come increased flooding, infrastructure and economic devastation, higher death tolls, and the countless personal tragedies that come with loss of life and home. A study done by researchers at the Massachusetts Institute of Technology in 2005 found that since the 1970s, hurricanes have doubled in intensity and duration, correlating that increase with higher sea surface temperatures. The frequency of category 4 and 5 storms has also doubled during that timeframe, a fact also attributed to the warming of the oceans.

While many businesses may not yet feel compelled to acknowledge the growing and continuing effects of global warming, one industry has launched its own frontal assault. During 2004 and 2005, insurance firms witnessed staggering losses as the amounts collected as premiums were overwhelmed by the massive outpouring of payouts in no less than ten major storms that devastated the Gulf and Atlantic coasts. Florida alone, where 70 percent of insured property sits on the coast, suffered eight destructive hurricanes in a fifteen-month period during the 2004 and 2005 hurricane seasons. When Hurricane Andrew hit Florida in 1992, insurance losses topped $26 billion. A dozen insurance companies became insolvent, while many others stopped writing policies altogether in the state. After Andrew, everything changed for the industry. Along the high-risk east and Gulf coasts, premiums skyrocketed. Between 2002 and 2006, rates in Miami Beach shot up 500 percent, while in Alabama, "the insurance premium for a 35-unit beachfront condominium building went up more than 10 fold."[69]

From the relatively hurricane-free 1970s up to the years just preceding Katrina, the industry watched as coastal building increased and a kind of collective amnesia set in. In Mississippi, New Orleans' eastern neighbor, ninety thousand people moved into three of its coastal and adjacent counties between 1995 and 2000. MIT professor Kerry Emanuel observed, "Despite centuries of hurricane disasters, our society continues to disregard collective experience and invite future tragedy by building more and more structures in surge-prone coastal regions."[70]

In fact, the coastal population in the United States jumped 28 percent between 1980 and 2003. In Florida alone, the increase was a staggering 75 percent.[71] By 2004, properties along the U.S. Gulf and Atlantic coasts were valued at $7 trillion. Looking the other way became the norm in Louisiana early on. As Tulane University historian Douglas Brinkley wrote in *The Great Deluge*, "Once Louisiana became part of the U.S. in 1803, entrepreneurial delusion became a mind-set in the region."[72]

Before the record losses became the new norm, insurance companies had a pretty good way of gauging risk. They used actuarial tables based on decades of weather patterns to calculate what was likely to happen in the future. But as the planet warms, and scientists warn that storms are likely to become more severe, the old rules no longer work. The result: the insurance industry believes global warming is real and getting worse, and it is responding accordingly, by getting out of the high-risk business of insuring coastal areas in times that seem increasingly unpredictable. The United Nations projects that climate change will cost the world's financial centers upwards of $150 billion annually for the foreseeable future.

"Allstate, one of the nation's largest insurance providers, has cut off coverage for 40,000 coastal homeowners in New York, and is no longer writing any new policies in Florida."[73] In February 2010, State Farm Florida announced it would begin cancelling policies for 125,000 of its customers in August, the midpoint of the hurricane season, because state regulators denied their request to raise premiums by 47 percent. Most of those customers resided in coastal areas.[74] The downstream effects aren't promising. As homeowners and business owners contemplate rebuilding, they face skyrocketing insurance premiums—if they can find insurers at all. "Without adequate insurance, businesses can't borrow money to keep their doors open and those on fixed incomes can't afford to stay in the homes in which they planned to retire."[75]

As losses become the new normal, the history of economic development along the Gulf Coast is being written on the wind. "Hurricanes and tropical storms represent the largest weather-related threat to economic stability along the U.S. coast."[76]

What might this mean to a world facing not only stronger storms but also rising seas? Considering that nearly half of the world's population lives within one hundred miles of the sea—and those who live in one of the world's great ports considerably closer—it appears likely that the warming climate and its effects will increasingly determine the places we can and can't call home. While living by the sea as we know it may well become a distant memory, for many who decide to risk it, it will at least become an exercise in living without a safety net.

A Hurricane Cassandra

That huge storm surge rode in on an ocean that was a foot higher than it would have been without climate change.
—BILL MCKIBBEN

While Katrina is (so far) the costliest hurricane in U.S. history (estimated at $146 billion in 2012 dollars), Hurricane Sandy may find a place in the history books as the wake-up call to a public still dithering about the reality of global warming and climate change—and the bigger, fiercer, more damaging storms that are becoming its calling cards.

Beginning with the hottest Marsh ever recorded, 2012 segued from one natural disaster to another. A summer of intense heat broke more than twenty-six thousand hot-weather records nationwide, spread drought across the country, turned more than half of the United States into disaster areas, and left record soy and corn crop failures in its wake. Hot weather and dry conditions created more than four dozen wildfires that raged throughout the summer, primarily from Arizona to Montana (the fires were so numerous that Google created a crisis map to make it possible to keep track of all of them)—one of which required nearly all the residents of Colorado Springs to evacuate because of the extreme conditions in Waldo Canyon.

The biggest natural disaster of the year—and the biggest since Katrina—began as a tropical depression on October 22 but was a category 3 hurricane at its peak, two days later, when it raked across the Caribbean, leaving sixty-nine people dead, on its way to the U.S. east coast. Sandy swept northeast, where it ran into an Arctic cold front moving in from Greenland, which pushed it to the northwest. In its path were the most heavily populated urban areas of the United States. By the time it made landfall, at high tide on October 29 near Brigantine, New Jersey, it was a category 1 hurricane with eighty-mile-per-hour winds. But by then its diameter had expanded to over a thousand miles; its area covered nearly two million square miles. Its impact was felt as far west as Chicago, where an adventurous few braved fifty-mile-per-hour winds and waded through the flooded bike paths to surf the twenty-foot waves coming ashore on Lake Michigan.

In the coastal and southern-most areas of New York City, the wreckage was widespread and the loss historic. The buoy set at the entrance to New York Harbor recorded the largest storm surge in New York history, 32.5 feet,[77] beating the previous record—set by Hurricane Irene only a year before—by 6.5 feet. The fourteen-foot surge at the Battery in Manhattan flooded streets, rail yards, tunnels, roads, construction sites (including Ground Zero), garages, and basements. Both the MTS subway systems and PATH trains were flooded, including seven trains that ran under the East River, the worst destruction in the subway's 108-year history. The force of the water carried ships inland, straddling them, in some cases, across railroad tracks. It shorted out power stations, taking out power to more than two million homes and leaving much of lower Manhattan in darkness. In Staten Island alone, two thousand homes were destroyed and half the borough was without power. Twenty-four people died there, twenty from drowning.

In New Jersey, a fifty-foot length of the famed Atlantic City Boardwalk was smashed and lost in the storm, its iconic Ferris Wheel buckled and broken, standing in the surf. Atlantic City itself was 85 percent under water. Half of Hoboken was flooded. Swaths of homes along the famed Jersey shore were pulverized. The cost of the loss in New Jersey alone was estimated to be $30 billion. Viewing the massive damage to the neighborhoods that dotted the shoreline, Governor Chris Christie called it "unimaginable."

Sandy's finale was as a freak snowstorm that dumped as much as three feet of heavy wet snow in an area that ran from the Carolinas north to Maryland and as far west as Ohio. Roofs buckled and collapsed from the sudden weight.

By the time it had blown itself out, after heading as far north as Toronto, 285 people were dead in seven countries; 24 U.S. states had been affected; 8 million homes were without power in 17 states; and a path of destruction from flooding, fires, and wind damage left officials speechless.

The damage came despite the heightened state of readiness all along the storm's path. After the numerous local and national errors with Katrina, government agencies at every level began to prepare well ahead of the storm. Seventeen states declared states of emergency. New York City mayor Michael Bloomberg ordered a mandatory evacuation of 375,000 residents from southern Manhattan. The National Guard had 61,000 personnel ready to respond to emergencies. FEMA deployed 4,000 personnel and set up two dozen disaster recovery centers in the most populous centers of New York and New Jersey. NOAA provided a hurricane app for smart phones to simplify storm and news tracking. Nearly 20,000 flights were cancelled during the days before and after the storm's arrival.

Despite the precautions and preparations, the damage was unprecedented. A theory about this began to emerge quickly. In its November 1 issue, only two days after Sandy hit, *Bloomberg BusinessWeek*'s cover story was titled, "It's Global Warming, Stupid."

Sandy featured a scary extra twist implicating climate change. An Atlantic hurricane moving up the East Coast crashed into cold air dipping south from Canada. The collision supercharged the storm's energy level and extended its geographical reach. Pushing that cold air south was an atmospheric pattern, known as a blocking high, above the Arctic Ocean. Climate scientists Charles Greene and Bruce Monger of Cornell University, writing earlier this year in *Oceanography*, provided evidence that Arctic ice melts linked to global warming contribute to the very atmospheric pattern that sent the frigid burst down across Canada and the eastern U.S.[78]

The way we usually measure a hurricane is by its wind speed, which is what the Saffir-Simpson scale (categories 1 to 5) measures. This works well in helping communities take measures to minimize damage to life and property, but wind speed isn't the only measuring stick for a storm's potential destructive power.

What made Sandy different was the energy at its core: the storm's massive size. Add to that the fact that, because of global warming, the atmosphere is warmer and thus holds more water vapor. The more water vapor, the bigger the volume of water that come ashore when a storm hits. And beyond that, East Coast sea levels have risen (from thirteen to sixteen inches in the New York area between 1880 and 2009), so storm surges are higher, flooding is more pronounced, and water seeps farther inland.[79]

Katrina pounded the Gulf coast with much stronger winds, but Sandy was twice as big as Katrina. University of Miami meteorologist Brian McNoldy said, "Katrina was capable of generating a locally higher surge, but Sandy was capable of generating a destructive surge over a larger length of coastline."[80]

This is the new climate reality that cities like New York must face: the unimaginable on a regular basis. New York governor Andrew Cuomo said, "We have a hundred-year flood every two years now."

Nowhere in the world is the rising number of natural catastrophes more evident than in North America. The study shows a nearly quintupled number of weather-related loss events in North America for the past three decades, compared with an increase factor of 4 in Asia, 2.5 in Africa, 2 in Europe and 1.5 in South America.

*Anthropogenic climate change is believed to contribute to this
trend. . . . Climate change particularly affects formation of
heat waves, droughts, intense precipitation events, and in the long
run most probably also tropical cyclone intensity.*
—MUNICH RE, the globe's largest reinsurer[81]

The Coming of the Whirlwind

Hurricanes like warm water. That's why the hurricane calendar falls
in the warmest months of the year. In late August 2005, nearing the
end of the hottest summer ever recorded, the waters that would soon
host three category 5 hurricanes in the Gulf of Mexico had reached
a very balmy eighty-seven degrees, a full five degrees warmer than
normal. Tropical depression 12 began over the Bahamas on August
24. When it dealt southern Florida a glancing blow a day later, it
was as a category 1 hurricane, Katrina. A million homes lost power
and eleven people died before it moved off the Florida coast and
spun into the Gulf of Mexico, where it met the friendly loop current
that runs deep and clockwise through the Gulf's warm eddies. The
heat in the water basically acted like "hurricane intensity engines,"
enabling the storm to feed off the warmth as it swirled in the Gulf
for three days, picking up moisture, wind speed, and slow-moving
intensity, revving itself up before turning northeast.[82] Loop currents
like the ones Katrina rode are warm, subtropical waters that flow
from the Caribbean Sea at the tip of Florida southwesterly through
the Yucatán Channel back into the Gulf of Mexico. They were the
alchemists that created the perfect recipe for Katrina's transformation into a storm 460 miles wide that would kill 1,800 people across
the Gulf Coast, nearly destroy an iconic American city, and wake us
up to the consequences of global warming.

By Saturday, August 27, Katrina was a category 3; on Sunday
morning, when the city's first-ever mandatory evacuation was
ordered, it began the day as a category 4 and ended the day as a
category 5. Winds were clocked at more than 170 mph. By dawn
on Monday, as it made landfall, it had dropped to a high category 3,

with winds at 127 mph (category 4 wind speeds start at 131 mph). Twelve hours after landfall, it was downgraded to a category 1, but the damage had been done. Over 90,000 square miles of coast between Louisiana and Alabama had been damaged or decimated, an area equal to the size of Great Britain. In New Orleans, as four tears widened in three levees, the bowl that was the city effectively tipped. An estimated 80 percent of the city was submerged, some areas under a dozen feet of water or more.

"Any hurricane acts like a vacuum as it drives across the ocean, literally pulling water up into its grasp. When the hurricane hits land, all that vacuumed-up water is let loose, in a great wave known as the storm surge."[83] In places Katrina's storm surges would reach nearly thirty feet as it rolled ashore, pounding everything in its path. At 8:00 a.m. on that Monday morning, Mayor Ray Nagin was interviewed on NBC's *Today Show:* "We will have significant flooding, it's just a matter of how much." Fourteen minutes later, the levee on the Industrial Canal began to collapse, inundating the Lower Ninth Ward. One minute after that, in nearby Waveland, Mississippi, the twenty-seven members of its police force fled their building and sought refuge in trees as the storm came ashore, water inside their office rising three feet in fifteen minutes. They endured and survived the slashing winds and debris of the storms, clinging to the treetops. Much of their small beachfront town was destroyed. Meanwhile, as they hung on, in New Orleans' St. Bernard parish, a few miles to the southwest, thirty-five helpless and bedridden patients at the St. Rita's Nursing Home, some of them tied to their beds, watched the water rise around them quickly. All drowned within the next half-hour.[84]

By 3 a.m. Tuesday, the power had failed at Methodist Hospital. Even back-up generators weren't working, since many hospitals had stored this equipment in basements—which flooded first. Volunteers and staff used hand pumps to keep patients on ventilators alive (they would do this hour after hour for two full days). The temperature inside the hospital was sweltering. But not everyone was affected just by heat. Many who clung to rooftops and tree branches, light poles and floating debris, got severe hypothermia from the high winds and water.

Everywhere the storm "created weaponry consisting of millions of pounds of airborne debris, cleaved from beachside buildings and out of unlucky houses. From garbage can lids to Ford 150 truck doors to Maytag refrigerators to 120-foot yachts, Katrina made shrapnel of everything." In nearby Biloxi, Mississippi, all ten of its floating casinos were pulverized.[85] Doctors said they saw not only cuts and punctures but also hands whose skin had been torn or shredded off, sometimes cut to the bone by debris and wind. "The result was that many people had hands swollen and raw like slabs of red meat."[86] Without anesthetics or analgesics, wounds were sewn up without anything to ease the suffering. Because of the insufferable heat and humidity, doctors and nurses shed their clothes and worked in their underwear, washing it out and hanging it on makeshift clotheslines to stay as hygienic as they could.

On Sunday, the day before Katrina made landfall, 18,000 vehicles were leaving New Orleans each hour. By Thursday, three days after Katrina hit, Baton Rouge replaced New Orleans as the largest city in Louisiana. Within a week, 1.7 million residents of the Gulf Coast would be scattered across all fifty states.

The damage was unprecedented. In Louisiana alone, 200,000 homes and 15,000 apartments were destroyed. Another 45,000 homes were declared unlivable. The parishes of St. Bernard and Plaquemines were 90 percent destroyed. In tiny Buras, a fishing village sixty-three miles southeast of New Orleans, where Katrina first made landfall, although everyone in the community had evacuated, every house was destroyed. The damages to the entire Gulf Coast were estimated at well over $100 billion. The loss to the area fishing industry was almost unimaginable: nearly three thousand vessels were destroyed. "And these were not just skiffs. A good-size Gulf shrimp boat could run to sixty feet." Besides the vessels, there was the devastation of the fishing grounds themselves, "the pulverizing of thousands of acres of oyster beds, some of them forty and fifty years old." The shrimp beds, also damaged, quickly repaired themselves, primarily because there were no fishing vessels left to trawl the water.[87]

By Thursday, 4,000 people were stranded on Interstate 10 without water, food, or medical supplies. Tens of thousands more still awaited help in the city's convention center, the Louisiana Superdome, and hospitals. It would be Friday or later before coordinated assistance began to arrive. In the interim, the U.S. Coast Guard and the Louisiana National Guard performed heroically, flying countless missions to rescue the stranded. The Ninth Ward and St. Bernard Parish were the hardest hit, with an estimated fifty thousand people awaiting rescue. A small flotilla of flat-bottomed boats manned by members of the Louisiana Wildlife and Fisheries took to the waters and was joined by local residents who showed up in rowboats, motor boats, pirogue canoes, and jet skis—and some even on foot, wading through the water—to rescue their fellow New Orleanians.[88] Bodies were visible for days, some still being discovered in abandoned houses more than a year later.

As bodies began being removed, reporters were told to stay back the equivalent distance of three football fields or face consequences—varying from arrest to denial of press access to future military operations.[89] Katrina's aftermath was very bad press. Forty-five dead patients were recovered from a New Orleans hospital a full week after an NBC cameraman had filmed them and reported his findings to officials.[90] Encountering the drowned is particularly gruesome, especially during very warm and humid weather, days or months after death. "What the mythic flood stories don't convey is the reality of decomposing flesh, a process that is accelerated when a body is waterlogged. The abdomen swells, the tongue protrudes and blood from the lungs comes flushing out of the mouth, nostrils, and eyes. A hideous, repugnant, rotten-egg stench, caused by the release of the methane-like gas, permeates the dead skin, making it especially awful for those who found the corpses after Katrina."[91]

But nothing could hide the truth. The American public was seeing it on every news channel. The storm's enormous size had rewritten all the laws of hurricane expectations. Clearly, the coastlines suffered the most. Bridges, beaches, wetlands, bayous, and byways were destroyed, and towns virtually erased from maps. In some places, only before-and-after satellite -maps could help people locate where they had once lived.

We hadn't been prepared, and no one seemed willing to step up and take responsibility. Danger filled the city. The water flooding the streets was toxic in countless ways, many unknown—not only from the thousands of barrels of oil, sewage, and chemical pollutants, but also from the poisonous brew that came from flooding the medicine cabinets, garages, and refrigerators of thousands of homes, restaurants, hospitals, pharmacies, grocery stores, and other buildings.

The death toll in New Orleans alone would eventually rise to 1,200, but a complete total will never be known. There is no accurate count for those who perished from diabetic coma, untreated high blood pressure, and other medical conditions, or from the heart attacks and strokes caused by the shock or hardship that registered on survivors later.

Before Katrina, New Orleans had a population of 453,000. More than half that number waited out Katrina whether they wanted to or not. After the storm, 378,000 would be displaced, either temporarily or permanently. Three full years later, 65,000 blighted lots in the city remained, and the population was estimated at 272,000, 60 percent of the pre-Katrina population. But by mid-2012, the numbers had improved significantly, with population hovering near 370,000, 80 percent of its pre-Katrina numbers for the first time.[92]

Prophets without Honor

Given the mythic and historical precedents available on Gulf Coast hurricanes, the personal experiences with past storms of city dwellers and city officials, as well as the warnings given to government bureaucracies on the likelihood of Katrina delivering a five-star disaster, how could this particular storm have taken everyone by such surprise? "If experts had prophesied a terrorist attack with that kind of accuracy, they would be under suspicion for treason," wrote Amanda Ripley in a *Time* magazine piece the weekend after the storm struck. "If Hurricane Katrina turns out to be the biggest disaster in U.S. history to date, it will also be the least surprising."[93]

The signals had been everywhere, if anyone had been willing to look. But in a post-9/11 United States, terrorism was getting the budget attention; the shuffling of agencies (FEMA was subsumed into Homeland Security and its funding cut) and the hiring of personnel without adequate emergency training—like FEMA head Michael Brown—didn't help.

The year before Katrina, FEMA had conducted an elaborate simulation called "Hurricane Pam," which had uncanny similarities with Katrina; it predicted much of what happened. But as accurate as it ended up being, nobody wanted to listen. Brian Wohson, a professor of engineering at Louisiana State University, served as a consultant on the exercise. "I'll be honest with you. I'm the researcher. I'm doing all the models, and sometimes I could say to myself, 'Am I Chicken Little? Could this really happen?' Even I was in denial, and I was the one running all the numbers."[94] One of the goals of the simulation was to determine how to deal with the hundred thousand or so poor and infirm residents who would need help fleeing the city. At disaster-planning meetings following the simulation, he said, "the answer was often silence."[95] Hurricane Pam might have impressed its participants, but the scenario didn't stick with them. Recommendations were still being assessed when Katrina hit.

While Hurricane Pam dealt with probable outcomes from rain and wind, it did nothing to alleviate another troubling and long-standing problem with coastal Louisiana: the loss of the state's protective wetlands along the coast, an environmental disaster all its own. Proponents of their restoration see the loss of the wetlands as one factor that made New Orleans so vulnerable—and one factor that could have been preventable. Louisiana has nearly three million acres of wetlands running nearly two hundred miles along the Gulf Coast and stretching eighty miles inland. Some of the wetlands' loss is a natural result of the shifting of the two-hundred-mile-wide

Delta plain of the Mississippi River, which is actually what created the barrier reefs and islands that comprise the wetlands in the first place.[96] Because hurricanes tend to gain strength over water and lose strength once they reach land, these reefs and islands once composed a buffer for inland areas, protecting them from a storm's harshest winds.

Their continuing disappearance is no small issue. According to King Milling, an America's Wetlands spokesperson, for every 2.7 miles of wetlands lost, you can count on a one-foot increase in storm surge. "Storm surges that used to be in the neighborhood of ten to twelve feet could suddenly be eighteen to twenty feet."[97] Katrina would create surges of twenty-two feet in pockets of New Orleans and a record-breaking 27.8 feet in nearby Pass Christian, Mississippi.

Between 1930 and 2005, southern Louisiana lost more than one million acres of wetlands across twenty parishes—an area equal to the size of the state of Delaware—both to coastal erosion and manmade interference. By 2005, the rate of loss had reached the equivalent of one football field every 38 minutes. Park Moore, Assistant Secretary of the Louisiana Department of Wildlife and Fisheries believes this is critical. "The impact of losing their wetlands was overwhelming. All the habitat for animals and invertebrates was disappearing along with a vital natural filter, which prevents pollution in the Gulf from toxic agents from oil and gas. Dredging killed the wetlands which, in time, would leave Louisianans more vulnerable to hurricanes."[98]

The manmade reasons for the destruction of the wetlands are easy to see: offshore oil platforms began to dot the Gulf in the 1950s, delivering millions of barrels of oil and trillions of cubic feet of natural gas to energy companies. Louisiana is a big part of U.S. energy production, providing a full 25 percent of the nation's oil and natural gas. Between them, Hurricanes Katrina and Rita destroyed 113 offshore platforms and damaged many offshore pipelines and processing facilities.[99] (Deepwater Horizon, BP's deepwater platform that blew out and sank fifty miles off the Gulf Coast in April

2010, was not installed until early 2010.)

Preceding the Hurricane Pam scenario run by FEMA, a number of magazines and newspapers crafted possible scenarios of a catastrophic hurricane hitting New Orleans. In 2005, John Barry's 1998 epic about the 1927 Mississippi River flood, *Rising Tide*, was "almost mandatory reading for the college-educated class in the Crescent City."[100] A five-part series written in the summer of 2002 by *Times-Picayune* writers John McQuaid and Mark Schleifstein, "Washing Away," marched lockstep through the reasons New Orleans was vulnerable and why preparations and changes to the current hurricane protection system were drastically—and quickly—needed. "Drowning New Orleans," an article published by *Scientific American* a full four years before Katrina, warned of such a storm's probable consequences.[101] It examines the effects of 1965's Hurricane Betsy and 1998's Hurricane George as the two storms that should have turned the tide on New Orleans's future.

When Betsy inundated parts of the city under eight feet of water, the city moved to upgrade the 350 miles of levees to withstand a category 3 hurricane. Good but no cigar, said the Army Corps of Engineers. "The Corps has been pushing for years for Category 5 protection," said Robert Flowers, former head of the Corps. "Decisions have been made to accept more risk."[102] The issue, they said, wasn't just bigger levees, but rather restoring the coastal wetlands.

But change comes slowly, even in the face of theoretical disaster. When category 5 Andrew missed New Orleans by one hundred miles, the city heaved a sigh of relief. When Hurricane George came even closer, waiting until the last moment to veer east, the truth became clearer, even to the most ardent naysayers. George was a near terror. "Its fiercely circulating winds built a wall of water 17-feet high topped with driven waves, which threatened to surge into Lake Pontchartrain and wash into New Orleans"—the exact scenario that would occur seven years later when Katrina topped the levees surges of twenty feet or more.[103]

That was enough for the state, local, and federal officials to sit down together and map out a serious plan to address the issue of their city's hurricane defense. Within months they had devised a bold plan called Coast 2050. Its goal: to restore the wetlands of coastal Louisiana by its target year. The first step in this plan would have involved rebuilding the marshland by creating river diversions at key junctures along the Mississippi, and then building control gates to allow freshwater and sediment to wash through marshes down to the Gulf. The second step would involve bringing in half a billion cubic yards of sand from Ship Shoal in Terrebonne parish, just west of New Orleans. The cost for the fifty-year program was calculated at $14 billion. The estimated cost of Katrina adjusted to 2013 dollars is around $120 billion.

In an editorial written less than a week after Katrina sank his city, writer Richard Ford described how words could not really express what it felt like to be a New Orleans native post-Katrina. "It's like Hiroshima, a public official said. But no. It's not like anything. It's what it is. That's the hard part. He, with all of us, lacked the words."[104]

The Way We Were

In March of 1804, in the time leading up to the actual signing of the papers finalizing the sale that came to be known as the Louisiana Purchase, Meriwether Lewis busied himself learning botany, zoology, and celestial navigation, as well as the rudiments of medicine from the nation's leading doctors. He also signed on his Army friend Captain William Clark to lead the expedition with him. With their boats built, the trip fully provisioned, and a crew hired, the journey that would see the first Americans set foot in what would become the western United States was ready to commence. The eventual cost to the American taxpayer would be $38,000. The expedition's assignment was twofold: to see what there was to see but also, and even more dramatically, to fulfill a quest that had haunted explorers for centuries: to find the Northwest Passage, the mythical intercontinental water route to the Pacific Ocean that would enable unfettered access to the markets of the Orient.

The Corps of Discovery, as Lewis and Clark's journey was called, saw things no American had ever seen before and much that we can no longer see. Everywhere their route took them, they witnessed wonder after wonder. There was a saying at the time that the eastern half of the United States was so heavily forested that a squirrel could start at the shore of the Atlantic Ocean and jump from tree branch to tree branch without ever touching the ground until it reached the Mississippi River. It wasn't until it got to the Great Plains that it would have to start walking. It took Lewis and Clark weeks to cross the mostly treeless Great Plains, a calm and dazzling display of fertile grasslands that presented a stark contrast to the Rocky Mountain passages that would challenge them almost to death near their trip's end.

Near what is now Bismarck, South Dakota, they discovered populations of Native Americans that dwarfed the populations then living in St. Louis and Washington, DC. At one point, as they maneuvered down a river, they had to pause to allow a herd of buffalo to ford across in front of them. They waited for an hour, awestruck by the size and power of the massive herd. In the Pacific Northwest, they saw what one crew member estimated as ten thousand pounds of salmon setting out to dry on the river's edge. All along the way they saved specimens of animals and plants no one of European descent had ever seen before, shipping them back to a delighted Thomas Jefferson.[105]

Across the ocean, the English poet William Wordsworth was observing the wholesale march into full-scale materialism, lamenting how the human eye was drawn increasingly to mechanical processes and economic progress and less and less to the quiet, redolent work of nature.

> The world is too much with us; late and soon,
> Getting and spending, we lay waste our powers:
> Little we see in Nature that is ours;
> We have given our hearts away, a sordid boon.

Writing at the dawn of the Industrial Revolution, which would span his century and the next, Wordsworth could not foresee the details, but he recognized the symptoms of people disengaging from their spiritual link to nature. As we were getting and spending, we were also losing and forgetting something whose simple sweetness would be a dim memory two centuries later.

As long as there have been civilizations on earth, humans have strived for more—to create, conquer, quest for, achieve, master, and invent, to continually reach beyond the limits of what we know and are able to do and even dream. Along the way, epochs came and went, civilizations were born and disappeared. Progress is nothing new, and it was not unique to the Industrial Revolution, whose chronological beginnings are at best arbitrary. But what was different at the beginning of the nineteenth century was how quickly we stopped exploring horizontally across the face of the earth and began exploring vertically. It was when we pierced the earth's surface to mine its riches that we really began to affect life on the planet as we had never done before—a spiral of effect and consequence that has shadowed us ever since.

Astrophysicist and storyteller Carl Sagan described humanity's time on this planet as the last minute of the last hour of the day of what he called the "cosmic clock"—11:59 p.m. and then some. On this cosmic clock, the Industrial Revolution is barely a blink, but its effects have sent our mother planet reeling in ways that can no longer be denied. The advantage we have over our ancestors who had yet to envision what a Pacific beach could possibly look like is just that. We have that capacity to see. While the families of the crew who set out from St. Louis in 1804 could only sit and wait for two and a half years to find out if their kin were even alive, much less what had become of them, we can hear from our far-off relatives almost instantly by phone. No matter where they are, we can hear their breathing through the receiver, hear their lives in our own ears.

Today, none of the conditions of Lewis and Clark's era still exist save one. We have not lost our hunger for exploration; it's just that we spend most of it digging for oil, gas, and coal—the discoveries that most interest us as twenty-first-century beings. And we have been wildly successful, creating a society that is mobile and connected in ways Lewis and Clark could never have envisioned. But while the Corps of Discovery spent their time in the unknown and learning what they could about the new territory and naming the new species they found, we have treated nature primarily as a thing to be used up. We have long since forgotten the gentle practice of naming what surrounds us to honor it and value its preciousness.

As chapter 1 points out, when we break the bond that exists between us and the earth that nurtures us, when we stop valuing what we can no longer name, the results are obvious. Just as Lewis and Clark thought they were going to find an intercontinental waterway that would take them to the markets of the Far East and found instead the destiny of the United States, we are new explorers who must dare to head into an unknown that we can feel but not yet see. We are being lured by our right brains as our left brains move in lockstep behind us and try to figure out a path that can work.

New Orleans, the port that made the Louisiana Purchase such a bright and shining possibility, has long had a reputation as a magical place. Its outrageous traditions, from its jazz funerals and above-ground cemeteries to its Mardi Gras celebrations, voodoo darkness, and polycultural historical roots make it unlike any other American city. Like a pulse, the mantra of the city calls out to celebrate life.

Once the Louisiana Purchase was complete, the Mississippi River officially became the country's tree of life, the artery that fed our other national parts, the body of water that thirty-one of our states feed directly into. The Mississippi Delta is effectively our country's root chakra, the bottom tip of the spiritual spine.

When New Orleans was hit by Hurricane Katrina, scattering its children to every state in the union, our nation's first chakra was shattered. Watching events unfold in excruciating slow motion, we no longer knew what we were capable of ignoring. Looking at this from an energetic and spiritual perspective, consider what it means to lose a precious commodity like the diversity of an entire city. When New Orleans drowned, it effectively dispersed some of the sweetness of our diverse history. How do we repair what has been so displaced, regather what is energetically ours from a sacred contract made by one of our country's ancestors?

We start by looking at what happened during Katrina as a fable, a tale of great meaning, a portent of things to come if we content ourselves by watching what is happening rather than venturing into waters that frighten us. One of the greatest ironies of this tale is still unfolding. Far away in the Arctic, because of global warming, for the first time in unknown eons, the ice pack has melted enough to create the type of northern passage that Lewis and Clark sought.

Thanks to increasingly widespread summer ice melt, a new northern sea route that runs from Norway past Russia to the Bering Sea was successfully carved out as a summer sea lane by Russian nuclear-powered icebreakers in 2010, and in August 2011, a Russian supertanker successfully negotiated the lane for the first time. A sister route, the Northwest Passage that frustrated Lewis and Clark and other explorers, is increasingly possible—even inevitable. Because of these new routes, exploration licenses are being issued in the United States, Canada, Greenland, Norway, and Russia. The prize they're after: the considerable store of minerals and fuel resources that once lay locked beneath the Arctic Circle and is now, incredibly, fair game for oil and natural gas exploration, not to mention the mining of precious metals. What this will enable, despite the hardships and harsh conditions in the largely untapped Arctic, says *The Economist*, is a twenty-first-century gold rush of epic proportions.[106]

Once again, as Inuit tribes and wildlife are being threatened with extinction, diversity and wholeness are threatened for the sake of what's expedient. The paradox is inescapable. It is the heating of the globe, much of it from the burning of fossil fuels that has endangered our life on this planet so completely. Yet the first response to that addiction with a full-scale assault to get more, like a heroin addict digging through a dumpster in hopes of finding a syringe with enough heroin still left in it, diseased or not, for one more fix, anything to postpone the inevitable pain of life without it.

In addition to the first chakra being the seat of our connection to the earth, it also represents, as Caroline Myss wrote in *Anatomy of the Spirit*, the seat of eye-for-an-eye justice, the idea of "what goes around comes around," and tribal consciousness. Tribes, say Myss, are rarely accountable for actions. As the country witnessed during the post-Katrina finger-pointing, it wasn't possible to find a single person or cause to hold fully accountable. The first chakra also corresponds to the first Sefirah in the tree of life in the Kabbalah, as well as to the Christian sacrament of baptism.[107] Katrina—the name comes from a Greek word meaning "pure"—offers us a new start, a clean slate, baptizing us into a new way of seeing, helping us to simultaneously bid farewell to our innocence and willful blindness and welcome the birth of new awareness.

Part 2

Waking Up

According to legend, when the Buddha arose from under the Bodhi tree,
he seemed to be engulfed in light. A Brahmin passing by
him approached him with great respect.
"Holy One, are you a God?"
"No, I am not a God," said the Buddha.
"Ah, you must be a Deva," declared the Brahmin.
"No, I am not a Deva," said the Buddha.
"Then it must be you are Brahma himself!" exclaimed the Brahmin.
"No," the Buddha assured him.
"Then you must tell me please, what are you?" asked the Brahmin.
"I am," said the Buddha, "awake."

Chapter 3

Oil Is One

When we try to pick out anything by itself, we find it hitched to everything else in the universe.

—JOHN MUIR

In the early hours of January 17, 1991, the United States, as part of a U.N.-led coalition, began a bombing campaign in Iraq against the regime of Saddam Hussein. The air campaign, which lasted for five weeks, was followed by a four-day ground campaign that drove the Iraqi Army from Kuwait.

Shortly after the bombing began, four hundred million gallons of crude oil dumped into the Persian Gulf, giving the world its worst oil spill (up to that time). The oil seeped out into the stretches of the Gulf, washing up on beaches, contaminating everything it touched, and killing untold numbers of wildlife, including an estimated twenty-five thousand birds. More than four hundred miles of the fragile Saudi coastline were drenched in oil. Because the circulation pattern of the Persian Gulf is slow and sluggish, scientists estimate the pollution done to waters could take a century to cleanse itself.

The United States accused Iraq of dumping the oil to create a barrier to a potential Marine landing. Iraq accused the United States of intentionally bombing oil tankers in Gulf ports. No matter. The effect was the same.

Near the end of the brief war, before the United States could declare victory and order a cease-fire, engineers from the Iraqi armed forces set fire to an estimated 789 of Kuwait's thousand oil wells, creating what experts gauge as the world's worst environmental disaster. Firefighters faced extreme obstacles, not only because most of the fires were far from water, but also because the U.S. air assault had left thousands of unexploded cluster bombs hidden in the sand where they fell.

Many of the wells were in Kuwait's Burgan field, second largest oilfield in the world. Only the Saudi Ghawar field is bigger. The wells would burn Kuwait's particular brand of light sweet crude for nine months, turning the area to smoke-choked permanent night. It would take ten thousand workers from twenty-seven countries to extinguish the blazes. As many as six million barrels of oil gushed into the air each day. The final estimated tally: one billion barrels.

A few million barrels were recovered. Much of what didn't burn pooled in more than three hundred lakes. In southern Kuwait, one such lake stretched for half a mile and reached depths of twenty-five feet. The Kuwaiti oil ministry estimated that the lakes contained twenty-five to fifty million barrels of oil, but over time, much of that sank into the sand, possibly with the bombs dropped to kill the tiny country's despoilers.

What didn't end up in lakes rose as smoke into the atmosphere and eventually into people's lungs. The smoke from the fires was so dense that it was clearly and quickly visible to NASA satellites stretching as it did from Baghdad to Iran. The noxious, cloying black rain of oil and smoke blew as far away as Turkey, Syria, and Afghanistan. Tons of soot covered the desert for months after the fires were extinguished. This sand and oil mixture turned patches of what was once tillable land into a substance called *tarcrete*. The combination of contaminants—soot, sulfur, and acid rain—covered agricultural lands as much as 1,200 miles in every direction. Eventually the damage made the soil so unfit that only weeds grew there. Once again, we humans were destroying the epidermis of the earth.

A dozen years after that first Gulf War, what many still remembered most clearly were the fires that marked its end. As a second Gulf War was about to get underway in 2003, the memories of what

Hussein had been willing to do to ruin a victor's spoils haunted people still reeling from the effects of the first war. When he was interviewed in January of 2003 by CNN, Dr. Meshal Al-Mesham, head of the Kuwait Environment Protection Agency said, "Right now in Kuwait we are noticing an increasing number of cases of cancer. We think it's related to what happened in '91 when we had the oil fires. A lot of people breathe very bad air."

Jonathan Lash, president of the World Resources Institute, a Washington-based think tank that focuses on environmental issues, seemed to concur when he wrote, "What many recall as a short-lived conflict resulting in the liberation of Kuwait was an environmental disaster—one from which the region and its people have yet to recover. The oil that did not burn in the fires," he added, "traveled on the wind in the form of nearly invisible droplets resulting in an oil mist or fog that poisoned trees and grazing sheep, contaminated fresh water supplies, and found refuge in the lungs of people and animals throughout the Gulf."[1]

At the end of his definitive history of the pursuit of oil, *The Prize,* Daniel Yergin wrote that while "our civilization has been transformed by the modern and mesmerizing alchemy of petroleum,"[2] that transformation came with a steep price. In our attempt to acquire and master it, it has acquired and mastered us. As we have pricked our planet's surface—like countless mosquitoes—we have found ourselves not just feeding but tethered to the consequences of our own gorging, nakedly guilty, sick at heart from its effects, but still hungry for more.

"When we decided to separate humanity from all of the rest of creation," says Thom Hartmann, "we created a schism that was deep and profound. When we decided that the world was here for us, separate from us, and it was our holy duty to control and dominate it, we lost touch with the very power and spirit which gave birth to us."[3]

If the universe had set out to teach us earthlings a lesson about our own willful blindness and neglect, our own creativity and brilliance, it could not have crafted a more purposeful journey for us or a more compelling story for us to learn about ourselves. At the center of that story sits the break that needs to be repaired: our ruptured connection with the earth. It is in the restoration of that spiritual birthright that hope and healing wait.

In a very real sense, it is the story of darkness and light, of best intentions and worst motives. It's about finally waking to a possible future in which our great-grandchildren await us with a single question: "What were you all thinking?"

The Opposite of Nature

Landing at LAX in one of the seven hundred thousand planes that come and go there each year, taking a shuttle to a rental car, then driving up La Cienega toward Hollywood in one of the twelve million vehicles that travel the L.A. freeways each day, you can begin to get a sense of how oil enables every mile of movement in the United States. As you head through Baldwin Hills and look up to your right, you see the paradox that is America's energy appetite. Puncturing the rolling hills that flank the 319-acre Kenneth Hahn State Recreation area, sometimes called the Central Park of Los Angeles, is a sea of pumping jacks bobbing up and down, pulling up the oil that has helped keep California's economy running smoothly, making it the eighth largest in the world. It's an example of our national energy schizophrenia: a lovely, pastoral slice of earth dedicated to nature surrounded by the symbols of what might be called the opposite of nature, the wresting from the earth of toxic gold.

No American city personifies the idea of America on the move better than Los Angeles. It is a city literally built on oil and criss-crossed with hundreds of miles of asphalt arteries that depend on a hydrocarbon diet to keep its mighty and diverse commercial heart beating. Without oil, like most of America, the city would come to a standstill.

California is also the most populous state in the country, and its thirty-six million residents and three million businesses pump enough noxious fumes into the atmosphere to give it a designation it would rather not have (and is trying hard to change): the twelfth largest emitter of greenhouse gases in the world.

Normally when you think of oil in this country, you might think Texas, Alaska, or Oklahoma. But California? Actually, yes. According to the Bureau of Land Management, the state remains the third largest onshore producer of oil and gas from federal lands, operating in six "super giant" fields. The first offshore drilling in the United States, in 1895, was near Santa Barbara. The La Brea Tar Pits in Los Angeles, a gift from the last Ice Age to the city's urban heart, was once a gathering place for settlers who collected oil from the pit's seeps to burn in their lamps, lubricate their wagon wheels, and seal their roofs.[4]

When the price for a barrel of oil peaked at nearly $150 a barrel in July 2008, it was accompanied by a steady rise in production. A lot of those pumping jacks that had been stilled were once again going at the oil for all they were worth. And during that summer, they were worth a lot. For all its bad raps, oil is still being pulled up out of the ground in record amounts, and it's still very big business. In 2008, the year of the great oil price run-ups, both Shell Oil and Exxon Mobil profits jumped to record highs: $31.4 billion and $45 billion, respectively. While the rest of the economy was sinking, the oil industry was doing just fine.

The pumping jacks you see all over the state resemble little mechanical dinosaurs, their heads bobbing up and down, pecking up the waste of their ancestors. It is that waste that transports, feeds, and moves the world. And we are still the mega-users. Even in the midst of their era of rocketing GDP growth, China and India can't touch us for oil consumption. While China uses about three barrels of oil per person per year, each man, woman, and child in America uses twenty-three barrels per year (and that's nothing—in 1978 each American guzzled thirty-two barrels). In India, the number is less than one barrel per capita.

The oil coursing through our national veins not only makes possible our transportation in all its mechanical forms, it also provides thousands of derivative products: everything from asphalt to nanosynthetics, part of a list that has spread like smoke into every nook and cranny of our lives. And its easy, cheap access has given us a silent entitlement, an esteem that is so deep in our national character that we'd rather be locked in bumper-to-bumper freeway traffic than surrender our beloved, gas-powered steeds to something as banal as a car pool. When asked by a *Wall Street Journal* reporter in late 2008 what it was like trying to wean Americans off their addiction to oil in the late 1970s, Jimmy Carter responded dryly, "It was like gnawing on a rock."[5]

No fun, that weaning. It's mother's milk that most of us are unwilling to do without. We Americans stubbornly love our oil and the vehicles that guzzle them. It's part of why we burn nineteen million barrels of it every day of the year. Its many forms of fuel— diesel, marine oil, jet fuel, heavy oil, and the light sweet crude that makes up our gasoline—make possible more than 80 percent of our transportation and much of the urban and suburban life that is uniquely American. Today, fossil fuels (much of it converted to electricity from coal-powered plants) heat and light our homes and businesses, run our factories and transportation systems, and keep us connected via the phone and internet. "Virtually every aspect of modern existence is made from, powered with, or affected by fossil fuels."[6] Without it, the modern American lifestyle—and economy— would nosedive in a free fall.

We couldn't eat either. Oil is not only the lifeblood of our transportation and industrial base; it's also the engine of modern agribusiness, inextricably involved in our food chain. Consider beef: the typical steer that spends an average of twenty-one weeks in a CAFO (concentrated animal-feeding operation), eating enough corn to reach about 1,200 pounds before he is slaughtered. Counting the amount of oil it takes to plant corn, fertilize it, spray pesticides, and then harvest and process it, that steer ingests the equivalent of nearly a full barrel of oil in his short, stuffed life. And that's just the carnivorous part of our diet.[7] (Nor is the easy solution for the world's omnivores to just stop eating meat. Nearly one-fourth of the world's population relies on livestock for some form of livelihood.

If we suddenly stopped eating meat, the world's unemployment figures would skyrocket.)

Most of the animal and vegetable material we eat travels an average of 1,500 miles before it reaches our plates. While the average
family of four in the developed world consumes about 1,070 gallons
of gasoline per year to keep their cars running, it takes another 930
gallons just to feed them.[8]

Oil runs the machinery that plants, harvests, processes, stores,
distributes, and prepares our food. It provides the raw materials
for the chemicals and pesticides that are sprayed on the crops that
feed both us and the animals we eat. Its byproducts fill every aspect
of our lives. And every day, acquiring and using oil becomes more
problematic. "Its volatile price erodes prosperity; its vulnerabilities
undermine security; its emissions destabilize climate. Moreover
the quest to attain oil creates dangerous new rivalries and tarnishes
America's moral standing. All these costs are rising."[9]

The two substances besides oil that make up the trio of hydrocarbons that form the backbone of our energy system—natural
gas and coal—are also critical players in our national infrastructure. And each is failing us on significant levels, which not only
endanger our economy, our way of life, and our national security,
but also—through the air we breathe, the food we eat, and the water
we drink—our health and the very future of life on this planet. Our
century-long dependence on them is at the core of our disconnection from our planet, and the way they became woven into a single,
central, controlling story is unique.

Spindletop: The Mother of All Salt Domes

It could be said that the twentieth century was birthed in oil, chris-
tened by a fount of green, then black, muck that shot out of a coastal
Texas salt dome on a January morning in 1901. The roar could be
heard in Beaumont, two miles away. Townspeople thought something had exploded and saw the two-hundred-foot plume that
announced the arrival of Spindletop, the world's first viable gusher

and the true beginning of the age of oil. In a single moment, the entire daily output of U.S. oil tripled. It would take nine days to cap the monster well "with a firmly-anchored valve," while nearly a million barrels of oil spewed across the hillock.[10]

If the twentieth century was really the American century, then historians will doubtless point to the breadth and depth of the natural resources that grace this country from ocean to ocean. But the drive to see what's on the other side of the horizon, to explore and test ourselves, is also an American characteristic. When Thomas Jefferson sent Lewis and Clark on that first land voyage to see what they could see, he perhaps inspired a tendency to quest that became part of our national DNA.

In 1978 William Least Heat Moon set out to recover from a divorce and found himself in a long meditation that carried him in his humble van across the so-called blue highways that cross the American landscape. "As a nation there are few things that draw us more strongly than a piece of roadway heading to we know not where," he said later. "This is the way we grow up. This is the way that we enter our history—get in a car and find the country."[11]

Our history became entwined not only with the car and the rite of passage it enabled but also with the hydrocarbons that ran it. Together, oil, coal, and natural gas became our energy spine. The American lifestyle is what rising nations want—and are increasingly getting. That freedom and access to the material things that make up the Western version of the good life are driving the growth of China and India, who today compete for the same resources we have long taken for granted. The truth is that if the rest of the world used the world's resources at the rate that the United States does, it would require three planets' worth of resources. Clearly, the earth can't accommodate another round of such hedonism. There simply are not enough of those resources to go around. China and India will not modernize via a fossil-fuel century as we—and much of the West—did.

One of the big drawbacks to our strategy of putting all of our energy eggs in one big oily basket is that oil is getting more difficult to extract and bring safely to market. "Our lifestyle, our entire world-wide modern civilization is possible only because we're rapidly using up a 300-million year old nonrenewable resource: ancient sunlight, principally in the form of oil, but also coal and gas."[17] The alternatives are dirtier and harsher on the environment, and capturing and distilling them often requires more resources than they produce. The era of the so-called easy oil is over. It's hard oil from here on out.

Oil and the Open Road

Today Americans drive more than 240 million cars. When Ram Dass chose the title *Be Here Now*, he might have been describing the state of being of the American driver: alone, behind the wheel of a car, on a road never before traveled. It is at once a skill in action, an adventure, and a leap of faith. We are gifted as no other country is, with a travelscape over three thousand miles wide that is criss-crossed with over three million miles of roads. The American open road is an adventure waiting to happen, an expanse that cannot be crossed by car in less than several days. It awaits our exploration—the unspoken birthright of every citizen. In our little (and not so little) metal steeds, shooting down a superslab highway at speeds that might have given our pioneer ancestors the bends, we can enter its larger or lesser paths, zone out and disappear—at least for a time.

Like Lewis and Clark before us, we quest, striking out for what Thomas Jefferson called the *terra incognita* of our own lives, finding our inner selves the way no one else quite can. It is our national meditation, the response to an endless curiosity about what's out there. In *Song of the Open Road*, Walt Whitman said the lure of the road is about testing yourself on your own, tasting freedom, experiencing firsthand how seeing what's outside of you changes what's inside of you. It is a kind of curiosity that he called "the profound lesson of reception." Listening, it turns out, is also an activity of the eyes.

Two years after Spindletop came in, exactly one hundred years after Lewis and Clark began the first American road trip, a retired thirty-one-year-old physician named Horatio Nelson Jackson made a similar critical imprint on our national DNA. Over drinks at the posh San Francisco University Club, he bet a friend $50 that he would be the first person to drive from San Francisco to New York, and he would do it within ninety days. It was not a task to take lightly. At that time, the only real coast-to-coast conveyances other than shoe leather and horseback were the exceedingly slow stagecoach, which could take three months, or the transcontinental railroad, which could do the job nicely within a week or less. But these were passive tours; Jackson was the first to set out on the road simply because the automobile offered him the freedom to do just that.

It was a perilous journey, one in which Jackson's car, a slightly used cherry red Winton with neither windscreen nor roof, broke down with great regularity, forcing the erstwhile adventurer to wait for days at a time for parts to arrive by train or stagecoach. But Jackson's original ninety-day estimate provided more than enough time. He arrived in lower Manhattan—along with his mechanic, Sewall Crocker, and bulldog companion, Bud—in the wee hours of July 26, 1903, a mere sixty-five days after he set out.

In short order, others set out to break his record. The open road became an American fever, despite the fact that finding gasoline was a daily hunt, camping out and cooking were the most likely amenities, mechanics were nowhere to be found (blacksmiths made most car repairs), and there were virtually no decent roads or maps to follow. Getting lost was part of the package.

Of the 2.3 million miles of roadway that existed in the first decade of the twentieth century, a paltry 150 miles were actually paved, and those all lay within city limits. Another 190,000 miles were surfaced with stone, gravel, shells, clay, bricks, or bituminous macadam. The rest were dirt paths, often full of rocks and ruts, used most often by horses, wagons, and livestock. Early automobile travelers followed stagecoach routes and railroad tracks and used the bridges and trestles built by the railroads.

The road system started to change as automobile manufacturers and suppliers began to see the wisdom of creating a highway system that could accommodate their products and fix them firmly into the American mainstream. In Indianapolis, on Memorial Day in 1911, an automotive entrepreneur and racing enthusiast named Carl Fisher celebrated the opening day of his new motor speedway. More than eighty thousand residents paid a dollar each to watch the new phenomenon, a five-hundred-mile car race around a 2.3-mile oval surfaced with more than three million paving bricks. This was the debut of what would become a fixture on the American scene: the Indianapolis 500.

Fisher had a passion for both automobiles and speed, and he was a born promoter. As both a headlamp manufacturer and a car dealership owner, he saw the necessity of an infrastructure that would enable the new automobile industry to grow. In 1913 he began to promote the building of the country's first transcontinental highway, the Lincoln Highway, stretching from Times Square in New York to Lincoln Park in San Francisco. He began raising the estimated ten million dollars required for its construction from private donations, including highly publicized checks from Theodore Roosevelt, Thomas Edison, and President Woodrow Wilson.

Perhaps Fisher's greatest promotion sealed the future for the American automobile when he convinced the U.S. Army to follow the Lincoln Highway (at that time still primarily composed of unimproved paths) on its first transcontinental motor convoy in 1919. The convoy was a multipurpose exercise. More than fifty thousand American servicemen had died in World War I, and half a million more Americans had succumbed to an influenza pandemic. The trip was meant to get people's minds off their worry and grief, to show off the Army's new, modern look, and to encourage recruitment. It was also part war game. After seeing what it had required to haul men and materials across Europe, they wanted to see how well we could do if we had to fight a foreign aggressor in our own land, using existing roads and bridges with the Army sustaining itself as it went—while also getting an idea of how well its new vehicles would function in "wartime" conditions.

Historically, this road trip was of particular importance, because of one of its staff observers. Having missed action in the recent war and feeling trapped and bored in what he feared would be a postwar letdown, Lt. Colonel Dwight Eisenhower volunteered to join as one of more than a dozen War Department observers who would submit a report on the convoy.

As it set off from Washington, DC, on July 7, 1919, the convoy was an instant success. Nobody had ever seen anything quite like it: a two-mile procession of eighty-one vehicles, including two trucks that carried spare parts, another that served as a blacksmith shop, two tankers carrying 750 gallons of gasoline apiece, a third carrying the same amount of water, motorcycles, staff cars for officers, five ambulances and kitchen trailers, a tractor, a three-million candlepower searchlight, a pontoon for floating large vehicles across rivers, and a monster vehicle called the Militor, which came equipped with a winch that could pull men and machinery out of every conceivable mishap.

Wherever the convoy stopped for the night, newspapers trumpeted the convoy's arrival and wrote glowing stories after its departure. Thousands of townspeople showed up to cheer its entrance and bid it farewell when it moved along its way. It was a slow trip. The roads were awful, only slightly improved since Horatio Jackson's days. There were no road signs, no means of direction, no way to know where you were or even if you were headed toward the town you hoped was ahead.

There were plenty of object lessons. Not only were most of the mechanics green recruits, they had never worked on engines before and had to learn as they went. The worn and narrow bridges often could not accommodate the heavy tanks and collapsed. The Army reengineered them and moved on, a boon for the fledging highway project. Heat and cold, rain and sandstorms plagued the trip, reinforcing the idea that these sorts of trips were hard enough in warm weather but would prove much more hazardous in colder conditions with fewer hours of daylight.

The closest thing to a map was the single printed guide that served as the convoy's reference, written by the few adventurers who had followed the paths in their automobiles. The scout who led the convoy was one of this small, stalwart group. Nobody else in the country knew the way. The convoy averaged five miles per hour. When it reached San Francisco on the morning of September 6, 1919, the entourage that accompanied it had grown so large that it took over half an hour for it to pass by. The town bubbled over with joy and pride, and the Pacific fleet, docked for the occasion, saluted the adventurers. The trip and its extreme challenges left a lasting impression on Eisenhower.

Twenty-five years later, as commander of Allied forces in Europe, Eisenhower saw clearly how Germany's modern highway system not only had enabled the Third Reich to successfully move troops and artillery throughout the country quickly but even made possible a two-front war. This convinced him that a robust highway system was essential for the United States. The "ribbon of highways" he envisioned would connect city and countryside as never before, enabling faster, more interconnected commerce while providing seemingly endless growth opportunities.[13]

A dozen years later, as president, Eisenhower signed an all-encompassing law calling for a 41,000-mile network of superhighways. It would take the next four decades to complete, and along the way it would seal America's postwar identity as a car-driving and oil-consuming nation.

The Merchants of Light

Decades before Lewis and Clark set out on their road trip, Pennsylvania's Seneca Indians were showing settlers how to use the black gunk that seeped out of the ground in some places to weatherproof their boots and canoes and even to apply it to burned flesh, inflamed gums, and saddle sores. The settlers dubbed it "Seneca oil," which eventually evolved into the "snake oil" sold as a cure-all in the 1800s. Although more and more of the stuff was needed to lubricate the machinery of the Industrial Revolution (lard couldn't tolerate much heat and friction), there was no other real widespread use for it until a bright scientist figured out how to distill kerosene from it.

For a country that had to make do with the feeble light of candles after the sun went down, the ability to light up a room with a single lamp catapulted kerosene, "the light of the age," to prominence, not just as an illuminant, but also as a potential commodity market. The challenge to entrepreneurs was this: how would a clever speculator find enough of this stuff to satisfy the public's growing demand, then get it out of the ground and transport it to market?

Such was the thinking of the first known American oil speculator, George Bissell, a dissatisfied school superintendent, self-taught lawyer, and linguist. While traveling through western Pennsylvania, he saw people harvesting oil from seeps and oil ponds. He knew that kerosene was distilled from oil and that salt miners often found oil before they found salt. It followed that if you drilled with the same kind of drill used for salt, especially in this part of Pennsylvania, the odds were good that you would find oil. He pitched his idea to some East Coast partners and convinced them that they could corner the kerosene market and get rich if they moved quickly.

One of Bissell's partners struck up a conversation with a down-on-his-luck ex–railroad conductor named Edward Drake; the partner liked Drake's can-do attitude and recommended him for the job. Drake accepted the job and prepared to venture to western Pennsylvania to secure the necessary land and begin drilling. Bissell attached the title of colonel to the front of Drake's name on the letters of introduction that went with him, in the hope that this bit of fakery would convey a measure of gravity and authority.

Shortly after he arrived in the spring of 1858, Colonel Edward Drake acquired a property with a known oil spring two miles from Titusville, Pennsylvania, from which three to six barrels of oil were gathered daily by traditional methods: skimming the surface of the pool or laying out rags to soak up the oil, then wringing them out into buckets. No one had ever drilled for oil before, but Drake followed Bissell's idea and set to work building a derrick and fashioning a steam engine that would pound the surface with a pole and pump up the oil. It didn't work.

After a year of Drake's failures, Bissell and his partners were growing impatient, then discouraged. In August of 1859, in despair and disgust, the fledgling Seneca Oil Company dispatched a final money order to the erstwhile colonel, telling him to pay off his remaining bills and shut the enterprise down. But before the message and final funding arrived, Drake and his tiny crew hit pay dirt, at 69.5 feet. The crude that ebbed to the top kept coming, coaxed up by a simple water pump. At first Drake and his driller found buckets, but the oil was coming up at the rate of twenty barrels per day, forcing the pair to scour the nearby town for whiskey barrels to store the oil. When those ran out, they built wooden vats.

Drake was experiencing a fact of life that went with success in the oil patch. Once you've got the oil coming up, you have to be prepared to store, market, and transport it. In short order, whiskey barrels cost twice as much as the oil they held. Drake's practice of drilling for oil caught on. Within fifteen months, seventy-five oil leases dotted the hillsides around Titusville with derricks. By the end of the Civil War, six years later, Pittsburgh would claim fifty-eight oil refineries, Cleveland thirty. Oil was being discovered in West Virginia, New York, Ohio, Colorado, and California. The first oil boom was on.

In the early days of that boom, oil was primarily sought out so it could be distilled into kerosene. As luck would have it, the type of oil produced in the country's first "oil patch" was perfectly suited for kerosene production, and it was also confined largely to the eastern part of the United States. By 1865, a young entrepreneur who owned Cleveland's largest oil refinery set out to bring order to the chaos that defined the early days of the oil age, and it made him the first American billionaire. John D. Rockefeller, the founder of Standard Oil, eventually was able to control every phase of the business, from production at the wellhead to refining, delivering and marketing the final product to the customer. At the beginning of the 1870s, Standard controlled 10 percent of all refining capacity in United States; a decade later, it controlled 90 percent.

Rockefeller's giant refineries produced one-fourth of the world's kerosene, all of which his company transported in their proprietary barrels via their own fleet of ships. His workforce was twice the size of the U.S. Army. Eventually his monopoly of the business would result in an antitrust suit that would break up the huge company, but Rockefeller was still the richest man in the United States thanks to "the light of the ages."[14] (In 1998, two of the companies that resulted from the division of Standard Oil would join again to become ExxonMobil, the world's largest private oil company.)

Superlatives seemed destined to follow this wild new industry. Fortunes were made and lost overnight. After Drake's find and the mad dash for other oil leases, overproduction drove prices from $40 a barrel to ten cents a barrel. Within the span of five hundred days, the town of Pithole, near Titusville, went from a dot on the map to an urban center with banks, telegraph offices, businesses, and more than fifty hotels. But as Pithole's oil fields were beset by swarms of locust-like oil crews, the oil quickly dried up, and the boom turned to bust. A plot of land bought for $2 million in 1865 sold for $4.37 a dozen years later.[15]

But the sheer scale of the 1901 Spindletop discovery dwarfed everything that preceded it. The eastern oil wells combined brought in 2,500 barrels per day; Spindletop brought in 75,000 to 100,000 barrels a day. When cynics told the two brothers who had been drilling the well that their find was a fluke, the story goes that they drilled three more and got the same output from them. Within three months, the town's population had tripled. Excursion trains brought the curious by the thousands on any given Sunday. By the end of the year, more than two hundred wells were operating under a hundred different oil companies.[16] From those oil fields arose the giants Gulf Oil and Texaco.

A string of big strikes followed. In Oklahoma, the massive Glenn pool was discovered near Tulsa in 1905, making that state the leader in oil production in the southwest for the next twenty-seven years, until the 1930s, when the vast East Texas oil fields were discovered—forty-five miles long and ten miles wide in places—in a little town called Kilgore. Dwarfing Spindletop and rivaling the later Saudi fields, the oil pumped from these fields daily topped half a million barrels. Derricks were built practically on top of one another. Oil seemed to be everywhere, even beneath the terrazzo floor of the Kilgore National Bank, which in short order shuttered its doors and became another derrick site.[17]

What made the oil fields of the American southwest so significant was not just their size or number but also the fact that while their oil—light sweet crude—was not really fit for making kerosene, it was perfect for fuel oil. The discovery of its many veins came at an opportune juncture. This type of oil would be poised to quench the thirst of a nascent automobile industry, and it would enable the rise of the United States as a superpower. Oil's rise as a commodity would also parallel the demise of its parent industry, kerosene—just as a new form of light was about to be introduced to the world, one that would change human culture forever.

The Birth of the Energy Age

At the same time that kerosene speculators were making and losing fortunes and helping to transform little hamlets into boomtowns, another source of energy was being harnessed. Many gifted minds were involved, the most notable being an inventor in New Jersey who would eventually hold more than a thousand patents, among them the phonograph, the stock ticker, the first commercial fluoroscope, an early motion picture camera, and the carbon microphone (which was used in Bell telephone receivers until the 1980s). The face of the country and eventually the world was about to be given the power to dispel the dark in an instant.

By 1879 Thomas Alva Edison had perfected the incandescent bulb, combining a long-lasting carbon filament in a vacuum glass tube that would burn for hundreds of hours, making it not only a vast improvement over kerosene but also a commercially viable venture. Within three years he had formed the first publicly owned electric utility, the Edison Electric Illuminating Company. After supervising the implementation of the earliest U.S. utility infrastructure,

Edison oversaw a dramatic demonstration that would whet the public's appetite for electricity: he lit up fifty-nine homes in an area in lower Manhattan, near his Pearl Street generating station.

It was the beginning of the age of harnessed power and the end of the age of kerosene. Electricity was safer and more dependable than kerosene lamps, which had claimed many lives from fires and suffocation. It surely dawned on some petroleum magnates that, although it would take decades to put the infrastructure for widespread electricity in place, if their lamp markets disappeared, petroleum might be consigned to merely providing lubrication for machinery.

But that was not to be. Through a synchronistic turn of events, the man who helped give the petroleum industry a new lease on life was, in fact, the chief engineer at Edison's own electric utility company. Edison's work seemed to put the future of petroleum on the skids, but his engineer, a visionary inventor named Henry Ford, was on fire with ideas that would not only save the petroleum industry but also transform the culture by putting the freedom to move great distances at will within the reach of the working class. The early twentieth century offered a dizzying number of automotive choices to a curious public, but Ford probably did more than any other single individual to help launch the era of the automobile and establish the markets for the fuel that ran it.

Steam-driven engines and vehicles had been seen as early as 1769, when Nicholas Joseph Cugnot invented the "steam wagon" as a transport vehicle for the French Army. The Stanley Steamer was in great demand briefly in the first decade of the twentieth century, and a Stanley model would set the speed record for a steam-driven car in 1906 (127 mph). A few years before, in 1899, French inventor Camille Jenatzy reached sixty-five miles per hour in his electric car, *Jamais Content.*

But the twentieth century market belonged to the internal combustion engine and the automobiles it would power. Steam engines could take a half-hour or more to heat up enough to generate the pressure needed to move their pistons (and passengers had to sit uncomfortably above the hot steam engines). Electric cars had a limited range, which made them perfect as taxis and trolley cars but less modern than the automobiles powered by the gasoline-guzzling third option, the internal combustion engine.

When Daimler and Benz introduced their first gasoline-powered automobile in 1895, fuel was hard to find, and the machines themselves were louder, dirtier, and more difficult to drive and maintain than either steam or electric cars. Nonetheless, they appealed to the public's new demand for speed, mobility, and access to the open spaces—no matter how often they broke down, or how few roads there were. The gasoline-powered automobile quickly became the dominant conveyance preferred by the public. In 1900 car registrations in the United States numbered eight thousand. By 1912 there were over nine hundred thousand; by 1920, over nine million.[18]

Henry Ford got the idea for the assembly line from an employee who had toured a Chicago slaughterhouse and noted how quickly and efficiently the animals were dispatched, then moved down a conveyor belt to be cleaned, divided, and packaged for market. In October 1913 the Ford plant in Highland Park, Michigan, began implementing the moving assembly line. Previously, it had taken more than twelve hours to assemble a car. With the new process, a car rolled off the line in one hour and thirty-three minutes. The era of mass production was underway.

The shorter assembly time allowed Ford to cut costs and make the Model T affordable to a much wider market. By the time Ford retired it from production in 1927, more than 15 million had been sold. Starting in 1914, Ford shocked Wall Street and the rest of the auto industry by mandating a higher wage for his workers, enough so that they could afford to buy the product they helped to make. Ford not only paid his workers $5 a day (the going wage was less than half that) after six months, but by 1926 he had also shortened the workweek to five eight-hour days. His reason: he wanted his workers to be able to buy the cars they were making and enjoy the countryside. The American middle class and the dream that accompanied it had been born.

As America moved into the Great Depression, the automobile industry breathed life into a staggering economy. It was easy to see why automobile manufacturing was such a boon to industry. By 1930 there were 23.1 million cars in the United States, and they used lots of resources—in some cases, substantial amounts of entire sectors. One analyst pointed out that automobile manufacturing had "doubled iron consumption, tripled the use of plate glass, quadrupled the use of rubber."[19] The world had never seen its like. It was the personification of a growth market. As a sheer consumer of raw materials, it had no equal in the modern world.

Changing the Face of War

Oil changed more than just the automotive industry. It was clearly the form of energy drawing the eyes of international industry. In 1901 the Santa Fe Railroad which mostly ran on coal—the previous century's golden child—had one oil-driven locomotive. By 1905, it had 227. Having ready access to oil also became a national security issue. In 1908 Great Britain, acting on the advice of Winston Churchill (who had been nervously observing the increasing military might of Germany), mandated that the Royal Navy convert from coal to oil and began the building the first of its five battleships that would run on oil. Britain also began to keep a presence in the Middle East to ensure ready access to oil, much like the U.S. Navy's Fifth Fleet does today in the Persian Gulf.[20] And they started the Anglo-Persian Oil Company (later called British Petroleum), in which the country held a 51 percent interest, making it the first state-owned oil venture.

Two Swedish armaments manufacturers, Ludwig and Alfred Nobel, came to the port city of Baku in Azerbaijan, then part of Russia, and brought oil refinery equipment, quickly becoming the premier group in the Russian oil industry. In 1901, when Spindletop instantly tripled America's oil output, the oilfields in Baku were turning out more than two hundred thousand barrels of oil per day, more than 95 percent of Russia's oil and half of the world's total oil.

Four years later, as the brief but violent Russian Revolution of 1905 (called "The Great Rehearsal" by Lenin for the full-blown revolution to come a dozen years later) erupted, oil field workers in Baku, hearing the speeches of Joseph Stalin, revolted, setting fire to the vast oil fields, marking the first time that political conflict had interrupted the flow of oil.[21]

World War I was the first war run on oil. Motorcycles, troop transports, mobile ambulances, and tanks all became part of the war machinery. For the first time, airplanes made three-dimensional reconnaissance possible and introduced aerial bombing and combat. Early in the war, when the German offensive came close to Paris, the entire taxi fleet was pressed into service to usher French troops to the front and save the city.[22]

Germany made a push to capture the Baku oil fields in 1918 and failed, and only a few years later, these vast quantities of crude became a key component in Hitler's thinking as he mapped out his plans to conquer Europe. Oil loomed more and more important as a resource. The machinery of war now officially ran on its products. Germany had vast amounts of coal, still the source of 90 percent of its energy by the late 1930s, but it had virtually no petroleum. It was with this in mind in 1932 that Hitler blessed the project of scientists at IG Farben, who in 1926 had bought the patent rights to a process that turned coal into a synthetic fuel. The Farben executives were looking for a patron for their process, which, although promising, was very expensive. The idea ignited Hitler's imagination. Here was a way for him to replace oil as fuel for his planned war machinery.[23]

Japan also had no natural petroleum resources, and before World War II, it got 80 percent of its oil from the United States. In 1931 Japan invaded Manchuria, part of its effort to commandeer the natural resources of Asia, including the oil-rich area then known as the Dutch East Indies (now Indonesia), whose vast reserves were already spoken for by Dutch, American, and British petroleum interests (from which Shell Oil would eventually emerge).

In June 1941, six months before the Japanese struck Pearl Harbor, Germany invaded Russia to attempt, once again, to secure the Baku oil fields. Both Axis powers saw how critical oil would be in fueling their navies, armies, and air forces. The earlier these fuel supplies were seized, the better. The attack on Pearl Harbor was an essential first step in securing the oil Japan would need to fuel its war machinery. With the U.S. Navy out of the way, it would have unfettered access to the oil fields in the Dutch East Indies.

But America's response was quick and overwhelming, entering the war with a distinct advantage that the Japanese could not hope to match: access to an unending supply of oil. By 1944, when Guam was the center of operations for bombing of Japan, 120,000 barrels were delivered daily. "At that same time, Japan's entire air forces on all fronts were consuming just 21,000 barrels per day—one-sixth of what was available just at Guam."[24] Oil was so abundant in the Pacific theater of operations that it was sprayed on the island roads to hold down the choking dust.

To accommodate this massive effort and the billions of barrels of oil it required for the American effort, a $95 million, 1,500-mile pipeline was built in a little over a year, stretching from the west Texas oilfields to the eastern seaboard, allowing a steady supply of oil to be loaded and sent overseas.

As the war progressed into its final stages, Germany's synthetic fuel needs grew larger. More plants were needed, and eventually concentration camp workers were recruited to complete them. Germany was getting 90 percent of its fuel from these plants, which made them a target of American bombing missions. By the end of the campaign—after nearly one hundred bombing missions—the fuel supplies that the German air force relied on had been reduced to less than 0.25 percent of what was needed. One spring night in 1945, Albert Speer slipped into Italy to assess what was left of the German Tenth Army. A convoy of 150 German trucks passed him, each pulled by a team of oxen. Germany surrendered soon after.[25]

By the end of the war, the allies controlled 86 percent of the world's oil supply. The Japanese resorted to running their jeeps on charcoal and using pine root for airplane fuel. A single round-trip mission required one hundred thousand roots. One effective solution was the kamikaze, the suicide pilot, who only needed fuel for the first half of the mission. Deadly efficient, kamikazes managed to do with a single plane what might otherwise have required several fighters—and much more fuel—to achieve.

When the war ended, oil even had a direct effect on the ends of the lives of the vanquished leaders. Rather than surrender, Japan's prime minister, Hideki Tojo, shot himself but botched the job. The American soldiers who had come to arrest him called for an ambulance, but none of the available vehicles had any gas. Eventually Tojo was taken to a hospital in time to save him from his wounds; he was later executed. Inside his bunker at the Reich Chancellery, a defeated Adolf Hitler shot himself in the right temple. His personal SS bodyguards doused his body with gasoline and set it on fire.[26]

Gas rationing ended in the United States within twenty-four hours after the end of the war was declared. And then the good times rolled again in earnest. Plenty returned to the American diet: beef, pork, sugar, chocolate, flour, milk, and eggs. Steel soon became available again. The American car industry, which had been retooled after Pearl Harbor to build war armaments, returned to production.

Fueling the Postwar Boom

After the war, oil and the automobile changed the landscape of the country. By the 1950s, suburban America had exploded, becoming the dream of the growing middle class. Development around American cities spread in every direction, with roads covering the country like a million threads. And with it came a mobile support structure: drive-in movies, drive-in eateries, drive-in cleaners, even drive-in churches, as well as motels, truck stops, billboards, and a new full-fledged industry: tourism.

As the cold war began to heat up between the United States and the Soviet Union, the need to keep the oil flowing was increasingly an American security issue. In the 1950s Iran booted out British Petroleum and nationalized its oil, taking all of BP's assets, including the world's largest refinery. Fearing that the oil would eventually go to the Soviet Union, the CIA and Britain's MI6 staged a coup, installing Mohammad Reza Shah Pahlavi in 1954. Likewise, American fears that the Soviet Union might take over the vast Saudi oil fields (for which engineers and U.S. oilmen had negotiated drilling rights) resulted in expanding influence there from among others, the Arabian American Oil Company.[27]

The industrial base of the United States was guzzling oil, and life was good. Besides its uses for fuel and heating oil, a cornucopia of other oil-based products began to emerge: plastics, synthetic rubber and fiber, asphalt, fertilizers, pesticides, clothing, paint, detergent, medicine, food additives, makeup, dyes, candles, and thousands of subcategories within these. Oil was being woven into every fabric of the American lifestyle.

In 1945 U.S. oil consumption was at 6 MBPD (million barrels per day). By 1955 the number of passenger cars in the United States had reached 48 million and oil consumption had reached 8.45 MBPD.[28] Americans were using fully one-third of all the energy produced in the world. Some of this was due to American consumption of gasoline, but much of it was due to the postwar explosion of business and industry infrastructure.[29] And U.S. oil fields were humming. By 1960 we were producing one of every three barrels pumped worldwide, and we were pumping out six barrels for every barrel we used. We were the hard-driving emirs of our own oil patch.

Emerging Uncomfortable Trends

In the 1950s, as America was discovering its postwar embarrassment of riches and enjoying its greatest period of prosperity, some interesting conundrums began to rumble through the culture. A geologist for Shell Oil named M. King Hubbert predicted that the domestic oil we were awash in was, in fact, running out and would hit its peak (the halfway mark in its total consumption) by 1971. In other words, as our growing population required more and more oil in the last quarter of the twentieth century, there would be ever-depleting supplies from our own oilfields.

This was hard news to hear—and it was largely ignored. Hubbert's deriders pointed to our uncanny productivity and our firm alliances with other oil-producing countries. The United States was basically a second Saudi Arabia. Our oil fields, though less robust, still supplied one out of every seven barrels produced worldwide. During the war, we had contributed six billion of the seven billion barrels required to defeat the Axis powers. And we were building deep infrastructure and protection agreements in the Arab world (with the United States agreeing to "offer military protection in exchange for drilling rights for U.S. companies."[30]) to ensure we would have access to their oil as well, just in case. Come what may, we'd have our oil.

Peak oil in the United States came and went without a blip on the national consciousness. Since then, U.S. Department of Energy annual reports have duly show that, as Hubbert had predicted, domestic oil production indeed peaked in 1970 and has declined ever since.[31]

But it wasn't just about supply and access to oil as a resource anymore. Other voices were being heard. Besides oil-industry prophets like Hubbert, writers like Rachel Carson and Aldo Leopold were making an out-of-touch public aware of the toxic effects that the chemical compounds of industrialization were having on the planet. When we poison the earth, they said, we ultimately poison ourselves. Nevertheless, these growing messages of dissent took decades to take hold.

But history quickly laid bare a weakness most of the population was unaware of. In October 1973, as the Yom Kippur War began between Israel and Egypt, the Organization of the Petroleum Exporting Countries (OPEC) met for its first summit to negotiate where to set the price of oil. As the tide of the war went against Israel, the United States sent military aid, infuriating the OPEC members. When the group met again in Kuwait, they voted a substantial increase in price, as well as a cut in production. The result in the West was chaos and panic. Not only did domestic gasoline prices rise 40 percent almost overnight, but supplies quickly dried up. Lines at gas stations stretched for blocks. For the first time since

World War II, controls were put on the amount of gas you could buy and sometimes the days you could buy it.

For Americans used to having easy access to all the cheap gas they wanted, anytime they wanted it, this was a sobering moment. For the first time, America as a twentieth-century imperial power was being challenged by an outside force—and suddenly it was uncomfortably clear that the most basic elements of our culture, our lifestyles and prosperity, had become dependent on the whims of others. What had once made us strong had, in a very short time, become our greatest vulnerability.

The first oil crisis in 1973 caused panic when we saw what life without easy access to oil might be like. But still nothing happened. By 1974, our freewheeling oil-baron days were in the rearview mirror: we were already importing 35 percent of our oil. In the course of that decade, a paradox began to emerge: the United States was becoming "an economic and military giant whose lifeblood was controlled in other parts of the world."[32]

In 1977, after just three months in office, Jimmy Carter became the first American president to raise public awareness of how our dependency on oil was jeopardizing our security and way of life. We were using more oil than we could produce, and our energy fate was becoming increasingly dependent on the decisions of other countries, most of which didn't particularly like us. We had, he told us, used twice as much oil in the 1950s as we did in the 1940s, and twice as much in the 1960s as we did in the 1950s. And in each of those decades, more oil was consumed than in all of the rest of history combined.

But no one wanted to listen.

In Alaska, BP, Arco, and Exxon were rushing to develop the huge reserves discovered underneath the North Slope; in the North Atlantic, the large fields of the North Sea were up for grabs, and a feeding frenzy ensued, with the United Kingdom and Norway eventually gaining control over most of the oil and gas reserves. OPEC continued trying to find the perfect price that would keep prices, supply, and demand in balance.

During his term in office, Carter gave five energy speeches, trying to enlist the aid and interest of the public as part of a first-tier response to changing our hydrocarbon-laden way of life. Wearing a cardigan sweater during the first of these televised speeches, he assured us that we still had time, but there was no time to waste. We needed to begin now to reverse our usage habits, start searching for fuel alternatives, and start practicing more energy conservation. Turn down the thermostats in the winter, he said, and up in the summer.

He modeled what he was talking about. He had solar hot water panels installed on the White House roof, ordered thermostats with controlled minimum and maximum temperatures installed in government buildings and had a wood stove installed in his living quarters. He created a cabinet-level Department of Energy and began to fund the fledgling solar and wind alternative energy industries. Between 1977 and 1982, U.S. dependency on foreign oil imports fell by 50 percent. This, in turn, helped swamp the world with oil by the mid-1980s, which not only weakened OPEC but helped facilitate the fall of the Soviet Union, which had overextended itself with more ramped-up infrastructure investment than it could then manage. "As a result," said Yegor Gaidar, director of the Institute for Economies in Transition in Moscow, "the Soviet Union lost approximately $20 billion per year, money without which the country simply could not survive."[33]

Calling the effort to conserve resources "the moral equivalent of war," Carter set the tone for his administration by implementing the first CAFÉ (Corporate Average Fuel Economy) standards for automobiles, which mandated a fuel-efficiency minimum (measured in miles per gallon in city and highway driving) that manufacturers had to meet for new cars and trucks. That sparked a surge of interest in saving energy, and the commercial world fell into step. As mpg information began to show up on the windows of new cars, energy-efficiency estimates began to show up on consumer goods. Everything from batteries to washers, dryers, and building insulation became more efficient. We also learned an important lesson:

that heightened efficiency gave us more service without a loss of performance, and as an added bonus, it often saved us money.[34]

Carter had reason to be concerned. Storm clouds had begun to appear on the horizon. By 1977, the year of that first speech and only six years after the United States hit peak oil, 98 percent of our imported oil came from OPEC or Persian Gulf suppliers. For the next eight years, although our rate of consumption continued to climb, our imports from OPEC and the Persian Gulf decreased steadily as we found other suppliers and conservation and higher energy efficiency in cars, appliances, heating and cooling systems and building materials became more commonplace.[35] Of his five energy speeches, perhaps the most famous was nicknamed the "malaise speech" in which he set the stage for what would actually ensue after his term as president ended.

By then his presidency had been nearly destroyed by the Iran hostage crisis, in which fifty-two Americans were held hostage for 444 days after the U.S. embassy in Tehran was overrun by supporters of a religious fundamentalist named Ayatollah Khomeini. After thirty-five years of the harsh rule of the shah (installed by U.S. and U.K. intelligence services to ensure the free flow of Iranian oil and provide a safe harbor to the many American and British production facilities housed there) that was strengthened by decades of massive U.S. military support, the Khomeini regime took control.

When morning dawned in America under the Reagan administration in 1981, U.S. demand for foreign oil began to rise again. Conservation was regarded as weakness, and with the help of a Democratic Congress, the new president was able to slash the budgets of the fledging alternative-energy projects and let the tax incentives for solar and wind companies lapse (putting a serious damper on financing for such ventures for years to come). Instead of America leading the way, Japanese and European firms enjoyed the financial and developmental fallout. When repairs to the White House roof made it necessary to remove the solar panels Carter had installed over the West Wing, the decision was made not to replace them.[36] Instead, they were sent to Unity College in Maine, where they heated hot water until they were retired in 2004.

The Reagan years saw the U.S. allegiances in the Middle East shift. The United States broke off diplomatic relations with Iran during the hostage crisis, and our relationship with Iraq became more friendly. During the eight-year Iraq-Iran War, the Reagan administration often provided covert intelligence and advice to Iraq to prevent Iran from overrunning its oil-rich neighbor. In 1988, the Iraq-Iran War ended in a draw, but it had been hugely costly for Saddam Hussein, who then tried to get Kuwait to forgive Iraq's war debts. Kuwait declined. Needing money to stem the tide of loss and debt, Hussein invaded Kuwait in the morning hours of August 2, 1990. Fearing that Hussein would move into nearby Saudi Arabia (and, some say, jumping at the opportunity to establish a military base on Saudi soil), the United States led a coalition of forces into Kuwait in February 1991. In one hundred hours, the Iraq army had been routed and vanquished. In defeat, Hussein gave orders to set fire to the Kuwaiti oil fields.

No one knows how far reverberations go or where consequences end. On a cool, crisp Tuesday morning in September 2001, nineteen young men, fifteen of them Saudis, commandeered four commercial aircraft on the American East Coast, crashing two into the World Trade Center towers in the financial district of New York City, a third into the Pentagon, and the fourth into a field in Pennsylvania. Armed with cheap box cutters and knives, the young men were disciples of Osama bin Laden, an Arab prince who had vowed vengeance in response to U.S. presence on Saudi soil since the first Gulf war.

In a speech made at the London Institute of Petroleum in 1999, then Halliburton chairman Dick Cheney lamented the Sisyphean task that oil companies had faced for a century:

> Producing oil is obviously a self-depleting activity. Every year you've got to find and develop reserves equal to your output just to stand still, just to stay even. For the world as a whole, oil companies

are expected to keep finding and developing enough oil to offset our seventy-one million plus barrel a day of oil depletion [in 2013 it was around 89 MBPD], but also to meet new demand. By some estimates there will be an average of two percent annual growth in global oil demand over the years ahead along with conservatively a three percent natural decline in production from existing reserves. That means by 2010 we will need on the order of an additional fifty million barrels a day.

And this was in the days before the growing resource appetites of China and India had begun to make headlines. Less than two years later, in April of 2001, Vice President Dick Cheney did an about-face from that earlier speech, setting the tone for the Bush Administration, while mocking the attempts of previous administrations. "Conservation may be a sign of personal virtue, but it is not a sufficient basis for a sound, comprehensive energy policy," Cheney opined. In fact, it had been.[37]

It took less than twenty years to put an end to the high-flying days when we were producing six times what we consumed. What Jimmy Carter—and Halliburton CEO Dick Cheney—had warned us about has come about. Our culture and lifestyles revolve around oil. It not only runs the machines that transport us on the land, sea, and air, it's woven into every fabric of our society, from pharmaceuticals, fertilizers, and pesticides to the thousands of synthetic formulations on which we depend in every corner of industry and manufacturing. And the acquiring of it has taken on new dimensions of risk and consequence.

What's your eco footprint?

How are your living habits affecting the earth (and what can you do to change them)? It's easy to find out. Take a quick quiz at the Global Footprint Network (www.footprintnetwork.org/en /index.php/GFN/page/calculators/).

The End of Easy Oil

Increasingly, the problem we are in is a global one. "In 1900 the world produced 150 million barrels of oil. In 2000 it produced 28 billion barrels, an increase of more than 180 fold."[38] Production figures are only half the story. The other half is all about how much we're using and the ways we are choosing to make up the difference.

In 2008 oil companies worldwide pumped 81.8 million barrels of oil out of the earth each day, while the world consumed 84.45 million barrels per day.[39] That means that annual consumption overran annual production by 967 million barrels—and that was during a year when high gas prices caused U.S. consumption to actually drop 475 million barrels for the year.[40] (Two years later, according to *The Economist*, increased Asian oil consumption helped account for the more than 5 million barrels per day deficit—or double 2008's numbers.)[41] So how is that deficit covered? By drawing from reserves.

This is where the oil drama gets a little fuzzy, because no one knows (or will admit) how much oil any one country really does or does not have. Persistent rumors abound that the Middle East's reports of how much oil it has are overblown. In general, most petroleum experts believe the globe's original total supply of conventional oil was about two trillion barrels. What remains is roughly anywhere from 850 billion to about a trillion barrels, although some oil analysts insist the lower end of that range is actually much lower than that.

And that's if oil consumption remains stagnant, which no one predicts it will. Increasingly, China is the elephant in the room. Because of China's increase in demand since 2004, there are no longer any "shock absorbers" to allay sudden peaks in demand. These used to exist, in the form of spare crude oil capacity, refining capacity, or discretionary oil product inventories. "These three reserves were the safety margins that the world oil market counted on. And year after year, as oil demand continued to increase at about 1 percent a year, these shock absorbers would absorb that gradual increase and ensure that prices went up only gradually—until 2004."[42]

That's when things really changed for the stability of the global oil supply. "At the start of 2004, the International Energy Agency predicted that global demand for crude oil would grow by 1.5 million barrels per day, that year. Instead," said Larry Goldstein, an oil industry expert from the Energy Policy Research Foundation, "it grew by three million barrels per day, and [demand in] China alone grew by over one million barrels a day."[43]

Three million barrels a day amounts to more than a billion additional barrels to add to what's already becoming a huge oil deficit. And that's the best-case scenario *only if demand stagnates.* With the gross national products of China and India growing at their present rates, no oil futurist expects that scenario to go anywhere but south.

Another problem is that those first trillion barrels were what the industry calls the *easy oil,* drawn from conventional sources, the deep, vast wells that were easy to extract from. The rest—much of which exists in parts of the world where the West is not well liked, including the Middle East and Russia—will not be so easy to get. This is the so-called unconventional oil. It's spread out all over the globe, some deep under the sea, some beneath the disappearing ice masses in the Arctic. Even if that oil can be extracted, which will be difficult enough, there are, as yet, no accessible storage facilities or close ports.

As the end of easy oil and higher global demand have collided, the search for new oil resources has reached manic proportions and locked humanity into a new time of wildcatting and oil glut. While experts agree that no new conventional oil fields will ever be found, we are not running out of fossil fuels, not at all. In fact, the International Energy Agency declared in 2012 that the United States will become energy independent by 2017 and a net oil exporter by 2030.[44]

How can this be?

The centrality of fossil fuel in our lives has added some new pages to the energy playbook—and some extremely powerful players: deepwater drilling; tar sands mining; and fracking of shale oil, natural gas, and oil shale (also called rock oil). All of these are part of the end of easy oil. As we enter the final chapter of our nation's history with fossil fuels, it's clear we are doing more than satisfying our craving for the riches and stability they bring to our economy. As we scrape the bottom of the fossil fuel barrel, we are playing with fire: with elements and techniques that can heat our planet to the point where there can be no recovery and no place for living things to survive. And yet here we go, headed straight toward an ecocidal brick wall at an ever-increasing speed.

Mining the Deep

The United States uses about 7 billion barrels of oil per year, and our own production of light sweet crude is in decline. If we are to satisfy our domestic needs without depending on the Middle East, the argument goes, we must reach into other North American sources, like oil or gas shale and tar sands from Canada—or the reservoirs of oil that lie farther and farther off our coast lines in the deep water.

Modern technology has given us high-resolution 4-D deepwater scanning, which has plotted vast areas of the ocean where oil reserves, although remote and risky to access, lie in wait. In 2009 British Petroleum's Tiber field in the Gulf of Mexico (with an estimated three to six billion barrels of untapped oil) seemed to disprove the experts' theory of "no new oil," but its discovery was problematic. No oil drilling is risk-free, but deepwater drilling comes with its own unique set of risks. It requires massive and highly sophisticated drilling rigs (called semi-submersibles), complicated monitoring and safety measures, and a very expensive and elaborate piece of equipment called a blowout preventer that has to sit on the well head to serve as an emergency shutoff valve, should the gases and pressures in the subsea floor below the well cause a blowout.

Today, 4-D deepwater scanning is so sophisticated that it can pinpoint oil reservoirs within feet of its location in the ocean substrata. The Gulf of Mexico now supplies nearly a third of our oil and natural gas, and 80 percent of that lies in the deep water, but to get to it, we have to not only go out farther but deeper. The U.S. Interior Department defines deepwater wells as those that are 500 feet or more below sea level; deepwater drilling refers to wells drilled in water depths of 1,000 feet or more.[45]

The coastline of our Gulf states sit on what amounts to a ledge that gradually falls off into a deep canyon. Like a net of tightly knit veins, the lines on oil lease maps that indicate new platforms are slowly edging farther out into the canyons and off the cliffs that lead down to the ocean floor. According to NOAA, there are currently more than 3,700 active oil and gas platforms in the Gulf of Mexico, and half of the acreage being leased for these platforms is for deepwater production.[46]

Unlike land drilling, deepwater drilling has to reach the seabed through thousands of feet of water before the real work begins, first piercing, then boring deeper into the seafloor. The actual distance to the oil can be several very treacherous miles. Once oil has been struck and a series of pipe and cement installations have successfully caught and maintained its flow, the derrick moves on to the next job.

When the Tiber field was drilled in the deep waters 250 miles southeast of Houston, the crew that safely and successfully completed it was elated. They had begun drilling four thousand feet below the surface of the water and drilled 6.6 miles beneath the seafloor, making it (at the time) the deepest oil well ever completed.

Three months after the crew had finished working on the Tiber field, the deepwater semi-submersible drilling rig had been disconnected and moved nearly three hundred miles northeast into the Gulf to its next project, lot 252 of a deepwater lease in the Macondo prospect, less than fifty miles off the Louisiana coastline. The rig was called the Deepwater Horizon.

The Deepwater Horizon was a state-of-the-art deepwater drilling rig made by Hyundai in South Korea. It stood four hundred feet long and three hundred feet wide, with a 242-foot derrick installed amidships. Powered by six massive Warsala 9,975-horsepower diesel engines that powered six 7,000-kilowatt electrical generators, the thousand-ton Deepwater Horizon was designed to operate in the severe weather common in the Gulf. Operating like a small, self-contained city, it could sleep and feed 130 people.

The task the rig and crew faced this time seemed less daunting than the Tiber project. The Macondo well was located eighteen thousand feet beneath the seabed, with an additional five thousand feet between the sea floor and the semi-submersible drilling rig.

On a balmy April night in 2010, the project had reached the last of the drilling phases. At 9:30, the Deepwater Horizon's 126 crewmembers were preparing to change shifts. The mood was celebratory. Those on board included officials from BP, Transocean (the rig owner), Anadarko, and Halliburton, who had gathered to acknowledge the giant rig's accomplishments, especially its seven-year safety record of no lost-time incidents. It had been called a lucky ship.

The year before, the Minerals Management Service (MMS) had recognized the giant rig as an "industry model for safety." In fact, "its record was so exemplary, according to MMS officials, the rig was never on inspectors' informal 'watch list' for problem rigs." That means that it wasn't inspected every month—as the federal agency required—and, in fact, had undergone "at least 16 fewer inspections aboard the Deepwater Horizon than it should have under the policy, a dramatic fall from the frequency of prior years, according to the agency's records."[47]

Suddenly a combination of mud, methane gas, and seawater blew up through a pipe conduit that connected the rig to the sea-floor. When the gas ignited, a powerful fireball shot up through the drilling floor. It was so enormous that it was visible for thirty-five miles. Reeling from the concussion, the men in the control rooms quickly activated the safeguards and alarms, but nothing worked, including the blowout preventer and emergency disconnect system, which were meant to activate shutoff valves to stop the high-pressure flow from the wellhead and to separate the rig and pipes from the wellhead so it could float free. Nor did the deck engine generators function, which meant the fire equipment was worthless. Even the shortwave radios didn't work.

Eleven men were killed in the explosion; their remains were never found. Many survived by jumping as much as seventy-five feet into the sea, while others managed to reach the lifeboats and were picked up by the nearby tender, the *Bankston*. Seventeen men were later hospitalized.

Observers reported that flames shot six hundred feet into the air from the rig. Nearby vessels poured water onto the burning rig, but with the highly flammable mixture blasting unabated from the seafloor, they could not get the fire under control.

Two days later, as President Barack Obama celebrated the fortieth anniversary of Earth Day with a speech in the Rose Garden, the rig's steel infrastructure finally collapsed and the Deepwater Horizon's flaming remains headed to the bottom of the Gulf of Mexico. As it sank, the riser pipe connecting the well to the rig bent and tore in several places, leaving an unrestricted flow of oil and natural gas from a wellhead nearly four miles below the water's surface. It was an unabated flow that no one knew how to stop, setting off the worst environmental disaster in U.S. history.

The United States government has long had close ties to the fortunes of the oil and gas business, because it owns the oil and gas in these deepwater canyons and collects royalties on everything produced. So it is caught in the middle, wanting to maximize production to maximize its royalties, but also obligated to keep the country's environment safe. If it stops or even lessens the production of oil and gas, it loses massive amounts of revenue.

Offshore drilling—and damage from oil spills and ruptures—is nothing new in America. In 1969 an oil spill off the coast of Santa Barbara fouled beaches and so enraged the populace that that single accident spawned not only Earth Day but also the National Environmental Policy Act, which required—for the first time—that the government review proposed drilling projects to determine their environmental impact.

After the 1989 *Exxon Valdez* disaster, public outrage over the range and extent of damage done to fishing fields, estuaries, beaches, and coastline spurred the federal government to create the Oil

Pollution Act, which established a liability trust fund to deal with the results of oil spills.

After the Deepwater Horizon disaster, with the addition of the fines specified in the U.S. Clean Water Act, BP was looking at maximum fines of $1,100 per barrel of oil spilled—or $4,300 per barrel if the government could prove gross negligence.

However, as oil exploration has become more widespread and its technologies more sophisticated and esoteric, government oversight agencies—perennially overworked and short on resources (and in line with the antiregulatory attitudes of most lawmakers and administrations)—have became completely dependent on the oil industry's expertise.[48] That's one of the reasons why BP was allowed to run the cleanup and repair of the well leak: as inept as their efforts were, nobody knew any better way to handle the crisis.

Within a few days of the disaster, BP had set up a video feed that allowed the public to view ten- to fifteen-second snippets of the flow from one of the spots in the torn riser pipe that were leaking oil nonstop. (Aware of their need to keep the leak estimates as low as possible, they chose the one leaking the least.) Since deepwater wells often release twenty thousand barrels a day under controlled conditions, most experts knew that BP's initial estimate of one to five thousand barrels per day was vastly understated. As weeks went by, and other views of the leaks became available, this figure was quickly challenged. Steve Weeks, a Purdue University professor of mechanical engineering, estimated the leak rate at as much as seventy thousand barrels per day.[49] BP denied this and kept to their much lower estimate.

As the flow of oil continued unabated, BP tried a variety of methods to stop the leak, many of them ridiculous, nearly all of them worthless. Having destroyed much of the area's fishing industry, the lifeblood of the region, BP started a program called Vessels of Opportunity, in which they leased thousands of fishing boats to aid in skimming oil and setting up oil booms to gather up the oil so it could be harvested from the surface by specialized vessels. With their livelihoods on hold, if not ruined, many fishermen had to work for their destroyers. They agree to sign gag orders and to work without protective equipment.[50] Their efforts weren't very productive. Estimates are that less than ten percent of the oil was removed by skimming or outright burning on the surface.

As tar balls began to wash up on beaches along the coastline and pictures of fouled marshes and oil-covered wildlife dying from lack of oxygen began to fill Facebook pages, Twitter feeds, and news broadcasts, public confidence in BP's ability to stop the leak worsened. BP's solutions weren't helping. First they tried a containment dome, a forty-foot tall structure meant to close in the leak so the oil could be siphoned off. It failed. This was followed by the Top Hat, smaller and equally worthless. Then came Top Kill, the famed "junk shot" of rubber balls, rope, golf balls and ground rubber that was supposed to be forced down the leaking pipe and stop the flow.[51]

Finally, on July 15, the flow was seemingly stopped by a containment cap called a capping stack. The public video feeds were turned off after the capping stack was in place, but it wasn't until September 19—a full two months later—that one of the relief wells finally curtailed the leak and the well was cemented in. (Since then, despite BP's protests to the contrary, leaks from the longitude and latitude of the seafloor rupture persist.)

While BP took credit for stopping the leak, no one will ever know how much oil was released into the Gulf of Mexico, largely because BP withheld its best estimates and spent so much time dispersing the oil at the leak source, which spread it out into the wider Gulf, doing long-term damage to every aspect of that body of water and its inhabitants. The government eventually estimated that the total amount of oil that leaked out was 4.9 million barrels.

Court papers provided from Transocean show that from the start, BP—ever mindful of the penalties that lay in waiting—had quickly gone to work to ensure that the actual flow count was minimized and that as little oil was in evidence as possible. On the day the rig sank, BP was already estimating that the daily flow could go up to 82,000 barrels. Two days later, Rob Marshall, BP subsea manager of the Gulf, wrote to BP manager Gary Imm, "Alistair

Johnston altered his Macondo well model to approximate open hole flowing conditions and calculated a rate of 82,000 barrels per day." Imm reportedly told Marshall, "A number of people have been looking at this and we already have had difficult discussions with the USCG [U.S. Coast Guard] on the numbers. Please tell Alistair not to communicate to anyone on this."[52] The day before, on April 21, another BP employee emailed a number of other employees that he'd used a modeling program to estimate a "worst-case discharge" case that hit 100,000 barrels of oil per day.

According to Transocean, "as BP admitted in the plea agreement, BP withheld this information from its May 24, 2010 submission to the United States House of Representatives Committee of Energy and Commerce. BP also withheld these estimates from Admiral Landry, the press, and the public when it estimated that the flow rate was between 1,000–5,000 [barrels of oil per day] in late April 2010."

On April 29, only seven days after the pipe ruptured and Deepwater Horizon sank, the company began injecting two types of Corexit oil dispersants directly at the leak site, effectively blasting everything into particles as it erupted into the water from the tear in the pipe, a move deemed highly dangerous by environmental experts, because dispersants are applied most often to oily residues after a cleanup of surface spills. They are not designed to be used four thousand feet below the surface. Applying them that deep meant there was no way to gauge their long-term effects or how far afield those effects would spread—and into what parts of the ecosystem they spread, once the currents caught them.

Corexit wasn't the only dispersant BP could have used, and in fact, twelve of the eighteen EPA-approved dispersants were judged more effective on the kind of crude oil that originates in the Gulf of Mexico. Two of those twelve were rated 100-percent effective in dealing with surface oil, while the two brands of Corexit used were rated at only 56- and 63-percent effective. "The toxicity of the 12 was shown to be either comparable to the Corexit line or, in some cases, 10 or 20 times less, according to EPA." But BP insisted on using the Corexit. Richard Charter, a senior policy adviser for Defenders of Wildlife, observed, "It's a chemical that the oil industry makes to sell to itself, basically."[53] Corexit is manufactured by Nalco, which formed a joint venture with Exxon Chemical in 1994. One of its board members is from BP, and a top executive is a longtime oil veteran from Exxon.

Word got out that airplanes and seagoing vessels were spraying the surface nonstop. Environmentalists, aware that Corexit is banned in the United Kingdom because of its toxic effects on shorelines and wildlife, were in an uproar. When the Coast Guard ordered BP to come up with a safer dispersant than the Corexit 9500 and the even more toxic and bioaccumulative 9527 (which can cause long-term damage to marine ecosystems[54]), BP ignored them. Finally the Coast Guard said BP could use Corexit in rare cases, but BP applied the toxic mess seventy-four times in fifty-four days.[55] A total of 1.5 million gallons of the two types of Corexit were sprayed on the surface and at the wellhead.

But "dispersed" doesn't mean the oil is dissolved and gone. While dispersing the oil kept much of it from rising to the surface (and therefore being in the "count" that the United States could use in its algorithm for charging BP for its spill liability), much of the oil either sank to the ocean floor or moved into deepwater columns in the Gulf of Mexico. A fifty-mile-wide dead zone soon formed around the Deepwater Horizon site.

Carol Browner, a top energy adviser to President Obama, went on ABC's *Good Morning America* four months after the disaster and declared, "The scientists are telling us about 25 percent was not captured or evaporated or taken care of by mother nature," but a report released by five prominent marine scientists disputed Browner's upbeat finding. Charles Hopkinson, a University of Georgia professor of marine sciences and the director of Georgia Sea Grant, said, "One major misconception is that oil that has dissolved into water is gone and, therefore, harmless. The oil is still out there, and it will likely take years to completely degrade. We are still far from a complete understanding of what its impacts are." Their finding concluded that up to 79 percent of oil did not disappear but remained, degrading much slower than the government claimed.[56]

An interesting side note: BP's Doug Suttles gave away the ballgame when an Internal memo revealed BP did indeed know what the real flow rate was, because the amount of Corexit they ordered wasn't the amount needed to disperse 5,000 barrels a day, but 70,000.

There is a saying that success has many fathers, but failure is an orphan. Every administration has seen its share of disasters, and the cozy relationship between regulatory agencies and those they regulate is just as prevalent in areas that cover how our coal, gas, and oil are captured, processed, and delivered, but one of the mechanisms that helped make this incident so disastrous goes back to the first months of the George W. Bush's administration, when Vice President Dick Cheney famously conducted an energy summit to lay out the details of the Bush era energy policy. Cheney's energy task force report resulted in Bush's executive order to accelerate energy-related projects. The Minerals Management Service, under the Department of Interior, quickly came under pressure to waive the compulsory environmental reviews to help expedite offshore drilling permits. Increasingly, waivers became the norm, with some applicants getting as many as four hundred per year.[57] The compulsory review documents the oil companies had to file became boilerplate. BP's, for instance, famously mentioned how its drilling practices would consider the needs of nonexistent walruses and seals in the Gulf of Mexico.

Eleven months after Deepwater Horizon blew up and sank, a Norwegian firm—which was hired by the Coast Guard to do a forensic analysis of the blowout preventer retrieved from the ocean floor—issued their report on what they believed was at fault. As expected, the most detailed explication involved the blowout preventer. Their conclusion: the force of the pressure from the gas and oil bursting through the seafloor was what bent the horizontal safety devices in the preventer so that they could not align and close properly, leaving the pipe open and impossible to close by any of the remote means at their disposal. If the blowout preventer failed as it did, catastrophe was inevitable. The blowout preventer on the Deepwater Horizon was what industry experts called a single-fail system. There was no backup.[58] This was perhaps a distinction without a difference since the Norwegian firm's findings showed that the nature of the condition itself, the pressure at the ocean bottom in extreme depths, was more than the blowout preventer could handle. Put simply, the blowout preventer didn't work.

In other words, currently there is no way to prevent what happened with the Deepwater Horizon from happening again. Or as one industry expert concluded: "The best way to control a blowout in the deepwater is not to have one."[59]

Shortly after the Deepwater Horizon incident, the Bureau of Ocean Energy Management, Regulation, and Enforcement (BOEMRE, formerly the Minerals Management Service) declared that no deepwater drilling permits would be granted without a report that showed exactly how a company would prevent a future blowout. But by early 2011, the BOEMRE was again handing out deepwater permits in the Gulf of Mexico. Their reason? The permitting agency reported that the oil industry was now complying with "rigorous new safety standards implemented in the wake of the Deepwater Horizon explosion." When the first permit was handed out in late February 2011, the BOEMRE press release stated its rationale: "This permit was issued for one simple reason: the operator successfully demonstrated that it can drill its deepwater well safely and that it is capable of containing a subsea blowout if it were to occur."[60]

And the recipient of that first permit: Noble Energy. Noble Energy is perhaps better known by the name of its major stakeholder: BP.[61]

But that might not even be the worst part. The required oil spill response plan Noble Energy submitted—the one that is supposed to include their updated approach to how they would control a blowout in deepwater—is dated September 2009, *seven months before* the Deepwater Horizon blowout.

Earlier Associated Press investigations show that the doomed rig was allowed to operate without safety documentation required by Minerals Management Service regulations for the exact disaster scenario that occurred; that the cutoff valve that failed has repeatedly broken down at other wells in the years since regulators weakened testing requirements; and that regulation is so lax that some key safety aspects on rigs are decided almost entirely by the companies doing the work.[62]

This is born from the certainty that the need for oil is so pivotal to the nation's economy and way of life that no regulation has any teeth. The technology they have spent billions perfecting is still geared to make money, not to prevent further losses or environmental devastation.

Videos and stills of the explosion's aftermath were filled with images of wildlife dead or dying from the oil and toxic chemicals left behind in the ocean. The environmental advocacy group Center for Biological Diversity filed a notice of intent to sue the Minerals Management Service over its lack of compliance with existing endangered-species laws. "MMS has given up any pretense of regulating the offshore oil industry," said the group's director. "The agency seems to think its mission is to help the oil industry evade environmental laws." During the period between January 2009 and the time of the Deepwater Horizon catastrophe, the MMS had approved "at least three huge lease sales, 103 seismic blasting projects and 346 drilling plans. Agency records also show that permission for those projects and plans was granted without getting the permits required under federal law."[63]

Bob Cavnar, a thirty-year veteran of the oil and gas industry with deep experience in drilling and production operations onshore and offshore summed it up. "There's no fundamental change to the way we drill the deepwater. We're doing it with the same equipment, the same blowout preventers on all the deepwater rigs that are in the Gulf that failed on the Macondo well. And the issue here is that these new regulations regulate an unreliable piece of equipment, and regulating something that's unreliable doesn't make it more reliable. It just makes it more regulated."[64]

Basically nothing's changed. Even now—after the negligence of this industry caused the nation's worst environmental catastrophe—it remains a monolithic power that rests secure in the knowledge that come what may, oil always wins. No matter the risk, no matter how recklessly they pursue it, no matter the cost to the environment or to those who must live with its consequences.

Oil is one.

Keystone XL: The Real Price of Remote Oil

Seventeen hundred miles north of the Gulf of Mexico, in Alberta, Canada, lies another fossil fuel with its own unique dangers. The tar sands fields in Canada and the American West have a kind of oil that is both grossly expensive to extract and something of an environmental nightmare. Producing tar sands, for example, requires not only massive amounts of water (2 to 4.5 barrels of water for every barrel of tar sands oil[65]) but also large quantities of natural gas to separate the oil, refine it, and transport it long distances down the pipeline, "enough fuel to heat six million average-sized homes every day." That number is expected to double by 2014 and by 2030, tar sands production is expected to require "about 92 per cent of the country's gas, leaving little to heat its homes."[66]

The mined product is actually bitumen, a sticky, tarry substance akin to the substance you'd use to tar your roof. (In fact, the Canadian First Nations traditionally used it to seal their canoes.) To move this gunky mass through a pipeline, it's often mixed with lighter hydrocarbons like benzene, a known carcinogen, to thin it out.

Getting at it means clear-cutting vast swaths of Canada's pristine boreal forest, one of the planet's most critical carbon sinks. Each barrel of tar sands oil requires the removal of four tons of trees, soil, rocks, and clay. Rivers and streams must be diverted, and wetlands drained.

As an industry, tar sands reportedly creates three times as much CO_2 as light sweet crude oil in its extraction and refining. Its burning produces a third more CO_2 than coal, and it takes two tons of tar sands to yield one barrel of oil. The mining and processing of tar sands also release sulfur dioxide, hydrogen sulfate, sulfuric acid mist, and nitrogen oxide into the environment, contaminating water, air, and nearby wildlife. The CO_2 emissions from the production and processing of tar sands doubled between 2000 and 2010 and are on track to double again by 2020.

As bitumen, it's heavier than the lighter crude we have grown accustomed to seeing in oil spills and it sinks, making it much tougher to access, much less clean up. In July 2010, a broken pipeline running through Michigan dumped 20,000 barrels of bitumen into Talmadge Creek, the Kalamazoo River, and Morrow Lake. A spill in 2011 dumped more than 1,400 barrels of tar sands oil into Montana's Yellowstone River.

On Easter weekend in 2013, two dozen homes had to be evacuated in a suburb of Little Rock, Arkansas, when Exxon's sixty-five-year-old Pegasus pipeline burst.[67] It quickly became clear that this was not just any crude oil, it was tar sands oil from Alberta, Canada. Many homeowners in the affected area were surprised to find out there was a pipeline running a few feet beneath their homes. According to a lawsuit filed two weeks later, 19,000 barrels of tar sands bitumen spewed across an area affecting homeowners 3,000 feet from the site. (Exxon claimed the leak was 5,000 barrels.)

Although Exxon blocked off the area to reporters, several people were able to visit the site and take video to prove that oil had indeed leaked into nearby Lake Conway, the source of the area's drinking water. Because tar sands is highly corrosive and is often mixed with benzene, there is no way to know what the long-term effects might be to the local population. After being told that the area was being cleaned up, one videographer brought back evidence of what Exxon was using to absorb the oil: paper towels.[68]

Tar sands is also the filthiest carbon-based product known to humanity, poised to dump geometrically more CO_2 into atmosphere —which is already dealing with twice as much CO_2 as it can naturally handle annually.

No one who is serious about fighting climate change
can want to see that oil out of the ground and into the air.
BILL MCKIBBEN

Despite its inefficiency and environmental drawbacks, the United States already gets from 18 percent to 20 percent of its oil from these tar sands, and until recently, few people had ever heard of them. A pipeline called the Keystone XL changed all that. If it's built, it will be something of an oil superhighway, stretching 1,700 miles across the U.S. heartland, crossing hundreds of streams and rivers—not to mention the critical fresh water supply of the High Plains, the Ogallala Aquifer—on its way to Gulf Coast refineries. If TransCanada, the pipe's producer, has its way, nearly a million barrels per day would zoom through the thirty-six-inch-wide pipe.

There is a reported 175 billion barrels of tar sands crude, primarily in central and northern Alberta, much of it near Fort McMurray. The amount of oil available makes Canada the sixth largest petroleum producer in the world, housing the globe's third largest reserves (behind Saudi Arabia and Venezuela). Tar sands oil has oozed out of the ground for thousands of years. It requires no exploration, as traditional oil wells do. There are no dry holes in this oil patch.

The process of tar sands extraction is more like strip-mining. Trees are cut, layers of wetland fen and peat are peeled back, allowing heavy-duty equipment to move in and dig through the layers of oil sands, which go down as far as four hundred feet. The sands (really a mixture of 85 percent sand, clay, and silt, 5 percent water, and 10 percent crude bitumen) are processed with warm water to skim off the oil. The sands sink to the bottom, the water that's left is fed into unlined open tailings ponds that are so large—the size of Manhattan—that they are visible from space. Syncrude, one of the largest tar sands mining monoliths, practices open-pit mining, using the largest trucks on earth. Each one is forty-five-feet high, comes equipped with tires fourteen feet in diameter, and weighs five hundred tons. A man standing next to one of these American-built monstrosities would barely come up to the tire hub. Its payload bucket is large enough to hold a three-thousand-square-foot home. Each four-hundred-ton load will convert to two hundred barrels of oil. Depending on whatever today's oil prices are, you can do the math and see why this is a petroleum gold mine. In places where the tar sands is even farther down, a process called *in situ* is used, in which steam is injected into the ground to melt the bitumen so that it can be sucked to the surface. WorldWatch Institute, an environmental watchdog group, calls tar sands "the bottom of the oil barrel."[69]

The Keystone XL pipeline came into public view in the summer of 2011. By then, an earlier version of the pipeline had been built between Hardisty, Alberta, and Patoka, Illinois. In its first year of operation, that first Keystone pipeline had a dozen major spills. After just two of these incidents, Department of Transportation pipeline regulators, noting that the pipeline crossed "high consequence areas" in seven contiguous states, issued a Corrective Action Order to TransCanada to take action "to protect the public, property, and the environment from potential hazards."[70]

After a second EPA supplemental environmental impact study gave the pipeline its second lowest rating, calling it "environmentally objectionable" (but still ignoring its major climate and safety issues), a group called Tar Sands Action launched one of the environmental movements largest and most impactful actions, a fifteen-day series of acts of non-violent civil disobedience in Washington, DC, that resulted in the arrests of 1,253 people.

In the hour before NASA's James Hansen joined more than one hundred others to be arrested that day in front of the White House in late August 2011, he talked to reporters in Lafayette Park about the environmental impact study that had just been released and how vague it had been on the environmental impacts caused by the pipeline's construction. But those weren't the environmental impacts he was concerned about, he said. As noxious as spills were, he wanted to address the less visible impacts—the vastly increased amounts of CO_2 in the air; the devastating effects on the globe's clean water supply, because of the massive amounts of water and natural gas needed to process and move the oil to port; the sheer inefficiency of spending the equivalent of three barrels of oil to gain five barrels of oil from tar sands; and the dangers to the critical waterways the pipeline would transverse, to name a few. This doesn't even include the losses the indigenous population and other Canadians are suffering and will suffer in much greater proportions: the loss of their pristine majestic arboreal forests, the contamination of water resources, and the huge upsurge in cancers the contamination is causing among indigenous populations (which are already on record).

Hansen has called the tar sands such a dangerous direction for our national energy policies that if the pipeline is approved, it is essentially "game over" for any attempts to stop the escalating rate of CO_2 now in the atmosphere. It was Hansen who first posited that the CO_2 levels need to be brought back to 350 parts per million to optimize the atmosphere's breathability and give the surviving species a chance to adjust to the damage already created by the current real-world level—now nudging 400.[71] (Bill McKibben's organization, 350.org, is dedicated to heightening awareness of the rising CO_2 levels and climate change.)

As the media continued to cover the arrests, the public outcry grew. A *New York Times* editorial recommended rejecting the pipeline, Desmond Tutu and the Dalai Lama wrote a letter to the White House with the same request, and protests spread across the nation. The Keystone XL pipeline suddenly became a political football, as members of Congress tried to force the president's hand to approve the pipeline.

The approval process for the pipeline has been under the purview of the State Department since 2004, when George W. Bush signed an executive order regarding oil pipelines that cross an international border. First, it requires the completion of an environmental impact statement (EIS). The State Department uses this EIS to assess the proposed project's economic and environmental plusses and minuses. The secretary of state then makes a recommendation to approve or disapprove the pipeline's construction based on these findings. Then the president can either sign a presidential permit or reject the proposed project.

By January 2012 President Obama had denied the pipeline permit (one reason being that the final EIS he had mandated hadn't been completed). As chapter 2 shows, the summer of 2012 was, to put it mildly, a record breaker. The term "climate change" was finally being used in connection with extremes in temperatures, more frequent and more violent storm systems, prolonged wildfires, and the crippling drought that devastated two-thirds of the United States.

But in August 2012, an election year, Obama green-lighted construction by TransCanada on the pipeline's southern section, from where it begins in Texas and ends on the Gulf Coast. Protests increased at spots all along the proposed route, where TransCanada had already begun laying pipe. By working with local and state governments (and in Texas, the railroad commission), TransCanada had already been granted eminent domain rights (substantiated by court order) to gain access to properties along the path, with or without the owners' consent.

Boom Times in the Bakken

In a wide swath of land that extends out of Canada and includes nearly all of the western half of North Dakota and the northeastern quarter of Montana lies a geological formation called the Bakken. Geologists and petroleum engineers have known about shale oil for a long time, and there have been many boom and bust times in the North Dakota oil patch. The issue with the Bakken formation has always been how to access it without spending more money than the oil would bring at market.

In recent years, highly technical advances in horizontal drilling and hydraulic fracturing (fracking) have given the 150 oil companies now there access to what geologists report as a twenty-five-thousand-square-mile sea of oil embedded in deep shale reservoirs that go down as far as fifteen thousand feet. What's different about oil in the Bakken is that it's trapped between these rock layers in tight reservoirs that may be only ten to fifty feet deep, so traditional vertical drilling provides short-term yields (this same limitation exists with thin pockets of natural gas now being tapped with a similar technology).[72] That dilemma has been solved by drilling vertically, then arcing horizontally and using sophisticated fracturing techniques to crack the rock, then capture the oil and bring it to the surface. Using this complicated process, each well can tap miles of oil-bearing rock that was previously too financially impractical to reach.

And that, in turn, has hatched a twenty-first-century oil boom in North Dakota. In 2008, the U.S. Geological Survey estimated the Bakken held from 3 to 4.3 billion barrels of crude, an estimate now thought to be low; in 2011, the agency announced it would fund a new assessment (due in early 2014).[73] Geological engineers already working the Bakken plays (as prospective oil patches are called) believe there's many times that much, enough to meet all the country's domestic needs for decades.[74] Locals have a name for their oil boom: Kuwait on the prairie.

In only a few years, this formation has begun to supply about 3 percent of U.S. daily oil consumption, making North Dakota the second biggest oil producer in the United States.[75] By November of 2012, production had reached 730,000 barrels a day. As the first oil wildcatter, Edwin Drake, quickly discovered, success in the oil patch must be quickly matched by a network of transport options to move the oil to market. In land-locked North Dakota, the transport of choice for all this oil is most often railroads, now carrying over a million barrels of oil daily.[76] But one of the ways the Keystone XL became the favored project of Montana and North Dakota is that TransCanada agreed to detour one of its pipelines to take on 100,000 barrels per day of Bakken crude from their states.

The byproducts that often come with oil drilling are salt, water, and natural gas. Because of the lack of pipelines to deliver the natural gas that comes out of the Bakken wells, oil companies in North Dakota are simply flaring it, letting it burn off. At most wells nationwide, the average amount of gas flared is 1 percent. In North Dakota, it's 34 percent. This is enough heat more than half a million homes, and the state is responsible for the three-fold increase in gas flaring in the United States. Before the oil boom, North Dakota was a dark spot on the satellite maps. Now these flares, some of which shoot twenty-five feet into the air, show up on the map as a cluster of bright lights.

Then there is the water. There are many complaints that dumped fracking water has destroyed agricultural land. State regulators can't keep up, both because of the sheer numbers of drilling sites and because fracking shale oil is pretty messy. Over the course of a week, a single well requires shooting about three million gallons of water and chemicals and millions of pounds of proppant into the wellbore under extremely high pressure to fracture the sandstone between the shale layers and retrieve the oil. After the fuels and water have been separated, some of the water is kept to be used again, either held in disposal wells or trucked to holding ponds. but not all drivers go to the trouble to cart the water back to the ponds; some dump it along the road or on nearby farmland.

Gas Fracking: Cracking the World Open

One of the most iconic images in recent years came from the Academy Award–winning documentary *Gasland*. A man turns on the tap at his sink, flicks his lighter, and jumps back as the water bursts into flame. For many, this was the introduction to the term fracking. Hydraulic fracturing, or gas fracking, is another of the fast-rising fossil fuel booms running rampant in the United States and around the world. Like shale oil fracking, gas fracking uses advanced drilling techniques that use extremely high pressure to inject saltwater and chemicals into deep shale rock formations, then mini-blasting the rock to make it release its payload of natural gas.

Since oil drilling began, drillers have noted that during the process, three things can come up: water, oil, and natural gas. (Salt is often a fourth component and was frequently the real prize early drillers sought.) Although so-called conventional natural gas has been around since the Pythia (the priestess at Apollo's oracle at Delphi) reportedly huffed it to see the future, until recently, shale gas, like shale oil, was not economically feasible. Shale gas exists in tight and narrow pockets. With vertical drilling, it's easy to miss these pockets or drill right through them. Even if you hit one, the narrow pocket is depleted quickly. With the advent of hydraulic fracturing (also called hydrofracturing) and horizontal drilling, it's a whole new ballgame. Even if the pockets are thin, they can extend horizontally for miles.

As with shale oil wells, gas wells are first drilled and lined with steel casings. During this first stage, which pierces the earth layer containing aquifers, an additional cement casing is used to keep the aquifers from being contaminated. Since the target area that contains the natural gas is several hundred or thousand feet below the aquifer, the industry argues that it's protected from any natural gas or chemicals seeping back up into the water table.

Once the pipeline has been drilled vertically (as much as eight thousand feet) and horizontally through the shale (as far as two miles) mini explosives anchored in the pipe are set off. A mixture of resin-coated sand (proppant), saltwater, and chemicals is injected under high pressure. It seeks out the fractured spots in the shale layer, expanding them and allowing the proppant to keep them open to release the gas. When the gas is recovered, it's still mixed with water, sand, and fracking fluid. The gas is heated and separated from the liquids in heating or condensate tanks. The retrieved gas is then transported via truck or pipeline to market. The water that remains after the gas recovery is stored in holding ponds. Some of it is used again, and some is dumped back into the earth into one of the 155,000 EPA-designated Class II injection wells.[77]

That's the general scenario. There's billions of cubic feet of shale gas, so the oil companies are ecstatic (most natural gas companies have been bought up by Big Oil: BP, Shell, and Exxon Mobil, among others); the American public thinks it's getting a clean, less-polluting "bridge" fuel as we say adios to coal and move slowly toward a world without oil; and landowners who lease their gas-drilling rights are making money—sometime lots of money. The oil companies' fallback reassurance to its critics is a familiar one: "we've been drilling for natural gas for decades, so it's a very old and steady technology."

Except it's not quite that simple. There are the other issues How clean is it, really? What's it doing to the water tables all over the country (and the globe)? What's in those millions of gallons of fracking chemicals that are now floating around underneath our countryside and towns?

Professor Tony Ingraffea of Cornell's Department of Civil and Environmental Engineering, takes issue with the industry's carefully tended "clean fuel" image. As an alternative to oil and coal, he says, these natural gas wells aren't just "the least worst, they're the dirtiest, the worst." First, natural gas is methane, a highly potent greenhouse gas that traps heat in the atmosphere much more efficiently than CO_2: over a twenty-year period, if emitted into the atmosphere unburned, as it is with these wells at various stages, it's a hundred times more potent than CO_2. Second, even small leaks turn into serious climate impacts over time. Third, the leakages aren't small. It's typical in newly fracked wells that large pockets of unburned methane actually vent into the atmosphere for days. "Data from Pennsylvania shows that this kind of leaking occurs in about one out of about twenty brand new wells." It also happens even more frequently in aging wells.

One of the photos Ingraffea uses in his lectures is a photo of Boston overlaid with a graph that shows methane leakage from aging pipelines across the city. The graph shows methane levels ten to fifteen times the background levels, demonstrating how profusely the city's aging pipeline infrastructure is leaking methane.[78] It's a sobering picture of the legacy these hundreds of thousands of new fracking wells might be leaving behind when they're old and gray. Ingraffea says that we're not making progress on climate change, thinking we can switch from coal and oil to natural gas. "We're making it worse."

These "fugitive methane emissions" are, in fact, a serious problem with fracking wells. A report done by Ingraffea, R. W. Howarth, and Renee Santoro of Cornell University looked at many of the aspects of natural gas as a so-called clean bridge technology. The report concluded that during the life cycle of a fracked well, from 3.6 percent to 7.9 percent of the total gas production is lost to the atmosphere as unburned methane. While that might not sound like much, there's a huge difference between conventional gas emissions and the emissions from this new, unconventional gas, the "clean fuel" being touted as our low carbon bridge from dirty old fossil fuels. It's "at least 30% more and perhaps more than twice as great as the life-cycle methane emissions we estimate for conventional gas."[79]

"The take home message of the study," says Howarth, is that "if you do an integration [study] of 20 years following the development of the gas, that shale gas is worse than conventional gas and is in fact worse than coal and is worse than oil."[80]

The Howarth report wasn't the only one reporting significantly higher methane emissions estimates. Even the EPA felt compelled to change its own estimates from its 1996 report, "Methane Emissions from the Natural Gas Industry," declaring that it had "significantly underestimated" the sources of potential emissions, because it had excluded the likely emissions resulting from the machinery required to produce, process, vent, and transport everything needed to service the wells.[81]

Creating, maintaining, and servicing each well is a decidedly energy-intensive process. It requires heavy equipment that uses fossil fuels, usually diesel. According to the Tyndall Centre report, "Heavy CO_2 emissions are linked back to the engine-powered fracking process, including the blending of fracturing chemicals and sand that are pumped from storage, and the high-pressure compression, injection and recovery of materials into and out of the well."

Each well has to have a well pad built and water either pipelined or transported in. Waste disposal sites and water containment areas have to be constructed. But even before any construction can begin, the site itself has to be prepared, often requiring clearcutting, and that means that roads have to be built.

Each gas well requires from three to five million gallons of water, or from fifty to a hundred times what conventional gas wells require.[82] According to the Union of Concerned Scientists, an additional four hundred million gallons of water is needed daily for post-extraction procedures, such as refining and transport, and the well requires more water each year it's in operation.[83]

It's not just the water used that's a concern. It's also what happens to the water while (and after) it's being used. Fracking uses some very toxic chemicals, but the problem starts with the well drilling itself. "Although fracturing fluids are more commonly known to contain chemicals linked to cancer, organ damage, nervous system disorders and birth defects, drilling muds or slurries [which lubricate the process] can contain a number of the same chemical constituents used in fracturing fluids."[84]

A report written by the National Resource Defense Council adds its own concern about the water resulting from fracking and what we do with it.

Hydrofracking and the production of natural gas from fracked wells yield byproducts that must be managed carefully to avoid significant harms to human health and the environment. These wastewater by-products are known as "flowback" (fracturing fluid injected into a gas well that returns to the surface when drilling pressure is released) and "produced water" (all wastewater emerging from the well after production begins, much of which is salty water contained within the shale formation). Both types of wastewater contain potentially harmful pollutants, including salts, organic hydrocarbons (sometimes referred to simply as oil and grease), inorganic and organic additives, and naturally occurring radioactive material (NORM). These pollutants can be dangerous if they are released into the environment or if people are exposed to them. They can be toxic to humans and aquatic life, radioactive, or corrosive. They can damage ecosystem health by depleting oxygen or causing algal blooms, or they can interact with disinfectants at drinking water plants to form cancer-causing chemicals.[85]

And the truth is that public water treatment plants aren't equipped to remove these contaminants from the water supply, should they leak in. Some of the levels of toxicity are so minute that public plants don't have the technology even to detect them. It should be noted that not only is most of this water never drinkable again, it's also consumptive water, meaning it's permanently removed from the natural water cycle. It's shot deep into shale laden with hundreds of chemicals and, over time, it leaks back up. Because the earth naturally contains radioactive matter and this is still a relatively new technology, the long-term effects of this now hazardous water have never been measured or quantified.

According to a report by the *New York Times,* in the 1980s, Congress was considering whether it needed to regulate the wastes that resulted from oil and gas drilling, so it turned to the EPA, whose researchers recommended tight controls because of the high toxicity of some of the waste. But when Congress got the report, those recommendations were left out, excised because of pressure from the White House's Office of Legal Counsel.[86]

That's been the pattern for decades. In 2002, for example, the EPA warned Congress that fracking could result in benzene contamination of drinking water. Then the *EPA reversed their position about fracturing causing benzene-contaminated drinking water.* The EPA also studied hydrofracking in 2004, when Congress was debating about regulating the process under the Safe Drinking Water Act. "An early draft of the study discussed potentially dangerous levels of contamination in hydrofracking fluids and mentioned possible evidence of contamination of an aquifer. The report's final version excluded these points, concluding instead that hydrofracking 'poses little or no threat to drinking water.'"[87]

In 2005, the Energy Policy Act exempted hydraulic fracking from any EPA oversight under the Safe Drinking Water Act. The Energy Task force removed any mention of these concerns from its energy plan.

Halliburton pioneered much of the technology used to frack oil and gas wells today and it's one of the leading providers of fracking supplies to the gas and oil industry. The Halliburton Loophole is the term used to describe the fact that "the gas industry is the only one allowed to pump undisclosed chemicals directly into the ground, even when adjacent to underground sources of drinking water." It's the one industry that is not regulated by the Safe Drinking Water Act, and it's covered by full or partial exemptions from the Clean Water Act, Clean Air Act, the National Environmental Policy Act, the Comprehensive Environmental Response, Compensation, and Liability Act (CERCLA or Superfund Act), and the Resource Conservation and Recovery Act (or the Toxic Release Inventory).

Bills have been introduced to both houses of Congress to force accountability on the gas industry, but none of those bills has been passed. In 2009, however, Congress mandated the EPA to investigate the health threats of fracking. A full report is due in 2014.

The industry stands by its claims that "no proven instances of water contamination have occurred due to hydraulic fracturing," but Dr. Ronald Bishop of State University of New York says that the industry uses an extremely narrow definition for "contamination," which includes only the part of the process "whereby hydrostatic pressure is used to force cracks in deep rock formations." This is a common tactic used by proponents of fracking: cherry picking a word or phrase to limit how the potential dangers of the process are defined. In this case, what's not being mentioned are the occurrences of "drilling damage, failed well casings, spills, erosion and sedimentation, or tanker accident."[88]

An internal document from Pennsylvania's Department of Environmental Protection lists dozens of instances of fugitive gas leaks causing house and well explosions, area evacuations, soil contamination, stray gas migrating into residences and businesses, much of it occurring because wells were improperly vented, were abandoned without plugging the boreholes, or had casing or cement failures.[89]

Although the exact makeup of chemicals used as fracking fluids is still protected as an industry trade secret—and currently no federal legislation requires their disclosure—we do know that natural gas drilling emissions include carbon dioxide (CO_2), sulfur dioxide (SOX), nitrogen oxides (NOX), carbon monoxide (CO), particulates, and volatile organic compounds (including benzene). It's also well known that, despite the fact that it's illegal, diesel fuel is often used in fracking.[90] Diesel contains benzene (a known carcinogen), toluene, ethylbenzene, and xylene (BTEX). The BTEX cocktail can damage the central nervous system, liver, and kidneys. Unlike fracking chemicals, diesel fuel is regulated under the Safe Drinking Water Act.

The industry routinely downplays the contents of fracking fluids, comparing them to the ingredients of everyday cleaning products and cosmetics. For example, industry champions like to point out that fracking fluids contain guar gum, which is also used in ice cream and candy. But the guar gum that helps thicken fracking fluid is also mixed with many ingredients not found in ice cream and candy, including biocides like Glutaraldehyde and DBNPA (Dibromo-3-nitrilopropionamide), both respiratory and ecosystem toxins. DBNPA is particularly lethal to organisms living in waterways, even at concentrations as little as parts per trillion, a level that isn't even detectable by modern technology.

Halliburton's home page is a little folksier about how they deliver these chemicals: "often with the help of a small percentage of additives that aid in delivering that solution down the hatch." This mirrors the language the industry likes to use, saying that most of what's used in hydraulic fracturing is water and sand—and that the chemicals compose only 0.5 percent of the total. But given the enormous amounts of water used in each well, that slim percentage translates into some daunting totals. Since each well takes between one and nine million gallons just to get it to the fracturing stage, for a typical well that could amount to thirty-four thousand gallons of highly toxic chemicals, potential endocrine disruptors, and biocides going into the earth at extremely high pressures, shooting their toxic tendrils out in unknown directions for unknowable amounts of time and to unknown effect.

It's this set of unknowns that makes for some real conundrums. When accidents and spills happen, medical and emergency personnel can't respond adequately—they don't know what's in the spills or leaks. Investigations into water and air contamination have been hindered and delayed, because researchers don't know what they're looking for or in what concentrations, so they can't test for specific chemical presence. "Environmental scientists say that without exhaustive information of fracturing fluids and how they are combined, it is impossible to fully assess their associated risks."[91] At the community and personal level, this is clearly a big issue. *If those involved in the shale gas rush do not know the dangers to which they are being exposed, there is no practical or effective way for them to deal with any downstream effects.*

And then there are the earthquakes.

Geologists from the U.S. Geological Survey report that a "direct correlation" can be seen between the earthquakes and wastewater injection disposal sites.[92] They aren't the only ones. Earthquake "swarms" have hit towns in Arkansas (more than eight hundred in one town alone), north-central Texas, New Mexico, Colorado, Ohio, Illinois, western New York, central Oklahoma (more than a thousand in 2010 alone), and West Virginia.

In 2013, *Mother Jones* interviewed William Ellsworth, a U.S. Geological Survey geophysicist, about the upswing of earthquakes in areas where fracking is on the rise. "Nobody is talking to one another about this," Ellsworth said. One of the things that concerns him, he said, is that a well might end up drilling through a fault "five miles from a nuclear power plant."[93]

Earlier, when EnergyInDepth, the lobbying group for natural gas, asked Ellsworth if he agreed that it's incorrect to correlate fracking and recent earthquakes, Ellsworth agreed. "It *is incorrect.* We find no evidence that fracking is related to the occurrence of earthquakes that people are feeling. We think that it's more intimately connected to the wastewater disposal."[94] One might retort that if there's a massive uptick in fracking wells (and the wastewater they produce), and if wastewater disposal is connected to the uptick in earthquakes, it's reasonable to assume that fracking is part of the problem, since wastewater doesn't show up on its own.

Wastewater from oil and gas wells is usually injected under high pressure into what the EPA classifies as Class II wells. There are at least 155,000 of them in the United States, and about 80 percent of those are involved with hydrofracking wastewater.

As daunting as the issues are, they are beginning to find their match in residents who live with the consequences of the shale gas boom. Just across the state line from Dimock, Pennsylvania, where the faucet famously caught fire in *Gasland,* a group of people from Vestal, New York, have formed VeRSE, Vestal Residents for Safe Energy. Their goal is to get their town council to ban drilling. New York State is having great success stopping fracking, with dozens of municipal bans and moratoriums already in place. The bans were challenged by energy companies, who argued that bans came under the purview of the state rather than local governments, but the New York State Supreme Court ruled against the energy companies. According to Sue Rapp, who helped found VeRSE, "many residents need little convincing, since they have seen homes in Pennsylvania with 500-gallon 'water buffaloes'—plastic tankards full of drinking water—sitting on their front lawns. She says that they've seen how property values plummet, banks revoke mortgages and natural landscapes are altered. Already, endless caravans of trucks barrel through their own town, kicking up dust as they head to Pennsylvania to service the gas industry."[95]

New York State Senator Terry Gipson has a section of his website dedicated to looking at the fracking issue. "Envision a time," he says, "when the trucks are gone, the lease money is spent, the trailers and the diners are empty, and all that is left is unusable farm land with a contaminated water supply. What will these people do then?"[96]

Increasingly, people aren't waiting to find out.[97]

Squeezing Oil from Rocks

Not to be confused with the shale oil being mined in North Dakota's Bakken formation, oil shale is basically rock that's infused with hydrocarbons. And according to the Bureau of Land Management (part of the Department of Interior), we have lots of it in the United States, reportedly 1.2 to 1.8 trillion barrels, but perhaps only about half that much could be retrieved. Still, as experts point out, that's more than three times Saudi Arabia's proven reserves.

But there's a big if connected to oil shale. Although a close relation of regular petroleum, during its formation millions of years ago, it wasn't heated as much as traditional free-flowing fossil fuels and ended up more rock than liquid—definitely not "easy oil." Oil shale has to be mined as any rocklike substance, then crushed, heated, and liquefied, before being put through final processing, making its per-barrel cost closer to $60.

Still, anything goes when it comes to oil resources. If it's out there, there's a good chance someone somewhere will come up with the technology to get it to the surface and convert it into a substance that will make our internal combustion engines go. Right now the technologies that would enable oil shale to be commercially feasible are unknown. But that doesn't mean it's not on the drawing board.

The biggest deposits of oil shale in the world are found in the American West in an area called the Green River Formation, which straddles the intersection of Utah, Colorado, and Wyoming. More than 70 percent of these reserves are on federally owned lands. In April 2013, the Bureau of Land Management made nearly seven hundred thousand acres in the three states available for potential oil shale leasing (along with 130,000 acres in Utah for potential tar sands leasing).[98]

Stay tuned.

Coal: The Eighteenth-Century Ideal

Although tar sands is the dirtiest and most toxic form of oil, over time, coal has been the most damaging fossil fuel globally, by virtue of its deeper presence and longer history as part of the world's energy supply. Oil runs our cars and shows up in every phase of our food supply, and natural gas figures in the widespread manufacture of fertilizer as well as heating and cooking; coal fills in the considerable space that's left. It's still the main source of electricity in our country, supplying more than half of our energy needs. It is a highly inefficient source (80 percent of its energy goes up the stacks), and it's responsible for nearly a third of our country's greenhouse gas emissions.

The United States burns about one billion tons of coal each year. Burning coal not only emits 20 percent of the globe's CO_2 load, but a host of other toxins—mercury, sulfur dioxide, nitrogen oxide, and particulate matter—all of which have been traced to creating and exacerbating respiratory ailments and heart disease, as well as raising the risk of heart attacks and strokes. Not only do these contaminants pollute our air, they eventually settle back down on the earth, sinking into our water resources and contaminating our food supplies.[99]

According to a 2011 report in the *American Economic Review* that assessed the air pollution damages caused by each U.S. industry sector, coal far outstrips its competitor industries. "The largest industrial contributor to external costs is coal-fired electric generation, whose damages range from 0.8 to 5.6 times value added."[100] Whatever useful energy coal might provide, its cost to our health and the environment is exorbitant and inevitable.

Consider the coal ash, a byproduct held in containment ponds near or around coal plants. These ponds bring a separate set of risks, especially when they fail. This is what the citizens of Harriman, Tennessee, awoke to on December 22, 2008, when a wall of the forty-acre containment pond that surrounded the Kingston Fossil Plant gave way, dumping a billion gallons of coal ash into the surrounding area. That flood not only buried parts of the town in lakes of toxic sludge, but it poured that sludge into the tributaries of the Tennessee River, the water supply for millions of people downstream in Tennessee, Alabama, and Kentucky. In sheer volume, the Kingston spill is nearly one hundred times greater than the amount of contaminant involved in the *Exxon Valdez* disaster, which dumped eleven million gallons of oil into the fishing waters of Port William Sound in Alaska, polluting 1,200 miles of shoreline. Like all such environmental events, no one can guess yet the physical and psychological downstream effects.

Overall, coal is finding fewer advocates who can make the case that it's a viable and intelligent energy source. It is being marginalized in an age when cleaner alternatives and the natural gas boom are moving in on its market share. Existing regulations for coal plants have stiff, two-pronged requirements: new coal-fired plants must be able to capture CO_2 emissions—and that technology does not yet exist; existing plants can be retrofitted to reduce both mercury and air toxins, but the costs can be prohibitive. The coal industry is getting the picture about domestic production as their share prices decline.

When Georgia Power announced in January 2013 that it would shutter a total of fifteen coal- and oil-fired generating units at four of its plants, it brought to 129 the total number of aging U.S. plants retired or put on the chopping block since 2002. Most of these plants were from forty-four to sixty-three years old and are located in the eastern half of the United States. "Today, more than three-quarters of U.S. coal-fired power plants have outlived their 30-year lifespan—with 17 percent being older than half a century," according to a 2012 report by the Union of Concerned Scientists. "As many as 353 coal-fired power generators in 31 states—representing up to 59 [gigawatts] of power capacity [about 6 percent of our daily electricity needs]—are no longer economically viable compared with cleaner, more affordable energy sources."[101]

Other countries are not so picky. The World Resources Institute reports that worldwide nearly 1,200 new coal plants are at least on the drawing board, with three-fourths of them in China (363) and India (450). While it's anyone's guess how many of them will actually go online, coal is still very cheap and in demand in both these rapidly developing countries. According to one U.S. agency's estimate, China burns almost as much coal as the rest of the world combined.[102]

While the figures are enough to make anyone's eyes cross, they cannot be ignored, because they affect the other essential fuel that sustains us: the very air we pull into our lungs hundreds of times each hour. Increasingly, this air is no longer life giving. In China alone, hundreds of thousands die each year from respiratory failure as a direct result of the toxins in the air. "In Beijing alone, 70 to 80 percent of all deadly cancer cases are related to the environment. Lung cancer has emerged as the No. 1 cause of death."[103] This is no mystery, considering that most of China's power is generated via highly inefficient and cheaply built coal plants. "Dirty" coal provides China with 70 percent of its energy and while its two-coal-plants-per-week pace of a few years ago has slowed, the country is still very much a coal customer.

Enter the coal of the Wyoming Powder River Basin. While domestic coal production in the eastern coal states like Pennsylvania, West Virginia, Kentucky, and Georgia is waning and its old plants are shuttering, western coal production is booming. The United States gets 40 percent of its coal from the Wyoming basin, a number that has grown since the late 1980s, when coal mining in the west became economically feasible. Unlike the coal of the eastern states, which is considered very dirty, given its high sulfur content, Powder River Basin coal has a low sulfur and ash content, making it much more desirable. Because of the decline in favor of domestic coal production, the Powder River Basin is eyeing hungry Asian markets. In 2013, five large export terminals were proposed—from California to Washington state—to accommodate the expected increase in business. Coal is cheap and plentiful in China and is not likely to be replaced any time soon with a different energy form. And according to data from the U.S. Energy Information Administration, by 2017 India is likely to be importing as much coal as China.[104]

But what happens in China doesn't stay in China. According to the U.S. Environmental Protection Agency, on certain days 25 percent of the pollution in the skies over Los Angeles can be blamed on the air that migrates eastward across the ocean.[105] And like the air blowing east from China, other contaminants collect in invisible but highly potent ways.

Coal's Killing Fog

Before oil began helping lubricate the machinery that made possible the industrialization of the twentieth century, there was coal in the nineteenth century, which made Great Britain into a giant of the Industrial Revolution's first century and powered the beginnings of U.S. industry. Coal has a brilliant, warm, reliable heat, but it has a nasty side effect. It chokes people to death.

The killing coal fog that encompassed London in 1952 effectively ended the age of coal in England. On the cold morning of December 5, smog (fog combined with coal smoke) encased the city, filling the air with particulate matter that contained sulfur dioxide, nitrogen oxides, and soot. The unusually cold weather had encouraged Londoners to burn more coal in their fireplaces. The combination of the additional smoke and the cold temperatures created the foggy shroud.

Unable to see a foot in front of them, people abandoned their cars where they stopped. Children got lost on the way to school. An opera performance had to be called off, because the air inside of the theater became intolerable. Bodies began to stack up in the morgue, and undertakers ran out of coffins. The Ministry of Health started taking a daily tally to determine how many more deaths were occurring than usual. Most of the deaths were attributed to respiratory illness—some people had chronic asthma or bronchitis, but others had died after the new onset of respiratory problems. The count reached more than 4,000, the daily totals rising from 250 on day one to 900 by the fourth day. The smog got everywhere, into homes and churches, through any crack. Some unexpected victims were a number of prize cattle ready to be shown at the Smithfield Show at Earl's Court. The animals started to have trouble breathing and then dropped dead, their lungs destroyed by the acid in the smoke.[106]

The World Health Organization has guidelines that stipulate 50 milligrams per cubic meter as the limit of acceptable air quality for short-term exposure. The numbers during the Great Smog were 1,600 milligrams per cubic meter.

Londoners had long been used to the inconvenience of the coal-induced fog, but this was different. "This was accompanied by an apparent disbelief that nothing could really be done to attenuate the pollution problem, especially given the public's awareness of the growing availability of alternative fuels to coal; all this in the waning, but still present post-war spirit of a fresh start and the opportunity to rebuild collectively."[107]

The City of London passed Clean Air Acts in 1956 and 1968 that required the conversion to smokeless fuels. Coal use as a domestic fuel was banned in urban areas.

Rainforests, Oil, and the Air We Breathe

Rainforests have been called the lungs of the earth. If that's so, then our global lungs are getting smaller and weaker. In the way Mother Nature set it up, trees everywhere, but especially those in lush rainforests, serve a critical purpose. They are our carbon sinks, their branches and leaves enabling the absorption of billions of tons of the CO_2 that finds its way into the atmosphere from manmade and natural sources. "Forests, especially in the lush tropics, suck and store carbon, which is released when trees are cut down or burnt."[108]

To put it simply, when they inhale, they take in CO_2. What they exhale is our oxygen. More and more these carbon sinks are disappearing, mostly for economic reasons. In the Amazon and Indonesia (which together contain 81 percent of the world's rainforests), the rush to clear-cut the valuable mahogany trees (also called "blood wood") is matched only by the mania to clear the way for agricultural land to grow biomass for oil alternatives, from corn to grass.

But tearing down forests to create oil alternatives is ludicrous. "The cruel irony is that deforestation will result in more [greenhouse gases] being released into the atmosphere than the use of biofuels will eliminate."[109] Deforestation doesn't just involve cutting. It also involves burning up what's left after the trees have been hauled away. That burning of the rainforests alone accounts for 20 percent of all the greenhouse gases dumped into the atmosphere annually.

It gets worse. Losing the trees also means being subjected to what they have long kept to themselves. "The amount of carbon stored in tropical forests is staggering—Brazil alone has nearly 50 billion tons—and its loss would ensure dramatic climate change. Scientists estimate that without a change in business as usual, more than half of the Amazon forest would be logged by 2030, releasing 20.5 billion tons of CO_2 into the atmosphere."[110] Not only do we lose their cleansing effects and life-giving oxygen, we gain more pollution.

Clear-cutting destroys the land for a short-term profit; it sets it up to erode and go fallow. With the trees gone, there is not only nothing to catch the CO_2 and convert it back to oxygen, there is nothing to absorb the water during the rainy season, so water tables decline. There is a delicate relationship between weather patterns, rainfall, and forests. When forests decline, the rainy season brings less rain. Destroying vast stretches of rain forest also destroys the diversity of plant and animal life; their mysteries and benefits are lost forever.

Once destroyed, these old growth forests cannot be easily restored. Despite any reassurances from clear-cutting advocates, replanting takes decades to begin to do the work of mature trees. The shallow root systems of saplings cannot capture enough water to help balance the rainfall needs of a forest, nor are they capable of holding soil in place to prevent erosion.

Because of this clear-cutting, Conservation International estimates that one species is going extinct every twenty minutes, over a thousand times faster than the norm throughout most of earth's history.[111] In that same twenty minutes, 1,200 acres of rain forest will disappear. "We have no idea how many natural cures, how many industrial materials, how many biological insights, how much sheer natural beauty, and how many parts and pieces of a complex web of life we barely understand are being lost."[112]

The cost to our ecosystems is steep; so is the loss of all that biodiversity. According to John Holdren, a Harvard and Woods Hole environmental scientist, "The biodiversity of the planet is a unique and uniquely valuable library that we have been steadily burning down—one wing at a time—before we have even catalogued all the books, let alone read them all."[113] Strands are being obliterated as the species web breaks and fails in spots. Like the burning of the library in Alexandria, we are being cut off from knowledge before we get to know what we are missing. "Destroying a tropical rain forest and other species-rich ecosystems for profit," says entomologist Edward O. Wilson, "is like burning all the paintings of the Louvre to cook dinner."

There was a time when we knew better. We have forgotten. As Thom Hartmann says, "Older [indigenous] cultures, with few exceptions, hold as their most foundational concept the belief that we are not different from, separate from, in charge of, superior to, or inferior to the natural world. We are part of it. Whatever we do to nature, we do to ourselves. Whatever we do to ourselves, we do to the world. For most, there is no concept of a separate 'nature': it's all us and we're all it."[114]

The Toxins among Us

According to a 2013 study published in the journal *Environmental Research Letters*, airborne pollutants and the uptick in human-caused ozone pollution kill 2.5 million people worldwide annually.[115] A new MIT study using data from the EPS's National Emissions Inventory, which catalogs emissions sources nationwide, estimates that air pollution kills 200,000 people in the United States annually,[116] more than five times the number killed in automobile accidents.[117] Air and water pollution together damage the health of people all over the world. "A joint study by the University of California and the Boston Medical Center shows that some 200 human diseases, ranging from cerebral palsy to testicular atrophy, are linked to pollutants. Other diseases that can be caused by pollutants include an astounding 37 forms of cancer, plus heart disease, kidney disease, high blood pressure, diabetes, dermatitis, bronchitis, hyperactivity, deafness, sperm damage, and Alzheimer's and Parkinson's diseases."[118]

As Rachel Carson, Aldo Leopold, and countless others have pointed out, what we put into the air and onto our soil affects everyone, and what everyone else does affects us. A report by a research team in the United Kingdom noted a rise not only in Alzheimer's and Parkinson's diseases but in motor neuron disease in general in six European countries as well as the United States, Japan, Canada, and Australia.[119]

From the late 1970s to the late 1990s, the number of annual deaths attributable to these brain diseases rose from three thousand to ten thousand. The death rates from these diseases, many of them from Alzheimer's, "more than tripled for men and nearly doubled for women. This increase in dementia is likely linked to a rise in the concentration of pesticides, industrial effluents, car exhaust, and other pollutants in the environment."[120]

In addition, a 2006 study done by the Harvard School of Public Health reported that "long-term low-level exposure to pesticides raised the risk of developing Parkinson's disease by 70 percent."[121]

The deadly neurotoxin mercury shows up now in virtually all countries with coal-burning power plants and many that have gold mines. "For example, gold miners release an estimated 290,000 pounds of mercury into the Amazon ecosystem each year, and coal-burning power plants release nearly 100,000 pounds of mercury into the air in the United States." The mercury from power plants in the United States, according to the EPA, "settles over waterways, polluting rivers and lakes, and contaminating fish."[122]

This contamination is so serious that in 2006 only Alaska and Wyoming did not issue any of the "3,080 fish advisories warning against eating fish from local lakes and streams because of their mercury content. EPA research indicates that one out of every six women of childbearing age in the United States has enough mercury in her blood to harm a developing fetus. This means that 630,000 of the 4 million babies born in the country each year may face neurological damage from mercury exposure before birth."[123]

Unborn U.S. babies are soaking in a stew of chemicals, including mercury, gasoline byproducts and pesticides . . . . The report by the Environmental Working Group is based on tests of 10 samples of umbilical cord blood taken by the American Red Cross. They found an average of 287 contaminants in the blood, including mercury, fire retardants, pesticides and the Teflon chemical PFOA.
—MAGGIE FOX, "Unborn Babies Soaked in Chemicals, Survey Finds," Reuters, 14 July 2005

Externalities: The Real Cost of Things

In the fall of 2008 Americans saw the cost of denial in dramatic detail as the markets that are the foundation of our system began to fray and collapse. Our banks, investment institutions, real estate market, and automobile industry all seemed to be coming apart at the seams. In a real way, we were reeling from the effects of a very long party at which no one wanted to look at the real costs of lowering federal income, wildly inflating government spending, and pairing that with stratospheric borrowing—much of it to enable what was by then a five-year war begun to secure oil fields in the Middle East. As trillions of dollars were flying everywhere and Americans watched their retirement accounts, jobs, and the very homes they owned begin to disappear before their eyes, one question was on everyone's mind: how did we not see this coming?

Much the same condition exists with our environment and the way the market has refused to acknowledge the real costs, the so-called externalities, that surround our willful denial of the state of our planet's resources. Nicholas Stern, once the chief economist at the World Bank, warned in late 2006 that the accounting for this would be expensive, in the trillions of dollars. Lester Brown points out that the market's refusal to acknowledge externalities shows that it "does not value nature's services properly. And it does not respect the sustainable yield thresholds of natural systems. It also favors the near term over the long term, showing little concern for future generations."[124]

As an example, Brown points to the real cost of gasoline. The current price of gas, he says, reflects what it costs to get the oil from the ground, refined, and delivered to the service station (and, most consumers would add, a very healthy profit for the providers). What it doesn't include are the costs of climate change, government subsidies, military costs to keep our supply free and secure, or the health care costs of the respiratory illnesses we cope with as a result of the polluted air we breathe. When you add those up, he says, the real price for gas is closer to $15 per gallon.[125]

Nor are these externalities common only to the United States. In 2008, China overtook the United States as the world's leading emitter of CO_2. It also leaves us in the dust when it comes to the amount of meat eaten (twice as much as the United States), the amount of grain (a third more) and steel used (three times as much).[126]

Environmental externalities have their own term: *green debt.* Pan Yue, vice-minister of China's State Environmental Protection Administration, wrote of China's green debt in 2006, pointing out that if all the environmental damage it has done in the last three decades were calculated, all of its GDP gains of that entire timespan would be neutralized. China had, he said, seen its Marxist philosophy only through the lens of class struggle. "We believed that economic development would solve all our problems." This, in turn, "morphed into an unrestrained pursuit of material gain devoid of morality. Traditional Chinese culture, with its emphasis on harmony between human beings and nature, was thrown aside."[127]

In an interview with *Der Spiegel,* Vice-Minister Yue spoke plainly about the pollution dangers his country faces. China's problems are frightening. The miracle that is Chinese progress, he predicted, will end soon, "because the environment can no longer keep pace. Acid rain is falling on one third of the Chinese territory, half of the water in our seven largest rivers is completely useless, while one fourth of our citizens do not have access to clean drinking water. One third of the urban population is breathing polluted air." According to the World Bank, sixteen of the world's twenty most polluted cities are in China. In the last fifty years, their population has doubled, to 1.3

billion, and the amount of land available for habitation and cultivation has been cut in half.[128]

Because of its scale, any single thing that China does packs a huge wallop. Just providing enough disposable chopsticks for its massive population (eighty billion sets) requires twenty million twenty-year-old trees per year.[129] With its forests disappearing at an alarming rate, and in an effort to discourage the use of the traditional mainstay and promote a greener alternative, the government passed a tax on their use in 2006, but it had little effect. Nor is that the only way trees are endangered. If China's size and ravenous appetite continue on its current trajectory, by 2030 China will need twice as much paper as the entire world produces today. And if by then it is at par with America in automobile ownership (three cars for every four citizens), it will need the equivalent of 98 million barrels of oil per day—about 13 MBPD more than the entire world uses today.[130]

It's all a set of unseen truths and consequences, things that happen whose cascading effects we cannot see or envision. That's because the earth is not composed of separate parts; it is a harmonious, synchronized body of interrelated pieces that not only fit but are symbiotic. We have stuck our finger into the center of all that and twirled to our heart's delight.

Slowly, the world is awakening to the reality that finite fuel resources by their very nature have no future in a world that is growing and constantly craving more. These fuels are not a sustainable option. So also is not caring. As the journalist and economist Dame Barbara Ward said, "To say we do not care is to say in the most literal sense that 'we choose death.'"[131]

These sprays, dusts, and aerosols are now applied almost universally to farms, gardens, forests, and homes—nonselective chemicals that have the power to kill every insect, the "good" and the "bad," to still the song of birds and the leaping of fish in the streams, to coat the leaves with a deadly film, and to linger on in soil—all this though the intended target may be only a few weeds or insects.

Can anyone believe it is possible to lay down such a barrage of poisons
on the surface of the earth without making it unfit for all life?
They should not be called "insecticides," but "biocides."
—RACHEL CARSON, *Silent Spring*

Different Kinds of Efficiencies

John Locke, one of the fathers of the seventeenth-century age of reason, may have helped set the tone for our hubris about nature when he said, in his second of *Two Treatises of Government,* that "land that is left wholly to nature . . . is called, as indeed it is, waste." Nature, to this way of thinking, was to be used. It was there for us, under our dominion. And that pretty much sums up the American mindset of the last half of the twentieth century.

If your only goal is to save time and labor and to maximize yields, oil gives us efficiencies that would have made our ancestors' heads spin. Even though the practices of modern agribusiness are highly wasteful, it takes about twenty minutes worth of fossil fuel energy to create one person's food for the day. If done by hand, the tilling, seeding, watering, harvesting, refining, and shipping for the same meals would take three weeks.[132]

Time is money. It's also the highly treasured currency of the American lifestyle. And to support that lifestyle—having everything available to us 365 days a year—we have spent ourselves into multiple forms of resource debt. Between surface water and underground aquifers, agriculture now uses a full 85 percent of our fresh water. Since World War II, our use of pesticides has increased by 3,000 percent. The toxic chemicals used to rid the soil of pests have the nasty habit of decimating all the members of the soil infrastructure, good and harmful—and each year, crop loss to pests has increased. As chapter 4 details, as we put increasing pressure on our soils to produce, they grow weaker. They are less able to nourish us, their yields less able to fulfill the nutritional requirements of our population.

The bottom line is that in the pre-green revolution days of the

1950s, our ultraefficient agricultural world used to produce 2.3 calories of energy for every calorie expended. We now get a paltry one calorie of energy for every *ten* calories expended. We've turned our productivity ratio upside down. We've turned our backs on the free energy that was our planetary birthright and spent wildly with the ancient blood of our prehistory. Just as our automobiles waste 85 percent of the energy in every gallon of gas, much of the oil we spend to feed ourselves is wasted. About 20 percent of the four million barrels of oil used daily in agribusiness is spent planting, harvesting, and tilling; the remaining 80 percent is spent transporting, processing, packaging, marketing, and preparing the food in our kitchens.

Growing food organically has many benefits, among them the fact that organic farmers use a third less fossil fuels than conventional farmers because they don't use chemical fertilizers and pesticides, both derived from fossil fuels. On the other hand, transporting an organic lettuce spring mix from the Salinas Valley to upstate New York still amounts to about three thousand food miles.

"The fossil fuel era freed human beings from the slower seasonal rhythms of an agricultural period and thus also from dependency on nature's constraints and divine intervention."[133] But it also broke our intuitive sense of how we were born to operate in concert with the earth. Once that sacred contract was broken, we went on a spending spree among the earth's resources, which finds us now in the woozy, aching aftermath of a gluttonous bender.

Facing the end of a way of life—even as a gradual shift—without envisioning what will replace it is unnerving, with good reason. The task before us, building a new energy economy, will be an undertaking of staggering scale and repercussions. "We need to take all our current energy assets—our coal-fired power plants, our oil pipelines and refineries, our tanker ships, our trains and planes and automobiles—worth well over ten trillion dollars and replace them all with an equally colossal and interwoven system of technology processes, and network (many yet to be invented), which by 2050 must be efficiently producing enough energy for 9 billion people, their companies and their lifestyles, all while emitting half the carbon per capita that is currently the case."[134]

Here's where the math inevitably breaks down, because, as Richard Heinberg and other resource analysts point out, much of what we are basing our calculations on today—fossil fuels, water, food, wood fuel—will likely not exist in the quantities they exist in today. By then they will have been decimated. The feedback loops are unchangeable.

Seeing Ourselves Anew

Breaking established and comfortable beliefs can have consequences. When Galileo broke with Aristotle's theory that the earth held the center spot in our solar system, the Catholic Church was sorely displeased. The idea that we actually circled the sun rather than it circling us was so radical and infuriating a concept that it took the Catholic Church until 1992 to reverse the proclamation that had originally banned his theory in 1616, leaving him an outcast who died in seclusion. It left people in a psychological state not unlike the one we are facing now. Without our egocentric beliefs that we are the center of nature, who exactly are we? Galileo didn't just help show us the earth wasn't the center of our solar system, he also set the stage for a bigger understanding—that the earth does not revolve around us. We need it. It doesn't need us. We're its dependents, not its sovereigns.

As we refashion our idea of twenty-first-century stewardship, we should see this as a surrendering to cosmic law, not giving up, but bowing in recognition of its mystery and our part of its whole. Spirit is in the theories of science as well as in the trees. When we look for ways to outdo nature, to fool it and coax more out of a day, we are not doing it in cooperation and fellowship with nature. Rather, we are operating from a hierarchical space, dictating terms and using the precious resources as though they were ours to waste, without any accountability or conscience.

At the same time that Edison was putting on his light show

in lower Manhattan, Albert Einstein was using his imagination to understand how light worked in a different form. He was enchanted less with its usefulness than its invisible properties and behaviors. He saw nature not just as the physical earth we can see but also as the laws that govern it. He saw beyond mere measuring and calculation to the elusive and harmonious randomness that is, paradoxically, a constant in our lives.

It is not easy to give up cherished ideas about who we are and how we work—though we are already doing it. In the 1980s, while Steve Jobs and Bill Gates were trying to convince us that computers and software were going to become essential, at first we could not see why or how. Our minds could not yet comprehend them as tools beyond being time-saving ways to do word processing and crunch numbers in spreadsheets. Nobody imagined being able to browse the Library of Congress in your pajamas at three in the morning because you couldn't sleep. Words like Twitter, Facebook, Google, YouTube, and blog were not yet in the global vocabulary, and the idea of exposing a single happening to the entire world in a moment was still incomprehensible. Nor could anyone foresee a television and computer embedded in a telephone that fit nicely in your pocket and carried in its tiny membranes a thousand times the capability of those early clunkers. Walking through the dawn of the computer age, we had no idea where we would end up. It took a little time and considerable imagination and revelation. But when the interest and energy of hundreds of millions of people get involved, things change.

"You are not going to see it coming," Bill Gates told *New York Times* columnist Thomas Friedman about where we find the solutions to our planet's energy crises. "The breakthrough will probably come out of somewhere you least expect, and we'll only know how it happened looking backward."[135]

If Gates is right, we won't really be able to identify the solutions until we see them in our rearview mirrors. Computers really matured when the internet and the world wide web gave us the beginnings of our new communications grid—an invisible matrix that most Westerners under age thirty have no memory of being without. Perhaps the new energy grid—the one that will power our transportation, heat and light up our homes and industries—will follow a similar path. By the time we replace the current grid with one that's invisible and clean and works in partnership rather than against nature, we will enjoy the sweet feeling of taking it for granted again. This is the invisible way we move into what's next, recognizing its shape only when we look back.

Becoming more conscious doesn't happen all at once. We become worthy vessels one insight at a time. Like the natives who could not see Columbus's ships when they first came ashore because they had no frame of reference for what they were looking at, we too cannot see the answers around us. We lack the template that helps us make sense of the information that surrounds us. Yet the answers are everywhere, not just inside our thinking, but beyond it. Whatever form the solutions eventually take doesn't matter. What matters is starting to engage the process.

Eudora Welty said, "The events in our lives happen in a sequence in time, but in their significance to ourselves, they find their own order . . . the continuous thread of revelation."

Where We Go from Here

As if to summarize the record-breaking summer he was already witnessing in 2012, climate activist and teacher Bill McKibben wrote a *Rolling Stone* article that framed the perils behind climate change in a new and compelling way.[136] McKibben used the findings of a little-known study by a group of climate researchers from Germany, the United Kingdom, and Switzerland that was published in *Nature* in 2009.[137] The lead writer on the report was a climate scientist named Malte Meinshausen. Citing data in the report, McKibben's article addressed a "factual void" in the climate change debate. If the nations of the world are to stay below the 2° Celsius temperature rise that scientists agree is the upper limit of what constitutes livable conditions, how exactly do we know where we are? How much carbon is yet to be burned, and how far along have we already gone?

McKibben's article delivered chilling news. As a planet we can dump roughly 565 more gigatons of CO_2, our so-called carbon budget, into the atmosphere before it tips the planet's heating past the 2°C mark. It should be noted that the 2°C mark is, at best, the least bad of the worst-case scenarios—and it still means four- to nine-meter rises among the world's oceans, according to James Hansen.

The startling bad news is that there are currently 2,795 gigatons in the proven reserves of coal, oil, and gas that the fossil-fuel companies are already planning to extract and burn. In other words, we have more than five times as much fossil fuel in play as the planet can tolerate before careening into unknown climate dramas that could compromise every life-form on earth.

According to McKibben, this isn't just on the drawing board as a possible option. It's surefire revenue that's already built into corporate share prices and downstream plans. Governments have grown accustomed to counting on these assets and crafted their long-term budgets accordingly—another way that fossil fuels have become ingrained in our lifestyles.

It explains why the big fossil-fuel companies have fought so hard to prevent the regulation of carbon dioxide—those reserves are their primary asset, the holding that gives their companies their value. It's why they've worked so hard these past years to figure out how to unlock the oil in Canada's tar sands, or how to drill miles beneath the sea, or how to frack the Appalachians.
—BILL MCKIBBEN[138]

The day after the 2012 elections, McKibben began a series of speeches around the country, called his Do the Math tour, barnstorming the country in a biofuel bus, conveying a single message to sold-out crowds in twenty-one cities: decarbonization of our economy is a moral issue. And the math he used from the Meinshausen report was intended to make his audience "understand they are going to have to intervene in a more powerful way." The bottom line according to the report is this: "In sum, 80 percent of all fossil fuel reserves would have to remain untouched to prevent uncontrollable warming."[139]

John Felmy, the chief economist for the American Petroleum Institute had a predictably different take on McKibben's message. "Oil, gas and coal are going to be used for the foreseeable future. It's inevitable. Instead of talking about an improbable fossil fuel scenario, we need to have a rational discussion about energy policy . . . focusing on things like improving efficiency."[140]

The problem is deeply entrenched. "As much as 30 percent of the value of some of the world's stock exchanges is in proven coal, oil and gas reserves, which energy companies are banking on mining and selling one day."[141]

HSBC, one of the world's largest banking and financial services institutions, released a report with similar findings, "that the largest oil and gas companies, including BP, Shell and Statoil, could lose 60 percent of their market values if governments proceed with tough carbon reduction targets and force companies to leave reserves untapped."[142]

McKibben said that what surprised him is that "the fossil fuel industry and skeptics haven't done the slightest thing to say the math isn't true." The IEA agrees with McKibben's thesis, that up to two-thirds of all known fossil-fuel reserves must be left unretrieved if we are to avoid a 2°C rise in global temperatures.

Because of its deeply ingrained place in our lifestyle, oil in America has long been the darling of our people. And whenever criticism was raised, oil's defenders have stepped in and done what was necessary to keep it in its place at the top of the pedestal of the American lifestyle. During the Bush Administration, the oil and automobile industries had a tireless champion, helping to stave off moves toward cleaner, more efficient engines, which would have hit both industries hard. If mandated, such increased efficiencies would have meant costly manufacturing changes to the automobile industry, and it would have begun, however slightly, to slow the driving public's per capita oil requirements. (The image of the CEOs from America's top three automakers testifying before Congress, in a direct appeal for funds as recession deepened into depression in the fall of 2008, was a jarring one.)

But to the oil industry, conservation has long been a four-letter word. Historically, the oil industry has been less than anxious to retool and change, especially since it had been enjoying a binge of profit from the SUVs and trucks it had been selling in record numbers—at least until rising prices at the pump began to change the public's car-buying habits.

Along with the two dozen barrels of oil that each of us uses in the United States per year, there are some sobering statistics about what all those threads of meaning spell out at the other end of the tailpipe (petroleum) as well as the smokestack (coal). The bottom line is that between all of our uses of hydrocarbon to heat, transport, and feed us, each American adds more than six tons of greenhouse gases into the atmosphere annually, part of the 6.2 billion tons that become a part of the underside of our atmospheric umbrella each year. Since the earth can absorb only about three billion tons a year, it's easy to see how all that extra CO_2 keeps making the future of our habitation on the planet harder and harder.[143]

Given the libraries of data we have accumulated, perhaps it's time to reweave the tapestry that was our collective species memory and rediscover the revelations that lie within it. We can learn much from the wisdom humanity relied on before coal and oil redefined what we could coax out of the earth. While fossil fuels freed us from nature's slower rhythms, they also enslaved us to an ever-thinning tether and a future we never dared envision. As it fed us with steady and ever-bigger transfusions of what Colombia's U'wa tribe calls the blood of Mother Earth, it also sucked dry the birthright of our topsoil and helped throw our planet's species diversity into chaos.

The path to healing our broken sense of where our center is lies in our willingness to be accountable for what and how we spend what the earth presents for all of us to share. Martin Luther King Jr. said, "The arc of the moral universe is long, but it bends towards justice." Increasingly, it also bends toward wanting to do the right thing.

As Barbara Kingsolver said at the end of her one-year experiment of living off the food she and her family grew themselves, "We so want to believe it is possible to come back from our saddest mistakes, and have another chance. . . . Something can happen for us, it seems, or *through* us, that will stop this earthly unraveling and start the clock over. Like every creature on earth, we want to make it too. We want more time."[144]

Chapter 4

Seeds of Discontent

A nation that destroys its soil destroys itself.
—FRANKLIN DELANO ROOSEVELT

As petroleum gets more expensive and the so-called three-thousand-mile Caesar salad gives way to food that is more locally derived, the intrusion of oil into the circulatory system that currently nurtures most of our food will slow. But if oil has become the lifeblood of modern agriculture, then biotechnology has become its heart. And it is on this stage of oil and biotechnology that key elements in a drama about the future of our food converge: the seeds with which the earth sustains us, the farmers who have traditionally been the stewards of the earth's bounty, and the GMOs (genetically modified organisms) being grown in increasing numbers across our farmlands by agribusiness.

Even before the introduction of GMOs in the late 1980s, American agribusiness played a big part in soil and water table contamination, in the disruption of historic ways of planting and sharing seeds, in the health and immune systems of our seed stores, in the health of both our population and global consumers, and in the disruption and depression in the lives of farmers—the men and women who serve as our sacred link to the food that comes from the earth.

The change in patent law, successfully lobbied for by the chemical and biotech corporations, has altered the character and integrity of our national seed supplies and threatened the health and bio-diversity of the most ancient seed archives on earth, from North America and the Middle East to Asia. This, in turn, is having a profound physical, monetary, and spiritual effect on farmers world-wide. The increasing demands of agribusiness are widening the gap between farmers' native ingenuity and the soil and seeds, and this loss of the hand-to-heart link between farmers and the earth must be examined.

The Seed Savers

Seed is a big deal. Its very meaning connotes totality, life producing life in a constant chain. All living things—from a fungus to a Super Bowl quarterback—begin as some form of seed. When it comes to the seed that, through the grace of good soil, water, and a coopera-tive climate, becomes the food that sustains us, keeping it whole and safe should be instinctual—and it often is.

From 1941 to 1943, during the nine-hundred-day siege of Leningrad in World War II, while more than six hundred thou-sand of its citizens starved, a cadre of Soviet botanists blockaded themselves inside a makeshift seed vault at the Research Institute of Plant Industry. Founded by the visionary botanist, biologist, and geneticist Nikolai Vavilov, the institute—under his leadership—gave the world its first seed bank, a repository for more than two hundred thousand types of seeds and plants. During the 1920s and 1930s, Vavilov and his researchers went on more than a hundred seed-gathering missions in sixty-four countries, combing the earth for seed samples and taking their botanical treasures back to Russia, where he created what was at that time the greatest living seed archive in the world.

During the siege, while their starving countrymen ate sawdust, grass, shoes, tree bark, their pets, the dead, and eventually nothing, the thirty-one people in the institute preserved their bags of rice, corn, wheat, potatoes, peanuts, and countless sacks of edible seed. They burned every stick of furniture in the building to keep the plants and themselves from freezing to death.[1] At night, when rats invaded in force, they beat them away with metal rods. Some of the plants they protected for posterity, like potatoes, had to be periodically planted and harvested. They took turns sneaking the potatoes out to the edge of the enemy lines and burying them to give them a chance—however slim—to reproduce, believing the front lines were the areas least likely to be tread upon.

When at last the siege ended, the liberators found fourteen of these brave botanists dead from starvation next to sacks of food, preferring to martyr themselves than let the Nazis—or their starving fellow countrymen—destroy their botanical heritage. The institute's rice specialist, Dr. Dmytry S. Ivanov, was found dead at his desk, with stacks of rice sacks beside him. Before he died, he reportedly said, "When all the world is in the flames of war, we will keep this collection for the future of all people."[2]

While they starved, their leader, Nikolai Vavilov, languished in prison, having enraged Lenin with his new-fangled ideas about seed gathering and genetic diversity. (Lenin could not tolerate either Vavilov's or Linnaeus's theories of humanity having "a common genetic origin in the African savannah."[3]) Vavilov died of starvation in prison in 1943, before the siege ended.

After the war, with much of their seed intact, the institute continued to thrive, and today its collection has grown to 380,000 gene types, representing 2,500 plant species. Vavilov was celebrated as a hero and even today his likeness is often found in seed archives around the world. The seed bank he spent his life enriching now bears his name, the Vavilov Institute of Plant Industry.[4]

The scientists who died saving Vavilov's life's findings during that terrible siege never knew whether their country would survive the war. But they did know there could be no rebuilding of their homeland without viable seed. Safe seed was ultimately more vital than who would win the war. Without it, there could be no future. Victors and vanquished alike would starve.

The Seed Safes

In a remote archipelago in Norway, only 480 miles from the North Pole, the Svalbard International Seed Vault began its slow work late in February of 2008, when it received its first shipment of a hundred million seeds from a hundred different countries—varieties of eggplant, lettuce, cowpea, wheat, sorghum, potato, rice, and maize among them. This "scientific Ark of the Covenant," created under the purview of the Global Crop Diversity Trust,[5] is the earth's largest high-tech repository dedicated to saving the world's seed heritage, and its goal is twofold: to serve as the archive of the current diversity of seeds available worldwide and to safeguard the future agricultural stability of every country on the planet.

Buried over four hundred feet inside a mountain, deep enough to be impervious to the ravages of global warming, terrorist attacks, and even nuclear explosions, the vault is reachable only through a stretch of tunnels separated by multiple heavy metal doors. The latest high-tech surveillance and refrigeration gadgetry protect it from intruders and temperature deviations and as an extra precaution, no single individual has all the codes necessary to enter.[6] Internal conditions are monitored and uploaded by satellite to the Nordic Gene Bank in Longyearbyen.

The choice of Longyearbyen isn't accidental. Serving as the capital of Svalbard, it is about as far north as humans can live and among its claims to fame are its telling celebrations. The Svalbard Ski marathon is billed as "the worlds' northernmost cross-country ski race." The Svalbard Museum is likewise the globe's northernmost museum. And during the second week of March, the local population celebrates Sunfest week, when the sun returns after winter's long dark nights.[7]

The naturally (some might say *unnaturally*) cold surroundings will keep the seed safely stored at 0.4°F, ensuring it will remain dormant. The remotely located vault was built so far underground that its creators estimate that seed will stay dry enough to allow wheat to endure for 1,700 years and sorghum for a whopping 20,000 years.

Even if the refrigeration fails and global warming becomes so severe that the polar icecaps melt, scientists say it would take two hundred years for the temperature of the vault to rise above freezing.

By the time the vault has reached its goal, it will hold over 2 billion seeds, divided up into about 4.5 million varieties. (The precise number will depend on how many counties choose to participate.) Built by the Norwegian government as a service to the global community, the purpose of the vault is to be the go-to site for any country in the world that is facing a crisis with its seed stocks because of drought, war, pestilence, or severe weather anomalies. Should some form of disaster strike, countries can "borrow" seed samples from the vault to kick-start their agriculture, not just for food and grain but also for essential herbs and medicinals.[8] The duplicates of these bits of "seed royalty" stored here never deplete the stock of originals. There is no charge to any country for the vault's storage services.

Today, scientists have it a little easier than the scientists who braved war, cold, and lethal hunger to save their seeds, but seed hunting and saving has a brave history.

From our earliest pioneering days, new seed strains were like gold. Early settlers had few crops to sell or subsist on besides native maize, blueberries, cranberries, hops, and sunflowers, and often brought seeds to the New World hidden in hat brims and dress hems. Thomas Jefferson famously smuggled rice out of Italy (a death-penalty offense) by sewing it into his coat lining and was one of a small coterie who received rice as an indirect gift from Captain William Bligh, who carried some of the seed back from Timor on his 3,600-mile ocean voyage in a twenty-three-foot launch, after being temporarily bounced from his job by Fletcher Christian.[9] Rice would eventually become a notable cash crop for swamp-laden U.S. coastal plantations.

The U.S. Department of Agriculture operates a network of twenty seed banks and has partnerships with other seed banks, including Svalbard. The seed archive at Fort Collins, Colorado, has been stockpiling seeds, plant tissue, whole plants and trees (as well as animal germplasm) since the late 1950s. It's sort of a lending library, storing both domestic and international varieties and is used as a backup resource when crops fail or to help restore food production after wars or natural disasters. It helped rejuvenate agricultural life for war-torn Cambodia and Rwanda, and for Malaysia when their rice paddies were destroyed by a tsunami. In poor countries, a single bad season can be devastating. One failed harvest can spell disaster not only for that year's food supply but also for years to come, if there are enough seeds left to be sown the next year. In addition to sending seed out, the center takes in an estimated forty thousand new seeds annually.

Ongoing wars across the globe demonstrate the need to have this sort of archive available, and they should be far from the sites of conflict. On September 10, 2002, less than a year after the U.S. war with Afghanistan began, the stores of precious seed that represented the agricultural diversity of Afghanistan were looted and destroyed. Each store was hidden within a private home, one in the city of Ghazni in the north and the other in Jalalabad in the east. It is common practice to back up seed stores by depositing duplicates elsewhere, but in war-ravaged countries, such practices often go undone.

What made this loss particularly tragic to the people of Afghanistan was that those seeds had evolved to be naturally drought-, blight-, or pest-resistant. Seed banks serve as "genetic reservoirs of adaptive traits," designed to keep the best of the best.[10] The looters weren't even after the seeds but rather the airtight plastic and glass jars they were stored in. The jars were upended, their contents spilled and exposed to the elements. Among the seeds lost were varieties of wheat, barley, chickpeas, lentils, melons, pistachios, almonds, and pomegranates. When scientists from Kabul examined the piles of commingled, scattered seed, they knew immediately there was no way to separate or identify them.

In countries like Afghanistan, where only 12 percent of the arable land is suitable for agriculture and only one-third of that land is irrigated, wide seed diversity is mandatory, because the topography is so varied. After decades of war and years of drought, how does a country begin to feed itself again? By importing seed, preferably its own. If it has been able to archive its seed in a seed vault, starting over is at least possible.

But seed banks are not always safe. Peru's National Agricultural Institute was raided in 1985, and their entire sweet potato collection was stolen by a starving mob. In 2007 the seed bank in the Philippines washed away in a typhoon, taking untold varieties of sweet potato, taro, and banana with it. Jars of seeds were reportedly seen floating in the ocean. Hurricane Mitch destroyed the national seed bank of Honduras in 1998, and an earthquake claimed Nicaragua's seed bank in 1971.

Prior to the 2003 bombing and invasion of Iraq by American and allied armed forces, scientists who worked at seed storage facilities in the Baghdad suburb of Abu Ghraib risked their lives to hastily smuggle a "black box" of what seeds they could save out of the country. Journalist Fred Pearce tracked what he called Iraq's "genetic holy grail. . . . and the future of agricultural prosperity of Iraq" to Aleppo, Syria, where he found "a battered old brown cardboard box sealed with tape, sitting on a shelf in a refrigerator."[11] While scientists from ICARDA (the International Center for Agricultural Research in the Dry Areas) planned to use the contents of the box to restart Iraq's agricultural future, it is feared that many seed strains, some that dated back four thousand years, were lost forever.

Scientists believe that a new, global five-year plan, backed by a $109 million grant, will help eleven of the world's largest seed banks expand their current collections, modernize their facilities, offer quick access to seed breeders, and be able to respond to sudden weather or political changes. This is what happened in Sri Lanka, when its coastal areas were flooded by the 2004 Indian Ocean tsunami. Breeders were able to quickly turn to salt-tolerant strains of rice that were stored in seed banks for just this purpose. With better seed banks, seed savers will be better able to respond to crises in politically fragile countries like Syria and Ethiopia, where so many of the earliest landraces exist, to ensure seed archives are not lost, as they were in Afghanistan.[12]

Losing seed varieties is exactly what all seed-saving initiatives are working to avoid. The Royal Botanic Gardens, Kew, south of London, is home to the world's largest collection of living plants and the massive Millennium Seed Bank. Its ultramodern seed vault houses over two billion seeds and has the world's largest collection of seeds of wild plants. Gathering seeds from more than fifty countries, it has successfully banked 10 percent of the world's total plant diversity. Categorized, checked for viability, cleaned, x-rayed, and put into the deep freeze, the seeds' metabolic processes are on hold, neither germinating nor dying. A logical and hopefully effective hedge against climate change, they wait to be retrieved in some future springtime, some time when they could pop up in a field in a climate zone they were never able to grow in before. Among the types of plant life the Millennium Seed Bank is trying to save are those of the tropical rainforests, whose diversity is unknown and which are being decimated at a rate that is almost impossible to keep up with. It is possible that this ultramodern approach can prevent (or at least slow) the extinction of plant species, if seed preservationists can capture seeds before an area is completely deforested.

Besides Fort Collins, Kew Gardens, and the Svalbard's so-called doomsday vault, large banks exist in Mexico, Colombia, India, Ivory Coast, Syria, Philippines, and Nigeria. More than 1,400 seed banks dot the world, each dedicated to keeping seed strains alive and safe. But of those, only a few dozen meet the necessary security, refrigeration, and sanitation standards required for long-term seed storage. According to a 2005 report by the U.S. Department of Agriculture and the University of California, many are in a very dilapidated condition.[13]

The Svalbard Vault is a joint mission of the country of Norway and the Global Crop Diversity Trust to reclaim and safeguard as many samples of seed as possible. They intend to continue their mission until they are satisfied that samples of all food and grass life across the globe are safeguarded.

Sites of the world's major seed vaults

Seed archive location	Archive contents*
Mexico City, Mexico	150,000 unique samples of wheat from more than 100 countries (90 percent of the world's diversity); 10,000 types of maize
Lima, Peru	7,000 samples of wild and cultivated potatoes; 6,000 of sweet potatoes
Los Banos, the Philippines	Nearly 110,000 samples of cultivated and wild Asian rice
Palmira, Colombia	64,000 samples of beans, cassava, tropical forages (legumes and grasses)—the world's largest and most diverse collections
Ibadan, Nigeria	More than 15,000 varieties of cowpea from 88 countries, a key cash crop and one of the region's main protein sources; composes about half the global cowpea diversity and 70 percent of Africa's traditional landraces, the continent's ancient domesticated seed varieties**

*   Samples from these archives began moving to the Svalbard Vault in stages, in February 2008.

** Table from CGIAR, www.cgiar.org.

At a time when more crops than ever are being grown on the earth's 1.7 billion acres of arable soil, why all the concern about saving seeds? Chiefly because of the havoc—much of it manmade—being wreaked upon them: global warming, drought, lack of foresight, poor resource management, failed crops, war, pestilence, natural disaster, not to mention genetic manipulation. Those 1.7 billion acres of arable soil will begin to shrink and turn saline, because of global warming and the rising of the oceans. The remaining land will have to bear the burden of feeding more people with less acreage. In India alone, its arable landmass will have to produce 30 percent more grain in 2025 than it did in 2000.[14]

In addition, today's agribusiness stresses monoculture and mass production, and scientists and seed activists say that this flattening and uniformity, coupled with the ocean of pesticides that have been dumped on our soils in the last sixty years, weakens not only the soil but the genetic diversity of seeds. That diversity is precious, and it's about more than mere variety; it's part of the natural heritage of our species, "a record of more than ten thousand years of human experience with crops, and of the struggle to produce food in changing ecosystems and climates."[15]

Much of our soil no longer contains any of the nutrients and organisms (sometimes referred to as "pests") that nurture plants, and therefore, us. The soil has been poisoned, ignored, exhausted for decades, often in the service of monoculture crops. Rachel Carson observed this over half a century ago: "Single crop farming does not take advantage of the principles by which nature works. It is agriculture as an engineer might conceive it to be. Nature has introduced great variety into the landscape, but man has displayed a passion for simplifying it."[16]

Engineering, indeed. Agribusiness assures us that simplifying and homogenizing are efficient ways to allow more food to be grown on fewer acres. We need that to feed the world. Simple, right? The experts disagree on all counts, saying that monocultures threaten our food supply, harm the soil by leaching it of essential nutrients, and ultimately impede the feeding of the developing world by running their own farmers out of business. More than 60 percent of people in developing nations still subsist on farming, and most simply cannot compete with big American agribusiness efficiency, its lower prices, thinner profit margins, and ever-present subsidies.

Monocultures also threaten the food supply because a hardy, differentiated seed stock is protection against global warming. "Maintaining the genetic diversity that exists among the wild plant population is absolutely essential if we are to have any chance of mitigating the effects of climate change," says Emile Frison, director general of Biodiversity International.[17]

The wild plant population is what keeps food strains strong. It is common in Mexico, for example, for small farmers to plant their corn near wild varieties to encourage cross-pollination, since the wild plants have proven their rigor just by surviving. If climate change removes these wild relatives from the gene pool, the threat to the genetic diversity that helps crops adapt is clear.

The truth is that since 1900, the world has lost much of its agricultural diversity. The U.N. Food and Agriculture Organization estimates that 75 percent of the world's varieties have gone extinct.[18] Other estimates run as high as 90 percent.[19] In the United States alone, the variety of apples grown has dwindled by more than 85 percent, from 7,100 to about 1,000. Between 1903 and 1983 we lost 80 percent of our tomato varieties, nearly 93 percent of lettuces, more than 90 percent of our field and sweet corn varieties, more than 98 percent of asparagus varieties. Just two varieties of apple account for more than 50 percent of the apples marketed, and half of the broccoli grown commercially in the United States comes from a single variety: Marathon.[20] In India, where now only a handful of rice varieties are grown, there were once two hundred thousand types.

So what? Who needs that much variety? According to plant geneticists and seed savers, we do. Frison agrees. As the global weather patterns change, he says, "We're going to need this diversity to breed new varieties that can adapt to climate change, new diseases, and other rapidly emerging threats."[21]

The outbreak of the wheat rust fungus called UG99 (named for the country of origin, Uganda, and the year of its outbreak) is a case in point, an example of what happens when diversity is limited. The UG99 fungus (which today has eight distinct races or strains) concerns agronomists worldwide, and not just because it is hard to control. The cost of control is well beyond the small farmer's means (fungicide application runs $100 for less than half an acre), and the blight is virulent and hardy, able to travel thousands of miles, from Africa to the Caribbean, on air currents in a matter of days. It's not hard to see how it can wreak global havoc in a matter of weeks. The effect on crop yields—at a time when demand for wheat is increasing with an ever-rising population—is sobering.[22] In the United States, the USDA is trying to develop strains resistant to UG99.

The Dangers of Lost Seed Diversity

The calamity that can ensue when our rich seed diversity is lost became painfully obvious in the 1840s during the time called the Great Hunger, when Ireland lost a full third of its population to a protracted potato famine brought on by a fungus-like pathogen called "late blight." (U.S. farmers still lose $6 billion annually to its modern, more aggressive equivalent.) Because Ireland's agriculture depended mostly on potato varieties that were very similar, when the blight hit one strain, it quickly spread, turning much of the potato crop into shrunken, rotted mush.

Potatoes were a staple of the Irish diet, its main source of calories. It's estimated that the average person ate as many as fourteen pounds of the tubers *per day*.[23] Although the Irish grew a number of other crops, a majority were poor tenant farmers working for their absentee British landlords, and most of what they grew was exported to England. With no crop diversity, no other hardy or wild potato varieties to step in and fill the gap, and no new seed to plant because the crop had perished, farmers had to spend what little money they had to buy food. Many struggled with the remnants of the killed crop and replanted what they could, but the blight continued for five long years. Without money to pay rent, many were turned out of their tenant farms, and with no way to grow or buy food, they starved. Mass emigrations began (including nearly a million to the United States alone). It's estimated that the island's current population (6.3 million in the Republic of Ireland and Northern Ireland) is still lower than its pre-famine levels.

Ireland's potato famine marked the first time in history that a crop had failed not just because of bad weather or the ravages of war, but because of a lack of variety. There was no Plan B. Having originated in the Andes and been brought back from the New World in the late sixteenth century, the tuber came first to Spain and later to England and Ireland; for the next two and a half centuries, all the potatoes grown in Europe were descendants of these first imported examples.

More than a century later, that lesson had to be learned again by both American and Soviet farmers, and the outcome changed agriculture and world economies in ways no one could have foreseen. In the early 1960s, southern corn leaf blight had begun to get the attention of agronomists in places as far flung as the Philippines and Mexico. By 1968 it was showing up in seeds in the Midwest. By the spring of 1970 it was in the Florida corn crop and by summer's end, with production losses becoming obvious in the nation's supermarkets, corn prices had skyrocketed. The cost to American agriculture exceeded a billion bushels—a full 15 percent of the nation's most important crop—and over a billion dollars in lost revenue. The main reason for the failure? Virtually all of America's corn crop was genetically identical. Just as in Ireland, an undiversified crop had to carry all the production weight. Like a single throw of dice, it was all or nothing.[24]

A year later, in the fall of 1971, as farmers in the Ukraine, the Soviet Union's breadbasket, faced winter, they felt confident that they would have a record wheat harvest the following summer. Their fields were seeded with the wildly successful, high-yielding strain called Besostaja. But what they hadn't counted on was the fickleness of the weather. January temperatures were too cold for the snow cover the crop needed and spring rains didn't materialize.

As the fears of drought became reality, Ukrainian farmers faced bleak harvests, while politicians were alarmed by the implications of perceived weaknesses in their food production system. Meanwhile, a Canadian economist had been keeping tabs on weather data and Soviet media reports and read between the lines. She determined that 30 to 40 percent of the Russian winter wheat crop—at least 20 million tons—would be lost to the harsh winter. Knowing how sensitive Besostaja was and that it was widely planted across nearly 100 million acres, she sent a report to the Canadian Wheat Board. What resulted was a secret deal between the Soviet Union and Canada that sent 27 million tons of grain to the Soviet Union to bail it out of its food crisis. At stake was a shortage not just of food for its people but also of feed for its vast populations of cows and hogs.

As the Canadians scored this trade coup under American noses at a hotel in New York City, a historic change began to take effect. By October the price of a metric ton of wheat had risen from $65 to $90. Then secretary of agriculture Earl Butz sounded a call to arms. American farmers got the message. His "get big or get out" and "plant hedgerow to hedgerow" resounded in their ears. The age of bigger and bigger farming was underway. Farmers went into debt buying more land, more seed, bigger and better machinery to plant and harvest, "and all the fertilizers, center-pivot irrigation pumps, and pesticides their land could absorb."[25]

This boom in wheat prices produced other consequences. As Butz extolled the virtues of bigger farming, he crowed about American abundance by referring to food as a weapon: a sort of "we have it, you don't" schoolyard taunt that did not go over well in some of the less agriculturally abundant corners of the globe. Some say that the first oil crisis in 1973 was in part a strategically pointed reminder to Americans that they didn't have the only natural resource worth coveting. Just in case we'd forgotten, two other conditions were now in play. Those shiny new combines wouldn't run on anything but the black crude that had suddenly gotten a lot more expensive. And our own domestic production capacities were quickly approaching peak, making us oil shoppers rather than suppliers for the first time in a hundred years.

The harsh winters that had decimated the Soviet summer wheat crop also hit vast areas of the developing world, and their import costs for grain doubled, to $6 billion. Resources had entered world politics with hard realities as the 1970s began to unfold.

Lost in the excitement of agricultural profit motive was another troubling truth. It was a lack of genetic diversity that had gutted the Soviet summer wheat harvest of 1972. While the Besostaja strain did well in the milder regions of the Soviet Union, it perished in the harsher winters of the Ukraine.

Nor did American farmers fare well. By the mid-1980s, the glut of grain on the world market sent prices into a free fall. Farmers faced rising debts in times of inflation and bloated interest rates. In record numbers, they went out of business. Between 1987 and 1992 alone, an average of 32,500 farms—most of them family run— were lost each year. The "hedgerow to hedgerow" planting continued, in an effort to increase output and make up for lost revenue. Increasingly, failed farms were bought up and folded into bigger and bigger farms. In some cases, the farmhouses themselves were burned to the ground and plowed over to create more space for planting.[26]

This scene played out again years later, as the 2008 growing season approached and farmers across America began demolishing old outbuildings to grow wheat, corn, and soybeans. "In the U.S., farmers . . . are razing old barns, ripping up sod and grassland, and uprooting fences—some in a routine attempt to improve land, others in an effort to make room for the grain boom." It was a full gallop response not only to rising demand for crops abroad, but to high hopes for the latest agricultural gold rush: corn-based biofuels.[27]

A Slow Process That Hit the Fast Track

Agriculture, it seems, no longer has much appetite for sitting still, but this was not always so. Stabilizing agriculture was a long time coming.[28] The idea of staying put rather than wandering as nomadic hunters took about two million years to develop. In the roughly twelve thousand years since the dawn of agriculture, civilization as we now know it—from written language and monumental architecture to trade and armed conflict—came into being. During much of that time, the most common practice for farmers was to save and share seed, selecting and cross-breeding varieties to make them heartier, adaptable, and more prolific. As centuries passed and the descendants of hunters and gatherers moved to the cities and towns and the population increased exponentially, more farmland had to be converted to accommodate this growth, making less land available—land that had to produce more food. The variety of food being grown slowly narrowed to a handful of crops, and those crops further decreased in diversity, with the result that the food supply became more vulnerable to drought and pests.[29]

"As the first link in the food chain, seed is a central factor in any nation's strategy for food security and self-sufficiency."[30] As long as the markets remained local, cultures could provide enough diversity to allow farmers to develop new breeds and conserve seeds and plant varieties. But as agribusiness has become more and more prominent worldwide, this diversity has been winnowed down to very few varieties. Using seed, says physicist and seed activist Vandana Shiva, "is the best way to conserve them; whichever economic system determines how plant species are used also influences which species will survive and which will be pushed to extinction."[31] In other words, use them or lose them.

Seeds have a resilience, a capacity to live and regenerate that is one of nature's safeguards. "When a fire destroys a forest, the species and plants that were lost will reassert themselves over time. Seeds that have lain dormant for decades and that germinate only when subjected to intense heat will come to life, burst into foliage, and bloom in the spring."[32] This was seen in the last decade in the regrowth in Griffith Park in Los Angeles. Less than a year after a fire devastated one-fifth of the park in May of 2007, the undergrowth so vital to preventing erosion on the hillsides had begun to regenerate itself and create a pelt of green.

We can count on the natural wisdom of seeds. What threatens us is the lack of wisdom of those who believe they have figured out a way to permanently alter nature by making it predictable and controllable, those who now engineer seed as a commodity goldmine.

The Seed Changers

In 1971 a General Electric engineer named Ananda Chakrabarty applied for a patent on a genetically engineered Pseudomonas bacteria to be used as an oil-eating microbe. General Electric saw it as a boon to cleaning up the crude oil spills that were becoming all too common. The U.S. Patent Office, operating on a longtime bias against patenting animate life forms, refused the application. General Electric and Chakrabarty persisted and eventually appealed the case to the Supreme Court. In 1980 a landmark 5–4 decision broke a long-term ban on patenting animate life forms, and the application was granted.

The situation was not without irony. "They had genetically engineered a micro-organism which could eat oil," says Frank Chapelle, a hydrologist for the U.S. Geological Survey. "As it turns out, all that became superfluous, even though the genetic engineering was brilliant. It turns out that natural micro-organisms were capable of doing the same thing."[33] The microbe, which had the annoying habit of snacking on lots of other things besides oil, was never used. Nevertheless, this case had enormous repercussions not for the oil industry but for the world's food supply. The floodgates to biotechnology had burst open, and what happened in less than a decade changed the way humanity would sustain itself. The era of GM food had begun.[34]

Scientists like seed activist Vandana Shiva took issue with the technology on several levels. She argued that nothing new was being produced; instead, existing material was merely being manipulated. "All that genetic engineers really do is 'shuffle genes around'; they do not create life," Shiva said. "Therefore, literally speaking, no life forms should be patentable. However, patent offices and courts have interpreted modification as creation. This allows the ownership of any altered biological material."[35] (Chakrabarty himself described the process in the same way: "I simply shuffled genes, changing bacteria that already existed."[36])

Another issue was summarized by lawyer and executive director of the Center for Food Safety, Andrew Kimbrell: "The (U.S.) Supreme Court's Chakrabarty decision has been extended and continues to be extended, up the chain of life. The patenting of microbes has led inexorably to the patenting of plants, and then animals." In other words, it gave corporations the right and power to own and control all the species of life on earth. By 1987, that included human cells, cell lines, genes—and seeds.

According to the late Wangari Mathai, coordinator of the Green Belt Movement and the winner of the 2004 Nobel Peace Prize, this is the plan of the multinationals. "This distortion has been deliberately created by blurring the meaning of invention so that corporations can obtain private monopolies on mere 'discoveries' of biological materials and their properties, such as umbilical cord blood cells and basmati rice."[37]

GM foods are foods that have had one or more elements of DNA altered. Every cellular organism has DNA molecules. Within the molecules of higher organisms are genes whose job is to carry our traits—our hair and eye color, height, and the facial features that make us look like our parents and siblings. These traits are passed on by reproduction. That's also the way they are passed on in the plant and animal world. Farmers and agricultural pioneers and botanists dating back to Luther Burbank crossbred crops or animals to develop the most desirable characteristics possible. That is not what genetic engineering does: it splices elements from outside the plant kingdom into their makeup. Jeffrey Smith describes the difference in *Seeds of Deception:*

> With genetic engineering, breeders have a whole new bag of tricks. Instead of relying on species to pass on genes through mating, biologists cut the gene out of one species' DNA, modify it, and then insert it directly into another species' DNA. And since virtually all organisms have DNA, scientists don't have to limit the source of their genes to members of the same species. They can search anywhere in the plant, animal, bacteria, even human world to find genes with desired traits, or even synthesize genes in the laboratory that don't exist in nature.[38]

Fortunately, many of the early examples of GMOs never evolved beyond laboratories. But recumbent bovine growth hormone (rBGH, also showing up in dairy products as rBST) is widely used in the U.S. milk supply, and much of the corn, cotton, canola, and soy crops grown in the United States are genetically engineered and show up in the multitude of genetically enhanced molecules that give our processed foods specific flavors and long shelf life. Many of the animals whose meat and byproducts (eggs, butter, milk) we eat spend their lives eating grains that are genetically modified.[39]

Michael Pollan's definitive writings on the origins of the modern meal describe the life cycle of agribusiness corn and farm animals; he reminds us that not only do we eat GMOs ourselves (most processed food, artificial sweeteners, and soft drinks include high-fructose corn syrup, which is derived from GM corn), they are eaten by what we eat. "We are what we eat eats," he says. The growth hormones and genetically modified bits of corn and soy that feed our food also ultimately feed us and reside somewhere in our cell tissue.

So what's the big deal? The corporations that patented their science and our own FDA have validated Monsanto's promise that this is safe, abundant food.[40] To that end, the FDA passed language in 1991 that said, in effect, that

- GM food is GRAS (generally regarded as safe) and substantially equivalent to non-GM food;
- no testing had proved otherwise;
- years of having GM food in our diets without apparent side effects is proof that it's safe.

These assumptions, however, present a jumble of catch-22s. Opponents of GM food—including scientists, political activists, consumers, and farmers—point out some glaring issues. First, the FDA failed to mention that there is no standard for comparison, because most testing has been done by interested parties who have invested large sums of money in engineering and selling these products. They also failed to mention that independent and even FDA testing (not made public for many years) proved that the products were anything but safe. In addition, because GM food was deemed substantially equivalent to non-GM food, neither testing nor labeling was required by law before they were offered for public consumption.

Citing food slander laws that went into effect after Amarillo cattlemen failed to secure a judgment against talk-show host Oprah Winfrey for saying on the air that she wouldn't be eating any more hamburgers after she found out about Mad Cow disease, corporations can sue food suppliers in some states for even labeling their products "GMO free," "no rBGH," or "no rBST."

It may be the corporations' dogged resistance to labeling that has caused the recent rush to judgment on GM foods. Polls taken since 2008 repeatedly show that more than 90 percent of those asked said they preferred labeling for GM foods. Who can blame them? The truth is that there is no sure way to tell whether food that has had its DNA moved around and altered is safe at all. There is much about this food that is inherently unpredictable. As Dr. Ignacio Chapela, a microbial ecologist at the University of California, Berkeley, said, "I think this is probably the largest biological experiment humanity has ever entered into."[41]

Monsanto should not have to vouchsafe the safety of biotech food.
Our interest is in selling as much of it as possible.
Assuring its safety is the FDA's job.[42]
—PHIL ANGELL, Monsanto's director of corporate communication

This gets to the heart of the issue that repeatedly arises with GMOs: we don't even know what we don't know. As the stories about the pervasiveness of high-fructose corn syrup in the American diet spread, consumer frustration grew. The corn-invested branch of the food industry tried to sidestep the issue by simply renaming high-fructose corn syrup "corn sugar." The FDA slapped them down in the spring of 2012 when it told the corn refiners who had made the change that they couldn't do that. "If the name had been changed," the FDA press release explained, "it would have given consumers the wrong impression that this product is 'natural.'" Which it clearly isn't.

Increasingly, the catch-22 with GMOs has inspired the public. They became concerned when they realized that they are not allowed to know what they are eating—and that in many states, it's against the law for them to be given that data. In 2012, a GMO labeling law was proposed in California. Proposition 37 inspired a new generation of food activists, and in the weeks leading up to the election, it appeared very likely that it would pass. But a late infusion of cash from companies like Monsanto and the Hershey Company helped doom the initiative. It lost 48.6 percent to 51.4 percent, helped by lopsided funding ($44 million against it; $7.3 million for it).

The biotech industry has long understood that the more the public found out about GMOs, the less inclined they would be to embrace them, so their approach has always been to minimize the discussion. Instead, the emphasis has been to stress how safe GMOs are, to insist that they are the same as non-GMO food, to discredit anyone who says otherwise, and to spend enormous amounts of money to convince an awakening public that—like Dorothy confronting the Wizard of Oz for his trickery—they should pay no attention to that man behind the curtain. Knowledge is power, and public knowledge is likely to be very bad news for an industry that has invested billions in their proliferation into every corner of the American diet. And the industry has long known the public's perception of their products. In 1974 Norman Braksick, president of Asgrow Seed (a Monsanto subsidiary) candidly told the *Kansas City Star*, "If you put a label on genetically engineered food, you might as well put a skull and crossbones on it."

The West Coast has led the way for a decade on dealing with GMOs. Marin and Mendocino counties in California and Jackson County in Oregon all passed initiatives that banned the cultivation of GMOs of any kind.

The failure of Prop 37 did not dissuade consumers. It galvanized them. By early 2013, similar labeling initiatives were underway in more than twenty states.[43] As if to confirm that, Ronnie Cummins, international director of the Organic Consumers Association, which spearheaded the Prop 37 initiative, said the fight for GMO labeling has just begun. "Prop 37 has awakened a sleeping giant. It has created a statewide and national movement with the potential to transform the entire U.S. food and farming system, part of a new political awakening in which grassroots forces have begun challenging the power of the corporate and political elite."[44]

It's only a matter of time before GMO labeling is mandated in individual states. "We can—and will—propose state laws and state ballot initiatives as often as we need, in as many states as we must," said Cummins, "until we have what 61 other countries have: truth and transparency in the form of mandatory GMO labeling laws."[45]

Others have tried to break the biotechnology industry's stranglehold on state lawmakers. In 2012 Connecticut legislators proposed a GMO labeling bill, then gutted it, fearing a lawsuit from Monsanto. Representative Richard Roy, cochair of the environment committee and the bill's sponsor, said, "Residents of more than 50 other countries get simple information saying that GMOs are present in a product. The freest society in the world cannot get that simple sentence."[46] On May 10, 2013, Vermont became the first state in America to pass a bill that will require labeling of all GM food in the state. But the bill cannot go to the Vermont Senate for a vote until 2014 and cannot become law until at least two other states adopt similar measures. At the end of 2013, governor Dannel Malloy made Connecticut the first state to actually mandate labeling, but the law cannot take effect until at least four other states get on board and do the same.[47] That's the power of this industry.[48]

In 1959, Dr. David Price of the U.S. Public Health Service said, "We all live under the haunting fear that something may corrupt the environment to the point where man joins the dinosaurs as an obsolete form of life. And what makes these thoughts all the more disturbing is the knowledge that our fate could perhaps be sealed twenty or more years before the development of symptoms."[49] Price was speaking at a time when the idea of atomic weaponry and its threats were growing but still new. But the anxiety he spoke of could easily apply today. We do not know what GM foods have done to us already, or when or even if we are ingesting them.

And that points to one of the most troubling issues surrounding GMOs: the possible cumulative effects that might manifest in our systems in decades to come, precisely because there has been no mandatory testing to track these effects over time. The breadth of potential risks to our health and genetic contamination may never be known. "We are confronted with the most powerful technology the world has ever known," said Suzanne Wuerthele, EPA toxicologist, "and it is being rapidly deployed with almost no thought whatsoever to its consequences."[50] Going even further, HRH Charles, Prince of Wales, has called GMOs the "biggest environmental disaster of all time."

Any politician or scientist who tells you these products are safe is either very stupid or lying. The experiments have simply not been done.
—GENETICIST DAVID SUZUKI,
Professor Emeritus, University of British Columbia

The Case of the Unknown Illness

In the 1980s an epidemic of unknown origin had doctors perplexed. People were showing up complaining of paralysis, mouth ulcers, shortness of breath, nausea, hair loss, and a host of other seemingly unrelated symptoms. Doctors were baffled and could find no common thread. The only shared complaint was severe, debilitating muscle pain, often coupled with a skyrocketing white blood cell count, a sure signal of a severe disruption to the immune system. The cases came and went without most doctors knowing the other cases existed. Then in 1989 a surge of cases in New Mexico got the attention of two doctors who sent their queries to Atlanta's Centers for Disease Control and Prevention. The common complaints suddenly presented a pattern and after some detective work, the common thread emerged. Each of the patients had taken supplements containing L-Tryptophan, an essential amino acid that is found in turkey, milk, and other foods, often used to combat insomnia and depression. (Think of drinking warm milk before bedtime to help you sleep.) L-Tryptophan, however, does not naturally cause these symptoms.

It was discovered that all the patients had taken the same brand of L-Tryptophan, one manufactured by a Japanese company called Showa Denko KK, which had genetically engineered the bacteria to create L-Tryptophan. The company's reason for using genetic engineering: it saved money. As explained in harrowing detail in Jeffrey Smith's *Seeds of Deception,* the only reason medical experts were able to determine the origin of the problem was the surge in symptoms, finally identified as an illness called EMS (eosinophilia-myalgia syndrome). Otherwise, the epidemic could have spread without anyone knowing about it. According to the Centers for Disease Control, the outbreak killed nearly one hundred people and sickened or disabled an estimated five thousand to ten thousand others. It is suspected that many more people suffered from the outbreak before it was identified but either they failed to report their symptoms or their reports were never connected with the epidemic.

Impurities in Showa Denko's genetically "engineered" tryptophan
happened to cause an illness—EMS—which was novel. The surge
of numbers therefore stood out and got noticed. If SDKK's [Showa
Denko's] poison had caused the same numbers of a common illness
instead, say asthma, we would still not know about it. Or if it had
caused delayed harm, such as cancer 20–30 years later, or senile
dementia in some whose mothers had taken it early in pregnancy,
there would have been no way to attribute the harm to the cause.
—L. R. B. MANN, D. STRATON, and W. E. CRIST,
"The Thalidomide of Genetic 'Engineering'"[51]

Testifying before a congressional committee in July of 1991, Douglas Archer, deputy director of the FDA's Center for Food Safety and Applied Nutrition, sidestepped the genetic engineering issue and instead used the moment to deride over-the-counter food supplements that the FDA had wanted to ban for years. L-Tryptophan is now available only by prescription. The fact that the only version of the supplement that caused any of the symptoms was the genetically modified one was not even raised by the FDA or questioned by Congress or the media, with one exception. *Albuquerque Journal* reporter Tamar Stieber, who had four friends stricken by the disease, followed the story back to its origin and won a 1990 Pulitzer Prize for her reporting.[52]

Fail: GMOs Enter the Marketplace

The Flavr Savr Tomato

Approved by the FDA against the advice of many scientists, a product named Flavr Savr tomatoes, created by Calgene, a Monsanto subsidiary, was the first genetically engineered food offered to the public. However, it turned out to have a short shelf life, and consumers did not like the way it tasted. It was soon removed from the market. In tests done with a group of forty rats before its product launch, some lab rats that ate the tomato developed stomach lesions, often seen as a precursor to cancer. Seven of the forty rats died inexplicably.

Pioneer Hi-Bred

In 1995 Pioneer Hi-Bred, a Dupont-owned seed company, took a single protein from a Brazil nut and genetically engineered it to enhance the protein nutrition of a new soybean to be sold as cattle feed. Because the animals would eventually be consumed by humans, and some humans have nut allergies, Pioneer ran tests to ensure that the protein they had used would not create allergic reactions in humans. To their surprise, it did—in three separate tests. This underscores an issue that is still problematic today. According to FDA toxicologist Louis Pribyl, "There are very few allergens that have been identified at the protein or gene level." He recommended that there be much closer scrutiny by companies who genetically engineer any plant that causes allergic reactions. His recommendations were ignored.[53]

To this day, testing on GMOs is voluntary. The FDA offers only guidelines, allowing GMO manufacturers to create their own test scenarios and conclusions.

StarLink

In the fall of 2000, StarLink, a brand of corn genetically bred to be used as animal feed and engineered with a mild pesticide in it, was inadvertently mixed into the nation's corn supply and showed up in many corn-based food products, including tortillas, corn meal, and taco shells. Unknown numbers of people experienced ana-phylactic shock, and more than three hundred food products were recalled. It is estimated that the cost to the manufacturer, Aventis, was $1 billion. The FDA allowed Aventis to conduct its own tests, and despite a double-blind test conducted and paid for by a public interest group that confirmed contamination by StarLink, Aventis eventually tried unsuccessfully to get the ban lifted so they could keep selling the product.[54] Although it was sold as yellow feed corn, USDA tests at the time showed traces of StarLink in 71 of the 288 companies they contacted; they concluded that it "may linger in the human food chain forever."[55] Indeed, a study published in August 2013 reported that the Saudi Arabian food supply is widely con-taminated with GM products, including StarLink maize, thirteen years after it was first detected in American food products and the company had promised to stop producing the product.[56]

Coming as it did in the early days of the move to sell GMOs to foreign markets, the StarLink debacle started a grassroots move-ment against GM food in the United Kingdom and then in the rest of Europe. Labeling for genetically engineered food—still not avail-able in the United States despite polls indicating that a large major-ity of Americans wants it—has been mandatory in the European Union since 2000. (A total of sixty-one countries worldwide now require labeling. See chapter 6 for a link to the site that shows the most current list.)

As of the summer of 2013, eight European Union countries had banned the cultivation of GM crops: Poland, Austria, France, Germany, Hungary, Luxembourg, Greece, and Bulgaria. Other countries (like Italy and the United Kingdom) allow it in some places but not in others. Europeans have wavered between being lukewarm to hostile about buying U.S. GM food, not only for human but also for livestock consumption. Portugal, Romania, Slovakia, the Czech Republic, and Spain (responsible for 88 percent of the European Union's GMOs) all allow the planting of transgenic crops. India, China, Canada, and Brazil are, like the United States, major stake-holders in growing GMOs.

New Leaf Potato

Although the New Leaf never constituted more than three percent of the nation's potato crop, Monsanto engineered it to contain several attractive traits: it promised to be disease- and bruise-resistant, herbicide-tolerant, to grow to a hefty size, and, with its own pesticide in residence, be able to ward off annoyances like the Colorado potato beetle. By 1998 the New Leaf was in the American diet, but that summer a distinguished biologist working for Scotland's Rowlett Institute, Dr. Arpad Pusztai, upset the apple cart. Pusztai was asked to give a perfunctory okay to plans for a genetically engineered potato that the Scottish Ministry had high hopes to produce commercially. He was already aware from his own research, however, that there were issues with the potatoes. Identical batches were giving differing results. Nutrition levels were not even, and substances in the potato that should have been safe for humans were damaging the immune systems of lab rats.

Since the accepted basic premise of GM foods was that they were stable, Pusztai knew something was wrong. Having created the model for testing GM foods two years before, he was disturbed by the patchy and slipshod testing protocols he was being asked to approve, and he declined. His concerns were overridden, and he was fired. A subsequent investigation exonerated Pusztai, but the controversy surrounding his firing created a storm of protest. For the first time, Europeans found out they had already been eating GM foods for two years. Now they also knew how poorly these products had been tested prior to being introduced into their food supply. In the United States, food manufacturers, including McDonalds and Pringles, yielded to consumer requests not to use the New Leaf potatoes in their products. Monsanto took the New Leaf off the market in 2001.

Later, when 80 percent of American and Canadian wheat buyers informed Monsanto they would not buy GM wheat, and more than two hundred American and Canadian groups representing farmers, corn growers, and wheat interests lobbied against it, Monsanto shelved plans to develop GM wheat in the short term, with good reason.[57] More than half of the U.S. annual $18 billion wheat crop is exported.

Given that GM wheat (unlike corn, soy, and cotton) has not been approved for any country and given the lack of enthusiasm in foreign markets for GM products in general, even Monsanto has to occasionally bow to market pressure. In the spring of 2013, however, the *New York Times* featured a story about an Oregon farmer finding genetically modified wheat growing on his farm. When he tried to kill the errant crop by spraying glyphosate (Roundup's main ingredient), it had no effect. After submitting samples for testing at Oregon State University, the farmer was told they contained the Roundup-resistant gene, a GM trademark.[58] This is a concern, because Oregon exports about 90 percent of its wheat.

It turns out that Monsanto's GM wheat was grown in field trials in sixteen states from 1998 through 2005 (though none in Oregon since 2001). For the record, the USDA cannot know for sure whether any of this wheat made it into foreign (or domestic) grain shipments. Given that this GM wheat pollen has been free to migrate for more than a decade, it's not clear what this might mean to future American wheat exports. The initial response from Korean and Japanese buyers was to cancel their wheat orders. Much of the wheat grown in Oregon is soft white wheat, perfect for the noodles that are such a staple of the Asian diet.

Farmers: GMO Crop Contamination and Farmer Liability

For his entire life, Percy Schmeiser has lived and farmed in Bruno, Saskatchewan, Canada. In 1998 he found a few tufts of canola (a wheat-like grain also known as rapeseed) growing around telephone poles near the highway bordering his 1,400-acre farm. What he did not know was that this canola was a proprietary, patented version of the grain manufactured by Monsanto. It was Roundup Ready seed, genetically engineered to withstand the spraying of the herbicide Roundup, one of Monsanto's most widely used and profitable products. Despite the fact that it had blown onto his land and taken root, he soon found himself embroiled in a lawsuit with St. Louis-based Monsanto over patent infringement.

Monsanto alleged that Schmeiser and his wife, Louise, had knowingly grown Roundup Ready canola on virtually all of their acreage and had not paid the chemical giant the $40 per hectare technology fee they claimed was owed them. Monsanto also charged them $400,000 in penalties, plus additional court costs. Tests revealed not only that more than half of their fields had been contaminated, but also that the entire seed archive that they had carefully maintained for five decades was tainted and had to be destroyed. After years of suits and appeals, the Supreme Court of Canada ruled in 2004 that the Schmeisers had indeed violated Monsanto's patent rights. (The court did not require the Schmeisers to pay Monsanto either damages or court costs.) The court further ruled that it didn't matter how the seed got into the Schmeisers' fields, whether blown in by wind, distributed by passing bees or birds, or dropped off the tires or flatbeds of passing trucks.

What was not considered was that the Schmeisers have been long-time seed savers and that, because of the Monsanto contamination, their entire life's work was ruined. "My wife and I took the position that a farmer should never ever lose his rights to use his seeds from year to year. And that was the basis we fought for—the rights of farmers," said Schmeiser. In his estimation, Monsanto's aim was to bring an end to seed saving and sharing, a way of life for farmers across Canada and the entire world. "The corporations want total, total control of the seed supply, which would then give them total control of the food supply. That's what GMOs are all about. Not more food [to] feed the hungry world, but control of the seed supply."[59]

In the wake of the court's decision, organic farming of soy and canola in Canada came to an end. It cannot be grown free of GMOs for the foreseeable future, because the entire crop nationwide has been cross-pollinated with Roundup Ready canola and soy. Schmeiser became an anti-GMO advocate and activist and tours the world sharing his story. He and his wife continue to farm canola. In 2005 he discovered their fields had again become contaminated with Roundup Ready canola. This time, he took Monsanto to court for damages. Three years later, in an out-of-court settlement, he prevailed. Monsanto agreed to pay cleanup costs and also agreed not to require a gag order. Most importantly, the company can be sued again if Schmeiser or other farmers discover further contamination.

Environment: Frankenfish and Gene Jumping

"We know," says Andrew Kimbrell, "how the introduction of a biological species into the wrong ecosystem" can create catastrophe.[60] In the 1950s the Nile perch was introduced into Lake Victoria and since then has devastated its ecosystem, driving to extinction some vital cichlid species and causing mayhem in the world's largest tropical lake and along one of Africa's most densely populated shorelines. The impact on the local economy was devastating. The enormous fish, which at maturity are six feet long and can weigh 450 pounds, devoured every other lake species and nearly destroyed the area's ecology. The perch had originally been introduced to Lake Victoria to increase fishing opportunities. The only problem was that no one thought about whether the perch belonged in such an environment or what the long-term consequences might be.

But what might happen if a genetically engineered fish were introduced into the U.S. food chain, and what if this fish were to merge with the native fish population in our oceans or fresh waters? This is a dilemma that may present itself if the FDA approves the lead product of a Massachusetts-based company called AquaBounty: the world's first genetically engineered salmon. FDA approval would give the company an enviable seat at the table of a $100 billion industry: aquaculture, commonly known as fish farming.

The AquAdvantage Salmon, as the company calls it, combines the growth hormone from a Chinook salmon with a "promoter" from an eel-like fish called an ocean pout that's spliced into Atlantic salmon DNA. The growth hormone from the Chinook instructs the Atlantic salmon DNA to keep growing all year, instead of just in the summertime. The result is a fish that eats less and can reach maturity in half the time of an "unenhanced" salmon (sixteen to twenty-six months versus thirty-six months), and is therefore potentially more profitable than regular farmed fish. But it lacks the key ingredient of a true salmon: wildness. Farmed fish—even non-GM farmed fish—often display a much paler color than the reddish orange flesh of wild salmon; their flesh is also streaked with thin white webs of fat. Some reports indicate that they are far less healthy than fish that live in the wild, and because many farms lie in netted cages in inlets and salmon spawning pathways, their pathogens can multiply quickly and leech out into the waterways, infecting or killing wild salmon that swim near them.

The greatest danger with these so-called GM Frankenfish is "gene jumping," a form of species contamination in which a species not intended to be targeted can be disrupted or even eradicated. The fish that are created with genetic engineering tend to live shorter lives and be less healthy, but they are larger. Their size makes these quick-to-mature GM fish more attractive to females, who will choose them over non-GM males, which live longer but are smaller, thereby short-circuiting the process of natural selection. Because of this tendency for female salmon to select bigger partners, the fear is that, should these GM salmon escape, the larger but weaker species would predominate within as few as six generations, and eventually the entire wild salmon population would be wiped out. This is a particular danger to the Pacific salmon, whose numbers have already been so greatly decimated that fishing bans are being enforced along the Pacific coast.

AquaBounty says this can't happen, because their engineered salmon are sterile, but according to the FDA's assessment of the environmental risks, only 95 percent of the salmon might be sterile, making the gene-jumping scenario less speculative. "There is the possibility that some of these fish could escape and reproductively interact with wild native salmon," said James Geiger of the U.S. Fish and Wildlife Service. "Any potential offspring could reduce the biological and ecological fitness of the native wild salmon."[61]

While the best of intentions is to keep these engineered salmon out of the native populations by confining them to these farms, mass escapes from fish farms into the wild are not unusual. Most fish farms have to be located near waterways to ensure fresh influxes of water, and vast numbers of farmed fish have broken free because of flooding—as many as 250,000 at a time. Once in the wild, there is no recalling them. It's a Pandora's box that can never be closed again.

And, following the custom that goes with GMOs, if approved, this first offering of a genetically engineered animal into the public food chain will not be labeled unless AquaBounty volunteers to do so. Without changes to existing labeling laws—or unless a package says "wild" on it—consumers will never know what version of salmon life-form they are eating. Several national retailers have committed to not offering any GM seafood, including Target, Meijer, H-E-B, Trader Joe's, Whole Foods, Aldi, Marsh Supermarkets, Hy-Vee and PCC Natural Markets.[62]

Us: GM Products We Live with Today

While most genetically modified crops are used for cattle feed, oils from all of the big four GM products—corn, soy, cotton, and canola—are on the market and are used as ingredients in many processed foods. Even if you don't count corn and soybeans in your daily diet, you're probably ingesting much more of them than you think, from vegetable oils to hidden sweeteners. One of corn's highest profile byproducts, high-fructose corn syrup (HFCS), is one of the most prevalent ingredients in packaged, processed, and fast foods—even in so-called low-calorie food—and its ubiquitous presence is frequently cited as one of the culprits in the last decade's uptick in obesity in America. Its presence also signals that a product contains GM corn. Only genetically engineered corn is used for HFCS. If a food is labeled organic, HFCS cannot be an ingredient.

Unless you eat organic food exclusively, it's likely that GM corn and soy products make up 30 percent of your daily calories.[63] In general, the more ingredients on a food label, the more GM corn and soy products are in the food being described.[64]

Recombinant bovine growth hormone (rBGH, or rBST, for recombinant bovine somatotropin). This is injected into dairy cows to increase milk production and turns up in many dairy products. While it may increase milk production, it also is a frequent cause of infertility and premature death in cows. The cow's udders can become massively swollen and infected and, unfortunately, some of the pus from these infections often gets into the milk from afflicted cows. Organic milk and milk products certify not only that the cows were not treated with rBGH but also that the cows were not fed GM corn or soy feed.

Bt sweet corn. Most GM crops are processed into sugars, oil, animal feed, and countless other ingredients we find on grocery shelves. Not this one. This corn is grown for direct human consumption (since the summer of 2013), and because it will not be labeled, consumers will not know whether they are eating GM or natural corn (unless they eat organic corn). Syngenta sold several varieties of Bt sweet corn to the public starting in 2002, but only on a tiny scale. Monsanto's variety will reportedly be grown on about 40 percent of the edible sweet corn acreage in the United States.

The truth is that every kernel on every cob contains both the Bt toxin that kills the insects that feed on the plant *and* Monsanto's Roundup herbicide, which makes the plant impervious to the multiple sprayings it no doubt endured. Whole Foods, Trader Joe's, and General Mills have all declared they will not sell or use GM sweet corn. On the other hand, Walmart, the nation's largest grocery retailer (with $129 billion of food sales per year), has said it will.

Despite claims from Monsanto and the EPA that GM corn would only harm insects (the herbicide in it reportedly kills them by breaking their stomachs open) and would be destroyed by the acids in the human digestive system—and is therefore safe to humans—a study done in 2012 at Sherbrooke University Hospital in Quebec

disproves that claim. Doctors found Bt toxin in the blood of 93 percent of pregnant women tested (67 percent of nonpregnant women)
and 80 percent of the umbilical cord blood of their babies.[65] Like
Americans, Canadians eat a lot of processed foods containing GM-
based HFCS, and much of the meat they eat comes from animals
fed with Bt corn. That's with the toxin one step removed. Now that
there's a direct delivery system into the human body with Bt sweet
corn, it is feared those numbers will rise.

GM sugar beets. GM sugar beets were granted USDA approval
and were growing by the fall of 2008 and, according to one estimate,
quickly garnered 95 percent of the sugar beet market. A 2009 ruling by a U.S. judge temporarily halted their cultivation, saying the
USDA had erred by releasing them before an environmental impact
statement (EIS) had been written. In July of 2012, with the EIS and
PPRA (plant pest risk assessment) done, the USDA green-lighted
them again, declaring that "from the standpoint of plant pest risk,
RR sugar beets are as safe as traditionally bred sugar beets." The
"RR" of course, stands for Roundup Ready.

GM alfalfa. During the 2005 and 2006 growing seasons,
glyphosate-tolerant alfalfa was preliminarily approved by the USDA
and grown on two hundred thousand acres in the continental United
States. A coalition led by the Center for Food Safety filed a lawsuit,
claiming the approval had skipped a mandated EIS and violated the
National Environmental Policy Act. This lawsuit brought to light
an intriguing truth: the petitions to approve GM alfalfa and sugar
beets marked the first time an EIS had been required on a GM crop.
With every previous GM crop, this requirement had simply been
ignored, and the crop was approved without one.

The lawsuit resulted in a court order that suspended the sale
of any future harvest resulting from these crops. The existing crops
from the 2005 and 2006 seasons were allowed to be harvested and
sold, and the existing plants monitored under "court-ordered stewardship," which basically meant that many farmers kept growing
them.

In early 2011, after more court battles and a final EIS, the USDA granted unrestricted approval of "alfalfa events J101 and J163," enraging health-conscious consumers, organic and non-GMO conventional farmers, and a public growing wary of GMOs in general. Organic food products, while not required to be 100 percent free of chemical pesticides (or even the inevitable accidental tainting by GMOs), must fall within a narrow window of error to maintain their USDA seal. GM alfalfa poses a serious risk to this certification, because windborne pollination will make the eradication of non-GM and organically grown alfalfa inevitable. Since organic alfalfa is part of the feedstock of meat and dairy animals grown on organic farms, the consequences of the contamination of their food chain and to the entire organic food industry are obvious.

The final EIS consistently sidesteps the environmental and food-safety issues raised in earlier lawsuits and places the onus of keeping their crops untainted firmly on the shoulders of the farmers who do not want their fields contaminated by GM pollen. The final EIS notes the probable harm likely to occur to the organic food industry and to conventional farmers who do not want their crops contaminated by pollen drift, but it does not address their concerns or the growing discomfort of the U.S. public about the viability of GM products. If one industry had plotted out a risk-free—and government sanctioned—way to eliminate another, this would constitute a perfect scenario.

Instead, in late 2012, the USDA convened an advisory committee to consider how non-GM farmers can still exist as competitors, and how to achieve "crop coexistence" between conventional (non-GM crops that are not grown organically), organic, GM, and IP (identity preserved or genetically pure) crops. One of the members of this committee observed the USDA's heavily favored bias in favor of GM crops. "Successful coexistence means the USDA must take its fingers off the scale in favor of biotechnology. Successful coexistence means that the USDA must accept that non-GMO agriculture is critical to the success of American agriculture and give it the recognition that critical means crucial. We are far from successful coexistence."[66]

Another committee member, Charles Benbrook, research professor at the Center for Sustaining Agriculture and Natural Resources at Washington State University, noted that the final report the committee compiled "does not embody significant compromise and it dodges key issues." For one thing, he said, it ignored any pretense of shared sacrifice in achieving coexistence. GM technology providers, he said, are being granted a "free pass and full immunity," while non-GM and organic farmers are being told to resort to crop insurance to offset the losses they would experience from crop contamination and loss of revenue.

As Benbrook points out, however, the leadership was unwilling to set any level of damage from GM crops that would act as "triggering" mechanisms that would enable insurance compensation to kick in. Most crop insurance compensation is triggered by definable events like drought or storm damage, not by something as amorphous as seed contamination. And since the USDA budget subsidizes up to 75 percent of the cost of crop insurance, covering gene contamination would be one more item for the U.S. taxpayer to shoulder in a time of growing austerity.

In his essay to the committee, Benbrook demonstrated the relationship between Monsanto and the FDA by including language from the first letter the FDA sent to Monsanto—on September 25, 1996 (for the approval of its MON810 Bt corn seed)—acknowledging its voluntary food safety assessment. This set the tone for what has basically become a revolving door approval process. Every approval letter sent out since then has basically been boilerplate.

Based on the safety and nutritional assessment you have conducted, it is our understanding that Monsanto has concluded that corn products derived from this new variety are not materially different in composition, safety, and other relevant parameters from corn currently on the market, and that the genetically modified corn does not raise issues that would require premarket review or approval by FDA.

Based on the information Monsanto has presented, we have no further questions concerning corn grain or fodder containing transformation event MON 810 at this time. However, as you are aware, it is Monsanto's responsibility to ensure that foods marketed by the firm are safe, wholesome and in compliance with all applicable legal and regulatory requirements.

—Letter to Dr. Kent Croon, Monsanto, from Alan M. Rulis, FDA Center for Food Safety and Applied Nutrition[67]

"Voluntary food safety consultations involving the FDA and technology developers are carried out during which the technology provider asserts that a new GE event produces food that is as safe as, and substantially equivalent to, non-GE crops," added Benbrook. "The FDA does not conduct an assessment of such assertions, and does not take a position on whether such claims are supported by sound science."

Nor has it ever and to date, not a single GM application has been denied.

Percentage of U.S. crops grown as GMOs

Cotton	94%
Soybeans	93%
Sugar Beets	90%
Canola (rapeseed)	88%
Corn	88% (no data on Bt Sweet Corn)
Hawaiian papaya	>50%
Zucchini and Yellow Squash	small %
Quest bran tobacco	100%
Alfalfa	Unknown
Kentucky Bluegrass	Unknown
Farmed salmon	As of early 2014, unapproved

This is by no means an exhaustive list.

GM potatoes. In 2013 the USDA once again invited comments on another proposed GM crop, this time from J. R. Simplot

Company, the potato supplier for McDonald's. The potatoes would become "frozen fries, potato chips and shoestrings, which make up approximately 50 percent of the potato market in the United States." But Simplot knows only too well that the first GM potato, NewLeaf, was yanked from the market after public lack of interest, but even if this version flops in the United States, the company is poised to ship them to Canada, Mexico, Japan, and South Korea.[68]

GM trees. Dozens of varieties of hardwood, softwood, and fruit trees are being genetically engineered too: chestnut, walnut, elm, pine, poplar, Norway or white spruce, eucalyptus, sweet gum, cottonwood, apple, orange, lime, cherry, even coffee. The aim has been primarily commercial: to find ways to grow trees faster and with appealing characteristics to growers. The Israeli company FuturaGene boasts that by altering the structure of plant cell walls, its GM eucalyptus grow 40 percent faster and proportionately thicker than traditional varieties. It believes it can offer a revolutionary source of pulp for paper and fuel, claiming its supply of fast-growing biomass can replace fossil fuels and green the world.

"Potentially, we believe this [development] can displace the whole fossil fuel industry. The technology can be adapted to any trees. We can have a whole new supply of fuel," says Stanley Hirsch, FuturaGene's CEO. China, which uses more than 20 million trees a year just for disposable chopsticks, is enthusiastically on board and has already planted more than a million GM pines, with no end in sight.[69]

Opponents face an uphill battle with a forest products industry that generates $400 billion annually. They claim that GM trees will harm biodiversity by contaminating soils and natural crops, encouraging clear-cutting of existing natural forests. Unfortunately, monoculture-style GE tree plantations sequester only one fourth of the carbon of native forests. So clear-cutting natural old growth forests and replacing them with genetically engineered ones not only releases massive amounts of carbon from the old trees back into the atmosphere, it also creates a net loss of the forest's ability to serve as a future carbon sink.

One group, the Forest Health Initiative, claims it has an altruistic rather than profit-based motive: it proposes to use GM technology to restore varieties thought lost to pest infestation and disease. They claim that by using a genetically engineered variety of the American chestnut tree, for example, they can bring the onetime forest staple back to the United States. Each of their three experimental field tests (one each in Georgia, New York state, and Virginia) has been modified with a gene that is believed to resist the parasitic fungus (Cryphonectria parasitica) that killed off the chestnuts in the twentieth century. If they can prevent the fungus that killed chestnuts, they say, their next project could include bringing back the elm tree, once devastated by Dutch elm disease. Their first trial with the chestnuts ends in 2016.[70]

GM crops in national wildlife refuges. Until 2012, and mostly out of public awareness, GM crops (mostly corn and soybeans) had been planted on so-called refuge farming programs in national wildlife refuges across the United States. In 2009 a coalition headed by the Center for Food Safety filed a lawsuit against the Fish and Wildlife Service (part of the Department of the Interior) and Ken Salazar, the department's head, charging that it had planted GM crops in violation of its own policy, which doesn't allow GMOs in a wildlife refuge unless there is a need for "accomplishing a refuge purpose" and GMOs are the only feasible alternative.

The 2012 decision was part of a series of lawsuits that resulted in the rollback of approvals for GM crops on seventy-five refuges across thirty states. The district court judge ruled that the Fish and Wildlife Service had to not only halt the plantings but also disclose their types and locations and monitor the sites, removing or destroying any volunteers (new plants germinating from the existing ones). The same coalition has won lawsuits and is engaged in litigation against GM plantings in other regions of the country. "This order underscores that GE crops must be tracked like toxic contaminants in order to nullify their effects," said one of the plaintiffs, Kathryn Douglass.[71]

GM rice with human liver genes. While getting preliminary approval from the USDA in 2006, this rice, once confined to the laboratory, has been grown on fields in Kansas since 2007. Engineered with human genes, it's not grown (or approved) for human consumption but is cultivated for a human immune system protein for use primarily in an antidiarrhea medicine for children, especially in developing countries where dehydration is a serious problem.

"This is not a product that everyone would want to consume," said Jane Rissler from the Union of Concerned. Given that the company is cultivating the plants outside, there is no way of preventing the pollen from attaching to whatever other crops might be growing downwind.[72]

This was a concern to St. Louis-based Anheuser-Busch when the company, Ventria Bioscience, proposed growing the rice in open fields in southern Missouri, where, despite company claims to the contrary, open pollination could alter the existing rice crops that the beer giant purchases for their product line. The specter of exposing customers to unknown human system proteins—coupled with unknowable side effects—may not have been one that the brewer was willing to take on. Anheuser-Busch, as the nation's biggest rice buyer, is a power to contend with, and when it threatened to stop buying Missouri-grown rice if Ventria moved forward, the company withdrew its plans.

No one knows what could happen to the human immune system if a product like this "pharmaceutical rice" gets into the food chain. "These genetically engineered drugs could exacerbate certain infections, or cause dangerous allergic or immune system reactions," said Bill Freese, science policy analyst at the Center for Food Safety. What's more, said Freese in a separate statement, "Use of these compounds has not been proven to offer any advantages over existing oral rehydration therapies."

Barring public upheaval or farmer boycott, a barrage of other GMOs will be petitioned for approval, and to date, every GMO that's been petitioned has been approved sooner or later.[73]

Biotech and Industrial Agriculture Myths

*Industrial Agriculture and GMOs Are the Solution
to World Hunger*

World hunger isn't the result of a lack of food. The UN Food and Agriculture Organization estimates that food grows in enough abundance globally each year to provide 4.3 pounds per person per day. "Industrial agriculture actually increases hunger by raising the cost of farming," writes Andrew Kimbrell, "by forcing tens of millions of farmers off the land, and by growing primarily high-profit export and luxury crops."[74] The loss of those farms is often cited as one of the main reasons for the millions of poor people in India going hungry each day.

Nor is GM seed more productive. According to a report published by the Union of Concerned Scientists in 2009, "The several thousand field trials over the last 20 years for genes aimed at increasing operational or intrinsic yield (of crops) indicate a significant undertaking. Yet none of these field trials has resulted in increased yield in commercialized major food/feed crops, with the exception of Bt corn." The report further explains that even the good news for GM corn was more likely due to improved breeding techniques, not genetic engineering. Ricardo Salvador, director of the Food and Environment Program with the Union of Concerned Scientists confirmed that GMOs are still falling short of their claims.

"We have actually taken a close look at their claims, such as boosting productivity, boosting yield, helping with environmental impact by making plants more efficient in terms of nitrogen utilization, helping plants deal with drought," explained Salvador. "In every case, our examinations have shown that the claims don't bear up to scrutiny. So the key thing to know about the yield curve that the agronomic world has been pushing over the last few years is that it has not been affected one bit by any of the traits we're talking about here."[75]

A recent UN report shows that small-scale farmers can double their food production within a decade simply by using sustainable and ecological methods for growing foods, what's called "agro-ecological" farming. This is low-tech farming that "enhances soils productivity and protects the crops against pests by relying on the natural environment such as beneficial trees, plants, animals and insects." According to the report, projects in Indonesia, Vietnam, and Bangladesh were able to reduce their dependence on insecticides for their rice by 92 percent, making the crop safer for consumers and cheaper for low-income farmers to grow. Olivier De Schutter, UN Special Rapporteur on the right to food explained, "Knowledge came to replace pesticides and fertilizers."[76]

GMOs Will Result in Less Pesticide Use

This is a slippery argument for companies like Dow and Monsanto to make, because pesticides are one of their main products. The truth is that pesticide use with genetically modified seed is frequently just as high or higher, and the health risks associated with having seed that has pesticides built into each cell (as is the case with Bt corn and Bt cotton) are unknown, because of a lack of FDA testing mandates and the corporations' ability to whitewash the testing process.

A study released in late 2012 in the journal *Environmental Sciences Europe* confirmed that pesticide use with GMOs has actually increased significantly, particularly since 2000. "It's been a slowly unfolding train wreck," said Charles Benbrook, the author of the study.[77] One of the reasons for this is that more weeds are becoming resistant to Roundup, and these so-called superweeds are requiring more spraying not only of Roundup but of many other herbicides as well.

The study focused on herbicide-resistant corn, soybeans, Bt cotton, and Bt corn. According to Benbrook, compared to the first five years the crops were planted, farmers are using twice as much herbicide per acre with Roundup's glyphosate, accounting for virtually the entire uptick. The study also found that GM corn requires from two to six Bt toxins to eradicate the corn borer and corn rootworm, and at least one of the "delayed release, systemic seed treatments" that has been implicated in the widespread Colony Collapse Disorder among honeybees. In addition, there has been "significant and historically unprecedented increases in fungicide use on corn" (from no more than 1 percent up to 11 percent of crop acres).

The pesticide contained in Monsanto's GM seeds is a glyphosate, a broad-spectrum herbicide that basically kills everything it's sprayed on except the crop that has been genetically engineered to resist it by having the herbicide gene inserted into its DNA. Thus, when Roundup is sprayed, the crop survives and thrives in neat, weed-free rows. That's the ideal, at least. Contrary to its claims, Monsanto's Roundup Ready crops require bigger toxic bailouts each year to get the crops to harvest. And according to the FDA, at least fifty-three of the pesticides used in massive quantities on today's major food crops to supplement Roundup are labeled as carcinogenic.

In response to Roundup's clearly weakening market potential, Dow Chemical and Monsanto have teamed up with a solution that involves still more chemicals: GM versions of corn and soybeans that would employ 2,4D (from Dow) "stacked" with Roundup's glyphosate. In their petition to the USDA for approval, Dow said the new seed types would be "stacked with glyphosate and other herbicide tolerance traits to generate commercial hybrids with multiple herbicide tolerances. This trait will provide growers with greater flexibility in selection of herbicides for the improved control of key broadleaf weeds."[78]

This "greater flexibility" in killing weeds is provided by 2,4-D, the most commonly used consumer pesticide in America, found on shelves in the gardening departments of Home Depot and Loews nationwide. It was also a major component of the Vietnam War–era favorite for killing anything that grew, Agent Orange. "If new genetically engineered forms of corn and soybeans tolerant of 2,4-D are approved," said Benbrook in the study, "the volume of 2,4-D sprayed could drive herbicide usage upward by another approximate 50%." That's because it's likely that new resistances will spring up and still newer superweeds and superbugs will result, requiring even bigger applications of chemicals until the next hybrid superweed or superbug comes along that requires even more. All of which means more leaching of toxins into water tables, rivers, and streams, especially the main water artery of the central United States, the Mississippi, to join the rest of the chemicals each year that make their way into the dead zone in the Gulf of Mexico.

As a barrage of criticism ensued about how much more pesticide and herbicide was being sprayed to combat superweeds and superbugs, in May of 2013 the EPA stepped in and gave Monsanto a little more breathing room by granting the biotech giant's request to raise the limits of pesticide residue allowed on many of the crops being sprayed with glyphosate.

GM and Conventional Crops Are More Profitable Per Acre Than Organic Ones

One of the selling points to farmers is that, although GM seeds are more expensive (the cost of Monsanto's Roundup Ready seed includes a per-acre or per-hectare technology fee), the increased output makes the cost worthwhile. Just as lower pesticide use with GM seed proved to be a myth, numerous studies also show that crop yields with GM seed are lower than non-GM seed. As costs for inputs (fertilizer and pesticides) continue to go up, the scenario grows ever less rosy. What is missing from the "high yield" data coming from agribusiness are the "externalities" that are often not factored into the bottom-line figures. These factors include health, environmental and social costs—including the loss of farming communities and their wealth of wisdom—and the subsidies that support agribusiness. As one food executive said, "There's money to be made in food unless you're trying to grow it."[79]

Organic food is changing that idea too. Being able to certify that your food is non-GMO has become a life or death issue to food manufacturers who want to be able to identify themselves as healthier alternatives and to be eligible to sell to markets like Whole Foods, which has declared that it will require labels on GM food by 2018 (anti-GM groups are suggesting they do it sooner). In the meantime, the stigma of not being certified organic is growing, and the increasing amount paid for certified organic crops is an incentive. "Two years ago, a bushel of non GMO soybeans cost $1 to $1.25 more than a bushel of genetically modified soybeans. Now, that premium is $2. For corn, the premium has jumped from 10 cents to as high as 75 cents."

The Non-GMO Project, the trailblazer in offering non-GMO certification, has seen demand for its services soar. In the month before California's failed labeling initiative, the group received 180 inquiries from companies wanting certification. "Nearly 300 more signed up in March, after Whole Foods announced that all products sold in its stores would have to be labeled to describe genetically engineered contents, and about 300 more inquiries followed in April" said Megan Westgarte, Non-GMO Projects' cofounder and executive director.[80]

One of the reasons organic farming is making progressively larger dents in conventional farming's market share is its productivity. Multiple studies demonstrate that organic farming, with its concentration on crop diversity, rotation, and lack of chemical inputs, is more productive, as well as being better for the soil. These studies also show that organic farming produces healthier food, and because it brings higher prices pound for pound at market, it's more economically viable.

The USDA began tracking the nutrient content of foods back in the 1950s, when the Green Revolution was getting a full head of steam. According to their figures, the nutrition value of nonorganic foods has steadily declined, making it necessary today to eat more food to get the nutrients our bodies need. Americans are increasingly overweight and undernourished (three out of five Americans are overweight; one in five is obese). On average, we are eating three hundred calories a day more than we were in 1985. About 90 percent of our calories come from sugars (lots from high-fructose syrup made from GM corn), added fat (much of it from GM soybean oil), and refined grains. Less than 10 percent of our calories come from the five servings of fruits and vegetables we're supposed to eat every day.

The effects on children are increasingly alarming. High-calorie, low-nutrient diets are being looked at as the culprits responsible for chronic diseases such as diabetes and cancer. Lacking the vitamins C, E, B12, B6, niacin, folic acid, as well as the minerals iron and zinc "appears to mimic radiation by causing single- and double-strand DNA breaks, oxidative lesions, or both."[81] All causes are seen as precursors to cancer.

As public demand for safer, more nutritious food grows, according to the Organic Trade Association, business for organics is good and getting better. In 1997 the organic food business wasn't exactly keeping big agribusiness up at night, nor was the public that interested. It had a mere 0.8 percent of the food market. But organic's annual share of the market has steadily increased. In 2006 organic food sales were up 16 percent over the 2005 figures. In 2012 sales hit $31.5 billion, accounting for 4.2 percent of total food sales. The market is consistently and exponentially enjoying nearly 10 percent annual growth, while conventional foods are seeing only 2–3 percent annual growth.[82]

GMOs Are Safe and Their Behavior Well Understood

The stories behind early GM crops like Pioneer Hi-Bred, L-Tryptophan, StarLink, and the Flavr Savr tomato contradict both of those claims. Since we are largely unable to know when we are eating GM products or byproducts, thanks to the inclusion of unlabeled GMOs in many foods, there is no way to know the genesis of potential illnesses, allergies, or worse.

One special issue to note: antibiotic resistance marker genes (ARMs). To create a GM crop strain, researchers must get foreign genes into the host DNA. To do this, they sometimes use a "gene gun," a .22-caliber device that blasts tiny bits of gold- or tungsten-coated genetic material into a dish containing thousands of cells, hoping with this "shotgun" approach to maximize cell penetration.

But how can they tell which genes have received the altered DNA? They can't. So they attach ARMs to each gene in the shot. Then they wash the blasted cells with antibiotic. The genes pierced with the ARM-toting gene will survive.

It's not a good idea to have genes in the body that are resistant to antibiotics. A study done in 2002 again proved that ARMs can and do survive the human digestive process and are therefore capable of reaching the human gut. Using test subjects who had colostomy bags, researchers found "a relatively large proportion of genetically modified DNA survived" the strong acids of the stomach and small intestine. Worse, this meant that the animals that ate the GM food that the test subjects ate had transferred them across species, another problem the biotech scientists said was impossible. The danger: that antibiotic-resistant genes could float around in our stomachs and guts for prolonged periods, making us resistant to the antibiotics we might someday need. And since we don't have food labeling that tells us when we're eating GM food, there would be no way to know if that antibiotic resistance in a person came from eating something that had ARMS in it.

GMOs Are Widely Successful

Because we don't label or strictly segregate GM from non-GM crops, overseas buyers have a problem with our genetically modified products—corn, soy, canola, and cotton. Public distrust of GM products has driven the United Kingdom and European Union to employ strict rules about labeling and content. Since there is currently no standard that defines a "GMO-free" product, France has passed a law requiring that any product containing more than 0.9 percent genetically modified ingredients be labeled as having GM content; a movement is afoot to drop that content to 0.1 percent. Some African countries won't allow our GM grain crops or seed on their shores anymore—not even as free food aid—because they fear contamination of heritage grains, a common danger with genetically modified seed. Because crops are open to the winds, their pollen is impossible to contain. Virtually all of Canada's canola has been tainted by GM crops for just this reason, and GM pollen has contaminated much of their honey, destroying their ability to sell to organic markets.

Ireland—a country that knows only too well the consequences of depending on monoculture—has declared itself a GM-free zone. As a nation, it has totally rejected the cultivation of GM crops. Only two GM field trials have been attempted on Irish soil: GM sugar beets, which were destroyed by activists in 1998, and GM potatoes, begun in late 2012 and still ongoing.

Only one crop, Monsanto's bestselling corn, MON810, is authorized for cultivation in the European Union, but it has never been grown commercially in open fields in Ireland. MON810 contains the Bt pesticide, which is embedded in the seed's DNA to fight the European corn corer, a parasite that's not even found in Ireland. Most MON810 is grown in the Spanish regions of Catalonia and Aragon, where open pollination has contaminated conventional corn crops.

All EU member states require labeling on any food or animal feed produced from and/or containing GMOs. Conscious of consumer rejection of GMOs, many EU food brands and retailers simply avoid using GMOs. However, a loophole in the EU labeling requirement allows animal products (meat, fish, poultry, eggs, and dairy products) from livestock fed GM feed to go unlabeled. Ireland imports about 2 million tons of nonorganic beef, mutton, pork, and dairy products annually, and most come from animals fed GM soy and corn. In addition, many Irish restaurants, pubs, fast food outlets, and caterers use cooking oils made from GM corn or canola without informing customers.[83]

Despite the clear mandate of its citizenry, Ireland faces the same governmental reluctance to face down the biotechnology industry as the rest of the world. In 2009, the Irish government agreed to a policy to prohibit cultivation and field trials of GM crops in Ireland and to introduce a voluntary GM-free label to enable farmers and food producers who avoid GMOs to increase their market share. The agreement, however, was never formalized into law.

How Did GMOs Get Past the FDA in the First Place?

When introduced to the public, GMOs were rated GRAS (generally recognized as safe) and substantially equivalent to non-GM food; that is, safe simply because there allegedly were no differences between the two food types. For all intents and purposes, the public was told, GM was the same as non-GM food. In May of 1992, the FDA spelled out the direction of its regulatory policy on GM foods: "The agency is not aware of any information showing that foods derived by these new methods differ from other foods in any meaningful or uniform way." And, it said, its scientists agreed.

That turned out not to be true. And we know this only because of the diligence of public interest attorney Steven Druker. Suspicious of the FDA claims that its scientists were on board with FDA talking points about the safety of GM foods, Druker filed a lawsuit to get the FDA to release documents proving their contention. During the discovery phase, Druker's office was inundated with fourteen thousand pages of documentation. "The idea was to flood us with so many documents we would never be able to read them all."[84]

But they read enough of them to find out that there had been many instances of dissension within the ranks of FDA scientists. An attorney named Michael Taylor, whose firm had once represented Monsanto, had become the FDA's deputy commissioner for policy. According to Druker, during Taylor's tenure, "references to the unintended negative effects of bioengineering were progressively deleted from drafts of the policy statement (over the protests of agency scientists) and a final statement was issued claiming (a) that [GM] foods are no riskier than others and (b) that the agency has no information to the contrary."[85] Taylor would later leave the FDA to become Monsanto's vice president for public policy. In July 2009, he was appointed a senior adviser to the FDA commissioner on food safety in the Obama administration. The next year he was appointed to the newly created FDA post of deputy commissioner for foods.

The FDA had some pet ploys, according to scientists within the FDA who tried to warn their superiors of the dangers of not testing.

One was that genetic engineering is no different from traditional breeding practices. This, said Linda Kahl, an FDA compliance officer, amounted to the FDA trying to "fit a square peg into a round hole." They were trying to force a conclusion for convenience. Not only were genetic engineering and traditional breeding different, she said, but "they lead to different risks."[86] FDA microbiologist Louis Pribyl agreed, contending that it's not clear that the creators of GM foods "will be able to pick up effects that might not be obvious."[87] Another ploy was to turn this idea that there is no difference between GM and non-GM food into a broad-based public statement of policy.

There is general consensus among the scientific community that genetically modified food is no different from conventional food.
—Speaker of the House DENNIS HASTERT, March 2003[88]

I want to make very clear that it is the position of the United States government that we do not believe there is a difference between GMO commodities and non-GMO commodities.
—MELINDA KIMBLE, U.S. State Department, May 1999[89]

VERSUS

The risks in biotechnology are undeniable and they stem from the unknowable in science and commerce. It is prudent to recognize and address these issues, not compound them by overly optimistic or foolhardy behavior.
—Editors, *Nature Biotechnology,* October 2000

Approval of new transgenic organisms for environmental release, and for use as food or feed, should be based on rigorous scientific assessment of their potential for causing harm to the environment or to human health. Such testing should replace the current regulatory reliance on "substantial equivalence" as a decision threshold.
—From the Expert Panel on the Future of Food Biotechnology, January 2001

The Distinction *Is* the Difference

The claim that there is no difference between GM and non-GM food—and therefore no need to label GM foods—continues despite growing public awareness and demands for transparency. In an interview in March 2008, Monsanto spokesperson Lori Hoag used that argument to justify her company's ongoing battle to keep labels like "rBGH-free" off cartons of milk coming from cows not injected with rBGH. Injecting cows with the hormone helps produce more milk, but the process also creates a number of troubling side effects that have concerned scientists, doctors, farmers, and consumers. These side effects include shorter animal life cycles and increased levels of mastitis, an infection of the udder. Because the mastitis is treated with antibiotics, there are increased chances of antibiotic resistance, as well as increased levels of Insulin-like Growth Factor-1, IGF-1, a hormone that has been linked to numerous types of cancer. "rBGH milk is supercharged with high levels of a natural growth factor (IGF-1), which is readily absorbed through the gut." High levels of this hormone present a double-barreled threat because it tends to "inhibit the body's normal ability to protect itself from microscopic cancers by the natural process of programmed cell destruction, known as 'apoptosis.' This promotes the growth and invasiveness of early cancers, and also decreases their responsiveness to chemotherapy."[90]

Despite being banned in every nation of the European Union, as well as Canada, New Zealand, Japan and Australia (and some dairies bowing to consumer pressure to make its products rBGH free), rBGH is still widely used in U.S. dairy products. Even though Monsanto sold its rBGH division to pharmaceutical giant Eli Lilly in 2008, the corporate branding runs deep. Monsanto is after all, as writer Jeffrey Smith said, the company "which told us that PCBs, DDT, and Agent Orange were safe." After a decade of rebuffs and reassurances from a company that has betrayed it so many times, a weary and skeptical public is holding its ground and demanding full disclosure. "The obligation to endure," says French biologist and moralist Jean Rostand, "gives us the right to know."

Public Distrust Is Driving More Openness

The Grocery Manufacturers Association estimates that as much as 80 percent of all processed food contains GMOs. Having them unlabeled makes it tricky to spot them. But the marketplace is a powerful mechanism, and the polls that show that an overwhelming number of U.S. consumers want their food labeled are convincing some manufacturers to simply opt out of using them. Yoplait and Dannon saw the trend early and stopped using dairy products from rBGH-treated cows in 2009. Many national dairy brands have followed suit, and the list is growing. Both Whole Foods and Trader Joe's say that products they sell under their own names are GM-free, as do Gerber, Heinz, Seagram, and Hain.

Farmers, too, have made their voices heard. In August 2009, 1,500 U.S. farmers sued Bayer CropScience for releasing an unapproved GM rice, apparently in 2006, and not telling farmers, the public, or the government about the contamination. (Bayer CropScience settled for $750 million against the claims of 11,000 American rice farmers.)[91] That same month, thousands of farmers from the southern and central provinces of Pakistan joined forces to ban the trial growth of Bt cotton seeds and GM presence altogether. Bt cotton seed is expensive; it cannot be saved and used for subsequent crops, because it is patented by Monsanto. It requires more water than indigenous varieties and, being a monoculture crop, it robs the soil of the benefits of crop rotation. A single bad season can mean devastation and starvation for farming families and whole communities.

It is consumer demand that is shining light on these issues, slowly bringing them into the public eye. In early 2010 a short piece in the *Huffington Post* described a report that claimed that three varieties of GM corn caused deaths in lab rats. This report caught fire with readers; it quickly acquired over 1,400 comments, more than 6,400 Facebook shares, and over 1,000 Twitter tweets.[92] Today biotechnology dominates our staple crops: 95 percent of all the soybeans grown in the United States and 80 percent of all the corn comes from patented seed, and every one of those seeds has a genetically modified pedigree.

But as opposition grows, it's also clear that the biotech companies have no intention of letting up. Their determination to capture and monetize the world's seeds through compulsory royalties, regardless of public will, is relentless. On November 19, 2012, the USDA released a report that basically absolves Monsanto from any contamination of non-GM crops by their GM seeds (freeing them from responsibility for the resulting loss of revenue), effectively pulling the rug out from under any further litigation of non-GM or organic farmers against Monsanto in the future. Their advice to farmers whose crops and seed stock might be ruined by GM pollination: get crop insurance.[93]

On the same day the USDA report came out, the so-called Monsanto Protection Act passed as part of the 2013 Continuing Resolution to continue government funding for a six-month period. The provision (also used in 2012), which was added to the House Agricultural Appropriations Bill, essentially "strips the rights of federal courts to halt the sale and planting of genetically engineered crops during the legal appeals process." This was a way to stop coalitions like the Center for Food Safety from filing lawsuits aimed at forcing a pause in cultivating GM crops until their mandated EIS process is completed. Although the provision is clearly meant for a single growing season, it sets a precedent that simply allows the biotechnology sector to subvert regulatory laws set in place for public protection for its own ends.

In May 2013, the European Union drafted a sweeping new regulation called the Plant Reproductive Material Law that effectively gives the European Union the power to control which kinds of vegetable, plant and tree seeds can be grown by individuals.

The Seed Healers

Thomas Jefferson once declared, "Those who labor in the earth are the chosen people of God." Philosopher and farmer Wendell Berry explains how his life's calling hobnobs with infinity.

*By farming we enact our fundamental connection with energy
and matter, light and darkness. In the cycles of farming,
which carry the elemental energy again and again through
the seasons and the bodies of living things, we recognize
the only infinitude within reach of the imagination.*[94]

Since agriculture began, we have counted on farmers to maintain
that fundamental connection for us, to spend their lives as part of an
ancient tapestry woven from a working partnership with the earth.
They are the gatekeepers of our survival, the stewards who have
been entrusted with keeping us alive with good, healthy food. Ours
has been a history of connection. What has happened to them has
affected us.

Today the gatekeepers are largely gone and with their absence,
spoiled by decades of cheap, plentiful, and unhealthy—but easily
accessible—food, we have lost our connection with that elemental
energy and are mindless of the origin of our nourishment and its
impact on our bodies. As modern food eaters, disconnected from
our nutrition, we are paying for that loss in ways that are outside of
our awareness.

Recall for a moment the story in chapter 1 of Harvard-trained
neuroanatomist Jill Taylor, who documented her own stroke, and in
its midst, found her connection to the whole. Each of us is, she said,
"the life force power of the universe, with manual dexterity and two
cognitive minds."[95]

What Jefferson and Taylor are talking about is our connection
to the whole, to the source of life and, taking it down a notch, to
the earth and our food. All around us are examples of both our connectedness and our separation. Just as the Hindus and Sufis say that
there are many paths to God because there are many people, we
could say that there are many paths to discovering our relatedness
to the whole and to each other because we are all different. The universe takes care that we have many routes available to accommodate
both our need and our capacity to see.

Thomas Jefferson's sense of connectedness to the earth (and to the farmers he admired) was as much a part of his body as his skin and eyes. It was informed and nurtured by his life and times in the playground of his eighteenth-century consciousness. The connectedness of Jill Taylor was delivered via her highly educated, late twentieth-century scientist's receptors. The delivery system was perfectly attuned both to getting her attention and to informing her curiosity with new perceptions, which forever changed the way she would see herself and others—not merely as beings with brains, but as spirits in human form.

Dr. Taylor's left brain dutifully recorded what was going on, and as its capacity to work broke down, her right brain slowly became the only mode of interpretation. As her right brain began to dominate, a new world opened up to her. What she experienced in her observation of oneness and how it relates to the whole was something that also captured Albert Einstein's imagination, when he said, "Our separation from each other is an optical illusion of consciousness"—a statement that neatly sums up the basic teachings of the Buddha. Just as we are not separate from one another, neither are the pieces of us separate from each other; rather, they are all just differently labeled parts of our "oneness."

Understanding how we work as energy beings provides us with a template we can overlay onto our lives to examine our mistaken belief in this separation. Looking at the world through that lens, we can better understand what has happened to the farmers and farmland and the food they've grown for us for the last half-century. We can better see how this break with the earth unfolded, not just on an economic or social level, but also from an energetic, spiritual perspective.

The Modern Origin of Our Break with Nature

Until the middle of the twentieth century, we had what Rachel Carson called a "soil community," an interwoven web of symbiosis between soil and creatures, each fed by the other.[96] Soil is like the earth's digestive system, a supremely efficient mechanism for creation and sustenance. She wrote, "The thin layer of soil that forms a patchy covering over the continents controls our own existence and that of every other animal of the land. Without soil, land plants as we know them could not grow, and without plants no animals could survive."[97]

And since World War II, that thin layer of soil has taken a pounding, a one-two punch. First the chemicals, then biotechnology. The so-called Green Revolution was launched on the back of one of the chemical luminaries of the war: DDT. In the 1950s, few questioned the sincerity of government oversight, and chemical companies were viewed as miracle workers—they cured disease and delivered plenty and affluence to the American landscape. The star of the now-infamous pesticide DDT had ascended quickly during the war years, because it had gained a well-deserved reputation as a supreme lice killer, a cheap, quick, easy way to keep GIs free of the vermin that tormented them in the field, when they had to endure long periods without clean clothes or baths. By killing lice, DDT was also credited with preventing typhus, which was carried by lice. Prior to World War II, typhus had been responsible for more deaths of soldiers and civilians alike than bombs, bullets, and starvation combined.

This first Green Revolution, by the way, bore no relation to today's movement toward environmental consciousness and sustainability. In fact, they could hardly be more different. In the 1950s, "green" essentially meant "go"—giving the gas to growth on a massive and unlimited scale. It meant production quantity and economic prosperity. It's no small irony that many of the goals of the modern Green Revolution are to reverse the philosophy and heal the effects of the first one.

With substances like DDT in their arsenals, farmers used and depended on chemicals to repel bugs and fertilize their crops as never before, with the aim of maximizing farm production to "feed a growing world," the postwar mantra. But slowly it became clear that this new wonderful world of chemicals was having unintended consequences. When Rachel Carson's *Silent Spring* was first serialized in the *New Yorker* in June of 1962, it set off a firestorm of protest from the chemical industry, chiefly from Monsanto, DDT's manufacturer. A public relations and media blitz ensued, and Carson was decried as a know-nothing alarmist. Still, the accuracy of her data could not be shaken. Birds had simply stopped singing in many parts of the country. Their corpses were found by the tens of thousands in American front yards and parks.

The culprit at fault was not easy to see. Instead, it was a mystery solved through a chain of evidence that led back to the wholesale spraying to ward off all sorts of pests, from gypsy moths to Dutch Elm beetles. But the chemical played no favorites, and its overkill tendencies became clear. Perhaps one-tenth of 1 percent of the insecticide sprayed actually prevented an infestation. That left the rest to settle onto leaves, trees, and shrubs, and to leech into the soil and the water table, into the wildlife, and, of course, into us. So pervasive was its spread into our ecosystem that DDT traces can be found in the mother's milk of virtually every woman on earth.

While Carson's book launched the modern environmental movement, its sad prophecy became all too clear. With the unbridled use of these pesticides came more unwanted consequences, among them the vast dead zones created by runoffs streaming down the Mississippi into the Gulf of Mexico, leaving in their wake a destroyed ecosystem affecting the topsoil, the wildlife, and all the area's natural resources. In the Gulf alone these areas span 7,700 square miles—roughly the size of New Jersey—of wetlands, marshes, and water bodies where, to this day, nothing grows. As more farmers plant corn to meet the growing demand for biofuels, the amount of nitrates leeching into the waterways from fertilizers could increase by another 34 percent by 2022.[98]

The bacteria in the surface foot of one acre of topsoil can weigh half a ton. What happens when the ecosystem in the soil is attacked by chemicals that are meant to kill one insect but at the same time also destroy much of the microbial life that works in symbiosis with the soil? What was once dark, loamy, rich-smelling soil turns to dusty clay. Robbed of their very nature, vegetables grown in such soil have little taste and even less nutritional value.

After the chemicals came the birth of biotechnology. With the advent of biotech came a new, even greater threat than chemical pesticides, made more troubling because of the extent to which its effects are unknown, unpredictable, and potentially untraceable. Genetically modified food and genetically engineered additives have changed the face of global farming, instituting uniform mono-culture where there was once diversity, taxing soil and its nutrients, and, some scientists believe, forever tainting the world with geneti-cally modified alterations to its systems. Biotech creates what one critic called "human health havoc."

The Cost in Despair

In 1910 the farm population of the United States accounted for one-third of the overall population. By 1969 that number had dwin-dled to a mere 5 percent. Today it is estimated that fewer than one percent of our more than 300 million citizens call themselves farm-ers (as an occupation, farmers are now bundled with ranchers and other agricultural managers in the census). And those dwindling numbers don't reflect the effects on rural communities when farm-ers leave. In the mid-1980s, when the United States lost 235,000 farmers, an estimated 60,000 other community businesses failed as well. A single farming area, McPherson County, Nebraska, has lost two-thirds of its population since 1920, including fifty-eight school districts and three entire towns.[99]

Between the advent of genetic engineering and the predomi-nance of corporate farming in today's agricultural landscape, it's small wonder that farmers have given up in historic numbers. While many farmers went out of business from the reverses that followed a boom of heavy investments in bigger equipment and larger farms, their exodus in more recent years has been tied to a combination of factors.

Contamination of crops. Four big cash crops have been genetically engineered for commercial use—cotton, soy, corn, and canola—and their pollen indiscriminately contaminates non-GM varieties of the crops, distributed by wind, rain, insects, and birds, even by trucks driving from a GM field into a non-GM field, rendering them unsuitable for many markets. This spells ruin for many farmers and has been the source of many lawsuits in Canada against Monsanto since their Roundup Ready canola has contaminated virtually all of that country's canola crop.

Loss of natural protection of Bt. Genetic engineering has resulted in the widespread use of an altered form of the natural pesticide Bt (Bacillus thuringiensis), making insects more resistant to the natural strain of Bt. With the natural pesticide no longer working, farming without the use of chemical pesticides becomes even more problematic. If farmers want to grow organic food, using chemical pesticides automatically decertifies their organic status and endangers their livelihood.

Inability to compete. Many small farmers who have tried to compete with agribusiness gave up because of the rising costs of inputs— seed, pesticides, herbicides, fertilizers—and continually lower profit margins. Failed crops wither away seed money. Since globalized trade took off in the 1990s, farmer suicides in India and China have risen precipitously. In America, after the disintegration of the family farm during the 1980s, suicide was the number one cause of death among farmers, more than three times the rate of the general population.

The first Green Revolution created a divide that has never been repaired: corporate agribusiness versus individual family farmer. Yield versus quality. Profit versus nurturing. As Wendell Berry said, "The standard of the exploiter is efficiency; the standard of the nurturer is care. The exploiter's goal is money, profit; the nurturer's goal is health—his land's health, his own, his family's, his community's, his country's."[100]

There is no way to measure the total impact of farmers losing their ability to keep us fed and healthy as land has been turned into a corporate commodity and food into something that no longer nurtures and sustains us. "For the farmer, the field is the mother, which feeds the millions of life forms that are her children."[101]

The New Earth Stewards

We as a nation are physically separated from our food. For the most part, we don't know where it comes from or who grows it. We are used to it being cheap and plentiful, showing up in tidy, blood-less packages. That plenty has turned into a potential curse, in part because we've lost track of whether what we are eating is nutritious or harmful. Even the most nutritious food eaten in excessive quan-tities can create health problems, and much of what is available in our well-stocked stores is downright unhealthy. By now we know that simply eating low-fat or low-calorie foods is not enough. We have to learn to look at the whole picture, including *how* we eat. Busy lives often mean quick meals, and today about one-quarter of the average American's diet is made up of fast food. The concept of eating a nutritious meal at a relaxing pace in a family or communal setting is almost a thing of the past.

For the last five decades, conventional agriculture has played an increasingly significant part in our diets. In the early 1970s there were six thousand to seven thousand items in the typical supermar-ket, about 40 percent of which were not present in 1960.[102] Today, *seventeen thousand* new food products go on the market *every year*.[103] If they are processed, the odds are high that they will have GM components in them, not to mention nonnutritious elements that can cause obesity. And much the same is true of almost all fast food. Because so much fast food and processed food tricks our taste buds with artificial sweeteners and flavorings, we can no longer count on our senses to tell us what we're eating and whether it's in our health's best interest.[104]

The onslaught on the American public's palate is relentless. The advertising budget for commercial food is $32 billion a year; for fresh food, a paltry $2 million. (McDonald's annual television bud-get alone is over $2 billion.[105]) Today it's estimated that as much as $10 billion is spent annually to make junk food attractive to chil-dren through traditional and online media. Not surprisingly, the studies supported by food producers that tout the health benefits of their products seldom match the findings of independent studies. "If a study is funded by the industry, it may be closer to advertising than science."[106]

While we can't rely on the images or data that advertisers use to sell us food and vouch for its nutritional provenance, we can count on vast resources, from libraries to the internet, to educate us. Understanding what we eat is not just proactive, it's essential. In the world of hidden food ingredients and altered components, knowledge is power. We have to count on ourselves, because for the most part we can no longer count on our former guardians, the farmers. When we lost the connection with farmers, we lost our connection with the soil, with real food, with what Michael Pollan calls "the circular flow of nutrients through the food chain."[107]

The 2014 CIA World Factbook listed the United States as fifty-first for life expectancy at birth, down a full ten points since 2008.[108] With two-thirds of Americans overweight or obese, it should come as no surprise that diabetes in people over seventy-five is expected to increase more than 300 percent by 2050, a grim comment on the health of the first generations to have lived their entire lives in a culture fed by industrial agriculture.[109]

It's important to remember that until the second half of the twentieth century, organic farming was the *only* farming. It was normal. But that kind of farming is often derided today by proponents of biotechnology. They say it's too slow, inefficient, and unproductive—even though statistics say otherwise.

At least one study indicates that organic food is simply better for you because of the way it is *not* grown. Using chemical fertilizers makes crops grow faster, so they have less time to accumulate nutrients other than the nitrogen, phosphorus, and potassium in the fertilizers. Faster growth, in turn, means crops don't develop with deep root systems that can reach down to where more mineral nutrients lie. Organically grown crops also contain more phytochemicals, compounds that make them naturally resistant to invasion from diseases and pests. The USDA has discovered that since the 1880s, when improved wheat varieties became common, the nutritional levels have dropped as yields have risen. So, although yields have tripled, iron levels have dropped by 28 percent and zinc and selenium by about 30 percent. We eat more food but get less nutrition. Starved for nutrients, we eat more. Craving but not satisfying the need for nourishment, we get obese.[110]

Local food advocate and master chef Alice Waters points out that we're operating under a system that does not have our best interests at heart. "You're told that food should be cheap," she says. "I think we have to learn to understand that we have been educated by a fast food system that cooking is drudgery, that it's much easier to go out and buy it."[111]

And therein lies one of the secrets to reconnecting. By learning more about what we are putting into our bodies, we reignite that most basic bond between ourselves and the earth. All of these issues surrounding our food have both physical and symbolic effects. Here again, the human energetic system provides the clues to a symbolic truth: this is what an energetic heartbreak is all about. As farmers lose their connection to the food they grow for us, to the seed it comes from, and to the consumers to whom they had been connected for thousands of years, we all lose our sense of connection with what nourishes us: the earth. That loss affects each of us through the other essential fuel of our lives—our food—leaving little aching voids in our bodies, minds, and spirits.

What is happening to our seeds and soil is happening to us. There is no separation. As we toxify the most basic and intimate components of our existence, our seed and soil, we toxify ourselves. Companies that believe they can treat the earth's most basic sacred elements and building blocks, our genes, with clumsy and faulty constructs crafted for profit, betray their own empty centers. We are organisms, not organs. We operate as systems, not as separate entities. The trillions of calculations our bodies make each second cannot be understood, much less diverted and modified without causing damning and unknowable consequences to our very cellular building blocks. Like Icarus flying too close to the sun, there is hubris here on a vast scale. Agribusiness is a powerful industry bereft of any wisdom but its quarterly bottom line, pitted against a timeless universe of action and consequence.

It's time for us to get involved; to demand more of ourselves; to open our eyes, our hearts, minds, and spirits; to fling the doors of perception off their hinges. We have to do it not because it's fashionable or because we need to expiate our sins, but because we want our species to survive. Like the heroes of Leningrad, who sacrificed themselves without knowing whether it would even do any good, each of us is called on to step up and do our part.

If the history of the third millennium is ever to be written, it will be necessary for the people who lived through it to make this time one of a new kind of accountability. An accountability not only at the individual level but also at the community, country, and global level. If you want to see who the new stewards of the earth are, look in the mirror. Look at the faces of the people walking down your street and in the aisles in your grocery store, and sitting across from you at the dinner table. That's us—known and unknown to each other, once shattered into countless pieces, finding our way back to wholeness.

In a time that sees us feeding ourselves at the expense of the soil and seed that is the source of our lives—an act that Rachel Carson termed *biocide,* a sacrifice of our own habitat—we must ask ourselves how any sane person can accept this. We can do better than live in a world that ecologist Paul Shepard called "just not quite fatal."[112] And as the last part of this book will demonstrate, doing so is well within both our reach and our own capacity for wisdom.

Part 3

Your Earth Calling

The world is a dangerous place to live,
not because of the people who are evil,
but because of the people who don't do anything about it.
—ALBERT EINSTEIN

Chapter 5

Reconnecting to the Earth

*We are bleeding at the roots, because we are cut off from the earth
and the sun and stars.*

—D. H. LAWRENCE

Now that you have walked through a mini-history of what got us
to the issues we face as twenty-first-century earthlings, what's
next is for you to find out where you fit into the solutions, how you
are being called to jump in and help out.

Finding your earth calling involves waking up, seeing differently,
and learning how to listen deeply to how the earth speaks to you. In
order to engage that inner process over time, this chapter includes
several spiritual practices to help you create and maintain a daily
spiritual foundation. These are intentionally earth-centric practices,
meant to help you let down your ever-churning cognitive left brain
and give your right brain a chance to chime in with its richness and
powerful ability to keep you heart-centered. One of the innate gifts
of being at ease in nature is its mystery, the way it draws you inexorably out of your hard-driving calculator into the part of you that
has faith in your perceptual ability.

Learning to pay attention and read the information that your
intuition is always receiving takes time. It happens in layers. Layers
settle in and attach. More layers follow. Ideas present themselves,
new understandings dawn. This is how we awaken, how consciousness is born.

Stepping into Your Soul's Journey

Finding your way to that spiritual trailhead is a process, an initiation into your own soul's journey. If your intention is earnest and humble, there is no wrong way to craft a practice. You can change things from time to time to keep it from becoming routine. There are countless ways to connect to nature, but the simple ones are the best. (And if words like soul or spiritual stop you in your tracks, simply consider these last two chapters as a doorway into becoming a better earth steward.)

It is one of life's paradoxes that as we age and separate from what nurtures us, an invisible bit of alchemy is set in motion. Our hearts begin to long for what our minds have forgotten—that sense of oneness, that absolute certainty of connectedness. That yearning is what drives us to respond to the sense that something is missing, because it is. We are not meant to feel separate and alone, shattered and distant from our cosmic tribe. On the physical level, we belong to many tribes: family, friends, school, town, nation, ethnic group, political party, planet, and so forth. But on a cosmic plane, we are universal beings. Returning to that sense of our own cosmic identity is part of each person's life quest.

Awakening to our place on the earth and our relationship with her begins not outside ourselves but inside, in the inner landscapes that reflect the chaos and longing created in our outer landscapes. As we strike out to discover all the ways that we can connect, both individually and collectively, we will become a species of new Magellans, laying out a healing path as a map for the generations to come.

It would seem that our time is calling us to awaken from our benumbed and bewitched state to a wonder at and reverence for the astonishing, miraculous and mysterious creation of which we are a part.
—Teilhard de Chardin

And luckily for us, we're designed for just that journey of discovery.

Each of us has what Duane Elgin calls a "literacy of consciousness," an innate ability to "know that we know." It is this kind of spiritual intelligence that helps us see and translate the clues that lie strewn throughout our lives. Looking back over the decades, each of us can begin to see the miracle that is our own life unfolding. We need only develop what he calls "the art of attention," to teach ourselves this cosmic vocabulary. "The importance of cultivating this core capacity is recognized by every major wisdom tradition."[1] No matter what belief system we grew up in, there is an avenue that takes us there. Our job is to train ourselves to have a "witnessing consciousness."

> *Life can only be understood backwards;*
> *but it must be lived forwards.*
> —SØREN KIERKEGAARD

Witnessing Yourself: Keeping a Journal

In the late eighteenth century, a pair of English gentlemen named James Boswell and Samuel Johnson set out from London to tour Scotland. During their travels, they each detailed their perspectives of their journey, creating the first travelogue, filled with the details of their day-to-day observations and experiences. The reading public was enthralled.

Today such public journals are called blogs. With our smart phones and a few minutes, we can plug in text, pictures, and video and transport people into intimate tidbits of our own histories.

The word journal comes from the French word for day, *jour*. It is a sip of your life, a tiny picture, a day's view. When joined with countless other tiny bits run into a series, it forms a mosaic you can recognize when you step back. For this reason, journaling your course through this kind of reawakening can be a way to follow the cracking open of your own consciousness. No, you don't need to be a writer (and you don't need to share it), and there are many approaches you can try—but the simpler, the better.[2] Here's how simple:

- Buy a journal (a ringed notebook is fine) and keep handy a pen that you like or set up a file on a tablet or computer.
- Pick a time of day and a timeframe in which to write (perhaps ten minutes in the morning or evening, maybe a half-page a day, etc.).
- Start now. Look out a window on your day, wherever you are. Note the first thing that draws your eye. That becomes your first insight into how you see your world. Build on it.

A journal can be multimedia: stick in magazine clippings, draw pictures, and add photos or whatever can fit between the pages. Get creative. It's your journal. Do what you want. What's great about journaling is that it gives you what something like a photo can't: the history of your growth, not just the visual memory. Uncaptured, it's like the photo op that got away. Once the moment has passed, that shaft of wisdom, that kernel of truth, disappears from your memory.

Journaling is a personal form of narrative. Unless it's your preference to be public, your journal need never be read by others. It can be, as journal-writing teacher Stephanie Dowrick says, "simply a vehicle for your inner wise self."

Journaling is particularly helpful when you are undergoing a transformation, a change in your life, a shift in your consciousness. It provides scaffolding, a framework on which you can attach seemingly unrelated meanderings over time. It is these seemingly miscellaneous pieces that collectively let you begin to form a new picture of yourself and even some of the ways the universe is trying to get through to you. Recording them creates a link between your mind and heart; it gives the pattern a chance to appear. This is part of the gift of the witnessing consciousness. You literally see yourself see yourself.

Waking Up: Learning to Look

Waking up requires more than opening your eyes. You must also train your eyes to see differently. This chapter suggests some of the many ways that you can wake up your innate connection to the earth—on ever-deepening levels—by seeing differently. In some, you'll fine-tune your eyes and ears; in others, you'll journey to the interior of your heart and mind. Each suggestion is a tool of awakening. As you work through them, note what occurs to you and make your own list.

Whichever place you start, what will most likely happen is that as you begin to tick off items, other ideas or questions will occur to you. The universe wastes nothing, especially energy. Once you invest your energy in listening to your heart and acting on what feels urgent to you, other ideas, other opportunities—some of them life changing—often present themselves. As you move your perception just a bit, the whole world begins to look different. One insight builds on another until life takes on a new perspective. That is the nature of grace. It comes as a bonus when your heart is open, your intent is genuine, and your attitude is humble.

Try something, then try something else. Start where you are. Honor your limitations, then find ways around them. Demand self-growth. Be ruthlessly accountable. Find your way to yes.

Your Place on Earth: Seeing Where You Live

We once were keenly aware of where we lived and who lived near us. Not so many generations ago, we understood the weather by looking up and smelling the air, by watching the wind and the sky and the ways the animals behaved. You didn't have to be a farmer to know what the earth was telling you. These sensing skills were "second nature" to us a century ago. We once knew the natural characteristics of the areas we lived in and had some sense of the human commerce that took place in them from dawn to dawn.

Learning more about where you live is essential to having a sensibility about your surroundings—to be able to perceive that they are not outside of us, but rather we are in the midst of them.

The ecologist Peter Berg first began using the word *bioregion* to describe the areas of land in which we live in terms of what he considers interdependent life forms: plant, animal, and human. "The bioregional perspective, the one I've worked with for nearly twenty years, recognizes that people simply don't know where they live."[3] One of Berg's goals is to help people "to become inhabitants again." This goes back to the process of naming things to help them have value to us. We cannot value what we do not name.

Once you value something, you never look at it the same way again. It changes you; it becomes a piece of you, however small. And because people today don't know much about where they live, or where their food, water, and energy come from, they don't feel a sense of kinship with it. That, in turn, means that they don't know what's healthy for the section of earth they occupy. Most of us don't know our area's history, why the streets, rivers, creeks, or parks have the names they have. Like our mountain ranges and old-growth forests, our neighborhoods, cities, and states have histories. The region you live in is steeped in the stories of countless lives lived right under the spot where you eat your meals, read your newspaper, surf the internet, and rest your body.

So if you name the components of your neighborhood, if you grow to love it and feel ownership of it, so that you say—in some form—"this is my tribe," it's not so easy for you to ignore it or let it be strewn with trash, sprayed with pesticides, or poisoned by the runoff from a strip-mining company that's contaminating the ground water.

That's the first part: get to know where you live. Learn what you can about the space that is providing you with oxygen every day of your life. You don't have to love all of it, you don't have to live there forever, but find some little thing to cherish about where you live. It has you in it. You have left pieces of yourself behind every time you exhaled a breath.

As Berg points out, if we know what is happening in our bioregion that is unhealthy or unsustainable, we can begin to make intelligent decisions about what to do as communities of involved, informed citizens. As resources become more precious and using them wisely and sustainably becomes the new norm, this kind of wisdom is essential. And since 75 percent of Americans live in cities today, "urban consciousness" is only going to become more important.[4] What you are likely to find out is that there are a lot of others In your region who have the same curiosity and concerns. The age of the urban warrior, defending and reinvigorating the health of his or her bioregion has quietly descended upon us.

Understanding your bioregion is an important piece in the process of establishing a connection to the earth, because it's the part of the earth where you and people you love spend your lives, where you dream and work and experience the passage of time. While Socrates admonished his pupils, "know thyself," more than two thousand years ago, today's eco-philosophers would more likely say, "know thy bioregion."

Learning Your Bioregion

How much do you really know about where you live? See how many of these questions you can answer without looking them up. If you can't answer some questions and decide to find out more, this list will take you a long way toward getting a sense of what's going on in your corner of the earth and how today's news stories—about global warming, oil and gas pipelines, GMOs, and the stability of the earth's food, water, and air resources—may be touching your life. The French philosopher Blaise Pascal said, "The least movement is of importance to all nature. The entire ocean is affected by a pebble." Every effort you make to understand the place you live in opens a door. Inside every door lies the gift of insight.

WATER
1. Where does your region get most of its water (reservoir, lake, river, or aquifer)? Has this always been your area's source of water? If not, what other sources has your area drawn from? What condition are those former water sources in now?
2. Get a map of your region and trace the water you drink, from precipitation to tap.

3. How long has it been since the main water lines in your neighborhood have been replaced? What are they made of (iron, stainless steel, clay, aluminum, PVC)?
4. Call your local water department to ask what chemicals are in your water.
5. How do you dispose of out-of-date prescriptions and over-the-counter drugs? What disposal practice does your water department recommend? Ask your friends how they get rid of their outdated pharmaceuticals.
6. How does your town rate the quality of your tap water?
7. What is the state of your area's water table? Healthy? High? Low? How long does your water department consider that your present water source will be sufficient for your town's needs?
8. How much rainfall did your area get last year? What about snowfall?
9. When was the last time your area endured a drought?
10. When was the last time a major fire burned in your area?
11. If there is a wildfire season in the bioregion where you live, how many wildfires have you had in the last five years? How many total acres were burned?

Trash

1. Where does your garbage go? How much of the methane coming from your city dump or landfill is being captured and recycled? How can you find out?
2. Where do your recyclables go?
3. In your town, is recycling a law, or is participation voluntary?
4. What are the rules about how it is to be presented for pickup (separated or not, contained in recyclable plastic, boxes broken down and tied, loose/not loose, and so forth)?
5. What day are recyclables picked up in your neighborhood?
6. For one week, weigh your trash—both garbage and recyclables. Make a list of ways you can begin to have less to throw out.

STUFF

1. Look at the clothes, shoes, bedding, and towels in your closets and drawers. How many come from outside the United States? Consider the travel miles involved.

2. Scientist Jane Poynter spent two years living inside Biosphere 2 outside Oracle, Arizona. After breathing clean, unpolluted air for two years, the first thing she noticed when she emerged into the earth's atmosphere in 1993 was, "People stink"—from all the chemicals we put on our bodies and clothes.[5] Identify the substances that you and members of your family use that contain any chemical additives: deodorant, perfume, hair spray and gel, aftershave, mouthwash, fabric softener, room deodorizers, laundry additives and detergents, toilet bowl cleaners, carpet fresheners, and so on.

ENERGY

1. What is the source for the electrical power and/or heat for your house or apartment?

2. If it's coal, where does your coal come from? If your coal supply is local, ask your utility company about the amount of CO_2 the plant injects into the atmosphere annually. How old is the plant? When is it due to be retired or retrofitted?

3. If it's nuclear energy—or you live near a nuclear power plant—where does the radioactive waste go? How old is the plant?

4. If it's natural gas, how far does it have to be piped to reach your neighborhood? How old are the gas lines? Does your gas come from fracked wells in your area? If so, how do they dispose of the fracking wastewater?

5. Do oil pipelines run through your neighborhood? If so, do they carry tar sands? How old are the pipelines?

6. Is any of your power from solar, wind, or geothermal technology? If so, by what percentage has it grown or declined in the last ten years?

7. Where is the closest wind farm or solar array to where you live? How much of your region's power comes from wind or solar?

8. If you own your home or condo, what would it cost in current prices to install one modern passive solar or photovoltaic (PV) solar panel on your roof?

WHO SPEAKS FOR YOU?

1. What are your local school board's plans on the greening of new or existing school buildings? How about civic buildings (police station, court building, firehouse, city hall, and others)?

2. What are the positions of your state and U.S. senators and representatives on alternative energy? What are their voting records? How much money have fossil fuel, nuclear, or "big ag" interests contributed to their campaigns?

YOUR LITTLE CORNER OF THE WORLD:
YOUR NEIGHBORHOOD

1. With two days' leeway, how many days has it been since the last full moon—or when is the next full moon?

2. Based on the various soil types, what soil series (sand, clay, and so on) is your home or apartment built on?

3. What is the industrial history of your area?

4. Name five native regional plants and the months that make up their growing season.

5. From what direction do winter storms, tornadoes, or hurricanes generally come in your region? Include all storm types that apply.

6. On the longest day of the year, when does the sun set where you live? What about the shortest day of the year?

7. Name five of the grasses that grow in your area. Are any of them native?

8. What spring wildflower is consistently among the first to bloom where you live?

9. Name five resident and five migratory birds in your area. When do they nest and produce young?
10. What primary ecological event or process determined the landform of your town or city?
11. What species have become extinct in your area?
12. From where you're reading this, point north.
13. What direction does your head point when you sleep?
14. Point to where the sun rises on your residence.
15. How many people live in your city or town? In general, is the population increasing or decreasing?
16. According to EPA standards, what is the air quality in your town, on average? How many days last year were environmental alerts issued?
17. What are the local or county regulations regarding the use of pesticides in parks and public areas? In yards? On farms? Golf courses? Are any warnings required for their use?
18. Do highway departments in your city and county use chemical pesticides and/or fertilizers on the green areas (medians, exits, greenspaces) along public highways and roads? If so, what kind? What do you know about their long-term effects on humans, animals, birds, insects, and the soil? (Hint: google them.)

Food

1. What are the main agricultural products of your region?
2. How long is your region's agricultural growing season?
3. If applicable, when are corn and wheat harvested in the summertime?
4. Although there are currently no state laws mandating it, does your state permit GMO labeling? (How to find out: go to a store that sells organic foods and see if there are "no rBGH" or "no rBST" or "no growth hormone" labels on containers of milk or cream.)
5. Where are the closest farmers' markets in your area? What months of the year are they open?

6. Do you belong to a CSA or food co-op? Do you know how to find one in your neighborhood or town?

7. Do you know how to plant and tend to a vegetable or herb garden? How to grow one without chemical pesticides or fertilizers?

8. Do you know how to start and maintain an organic compost heap?

9. Can you name at least two farmers who raise organic meat or grow organic vegetables or wine grapes near you?

10. Do you know how to shop for fresh, chemical-free produce?

11. Where did your last purchase of fresh fruit come from? How about the ingredients for your next salad? The last vegetables you served? If your produce came from other countries, what do you know about their food safety laws?

12. A "locavore" is someone who eats food that comes from within about one hundred miles of home. Become more aware of how you nourish yourself. Begin by taking stock. Examine the contents of your cupboard, refrigerator, and freezer. Note how many items come from more than one hundred miles away.

13. Contact the office at a neighborhood school and track the ingredients of a typical lunch. How much of the food is processed or otherwise includes GMOs? How much is fresh and local? Organic?

The quieter you become, the more you are able to hear.
—RUMI

Waking Up: Learning to Listen

"The human heart," says Yale theologian and ecologist Mary Evelyn Tucker, "is waiting to participate in dialogue with the earth. The human soul is poised to recover the language of the sacred that brings us back into contact with the great rhythms of the natural world."[6] Richard Louv writes that we should no longer think of being limited to just the five senses of taste, hearing, sight, smell, and touch. Today, scientists postulate that we have as many as thirty, "including blood-sugar levels, empty stomach, thirst, joint position, and more."[7] Really listening means being able to hear deeply—and that requires teaching ourselves listening as a skill. Fortunately, nature offers us many ways to do that. Here are some suggestions.

1. Watch the movie *Into Great Silence.* Note: When you watch it, don't think your television is muted. As the title suggests, it invites you into a relatively sound-free world, especially in the first half. If you watch it with someone, agree to not speak during the film. Make sure your phones are turned off. Give yourself the chance to emulate the experience of monastic life. What resistance do you notice? Jot these down in your journal.

2. Find a nearby nature space that you love that you can use in some of the practices listed.

3. Learn to be patient with yourself, not just because it helps slow you down (which helps you see more clearly) but also because it's practical and healthy. Being patient helps keep you grounded and present to your practice. As the Buddhist master Thich Nhat Hanh advises, "In order to understand, you have to take the time to look deeply and to listen deeply." Give yourself time to let things unfold naturally. Otherwise, you can exhaust yourself. Learn the pacing that's best for you. Honor your spiritual "bandwidth."

4. Learn yoga, tai chi, or chi gong to become more attuned to the way your body speaks to you. Each of these practices helps you identify how energy flows in your body when you are relaxed and not distracted.

5. Set aside a small space that can become your altar. Add things that you cherish, that nurture your spirit: snapshots; icons or statues; likenesses of religious or spiritual figures; stones; shells; crystals; candles; a bundle of sage and a

receptacle in which to burn it; a child's baby shoes or gradu-
ation photo; a souvenir from a sacred space you visited; a
bottle of holy water; a prayer bookmark; books of poetry,
prayer, or inspiration that you value. The list is a personal
one. Prepare it with the reverence appropriate to a sacred
space. This will be where you can meditate or pray, a place
from which you draw spiritual strength and sustenance. If
space allows, you can adorn it with a prayer shawl, a scarf,
or a small gong; play some sacred music or include some
recordings of nature sounds; and add a chair and a lamp.

6. Find a quiet place outside where you feel perfectly safe. Put
a sleep mask or dark material over your eyes. Sit upright
and breathe. Pay attention to how your senses come alive.
What do you hear and smell, what makes your ears prick
up, your skin react? What does the air feel like? Discover
how quickly your perception shifts and awakens your innate
ability as a human to hear deeply. Listen to your heart beat
and your lungs inhale and exhale.

Looking + Listening = Seeing

Author Sue Monk Kidd was facing a dark period at midlife,
feeling constricted by the life she thought she'd always wanted
to lead and bereft at the emptiness she felt. Culminating in
what she described as "holy quaking" jarring her into action,
she took a walk one cold winter afternoon, finally settling with
dark, brooding thoughts on a park bench. As the wind blew,
her attention was drawn to a tiny chrysalis hanging at the tip
of a dogwood branch. Knowing instinctively this was a sign
she should pay attention to, she broke the twig and brought
its prize home. As she spent months watching the cocoon go
through its stages of transformation, she went through a transformation of her own.[8] She was struck by what writer John
Shea said: "When order crumbles, mystery rises."[9]

The caterpillar encases itself with a cocoon and waits, and

while it waits, its transformation includes an absolute meta-morphosis into another creature with entirely different DNA. It dissolves into its destiny, and what it becomes is nurtured by what it was. The budding butterfly feeds off the goo that the caterpillar dissolves into. At the appointed time it will slice open its cocoon, climb out, dry its wings, pump them up, and fly away. Within that cocoon, the caterpillar dies to its old life to enable its new form. It cannot rush the transformation or outguess the wisdom of its timing. If transformation is what we seek in the world, we have to begin with ourselves. Mahatma Gandhi understood this when he said, "Be the change you want to see in the world." You can change nothing but yourself, but changing yourself is everything.

Biodynamics: The Earth's Healing Power

On a trip back to the family farm of his youth in August 2009, Nicholas Kristof wrote about the spiritual downside of modern industrial agriculture. By turning farms into assembly lines of efficiency and animals into commodities, he said, we have lost something precious. "It's not just that it produces unhealthy food, mishandles waste and overuses antibiotics in ways that harm us all. More fundamentally, it has no soul."[10]

In 1922, a Hungarian-born cultural philosopher, architect, sculptor, and mystic named Rudolf Steiner had not only made the same observations, but, because he was adept at hearing and seeing how the earth worked, he had built a new theory of agriculture around that very thesis. Steiner was a popular lecturer on a wide variety of topics, including those that focused on the ways plant growth is affected by spiritual and cosmic influences. Besieged by requests from farmers concerned about the declining health and viability of their seeds and soil and the declining quality of their food crops, Steiner agreed to help them. In 1924 in Silesia, Germany (now Poland), he delivered a series of eight foundational lectures on a new principle of agriculture he called "biodynamics." He talked about how the health of the soil was a key piece in the health of the food chain. Sick soil meant sick food, sick animals, and sick people.

Steiner, who by then was in his sixties, had been talking about these principles of holism and the importance of practicing them for decades. During the lectures, one of his students rose to ask why so many people, even given the specificity of his solutions, found it so hard to stick to the practices.

Steiner responded simply, "This is a problem of nutrition. Nutrition as it is today does not supply the strength necessary for manifesting the spirit in physical life. A bridge can no longer be built from thinking to will and action. Food plants no longer contain the forces people need for this."[11]

To Steiner this was already old stuff. Even then—nearly a century ago—our food lacked soul. And lacking soul, it failed to nourish us on all the levels critical to our survival—both physical and spiritual. What was true then is more radically true now. What Steiner discovered was one way back from that invisible but potent truth. What we needed was a way to confront our spiritual starvation and heal it. Happily, that path back to health would also reconnect us to the roots of our very life force and what might be called the next step in our spiritual evolution.

Biodynamics comes from the Greek for "life" (bios) and "energy" (dynamis). It is a farming technique that employs spiritual and physical farming practices and, although it's similar to organic farming in that it does not use any type of chemical fertilizer or pesticide, it has a different philosophy, seeing farming as a closed, self-nurturing system of soil, plants, and animals. It practices the restoration and healing of the earth and working in cooperation with its natural cycles, with the farmer playing a key role as a humble and informed steward. Seeing the earth as a living organism and a part of an intelligent, living cosmos, biodynamic agriculture observes the celestial rhythms of the moon and sun for planting and harvesting and for making what are called the nine biodynamic preparations.

> *To live, we must daily break the body and spill the blood of Creation. When we do this knowingly, lovingly, skillfully, reverently, it is a sacrament. When we do it ignorantly, greedily, clumsily, destructively, it is a desecration.*
> —WENDELL BERRY[12]

Each preparation has a specific healing role, from the specially prepared manure to the finely ground quartz meal of silica powder to the ancient medicinals—yarrow blossoms, chamomile blossoms, stinging nettle, oak bark, dandelion flowers, valerian flowers, and horsetail. Some, such as valerian flowers and horsetail, are used as compost sprays. Others are buried in the earth for six months to a year to decompose. When dug up, each performs a different, significant role in the healthy decomposition of the compost and in the treating of the soil and plants during the growing season.

Biodynamics is designed to heal and empower the immune system in every molecule of soil and plant life, to waste nothing, and to be a fully sustainable system. A biodynamic farmer's aim is to understand the laws and forces of nature and to work in harmony and cooperation with them to cure the soil naturally of the toxins that have been deposited in it—and heal our own hungry, disconnected spirits in the process.

> *Harmony with land is like harmony with a friend;*
> *you cannot cherish his right hand and chop off the left.*
> *That is to say, you cannot love game and hate predators;*
> *you cannot conserve the waters and waste the ranges;*
> *you cannot build the forest and mine the farm.*
> *The land is one organism.*
> —ALDO LEOPOLD[13]

Findhorn: Mother Nature as Miracle and Mystery

On a snowy November day in 1962, three people in north-eastern Scotland took a bold step that changed their lives and set the world thinking differently about how humanity might be able to relate to nature. It was only two months after the publication of *Silent Spring* set the world blinking with disbelief about something called DDT, and only days after the Cold War powder keg called the Cuban Missile Crisis had ended in the United States, introducing more than a decade of revolution and unrest.

The trio, Peter and Eileen Caddy and their friend Dorothy Maclean took up residence—along with the three Caddy children—in a thirty-foot travel trailer to begin a simpler life, one that connected them not to business and the making of money but to restoring beauty and love to the planet. Although Peter built a tiny annex for Dorothy, for the next seven years the six of them effectively shared this space.

In the prior five years, Peter Caddy, a former RAF squadron leader, had enjoyed the good life as the manager of a large hotel in nearby Cluny Hills. During his tenure, the hotel had prospered; it had been elevated from a three-star to a four-star rating. He and his family lived in the lap of luxury, enjoying all the amenities of a resort hotel, complete with a full five-course dinner each night. Their future seemed secure. Yet by 1962, Caddy was unemployed, living on public assistance—the modern U.S. equivalent of about $600 per month—to feed his wife and children and their friend, on a spot he described as "surrounded by gorse and broom, sitting on sand between a rubbish dump and a dilapidated garage."[14] The area, overlooking the Firth of Moray, was called Findhorn Bay.

What followed for Peter, Eileen, and Dorothy was an adventure in faith. As hard as the next years were, they believed completely—being deeply spiritual people—that their lives were being led purposefully. Each night, Eileen rose at midnight and meditated for hours. She faithfully wrote down what came through to her, guidance that told them what they were being called to do—create a garden—and exactly how they were to do that, down to the tasks to be done each day and even what food and drink was best for them. The fact that none of them knew anything about gardening didn't seem to bother anyone.

With winter quickly advancing, they spent the next months preparing their garden space. Acting on guidance was nothing miraculous or new to them. They believed that during their years at the hotel that this same guidance had enabled Peter to raise the hotel's standing and triple its yearly income.[15]

Peter was to be the Adam in this Aquarian Garden of Eden, creating the structures they would need, procuring the materials and managing their labors. As they worked, preparing the ground for the spring planting, they began to be aware of an energetic and powerful connection to the soil. A few months after they had started their work in the garden, Dorothy, who had been the Cluny Hotel secretary, began to receive impressions in her meditations from the spirits in the garden. As she learned, there was a spirit, or "deva," for each kind of vegetable and fruit, for the trees, weeds, grass, sand, wind—every single element they were surrounded by. She passed this information along to Peter and Eileen. From these spirits, they learned how crucial it was to have complete cooperation and trust between humans and nature.

The soil on their windswept half-acre was an impossible mixture of sand, hard grass, and rock. It seemed a poor host in which to grow anything, much less a vegetable garden. Besides the seemingly barren sand, it appeared unlikely that anything could take root or survive, much less thrive, against the wind's constant barrage. Still they tilled their little patch and followed the guidance each of them was receiving, working the soil over and over, literally willing life into it. As Peter said, "Every square inch of soil was handled by each of us several times."[16]

They built fences and poured concrete walkways, all with raw materials that fell into their laps. It was hard and exhausting work. There were setbacks and corrections, but by May the first radishes, turnips, and lettuce were appearing. By the end of June, the garden was thriving. Neighbors gawked in disbelief at the appearance of a garden in such a hostile environment. They were witnessing the healing of the soil and the resulting health and vitality of new plant life.

During their second winter, Peter got permission from the park owner to rebuild the soil in the uneven, sloping area to the south of their garden, where they planted berry bushes and apple trees. During that growing season, they grew sixty-five different types of vegetables, twenty-one kinds of fruits and forty-two different herbs. But what was more significant was the size and vitality of what came out of their garden. In the second summer, one of their red cabbages weighed thirty-eight pounds, another forty-two. A single white sprouting broccoli plant was so large that the whole family ate cuttings from it for months. When it came time to pull it up, it was almost too heavy to lift out of the ground.

> *With all visitors coming to Findhorn there was*
> *this kind of give and take: our technical knowledge was*
> *broadened, their spiritual horizons were extended.*
> —PETER CADDY

It began to occur to them that there was a bigger reason for their success, beyond beginner's luck. Perhaps, Peter thought, "something spectacular was needed to draw attention to our garden, to pave the way for a time when we might openly talk about our conscious cooperation with devas and nature spirits"—something they were not yet openly discussing. "People thought us strange enough as it was." With the eye-popping bounty growing out of little more than sand, rumors of this unlikely garden began to draw attention. A soil analysis by the county horticultural adviser proved that the thin and unlikely looking soil was, in fact, perfectly balanced. Support from Sir George Trevelyan and Lady Eve Balfour (author of *The Living Soil,* a groundbreaking book on the interrelatedness of all life and humanity's need to honor that link) helped begin conversations about topics that people had previously not felt comfortable discussing.

Here were these rank amateurs getting vegetables and trees to grow where logic said they could not and in a climate that most believed was forbidding—though the soil was somehow perfectly balanced and the vegetables thrived, growing in unmatched size and quantity. All of this was happening in a world just waking to the fact that all was not well with its air, soil, and water because of the amount of the contamination being dumped upon it. Here was quiet unmistakable proof that human beings working in cooperation with the forces of nature could achieve miracles.

The ancients, of course, accepted the kingdom of nature spirits without question as a fact of direct vision and experience. The organs of perception of the super-sensible world have atrophied in modern man as part of the price to be paid for the evolving of the analytical scientific mind.
—Sir George Trevelyan,
writing about the phenomenon he witnessed at Findhorn

In 1969, a U.N. agricultural expert and agriculture professor, R. Lindsay Robb, visited Findhorn just before Christmas and quickly realized something besides dedicated gardening was responsible: "the vigor, health and bloom of the plants in the garden at midwinter on land which is almost a barren powdery sand cannot be explained by the moderate dressings of compost, nor indeed by the application of any known cultural methods of organic husbandry. There are other factors and they are vital ones."[17]

Those vital factors—the communication and cooperation with nature via each participant's intuition or inner guidance—continued to make Findhorn a destination for spiritual seekers and garden enthusiasts, drawing horticultural experts and teachers from around the world. In 1970, eight years after Findhorn's humble beginnings, American spiritual philosopher and teacher David Spangler was invited to help envision its future. During the next three years, Findhorn's role would grow from that of garden to an education center, fulfilling the role of the keepers of wisdom—to learn by living and then teach their lessons to others. It was time for Findhorn to move into its next stage of growth, into the education of the human consciousness and what Peter Caddy termed "the transformation of the human soul."

Now, looking back, a clear pattern and plan can be discerned,
each apparent challenge seen as teaching the perfect lesson.
A man quite untutored in the techniques of gardening was
placed in this unpromising terrain and challenged to create a
garden. He was provided with all the necessary channels and
situations necessary to revive in him the
spirit of true cooperation with nature, under the guidance
of the God within. And the garden grew.
    —PETER CADDY

In the half century since, as Peter Caddy sensed, Findhorn's identity has continued to evolve, its history and humble beginnings serving as the healing foundation for everything that has been built upon it since. It did evolve into a place of leadership in the teaching of human consciousness and the transformation of the soul. In 1997 Findhorn was given official NGO status by the United Nations. Today, it is a famed source of wisdom and education, an experiential learning center that lives its creed—to discover what it truly means to live an ecological, sustainable, and responsible life in the twenty-first century. Its community has the lowest ecological footprint in the industrialized world (half the average energy usage in the United Kingdom). Its Living Machine, the first sewage treatment facility of its kind in the United Kingdom, cleans wastewater without chemicals by filtering it through a greenhouse, where bacteria, plants, and various aquatic animals purify the water. It has received a Best Practice designation from the United Nations Centre for Human Settlements.

Having grown way beyond the half-acre garden that its three founders launched, the Findhorn Ecovillage not only contains the original trailer park, but also a campus—the former Cluny Hill Hotel—as well as an arts center, a publication company, a bakery, and other facilities. It provides two hundred classes each year to community members and visitors. Its membership now numbers three to four hundred people at any given time. The ecovillage contains other similar-minded organizations, including Trees for Life, the nonprofit whose aim is to repopulate the ancient Caledonian Forest in Scotland and the Moray Steiner School (one of 890 Steiner schools in the world), which practices the educational tenets of the philosopher and father of biodynamics, Rudolf Steiner.

"In a period where there is a lot of hand wringing and disempowerment, [Findhorn] is a project where people have moved beyond the politics of protest to actually create something that models what they would really like to see. That is in a sense a model of what the world could look like if we pull all our different images of sustainability into one place."[18]

In the foreword to a book written by the Findhorn Community in 1975, the poet and cultural historian William Irvin Thompson wrote about Findhorn's timely, powerful, and gentle legacy, how—with patient hands and open hearts and minds—a few people put us back in touch with a deep connection we had forgotten we had.

Whether we speak of kachinas, devas, djin, angels or sprites, we are invoking a cosmology that is much the same around the world. Industrialization tried to drive that cosmology out of men's minds, but now that the failure of the Green Revolution has dramatized the failure of the industrialization of agriculture, the underground traditions of animism can surface without any sense of embarrassment. It is the proponents of the agro-industry who need to be shame-faced now.

The landscape of the New Age is not a regressive Crunchy Granola fantasy of nineteenth-century American agrarian life. We are not going back to what Marx called "the idiocy of rural life"; we are going back to nature with the consciousness of civilization behind us and the adventure of planetization in front of us.

Modern man knows how to talk back to nature, but he doesn't know how to listen. Archaic man knew how to listen to wind and water, flower and tree, angel and elf. There is a weakness to bigness and power, and all the little cultures have returned to tell us that.[19]

Beginning an Earth-Based Spiritual Practice

At the beginning of his organization's training seminar, Climate Reality Project founder Al Gore defines the environmental crisis as both a moral and a spiritual crisis. "Whether or not you are religious, you have a spiritual life."[20] Connecting with nature works seamlessly with a personal spiritual practice. A spiritual practice is just that: a regular commitment to spend time nurturing your own spiritual life. It is a form of ritual that helps ground you and keep you connected to the sacred in your life, to the bigger cosmos of which you and everything else are a part.

A spiritual practice is a singular and personal commitment. It must fit your own spiritual needs. Its power is in its regularity and the sincerity of your commitment, not in how much time and energy you put into crafting it. It can be as simple as a pause for prayer at some point in the day. Some find it most meaningful to start each morning (or end each day) with a short inspirational reading followed by a few minutes of prayer or meditation. Others commit to regular service to others, either on a global or local scale. While it's helpful to start with someone else's ideas of what this practice should consist of—like spiritual training wheels—with time and dedication, your own sense of what you need will rise.

There are as many ways to reconnect with the earth as there are people on the planet. Each of us has a unique link, like an energetic fingerprint. Beginning a spiritual practice is a serious undertaking. Set aside a moment each day for prayer or meditation to help get your left brain out of the way and make room for your spiritual senses to engage. You're about to engage in a process of mystery, so take a moment to let your focus drift. These practices are meant to help reconnect you to the earth you came from, to awaken you to the life you have been given, to make you more conscious. The more conscious you become, the more consciously you can contribute.

Begin with the following prayer (you can substitute "heaven" or "the universe" or "divine spirit" or another form of address for "God" if you wish). "God, let me hear you call me. Show me the reason you gave me life at this time and in this place. Let me know the way I am being called to serve. Help me listen. Thank you. Amen."

Getting Started: Reconnecting to the Earth

Reconnecting to the earth also reconnects you to your senses, the nature that is always in you. When you turn your senses over to nature, it heightens your awareness of everything. This list will help you get started. Use one for awhile then switch to another, rotate a few, or stick with one you like. Find what works and feels right. There's no wrong way to do this. This process helps you discern what's comfortable and do-able for you. Add to this list as new ideas or variations arise.

1. A perfect way to start: David Suzuki's thirty-by-thirty challenge. Spend thirty minutes outside for thirty straight days. Walk, run, explore, or just sit out in nature, and let it have its way with you. Reconnecting with the earth is just plain good for you. As his website shows, scientific research proves that after just two minutes, being in nature begins to relieve stress; within two hours, your memory and attention span improve; and after two days in nature, cancer-fighting white blood cell levels increase by as much as fifty percent.

2. On your nature walk, see if you can identify three trees. Stumped? No worries, there's an app for that: Leafsnap (http://leafsnap.com) is an "electronic field guide" that lets you take a picture with your smart phone and dig into a database that will eventually include all tree varieties in the continental United States.

3. Branch out and be with nature at night. It's a whole other world. Note how your nonvisual senses perk up.

4. As part of your practice, spend a few minutes each day with books of daily meditations or prayers. These help center and

ground you. When possible, be out in nature when you read or listen to these.

5. Develop a walking meditation practice. How often have you solved a problem or received an inspiration just by walking quietly by yourself? Why? Because outside, when you are in contact with the earth, you are closer to your own life source, a wisdom as old as time itself. We might not be able to say why, but we crave it and feel ourselves calm down and relax when we are within its energetic grasp. Creating a walking meditation allows you to engage this connection, to give your intention to it, to invite it in and be totally present to its healing grace. As the Buddhist master Thich Nhat Hanh affirms, the rules are simple. Have no goal. Just let yourself be happy as you walk. "Each step brings you back to the present moment which is the only moment you can be alive." *Suggestion:* google "walking meditation" for YouTube videos or read his book, *The Long Road Turns to Joy: A Guide to Walking Meditation.* Note what rises as you walk. What sorts of things cross your mind? Note these in your journal.

6. See what is happening to the world near you. Consult a county map and trace where the waste output from a nearby industrial plant (food processing, clothing, bottled water or equipment manufacturer, coal or nuclear plant, etc.) dumps out into a river or stream. If you can, follow it to where it empties. Sit by that site. Close your eyes and concentrate on your breathing. Listen.

7. Native American James Gosling was asked what it was like to go to an area that has had its timber clear-cut: "I couldn't breathe," he said. "It was as if the earth had been skinned. I couldn't believe anyone would do that to the Earth."[21] Go to an area that has been clear-cut. Sit by that site. Close your eyes and concentrate on your breathing. Listen.

8. Scientist David Suzuki says, "From our first cry announcing our arrival on Earth to our very last sigh at the moment

of death, our need for air is absolute. Every breath is a sacrament, a sacred ritual." Go to a botanical garden and breathe the oxygen it produces. Think of how the trees in that enclosed space are silently converting carbon dioxide to oxygen and how dependent each of us is on their survival for our own survival.

9. Go online or call your state parks department and find the closest state park. Spend time sitting in the midst of greenery and trees. Sit under a tree and close your eyes. See how many sounds you can identify. What does the air smell like? What does the wind sound and feel like? Pay attention to how your body feels. What part of your body responds to the experience?

10. When the naturalist John Muir first laid eyes on what one day would be named Yosemite National Park, he was so stunned by its beauty that he would spend much of the rest of his life tirelessly working to expand its territory and save it from the encroachment of developers. His passion about what he called "the heart of the world" was one of Theodore Roosevelt's inspirations for creating our national park system. If you can, visit one or more of the sixty-two U.S. National Parks. Spanning more than ninety million protected acres, these national sanctuaries are perfect spots in which to immerse yourself in nature, slow down, and listen to your life. Many have campgrounds and/or cabins. If you can spend the night, do so. Give yourself time to let the sounds, smells, and rhythms of nature that are unique to each park filter into your consciousness. (If you want to learn more about the evolution of our parks system, watch the 2009 PBS documentary series by Ken Burns, *The National Parks: America's Best Idea*.)

11. If a state or national park is too inaccessible, sit in a garden or a wooded area, on the seashore, or just on a porch, park bench, dock, or any other place where you can be outside in relative quiet. With your eyes closed, let the sounds seep

into you. Note how your breathing slows and your stress level declines.

12. Take a walk every day that you can. Set aside the time as a discipline. Turn your phone off or leave it at home. Listen instead to the sounds that fill each block as you walk. This is the environment you live in—your bioregion. It keeps you alive. You are part of one another. Feel that.

13. Go hunting with a camera or a tape recorder. Take pictures that record your experience. Set your tape recorder near a lake or a stream and record the sounds. Share on your website or social networking sites.

14. Sit on a porch or under a safe overhang during a rainstorm and feel the power of the electricity in the air, the storm's rhythm, how the earth absorbs the sounds of thunder, how the fury and wind eventually settle into rain, how the air feels afterward, how the sounds change. Feel how your body responds.

15. If you live where there is snowfall, go outside briefly each hour during a snowstorm to see how slowly the snow turns the world clean and quiet. Notice how it alters the way your landscape appears and sounds, masking the landmarks that are so familiar to you during other times of the year.

16. Have a dawn and sunset practice outside in which you pay homage to your life, to the air you breathe into your lungs, and to the earth that sustains you. Thomas Merton referred to sunset as a moment in nature that is a kind of Sabbath of the body, a brief period of sustained receptivity. The dawn and sunset of each day are sacred and mystical moments, short and filled with grace. Allow yourself enough time on each end to appreciate the few minutes' duration of each transformation. Thomas Berry said, "Our moments of grace are our moments of transformation." Think of them together as the completion of a cosmic breathing cycle: one inhalation, one exhalation. Allow yourself time to soak up and breathe in their sweetness.

17. At least once a month (when the moon is full or new, for instance), spend time gazing at the night sky, away from the city lights, if possible. When the moon is full, watch its trajectory. When it is new, appreciate the darkness of the sky, how regular and dependable life's cycles are. No matter how many times we look at the moon, no matter how many times we look at the stars, we are captivated, in awe, under a spell. Each of us is a little different every twenty-eight days. The moon's placement in the sky is a little bit different too. Even so, it has been the constant through time, through our own lives and the lives of everyone who came before us. The moon and stars have always been there, our tether to the past—and the future generations' tether back to us. It's our commonality. The Greek philosopher Heraclitus once said, "For those who are awake, the cosmos is one."

18. Go to the website of the Hubble Space Telescope (http://hubblesite.org) or to an observatory and see pictures taken by the Hubble Telescope to begin to appreciate how vast the cosmos is. Remember the Serbian proverb, "Be humble, for you are made of earth; be noble, for you are made of stars." This magnificent creation is what you are a part of.

19. Download NASA's free Earth Now app on your Apple or Android device and see up-to-date visualizations of how climate change is affecting our planet: choose a "vital signs" datamap of air temperature, sea level, water vapor, carbon dioxide (CO_2), carbon monoxide (CO), ozone levels, and more, with accompanying data and sources. Use your finger to spin the globe to get a 3-D 360-degree tour.

20. Practice gratitude. Take a gratitude walk in a place that you cherish. Talk to nature. Say thank you. Say a gratitude prayer when you wake up and before you go to sleep. You are breathing and alive. Find the gratitude there. The mystic Meister Eckhart said, "If the only prayer you ever say in your entire life is thank you, that will be enough."

21. Learn the birds indigenous to your area and watch for their

comings and goings. As you become more aware of the birds that visit you, you may also want to create a bird sanctuary, matching plants, trees, and bird feeders to the bird species that you want to draw to you. Make a daily ritual of putting out food and water for them. Go online and consult your local university agricultural extension service or local nature clubs to find out which trees or plants in your area attract particular types of birds, butterflies, and bees. Know that nature yearns to connect to you as you do to it.

22. Find a Buddhist or Catholic monastery near you that allows weekend retreats. Arrange for one (they are usually very modestly priced). While there, spend as much quiet time outside as you can. Leave your computer at home. Leave your to-do lists and your work at home. Leave your phone off as much as possible. Honor the healing stillness you have arranged to immerse yourself into. Some monasteries offer spiritual guidance during your time there. Consider arranging an appointment with one of the on-site community members during your visit.

23. Spiritual practice often stirs deep mystery in each of us. As time passes, you may begin to sense that you need to explore your own spiritual life more deeply. Begin working with a spiritual director or mentor—someone who is trained to help you learn to listen deeply—to help you recognize and understand the transformations and insights that will begin to unfold in your life. As spiritual director Jim Curtan says, "Enlightenment is an accident. Spiritual direction makes you accident prone." Having a good guide to accompany you is a gift. Each person's need dictates how often you meet, but once or twice a month is common. Don't let a director's location deter you from working with him or her. Many spiritual directors work mostly with in-office visits, while other directors live varying distances from their clients and work primarily via phone or online (using Skype or FaceTime, for example). Finding a director is an act of faith

and involves listening to your own inner guidance. If you have friends who work with a director, see if their director can recommend someone. Also ask at your place of worship or check with local archdioceses, synagogues, or churches. You may also inquire at Buddhist centers, yoga centers, or clinics that practice alternative and holistic medicine.

24. According to many indigenous societies, including Native American ones, everyone has a spirit animal. Determine what yours is. Learn about it. Invite that spirit to tell you how it has influenced your life and ask it to be present with you in your daily practices.

25. Bring a heightened awareness of trees into your life. Trees are our carbon sinks. They breathe in CO_2 and breathe out oxygen. They hold water and through their numbers determine what areas will get rainfall. Without them we could not live. Trees have long held sacred connections to spiritual beings. Think of Buddha and the Bodi Tree, Christ being crucified on a cross made of timbers, and the Tree of Life celebrated in the Jewish tradition. Trees are a compound connection with both the roots that dig into the earth and the branches that reach to the heavens. Find a tree in your landscape or nearby park that has caught your eye and visit it often. Speak to it, sit under it, touch it, tune into it, thank it. Enjoy how the sun filters through its branches and leaves. Lean against it while the wind blows and feel it move. Note what it smells like. Learn its branches and crevices. Honor it as a living thing, helping to fill your lungs with clean air.

26. Museums are full of the work of artists who have tried to capture the ephemeral, changing nature of art on canvases and in sculpture. Nature is elusive; it never stands still. There is a great tradition of using art in your landscape, of honoring nature's capacity to stir wonder and act as a canvas and backdrop for companion works of art that are manmade. Whether you fill your garden with solar lamps, gazing balls, angels, ornamental iron, sculpture, chimes,

shepherd's hooks, or ironworks, art is a beautiful way to enhance your landscape. It can add perspective, harmony, balance, and charm. More importantly, art creates awe in us. "Art," says Matthew Fox, "is the only language we have for awe." The role of the artist, he says, is to teach us to "behold being, to go into grief, and show us the intrinsic power of creativity."[22]

27. In a nature space you love, practice some form of exercise that stresses mindfulness and regulated breathing, such as tai chi chuan or yoga. Being in nature when you practice such bodywork enhances the experience, bringing you closer to the earth. Tai chi, for example, is often called moving meditation. It encourages your body to enter into timeless flow. It is a present-time experience. You cannot practice its movements and be thinking about anything else or you will break your rhythm and lose your place. It is a practice that simultaneously inspires deep mindfulness, awareness of your balance and center, and the interconnectedness of the parts of your body and the heat of energy, or chi, moving through your body. This kind of slow, purposeful physical exercise done on the earth's surface could be described as mindfulness within mindfulness—or connection within connection—and it is a very powerful way to both honor and receive input from the earth.

28. During a nature walk or a time outside by yourself, engage in a practice that Richard Rohr teaches: find something in nature that represents the presence of God to you. Whatever form it takes—tree, bird, rock, wind, rain, animal—just acknowledge its presence and innate sacredness.

29. Make a habit, whenever possible, of doing your journaling in a quiet space outdoors. If you cannot be outside, try to locate yourself by a window (open, if possible), so you can at least look outside.

30. If you live near a cemetery where relatives are buried, visit it and tend to a loved one's grave. Spend time in the stillness

and ask your ancestors for guidance. If you do not, find a beautiful graveyard and meditate in its sacredness and stillness.

31. Get a massage out in nature. (For example, the Esalen Institute, in Big Sur in Northern California, is well known for offering massages in a spectacular cliffside setting.)

32. Abraham Joshua Heschel said, "Mankind will not perish for want of information, but for want of appreciation." We are the first generation to be disconnected from the stars and skies that humankind has always turned to in awe. Because of pollution and bright city lights, we are often cut off from the sight of the cosmos to which we belong. Whenever you can, do any of these practices under a full night sky and feel the moon and the stars above you and the earth beneath you. It completes a magical and mystical circle that each of us relates to without knowing why.

33. Find a labyrinth you can walk. Although ancient labyrinths also included square or rectangular shapes, modern labyrinths are most often circle formations composed of parallel paths that slowly wind toward the center and then wind back toward and exit near the entrance. Much like the practice of an internal martial art, which requires reverence, focus, and mindfulness, the act of walking a labyrinth takes you out of your day to day into something of an altered state. Walking a labyrinth is often seen as a symbolic journey inward and many find it a meaningful form of meditation, especially when you walk an ancient labyrinth, such as the famous labyrinth on the floor of the Chartres Cathedral in France, on which people have been walking in varying contemplative states since the thirteenth century. As sacred sites, ancient labyrinths are often the site of mystical insight and revelation and as such represent a potent cosmic force. If you need help finding one, google "find a labyrinth" (or go to http://labyrinthlocator.com) and select a labyrinth you would like to visit based on type, material, category (church,

art installation, farm, historic monument, etc.) and proximity to your zip code. If there is no labyrinth near you, contact a Catholic, Episcopal, or Unity church near you. They may know of one that is within a reasonable distance. You can also build a small-scale labyrinth in your garden or yard. Consult gardening books to help plan how to tier the plants to achieve the height and effect you want.

34. In your favorite nature space, pray. Pray for the healing of yourself, of friends, of the planet. Finish this sentence. "When my life is over, I want my legacy to the earth to be . . ."

35. Once you have found a nature spot that you hold dear, go there and offer a prayer in which you ask the earth's forgiveness. You can create a forgiveness prayer of your own or use the following one as a model. Practicing an act of contrition with humility and sincerity in nature is a sacred act of atonement and renewal.

Forgiveness Prayer

Every person on earth has helped contribute to the condition of our planet. Find a place in nature where you would feel comfortable reading this out loud to yourself. As you read, pause to look around you. The earth will hear you.

This request for forgiveness is dedicated to all of the earth, to all living sentient beings, as well as to all those no longer alive that we never knew, never mourned, and never championed. We ask on behalf of ourselves, as well as others who have gone before us or those who cannot yet speak for themselves.

Forgive us for our selfishness, for not seeing beyond our own blind sense of entitlement. Replace that with the sense of honor, awe, and connection we were born with and have lost. Help us see beyond our own immediate needs to the needs of future generations that are yet unknown to us. Let us be worthy of that stewardship.

Help us reconnect and rebuild our own shattered pieces back into a whole that is in union with you.

Forgive us for betraying you, for turning our backs on your anguish, for knowing better and doing the wrong thing anyway. Return us to a sense of integrity and intentionality. We long for a new generosity of spirit. Help us find it.

Forgive us our ego and arrogance, for looking you over and seeing you only for what we wanted for ourselves. We are visitors, guests on this planet. Help us remember to be humble and dependable caretakers. Fill us with a longing to leave you—the earth we came from—healthier than we found you.

Forgive us for the grief and loneliness we have caused, the feelings of disenfranchisement, vengeance, the loss of preciousness of what you represent in our lives. Help us find our place again and rekindle those feelings of recognition and joy that we have lost and long for.

Forgive us for our destructive addictions and thoughtless, expedient choices, for feasting carelessly at what we chose to believe was an endless and limitless trough, as if you were ours to devour without thought to anyone but ourselves or any time but ours. Help us gain the gift of wise choice, to be dependable gatekeepers of the gifts you hold ready to share with us.

Forgive us for not seeing clearly, for being unwilling to see or hear what was happening to you and to all of our fellow creatures. Help us use our gifted brains in balance both to learn the truth of what we have done and to intuit ways to begin healing. Help us see the way to support and celebrate those who champion you.

Forgive us for waiting so long to see the totality of what is unfolding around us. We have ignored so many voices, derided the wisdom of so many who tried to warn us. We seek now to find a path back to our sacred connection to the energy that is yours, to spend our days working in renewal and rebirth, to pour new, healing thinking into the collective, doing our small part in adding to a path that others can follow and then endow to those who follow them.

For all these things we most humbly ask for the courage and

wisdom we need to step into our new roles, as we strive to become both spiritually accountable and joyfully responsible in this new world unfolding before us.

As we end this prayer, we are mindful that forgiveness is a process that falls away from us in layers and that it must always begin with us forgiving ourselves.

Peace to each and all.

> *Forgiveness is the fragrance the violet sheds on the heel*
> *that has crushed it.*
> —Anonymous

Chapter 6

The Alchemy of Action

Action springs not from thought,
but from a readiness for responsibility.
—DIETRICH BONHOEFFER

O n some level, we know what we are being called to do. Each of us has a mystical fingerprint that identifies our life's calling and an inner music whose pull we cannot resist. That mystical fingerprint is unique and powerful. It beckons in a way that may be soft but is always undeniable. If we would listen—and look around—we'd find ourselves surrounded by others on the same journey of discovery, breathing together with us. The reason is simple—because, like you, as they looked around their lives and saw a need—they couldn't *not* act. This is often how our spirits wake us up, not with a shrill alarm, but with a sudden understanding of the simple but profound ways that calling shows up. And there are about seven billion ways it can reveal itself.

Everyone has been made for some particular work,
and the desire for that work has been put in every heart.
—RUMI

Knowing isn't enough; neither is being willing.
We must do.
—JOHANN WOLFGANG VON GOETHE

What Moves You?

Like a fingerprint, your earth calling is unique. Wherever you live and whatever your age, you were born for these times, and you are not traveling alone. And you have so many choices and entry points, the first dilemma is an easy one: just pick something and start. Everything you do will inform you about where you go next. The operative word is *do*. Act. Stretch yourself. Learn. Move. Get involved.

The universe abhors a vacuum and loves action. As Goethe said, it's great to know, to have the data and even wisdom at hand; it's also great to have a willing heart, but what ignites change is action. Action is any movement's oxygen and lifeblood.

So begin with a single question: What moves you? What makes your heart pound? What can you simply not look away from? What are you willing to risk? Rabbi Michael Lerner says that at times of social evolution, people often hang back from acting, because they don't want to be the first ones to move away from the tribe, to risk humiliation by acting too quickly. Not everybody is comfortable risking arrest to save a great tree from being felled or an oil pipeline from being built or a whale from being hunted. That's okay. Step into the waters slowly. Just get wet.

Some people like to march, others like to write letters to the editor or wield power as armchair activists with online networks. Others are "boots on the ground" networkers who are more comfortable making speeches, rallying people, negotiating with municipal authorities, mediating disagreements, or just keeping the pizza coming at planning meetings.

What are you good at? Are you a networker, a nurturer, a born leader, a visionary? Are you politically or socially connected or know people who are? Are you good at raising funds, compiling data, writing press releases, answering phones, assembling meals, handling logistics, hosting meet-ups, making signs, training others? Do you have computer and website management skills? Are you good at photography or shooting short videos and popping them up on social media sites? Make an honest assessment of what you have experience doing, are willing to do, or just want to learn. Then jump in. You'll find your place. There are thousands of nonprofits, NGOs, and green organizations that need dependable volunteers to handle the bulk of the day-to-day management of the business of climate activism.

As you serve, you will be served right back by a growing understanding of where you fit, so give it time and use your awakened senses for guidance. It will come. Everyone alive has a place at this table.

> *Let yourself be silently drawn*
> *by the stronger pull of what you really love.*
> —RUMI

Start with Dirt

Our cultural stories give us the central clue to why being grounded in the earth—particularly gardens—is so key to us. They represent innocence and wholeness, nurturing and security, tranquility and new beginnings, the centrality of life and its cycles of birth and death, stasis and reflection, hope and inspiration. They embody the promise of seed and fertility, the perpetuation of life, and even creation itself. Many cultures have creation stories that trace our physical origins back to the earth and its bounty: wood, cornmeal and seeds, even mud brought from the bottom of the ocean by a water beetle, or—according to the lore most familiar to Westerners—simple garden soil.

> *With the sweat of thy brow shalt thou eat bread*
> *till thou return to the Earth, for out of it wast thou taken,*
> *for soil thou art and unto soil shalt thou return.*
> —GENESIS 3:19

As the Bible describes, the first inhabitants in this divine creation were Adam (from the Hebrew *adama*, "earth" or "soil") and the product of his rib, Eve (from the Hebrew *hava*, "living"). As geneticist David Suzuki says, "Together they make the eternal connections: life comes from the soil; the soil is alive."[1] So our first identity as an earthling is literally that—a little being of earth.

Gardens are frequently spots where stories of spiritual unfolding occur. According to legend, it was while he was on his way to the garden of his parents that the young Buddha-to-be was struck by the suffering and fleeting nature of life and dedicated his life to the search for enlightenment. It was in the garden of Gethsemane that Jesus frequently congregated with his disciples. It was his sanctuary for prayer the night before his crucifixion. A garden is often seen as a place to rest and listen for guidance, a place to restore oneself.

Francis Bacon spoke of the divine signature present in the very idea of a garden: "God almighty first planted a garden: and, indeed, it is the purest of human pleasure." A garden is both a sacred undertaking and a source of joy. It's fun to feel the soil on your hands, to stand barefooted on the earth, to lie on the ground at night and look at the stars. There are many different kinds of gardens, and they all provide a type of nurturing—some for body, some for soul, some that do both.

We are stardust. We are golden.
We've got to get ourselves back to the garden.
—"Woodstock" (written by JONI MITCHELL)

Plant (or Help Tend) a Vegetable or Flower Garden

Start here, by getting your hands into the dirt. Remember that you are tending to the skin of Mother Earth. You are piercing it with an intention of love and healing. Whenever you fall to your knees in the garden to make it ready for planting, you are engaging in a form of supplication—the ultimate humble act—and when you dig your hands into the dirt, to turn it over, caress it, expose it to sun, and clean it up, you are living your intention and honoring your bond. That act is a hand-to-heart connection that ignites a bond with the earth and begins an alchemical process, a relationship, a partnership of shared healing.

Begin by looking at every little thing as sacred—because everything *is sacred* In the Talmud, there is a saying: "Every blade of grass has its angel that bends over it and whispers, 'Grow, grow.'" Every stone, every plant, every bird, every tree is sacred. Once you begin to look at nature differently, your entire field of focus shifts. Challenges that seem like roadblocks start to look different.

1. Pick your spot. It doesn't matter whether you start with a houseplant in your window or a plot of ground in your back yard.
2. Set your intention. Bless the space that you cultivate and invite the spirits of nature to be with you and guide you.
3. Promise to tend to the garden regularly as part of your spiritual practice.
4. Clean the area with reverence, as you would tend to the body of a loved one. Spray a biodynamic detox on it to help it heal from the contamination that has accumulated from chemical fertilizers and pesticides, loss of topsoil, and neglect. (Biodynamics is a fast growing but little understood philosophy about food and how it's grown; see chapter 5). *Note:* If you use this detox, you must never use chemical sprays, fertilizers, or pesticides on that soil or plant at any time after that. Biodynamics requires the conscious cooperation of the user with the laws and agreements with nature made by the person who created the mixture and sold it to you. (To find a biodynamics provider, search www.biodynamics.com. If you're looking for biodynamic herb and vegetable seeds, try http://turtletreeseed.org.)
5. Before you plant any seeds or transplant any seedlings, roll some organic cow manure into the prepared soil.
6. If you're planting food, plant heirloom or organic seeds and plants that have not been genetically modified. (You can also grow food from leftover food in your kitchen, such as

potatoes, onions, celery, leeks, and garlic. See http://wakeup
-world.com/2012/10/15/16-foods-thatll-re-grow-from
-kitchen-scraps for more information.)

7. Water when needed (look and listen). Touch the plants as
   they grow. Weed as necessary.

8. Minimize what you feel you have to buy to create your garden space. Use what you have, such as old stakes if your
   plants need support as they mature, and the tools and imple-
   ments you have used before. Don't waste money on prettify-
   ing the process. Spend it buying good-quality organic cow
   manure and healthy, unmodified heirloom seed stock.

9. Share what you grow. Compost what's left over. (Google
   "composting" for ideas on how to maximize your output; see
   the documentary *Symphony of the Soil.* You'll be amazed.)

10. Practice mindfulness and being present. Listen to the earth.
    Open your mind and heart to its guidance.

11. Keep a garden journal. Take pictures or, even better, shoot
    short videos to record your progress. Share them on your
    website or on social media sites like Facebook and YouTube.

> *In the garden more grows than the gardener sows.*
> —SPANISH PROVERB

Here's the divine paradox of the garden: When you work in the
garden, the garden works on you. Use your newly refined mindfulness and

- trust this process,
- trust there will be a connection,
- let its influence unfold in you.

This unfolding is the subtle way that the universe gives us direction. Through this process of covenant—of you making a sacred
agreement, then honoring it—you show yourself and creation that
you can be counted on, that you are sincere. By honoring your agreement, you learn to trust your own spiritual will and its capacity to

be dependable and disciplined. In short, it's how you build what Caroline Myss calls a "spiritual backbone."

Once you set that process in motion—once you put your hands into the earth, give it your sweat and love and attention, and nurture what rises out of it—something will shift in you. The influence of that connection you have reestablished only begins in the contentment you feel or the joy at seeing food or beautiful flowers begin to thrive under your stewardship. Depending on your own capacity to listen, there is no limit to what this process will stir up in you and how it will open your heart and inform you at subterranean levels.

Begin to think of a garden as an ecosystem. Consider what a natural multitasker Mother Nature is. As master gardener Toby Hemenway says, "Nothing in nature does just one thing."[2] A tree planted solely for shade performs many other services for a yard. It attracts pollinators—butterflies, bees, and other essential insects—provides food (nuts and fruit) and spaces for bird's nests, pulls groundwater into its roots, cleans the air by absorbing CO_2, and covers the ground with fallen leaves and twigs that form soil-enriching compost.

So too, a garden can offer food, herbs for healing and cooking, colorful flowers that lift our spirits and please our eyes (and also draw pollinating insects to continue the cycle of life). Fruit arbors not only give us delectable jams, healthy snack food, and wines but also serve as beautiful natural borders and accents to our yards. Gardens not only provide edible landscaping and a way to heal the piece of bioregion you live in, they can also be a space to spend time in, not just for weeding and tilling, but also for respite and healing.

Any time that you are participating in a process of creation that involves the earth, you are in a kind of cathedral, a sacred territory. If you can, visit some of our national gardens—our national parks and preserves. These warrant a special kind of respect.

Become personally invested in your bioregion, wherever you live. Every state has its own unique beauty, whether its primary feature is mountains, coastline, desert, woods, or prairies. Wherever you live, love what is local to you.

On the undersurface of every leaf a million movable lips are engaged
in devouring carbon dioxide and expelling oxygen.
—PETER TOMPKINS[3]

Plant a Meditation and Healing Garden

Consider why Zen gardens are so special and, in general, why gardens tend to be the sought-after sights for the healing that a quiet, peaceful space encourages. Being able to meditate in a natural setting, especially one you have helped to craft yourself, gives you an opportunity not only to connect with your earthly roots but also to hear where you are distracted and to learn discernment. You will begin to detect and differentiate the voice of your intuition and spirit.

Depending on how much space you have, or whether you support a community garden that also wants this option, a small, untrafficked spot can be set aside as a place where visitors can meditate or pray. Fill the space with healing and aromatic herbs and soft, welcoming plants (for example, lamb's ears, bunny tails, and ferns—plants that are soft or willowy—yellows, whites, lavenders, violets, and greens). There are hundreds of ways to lay out such a space, but typically they are built in circles, squares, or rectangles, flanked with trees or shrubs, a bird feeder or bath, and a fountain or other water element.

Meditation gardens can double as healing spaces. When you surround the space with flowers and healing herbs and set down flagstones to form a defined center, a person sitting on a chair or bench in that small courtyard can experience the sense of being surrounded by the healing power of nature. To complete the balance of the five elements, according to Chinese thought (earth, air, water, metal, and fire), add a piece of metal sculpture and some plants which represent the fire element—thistle, yucca, cactus, or nettle.

1. Consider how to convert your yard into what Michael Pollan calls an "edible landscape." Instead of having an ornamental

landscape that's merely beautiful to look at, make it earn its keep. Turn it into something that feeds more than the' eyes, blending flowers and food. Contact your local university's agricultural extension service for recommendations or classes or just google "edible landscape." Once you have mastered the concept, teach others.

2. As you get familiar with the seasonal rhythms of the earth in your own area, visit a neighborhood elementary school and volunteer to teach the children (and the teachers) how to cultivate a community garden.

3. Make a plan to restock your pantry, refrigerator, and freezer with food that contains no preservatives, chemicals, or processed ingredients (including anything containing high-fructose corn syrup or GM additives). Learn more about where you will find GMOs in the food that fills most grocery stores. *Your Right to Know: Genetic Engineering and the Secret Changes in Your Food*, by Andrew Kimbrell is a must-have reference book.[4]

4. If your state allows GMO labeling, ask the management at your regular grocery store to stop carrying dairy products that contain rBST or rBGH. If GMO labeling is against the law in your state, call your state and local representatives to register your displeasure, and go online to find out where you can join groups that have helped overturn so-called food-libel laws in other states.

5. Plan a potluck dinner, inviting everyone to bring food that comes within fifty miles of your town and is free of pesticides, chemicals, or GMOs of any kind. Find meat from animals not fed GM corn or raised in a CAFO (concentrated animal-feeding operation). Keep in mind that before the 1950s, this was the only kind of food that people ate.

6. Contact a local organic farm and volunteer to weed, pick crops, or sell produce for part of a day. Industrial agricultural farms are generously subsidized by the U.S. government. Volunteering offers local farmers a goodwill subsidy

that costs the taxpayers nothing, while it builds community and offers nonfarmers a way to show gratitude and to participate in the process that brings healthy, nourishing food into people's lives. Don't know where to start? Contact World Wide Opportunities on Organic Farms (www .wwoofusa.org or www.wwoof.net) to find out how you can volunteer to work with organic farmers locally or internationally to share knowledge and help create a global consciousness about the benefits of ecological farming. (If you are a farmer, you can also learn how to use your farm to host volunteers.)

7. Join an organic CSA (community supported agriculture). When you sign up with a CSA, you pay a farmer an annual subscription for the regular delivery (usually weekly) of fresh produce during the growing season. It's a way to invest in a steady stream of good, organic food from a local farmer and give him or her the security of regular income. The relationship benefits both parties. Besides getting good, reliably healthy food, you create a relationship with someone who grows what nourishes you and your family; you, in turn, help that farmer grow food on one more patch of ground that doesn't pollute the earth with chemical fertilizers or pesticides. (To find a CSA near you, go to www .localharvest.org.)

8. Find out what farmers' markets are near you and patronize them during the harvest months. These markets thrive through community participation. If possible, bring your friends and neighbors and make it a weekly celebration of what's being grown locally for you by people you actually begin to know. Farmers' markets are the best way to eat like a locavore. (To find out where your local farmers' markets are and many more resources that track the movement away from "fast," processed food to healthier, locally sustainable food, check out www.slowfoodusa.org, www.localharvest .org, and www.farmersmarket.com.)

9. Volunteer to organize an organic community garden in the yard of a church, school, or senior residence center—or in an abandoned lot or other open space that is not being utilized. Include edibles and flowers.

10. Replenish the earth's carbon sinks by replacing some of the trees being devastated by clear-cutting and disease. Give everyone's lungs the tiniest boost. You can buy trees from www.americanforests.org (as cheap as $1 per tree) and choose where you want them planted.

11. Add some non-GM trees to the planet by planting a tree farm (it's easy). The Arbor Day Foundation will ship your choices at the right planting time for your climate zone. Contact www.arborday.org for details.

12. Join "re-greening" organizations that plant shade trees and fruit orchards to counter CO_2 emissions. While many online sites offer you an opportunity to plant trees to supplement those being lost to tree harvesting or natural disaster, some organizations let you do hands-on work. There is no substitute for the experience of midwifing new growth going into the earth. Become a volunteer and offer to return at regular intervals.

13. Learn about the plight of the many endangered indigenous and healing plants that are being threatened in North America from United Plant Savers. Offer to work at their 360-acre botanical sanctuary in Ohio as a volunteer. (See unitedplantsavers.org to learn about interning opportunities and seminars available.)

14. If your local parks or greenspaces are sprayed with chemical fertilizers or pesticides, petition your park board to forbid their use. This is a form of what Andrew Harvey calls "sacred activism." Each human being on the planet can take personal responsibility for caretaking one piece of the earth that speaks to his or her heart: one creature, one tree, one piece of a habitat, one part of a vacant lot, one mountain footpath, one bend of a riverbed. Begin there.

15. Use organic pest remedies (google "organic pest remedies"). Here's one for aphids: fill a sixteen-ounce container with onion and garlic scraps. Top it up with warm water and let it sit in the sun for a couple of days. Strain out the scraps and bury them around the affected plant. Use the newly aromatic water to spray the plant leaves and stems.

16. Cultivate a flower garden of your own that offers a sanctuary for butterflies. Keep in mind that scale is not important. This can be a full-fledged garden whether you have acres of yard or one flowerpot on your fire escape or porch.

17. Plant milkweed! It's the stuff that butterflies thrive on and must have in order to carry out their yearly migrations (see sidebar).

18. Offer your newfound wisdom to others. Find ways to teach others how to do any of these practices—especially children. Show them how to plant and tend to a garden. Pass along what they can also pass along. This begins anew the traditions that honor the earth.

19. Teach dog and cat owners how to fertilize their yards without using chemical pesticides and fertilizers that can injure and kill their animals.

20. The geneticist and ecologist David Suzuki says, "One way or another, we are Earthenware." Earth frames our cradle-to-grave life cycle. It is our life source. Take a pottery class to learn how to throw pots and create with earthen materials. During the wintertime, if you cannot get outside easily or the weather is too inclement, keep some earthen clay on hand to mold. Keep it in an airtight container and save the scraps. Working with clay is a powerful way to help keep you connected to the earth.

21. Is that tuna you're eating the good kind? What about that farmed salmon or tilapia? If you enjoy seafood, find out where it came from. Many species have been harvested nearly to extinction. Make a decision to eat only those fish that are sustainably caught or raised. Sea Choice provides a card

that lists sustainable choices and what should be avoided (www.seachoice.org/wp-content/uploads/2012/04/SC _card_2012_5panel_web.pdf). Let your seafood supplier know you want the details.

22. Stay aware! By the summer 2013, persistent CO_2 readings of 400 ppm were recorded at Mauna Loa in Hawaii. (You can plot ongoing change in CO_2 concentrations at http://keeling curve.ucsd.edu/ and on Twitter @keeling-curve.)

23. Want to move beyond growing vegetables? Try keeping bees or chickens! With bees, you'll be helping out our most dogged pollinators, and with chickens, you can be assured of great manure for your garden and fresh eggs to boot. Ask at your local city or village hall to see if they're allowed. Then get busy. Online resources for beekeeping and growing poultry abound.

24. Periodically take a day off and appreciate that progress is being made. No lasting social change happens overnight. Even if some days see dramatic action (say, with the fall of the Berlin Wall), often it takes years to make that one day happen. Generations of people put their energy into creating that change. Many of them did not live to see the change they were working for (think of Martin Luther King, Jr.). There are so many issues facing us earthlings these days, it can feel overwhelming. So pace yourself. Take a day or a week to recharge. Get a massage. Go on a picnic. Watch a movie that makes you double over with laughter. Make a date with a loved one. Your causes will survive without you for a while, and the pause will help invigorate you.

25. If you're looking to know more about all things organic, from political food happenings to great tips on seeds, organics, and GMOs, check out the Organic Consumers Association (http://organicconsumers.org) and the many listings in the table at the end of this chapter.

26. Start or join a community garden. Information can be found at the Let's Move website (www.letsmove.gov/

community-garden-checklist) or through the American Community Gardening Association (www.community garden.org). You can also see their Facebook page for up-to-date information.

27. Watch *Chasing Ice*. It's the single best way to understand what's happening with our polar icecaps and the Greenland ice sheet. If you can't find the movie, google "James Balog" for a brief lecture on YouTube that will feature most of the more shocking moments in this incredible documentary (www.youtube.com/watch?v=bAbDDA3otfc is a good one).

28. Stumped about how to respond to climate change deniers? If *Chasing Ice* doesn't work, take them (or just go yourself) to the Climate Reality Project's site for dispelling myth (https://realitydrop.org or @RealityDrop on Twitter).

> *Maybe we want to start thinking of trees as part of our public health infrastructure.*
> —U.S. Forest Service researcher

Create a Monarch Waystation

We need our pollinators. A third of our food comes from plants, so without butterflies, bees, bats, wasps, and others, we'd have a lot less to eat. Monarch butterflies are particularly in danger because they are losing key elements of their ecosystems due to land development (in the United States, six thousand acres of land are converted to development daily), mowing, and pesticide spraying by highway departments. During the breeding season, monarchs need milkweed plants—which provides adults with the nectar they need during reproduction and which they use to rear their larvae. Monarchs also need nectar sources to fuel their long migration to and from Mexico, and over the winter, they need shelter and water. All of those resources are being lost to development and to chemically intensive agriculture. By creating a monarch waystation, you help these critical pollinators make their long journeys each spring and fall. All you need is some seed or milkweed plants (easy to get) and a little attention, and Mother Nature will take care of the rest. And, lucky you, you'll get to see your hungry visitors twice a year. (There are a number of resources, such as http://monarchwatch.org, www.fs.fed.us/wildflowers/features/panels/ManisteeMonarchWaystation.pdf, and the popular Milkweeds for Monarch Waystations page on Facebook: https://www.facebook.com/pages/Milkweeds-for-Monarch-Waystations/595805343782652.)

If we surrendered to Earth's intelligence,
we could rise up rooted, like trees.
—RAINER MARIA RILKE

Be a Conscious Consumer

Our hyperconsumerism is clearly one of the major roadblocks to sustainability. While it's obvious that recycling paper and plastic and composting our coffee grounds won't solve the climate crisis (in fact, modifying our consumer habits should be the bare minimum we expect of ourselves), everyone has to begin somewhere, and even small acts wake us up to bigger truths.

At Home

There are hundreds of ways to reduce (and even pay for) your carbon footprint. The obvious ones include keeping your car tuned up, turning your thermostat lower in the winter (wear layers, make your body work a little) and higher in the summer (use fans and cross-ventilation and hydrate yourself), turning off power strips (and your computer) at night, having your house graded for its energy efficiency, and so forth. As they need replacing, begin to buy energy efficient appliances (as well as cars, lawn equipment, HVAC units, and water heaters). Before long, they will be the only models you'll find available, so why not be ahead of the curve.

1. In the grocery store, choose items with less packaging. Packaging is not only wasteful, it also adds to the item's cost. If it's too bulky, write the manufacturer and suggest they become more eco-conscious. If you see grandiose packaging at your grocery store, mention it to customer service. And be sure to thank them if they just happen to be getting it right.

2. Get in the habit of taking your own leftover paper bags, cloth shopping bags, and soft coolers to the grocery store with you. (And unless you are unlike most mortals, put them inside the car rather than the trunk, so you don't forget them.) If you still have a supply of paper and plastic bags from the days you weren't eco-conscious, recycle the ones you're not using.

3. Think twice before shopping at big box stores. Determine whether you're really saving by buying larger quantities, especially items with a limited shelf life.

4. Learn to compost your food waste and find out what works best—raw vegetable and fruit scraps, yes, leftover stew, no (unless you do vermicomposting).[5] See the documentary *Symphony of the Soil* for some great wisdom on composting.

5. Patronize restaurants (and food trucks!) that use organic and locally grown food (and encourage others to start using such foods). Organic growers use fewer fossil fuels than conventional farms because they don't use petroleum-based herbicides or pesticides. Ask if a restaurant's fresh fish and seafood is farmed or wild (in general, wild is better, but be sure it's a sustainable fish choice).

6. Wean yourself from paper products. Try going a week without paper towels or plates (use real ones). If you use disposable diapers, consider that according to a study by the Union of Concerned Scientists, about eighteen billion disposable

diapers (serving both babies and incontinent adults) hit landfills annually, comprising about 7 percent of their mass. They don't break down in landfills (even the biodegradable ones) and are made mostly from wood pulp and petroleum-based synthetic-polymer. Cloth diapers require hot-water washing and because of that are often seen as poor alternatives to disposables. On the other hand, they can be recycled after their useful life is over and don't clog up landfills. They now come with snap closures and tailored leg openings. If you do go the cloth route, use organic cotton, so you're not putting pesticide toxins next to your baby's skin (most cotton in the United States is GM and contains pesticide in the DNA of its seed).[6]

7. Eat less meat. Meat requires more than fifty times the acreage and eleven times more fossil fuels to produce a gram of protein than plants do. That's because it takes about thirteen pounds of grain to produce a pound of meat (70 percent of the grain and cereal grown in the United States goes to feed animals). And that grain requires lots of fossil fuels for the machines that till, irrigate, plant, and harvest it (and spray it with pesticides, if it's not organic), and then it needs more fuel to store, ship, and package it. And once the animals have ingested all that grain, there's the oil needed to ship the fattened animals to the slaughterhouse, slaughter them, operate the processing plants, transport the tidily packaged meat to grocery stores, and keep it cold or frozen until it's sold and used. Then there's the water needed to hydrate the animals and clean up their urine and feces (and remains, post-slaughter). About half of the water we use in the United States goes to keeping animals in our food chain. Besides that, eating less (or no) meat is healthier for your body. (Dr. T. Colin Campbell explains many more reasons in his books.)

8. Furnish your house with sustainably harvested or reclaimed wood items.

9. Establish a "recycling center" in your house or apartments. Small spaces or containers are a great start.

10. Landscape with hearty, indigenous plants that don't require much water. There are many books that show you how to turn your yard into a permaculture zone.

11. Start a "green team" at work. As vehicles and office equipment age, replace them with more energy-efficient ones.

12. Become familiar with emission-reduction targets and practice them at home and work.

13. Stop drinking bottled water (unless your municipal water is really unsafe). In 1976 Americans drank about 1.6 gallons of bottled water per person each year. Today it's thirty gallons. In many cases, bottled water is actually inferior to tap water. People in the United States drink half a billion bottles of it every week, despite the fact that it's about two thousand times as expensive as what we can pull out of our taps. (Would you pay $6,000 for your morning vente of Starbucks?) And here's the joke on us: about a third of it is really tap water anyway (think Aquafina and Dasani). The Energy Policy Institute estimates that each year it takes fifty million barrels of oil to pump, process, transport, and refrigerate bottled water (enough to fuel nearly three million cars for a year). When we toss the empty bottles out, about 80 percent either end up in landfills, where they will stay around one day short of forever, or are incinerated, dumping toxins like chlorine gas and ash laden with heavy metals into the air. The other 20 percent are downcycled or turned into other products and thrown out again (dumped in India, for example). We've all become accustomed to carrying our water around, so buy a refillable bottle and keep it handy.[7] Filter your water with a good inexpensive portable system like ZeroWater.

14. Work to bring more drinking fountains to public places or to have bottled water banned in your village, town, or city.

On the Road

1. Avoid idling. It creates way more CO_2 and wastes billions of dollars in oil every year. In New York, where car service is an industry and cars idling for hours rarely raise an eyebrow, a 1971 law limits idling to three minutes (or risk getting a $220 ticket). The problem is that the law isn't being enforced. And yes, somebody took this issue on, trying to get people to stop idling their cars and made a documentary about it—with predictable responses (see www.idlethreat movie.com).

2. If your city has it, take public transportation at least one day a week.

3. Take a "staycation" this year rather than driving or flying to a destination.

4. When taking a road trip, pack meals you make yourself and use refillable water bottles to minimize trash (and save money on fast food).

5. Drive within the speed limit. You'll burn less gas and statistics show that it's safer.

In Your Neighborhood

1. Begin a climate change discussion group at your local library, community center, or place of worship. Often groups that sponsor garden clubs will welcome information about how their flower, vegetable, and bird populations are being affected by increased warming and changing weather.

2. Request a free climate change lecture (see http://climate realityproject.org).

Pushing the Comfort Envelope

1. Buy only organic cotton. Yes, it will cost more, but you won't be wearing clothes that have pesticides built into each thread—which is true with garments made with GM cotton.

2. One weekend a month, use a bicycle or walk for errands within a one-mile radius of your home.

> *Act as if what you do makes a difference. It does.*
> —WILLIAM JAMES

Sustainable Facts

- In 2013, McDonald's ensured that 99 percent of its three hundred million Filet-O-Fish sandwiches will come from Marine Stewardship Council (MSC) qualified sources.
- Starbucks now gets 93 percent of its coffee (545 million pounds in 2013) from ethically qualified sources; by 2015 it will be 100 percent.
- By 2017, Walmart will buy 70 percent of its products sold in the United States only from those who use the giant retailer's own sustainability index.
- By 2018, all Whole Foods grocery stores will require GM labeling for products with GM ingredients.

Grow Hemp (If It's Legal)

Hemp has been around for thousands of years. No, it's not the same as marijuana; it is a cousin of cannabis, and it doesn't get you high. (The THC in hemp is 0.2 percent, while in marijuana it's 10 percent or more.) Hemp is a versatile industrial substance that, until the twentieth century, was used for everything from ropes and sails to plastics, oil, fiber, and paper production. Because hemp plastic was lighter but stronger than steel, Henry Ford constructed resin-stiffened hemp fiber and used it in the door panels on his early Model Ts (and he ran the car on ethanol made from hemp). Dr. Oz has even touted hemp milk on his television show. Hemp is said to be high in omega-6 fatty acids and contains all of the essential amino acids. Its seeds are sold in many forms as a healthy snack food. Today it's also gaining a following as a sort of miracle building material that can generate a negative CO_2. Hempcrete petrifies over time and can help buildings last for hundreds of years.

Our forests are being decimated for timber, and they take years to replace, but hemp grows to maturity in months and contains four times the cellulose per acre than trees. Hemp's stock as a crop will probably increase in value and popularity as states relax their laws on growing of hemp and marijuana. For more information, see the USDA's video, *Hemp for Victory* and the first part of *When We Grow, This Is What We Can Do*, a pro-legalization documentary that makes a strong case for growing hemp.[8]

> *Do the best you can until you know better.*
> *Then when you know better, do better.*
> —Maya Angelou

Use Social Media to Share Your Experiences

Today anything worth sharing can be instantly broadcast to others. Use social networking sites like Twitter and Facebook to raise consciousness about the planet and the thousands of opportunities to wake up and be of service. Many green, food-related, ecology, and earth-friendly sites have fan clubs you can subscribe to on Facebook and on Twitter, as well as on other sites. You can link to them from Facebook, sign up to get tweets from others, send tweets on your own, gather and follow fans, and generally draw others to your interests. This is an instant way to distribute news, keep tabs on newsworthy stories, and share information others send to you.

Getting Started on Your Activism

The lists that follow are a starting point. There are countless sites online, and you can find them in lots of different ways. You'll see them listed here with their website, and their Twitter and Facebook pages. You may want to include others like Google+, Pinterest,

StumbleUpon, and the others that will join them over time. And don't forget YouTube, which is becoming the biggest open classroom in the world. The information you can find online today is staggering, so these are meant to help you get a sense of what's out there. In two words: a lot. Facebook and Twitter are not just good ways to keep in touch. They are also terrific ways to drill deeper into topics that interest you. You can find out how to do nearly anything by cross-referencing several of these tools.

Most of these sites actively seek volunteers. If you can't find a way to contact them via the site, consult their Facebook or Twitter pages.

> *The conversation on climate is evolving rapidly*
> *partly because Mother Nature has joined the conversation*
> *and has a powerful voice.*[9]
> —AL GORE

Earth-Advocacy or Green Organizations

Climate Change Now tracks multiple related issues and actions: "Climate Change information, protests, videos, information."
www.goodactionnetwork.org
@GoodActionNetwk

The Climate Reality Project was founded by Al Gore in 2005 to train climate leaders to present the updated version of the slideshow featured in the 2007 documentary *An Inconvenient Truth*. All members are qualified volunteers, trained by Gore; the presentations are free on request.
http://climaterealityproject.org
@climatereality
Facebook: Climate Reality

Conservation International is one of the largest U.S.-based conservation organizations; dedicated to the protection of nature and all its biodiversity.
www.conservation.org (blog.conservation.org)
@ConservationOrg
Facebook: Conservation International

Earth Day Network: Yeah, that Earth Day, begun in 1970 in response to an oil leak off the coast near Santa Barbara. It's now an internationally recognized day of action and awareness. The website is a deep, rich resource for all things related to the environment. Just go browsing. You'll learn a lot.

www.earthday.org
@EarthDayNetwork
Facebook: Earth Day Network

Edible Wild Food promotes the foraging principle that wild edibles (weeds, flowers, shrubs, trees, vines, and herbs) are easy to find and full of nutrition and have a number of other benefits.

www.ediblewildfood.com
@EdibleWildFood
Facebook: EdibleWildFood.com

Energy Action Coalition is made up of forty youth-led environmental and social justice groups composed of young activists who "refuse to accept solutions that fall short of scientific fact or come at the expense of developing communities. EAC is poised to deliver on our vision of a clean and just future, and build the sustainable new green economy that will be our generation's legacy to the world."

www.wearepowershift.org
@energyaction
Facebook: Energy Action Coalition

Environmental Defense Fund began in the late 1960s in New York after successfully winning a statewide ban on DDT, after research showed it was damaging the Long Island wildlife and ecosystem. The organization has been a part of much environmental legislation since, from the Clean Water Act to the blocking of dirty coal plants. The nonprofit works with corporations to encourage voluntary sustainability practices and does not take contributions from them. Its projects span a wide range of environmental issues from fracking to smart grids.

www.edf.org
@EnvDefenseFund
Facebook: Environmental Defense Fund

Friends of the Earth Dirty Fuels is part of a larger whole, the Friends of the Earth, founded in 1969, on the eve of the first Earth Day, by David

Brower, an environmentalist and former executive director of the Sierra Club. The organization has long been involved in dealing with a wide range of issues—from nuclear power and Agent Orange during Vietnam to the sale and lease of public lands in the West to current issues with fracking and dirty fuels like tar sands.

www.foe.org/projects/climate-and-energy/tar-sands
@FOE_dirtyfuels
Facebook: Friends of the Earth U.S.

Global Crop Diversity Trust is the only worldwide group dedicated to the protection and conservation of the diversity of crops as well as the seed security of our planet. It helps fund Russia's Vavilov Seed Institute and the Svalbard Global Seed Vault in Norway.

www.croptrust.org
@CropTrust
Facebook: Global Crop Diversity Trust

Greenpeace is probably the most well known environmental organization in the world. Founded in 1971, they are an NGO with offices in forty countries. Its mission is to protect and nurture all forms of life through the use of direct action, governmental and corporate lobbying, and scientific research.

www.greenpeace.org/international
@Greenpeace
Facebook: Greenpeace International

Habitat for Humanity is a nonprofit, Christian housing ministry with a simple vision: to provide everyone with a decent place to live. It works entirely through volunteer labor and donations and can frequently be seen building homes in areas decimated by hurricanes and other natural disasters.

www.habitat.org
@Habitat_org
Facebook: Habitat for Humanity

The I Matter Movement was begun in 2009 by then thirteen-year-old Alec Loorz and his mother to give a voice to the next generation about the very different climate-changed world they will live in. As a teen activist, Loorz has spoken at Earth Day and TED events about getting the government to declare the atmosphere a public trust that should be cleaned up and maintained for his generation and those to come (he also took the government to court on the issue). The movement has an annual march the second week of May to raise awareness about climate change to get adults to see the future of America's youth as a priority that's at least as important as jobs and the economy.

www.imatteryouth.org
@iMatterMovement
Facebook: The IMatter March

Interfaith Power and Light works to help congregations be faithful stewards of Creation "by responding to global warming through the promotion of energy conservation, energy efficiency, and renewable energy." From its Twitter page: "We are mobilizing a religious response to global warming. Love God? Heal the Earth."

http://InterfaithPowerandLight.org
@interfaithpower
Facebook: Interfaith Power & Light

The National Park Service is the steward of the more than four hundred U.S. national parks, monuments, and historic sites, battlefields, military parks, lakeshores, recreation area, scenic rivers and trails, and the White House.

www.nationalparkservice.org
@NatlParkService
Facebook: National Park Service

The National Resources Defense Council (NRDC) is an NYC-based nonprofit/nonpartisan advocate for environmental protection. With over a million members and a staff of more than four hundred scientists, lawyers, and environmental policy experts, NRDC is one of the United States' most powerful environmental safeguard groups. It works with both environmental groups and corporate interests to craft sustainable paths for the use of natural resources.

www.nrdc.org
@NRDC
Facebook: NRDC

Nature Conservancy is the Americas' best-funded environmental nonprofit, working to conserve land in more than thirty countries (and all U.S.

states), protecting more than 119 million acres of land and 5,000 miles of the world's rivers.

www.nature.org
@Nature_org
Facebook: The Nature Conservancy

The Sierra Club was founded by naturalist John Muir in 1892. Today it's the largest environmental organization in the United States and is often allied with 350.org on activist issues.

http://sierraclub.org
@sierraclub
Facebook: The Sierra Club

Tar Sands Solutions Network is a report of what the tar sands mining is doing not only to the climate but also to the health and welfare of the Canadian people. It represents a network of groups including First Nations, environmental groups, landowners, farmers, scientists, leaders, academics, and grassroots groups through North America.

At http://oilsandsrealitycheck.org there is a slideshow that delivers succinct facts on the effects by climate, economy, human rights, land, species, air, and water.

http://tarsandssolutions.org and http://oilsandsrealitycheck.org
@TarSandsSolns @dirtyoilsands
Facebook: TarSandsSolutionsNetwork

The U.S. Fish and Wildlife Service is the U.S. government agency of the Department of the Interior that oversees fish, wildlife, plants, and their habitats.

www.fws.gov
@USFWSHQ
Facebook: U.S. Fish and Wildlife Service

The World Wildlife Fund is the world's leading NGO focused on wildlife conservation and preserving endangered species.

http://worldwildlife.org
@WWF
Facebook: WWF

It is for us to pray not for tasks equal to our powers,
but for powers equal to our tasks.
—HELEN KELLER

How to Fight Fracking

Americans Against Fracking is a national coalition dedicated to banning fracking. They support local, state, and federal efforts to ban fracking, as well as opposing practices that help facilitate fracking, like natural gas exports, frack sand mining, and pipeline construction.

www.americansagainstfracking.org
Facebook: AmericansAgainstFracking

Food & Water Watch works to ensure the food, water, and fish we consume is safe, accessible, and sustainably produced.

www.foodandwaterwatch.org
(for fractivist tools, http://foodandwaterwatch.org/water/fracking/
fracking-action-center/activist-tools; http://foodandwaterwatch.org/
water/fracking/fracking-action-center/local-action-documents/)
@foodandwater

FrackAction is an NYC-based grassroots organization working to protect the public and the planet from the dangers of fracking. It promotes advocacy, community organizing, and building public awareness about fracking and what can be done to stop fracking.

www.frackaction.com (New York state)
@FrackAction
Facebook: Frack Action

Josh Fox, director of *Gasland 1* and *Gasland 2.*

www.gaslandthemovie.com
@gaslandmovie
Facebook: GASLAND

Riverkeeper is the safeguard organization for the Hudson River, which nine million people rely on for their drinking water. For nearly fifty years, Riverkeeper has been New York's clean-water cop, protecting the state's water and bringing to justice hundreds of environmental lawbreakers.

www.riverkeeper.org
@riverkeeper_ny
Facebook: Riverkeeper

Safe Water Society is a grassroots group and clean-water advocate for families living in the Marcellus shale area, an area highly affected by the hydraulic fracturing of shale gas wells. Located in Lehigh Valley, PA.

http://safewatersociety.org
@SafeH2OSociety
Facebook: Safe Water Society

ShaleShockMedia is an online network of artists and media activists working to stop fracking.

www.shaleshockmedia.org
@Shaleshock
Facebook: Shaleshock

Waterkeeper Alliance is a global network of two hundred Waterkeeper Organizations dedicated to cleaning up rivers, lakes, and coasts through aggressive grassroots action "for swimmable, drinkable, fishable water worldwide."

www.waterkeeper.org
@Waterkeeper
Facebook: Waterkeeper Alliance

GMOs and Global Food Security

Center for Food Safety monitors and challenges modern food-production technologies and supports organic and other sustainable agriculture practices. It serves as a watchdog on the USDA's open-door policy of approving GMOs and its many successful legal cases "collectively represent a landmark body of case law on food and agricultural issues."

http://centerforfoodsafety.org

To see their Food Industry Guide to Front Groups, see "Best Public Relations Money Can Buy," at www.centerforfoodsafety.org/files/front _groups_final_84531.pdf

@TrueFoodNow
Facebook: Center for Food Safety

Earth Open Source is a nonprofit organization dedicated to the global food system. They advocate agroecological farming techniques that conserve resources and produce healthy, toxin-free foods.

http://earthopensource.org
@EarthOpenSource
Facebook: Earth Open Source (EOS)

Fight against GMOs is an online resource of all things GMO. Operated by a powerhouse crew of two, they have created a virtual lexicon of up to the minute information about genetically modified organisms.

http://fightagainstgmos.com
@FightAgainstGMO
Facebook: Fight Against GMOs

Food Democracy Now is an online community dedicated to building and maintaining a sustainable food system free of the influence of big agribusiness.

http://fooddemocracynow.org
@food_democracy
Facebook: Food Democracy Now

Food Politics highlights the work of award-winning health, nutrition, and food-safety educator Marion Nestle. Besides her own sizable body of work, her website features a links page that is an education unto itself.

http://foodpolitics.com
www.foodpolitics.com/links
@marionnestle
Facebook: Marion Nestle

GMO Evidence is a worldwide user-friendly library of evidence of harm caused by GMOs to animals and humans. (Based in the United Kingdom)

http://gmoevidence.com
@GMOEvidence
Facebook: GMO Evidence

GMO Free USA is a Connecticut-based group dedicated to making food manufacturers reveal if they are using GMO ingredients in their products. The organization's goal is to implement nationwide boycotts of companies that refuse to stop using GMOs.

http://gmofreeusa.org
@GMOFreeUSA
Facebook: GMOfreeusa

GMO Inside is a coalition that believes that consumers have the right to know what's in their food. The site educates about foods containing GMOs and describes non-GM and organic alternatives.

http://gmoinside.org

@GMOInside
Facebook: GMO Inside

GMO Journal is an online publication that covers all aspects of the GMO debate. They cover policies, laws, and regulations as well as the impact GMOS have on an individual's health and the environment. They also address the moral implications of GMOs as a new food technology.

http://gmo-journal.com
@GMOJournal
Facebook: GMO Journal

GMO Seralini is based on the scientific research and findings by Professor Gilles-Eric Seralini on a long-term study of the safety and health impacts of GMO food and their associated pesticides on lab rats over their lifespans. (Industry studies covered only ninety days of the typical two-year rat lifespan, so could not reflect realistic responses over time.) Warning: graphic images

http://gmoseralini.org
@gmoseralini
Facebook: GMO Seralini

GM Watch is an organization committed to countering the influence and propaganda of the biotech industry.

http://gmwatch.org
@GMWatch
Facebook: GMWatch

The Institute for Responsible Technology "is the most comprehensive source of GMO health risk information on the web." Founded by GMO watchdog Jeffrey Smith (and author of *Genetic Roulette,* among others), this is a website you could get lost in, but by the time you come out, you'd know a lot about GMOs. Download their free Non-GMO Shopping Guide or their free ShopNoGMO app.

http://responsibletechnology.org
@IRTnoGMOs
Facebook: Institute for Responsible Technology

Just Label It represents the rights of the consumers to know what they're eating by promoting transparency in labeling of GMO foods.

http://justlabelit.org

@justlabelit
Facebook: Justlabelit.org

Non-GMO Project is a nonprofit started by natural food retailers. It is currently North America's only third-party organization that verifies and labels GMOs. They work to educate consumers and corporations on the impacts of GMOs as well as providing healthy non-GMO alternatives.

www.nongmoproject.org
@NonGMOProject
Facebook: Non-GMO Project

The Organic and Non-GMO Report is the only news magazine dedicated to GMO awareness and all facets of the issue. You can learn how to create non-GMO products from "seed to shelf," find non-GMO ingredient sources, connect with food buyers that don't use GMOs, and monitor and stay informed on global GMO issues. It also publishes the Non-GMO Sourcebook.

http://non-gmoreport.com
@nongmoreport
Facebook: The Organic & Non-GMO Report

Healthy Living, Eating, and Gardening Organizations

Alice Waters is owner and founder of Berkeley's Chez Panisse Restaurant and Foundation and an ardent advocate of organic food and teaching others how to eat and cook more healthfully. The foundation's primary work involves the Edible Schoolyard program at the local Martin Luther King, Jr. Middle School. It teaches children to grow, harvest, and prepare foods from the one-acre garden. An offshoot has been the School Lunch Initiative, which aims to bring a wholesome school lunch to the ten thousand students in the Berkeley School District.

http://edibleschoolyard.org and www.chezpanisse.com
@AliceWaters
Facebook: Alice Waters

Environmental Working Group provides a Shopper's Guide to Pesticides in Produce (requires $10 donation) based on your zip code. Regularly updated with the latest news, including the Dirty Dozen Plus and the Clean Fifteen, the fruits and vegetables with worst and best pesticide residue ratings.

www.ewg.org/foodnews

@EWGFoodNews
Facebook: Environmental Working Group

Farm and Field to Table is an online resource that advocates local food production and exchange as a means of strengthening community health and increasing cooperation between neighboring groups.
www.Farmandfieldtotable.org
Facebook: Farm and Field to Table

Food Corps helps kids grow up healthy by educating them about nutrition and healthy foods. They bring high-quality foods to schools in low-resource areas and teach children how to build and maintain their own organic gardens.
https://foodcorps.org
@FoodCorps
Facebook: FoodCorps

Frugally Sustainable is an Arizona-based website with tips on healthy living, nutrition, and herbal and natural garden remedies.
http://frugallysustainable.com
@FrugallySustain
Facebook: Frugally Sustainable

Leopold Center for Sustainable Agriculture, named for conservationist and educator Aldo Leopold, is a research and education center focused on making farming both sustainable and profitable.
http://leopold.iastate.edu
Facebook: Leopold Center for Sustainable Agriculture

Local Harvest is the definitive online public directory of organic farms, farmers markets, organic restaurants, and other local food sources in the United States.
www.localharvest.org
@Localharvestorg
Facebook: Localharvest

Month without Monsanto looks at the prevalence of Monsanto in our daily lives and how hard it is to live for an entire month "without eating, wearing or washing with any Monsanto products." It's part of the Digging

Deep website, whose bloggers research "the companies, organizations, policies and practices shaping our diets."

http://diggingdeepcampaign.com/a-month-without-monsanto
@WithoutMonsanto
Facebook: Month Without Monsanto

Mountain Rose Herbs, based in Eugene, Oregon, has been selling organic products and advocating organic agriculture since 1987. Their commitment to organic excellence, quality control, and ethical business practices makes them a gold standard for young green companies to aspire to.

www.mountainroseherbs.com
@MtnRoseHerbs
Facebook: Mountain Rose Herbs

Organic Gardening magazine was started in 1942 by the late Jerome Irving Rodale, one of the first advocates of organic farming. Now in its eighth decade, it continues to educate people on organic gardening techniques, identifying beneficial insects, the merits of composting, and much more.

www.organicgardening.com
@ogmag
Facebook: Organic Gardening Magazine

Pure Herbalist tells you all things herbal, from how to create a medicinal herb and spice cabinet for emergencies to general information on natural, organic, and holistic herbs and their various uses in cooking, handicrafts, natural beauty, and homeopathic and holistic remedies.

http://pureherbalist.com
@PureHerbalist
Facebook: Pure Herbalist

Slow Food is a global, grassroots organization with supporters in 150 countries. "Promoted as an alternative to fast food, it strives to preserve traditional and regional cuisine and encourages farming of plants, seeds and livestock characteristic of the local ecosystem." (One of their officers is seed activist Vandana Shiva.) Read about Food Sovereignty and the manifestos on food, seed, climate change, and food security on their website. Their Stop the Crop initiative works to promote "a sustainable GMO-free future" for the world.

http://slowfood.com and www.slowfoodusa.org
@SlowFoodUSA

Facebook: Slow Food (See also Tierra madre)

So Delicious Dairy Free provides dairy- and gluten-free milks, ice creams, yogurts, and coffee creamers (includes store finder).
http://sodeliciousdairyfree.com
@So_Delicious
Facebook: So Delicious Dairy Free

The Farmers Market Gazette is a food ezine that focuses on farmers' markets, greengrocers, and organic food suppliers and farmers across the country. You can learn about the merits of organics, the detriments of fast food, and how to start a food truck business.
http://farmersmarketgazette.com
@Gazette_Editor
Facebook: The Farmers Market Gazette

The Greenhorns is a grassroots nonprofit dedicated to the young farming community. The organization works to recruit farmers, support them, and help promote their efforts.
www.thegreenhorns.net
@greenhorns
Facebook: The Greenhorns

Tree Hugger is like a google homepage for the green movement. Everything from environmental news and trends to healthy recipes and green fashion, initiatives. This site has it all.
www.treehugger.com
@TreeHugger
Facebook: TreeHugger

World Wide Opportunities on Organic Farms shows you how to be a volunteer on an organic farm, whether it's in the next county or on the next continent. This helps you learn about organic farming by actually *farming*. You can also learn how to teach organic and sustainable farming practices on farms in dozens of countries around the world.
http://www.wwoofusa.org (US) http://www.wwoof.net (international)
@WWOOFUSA
Facebook: Wwoof-Usa

Ocean Conservation and Action

Antarctic Ocean Alliance's goal is to establish a network of protected areas in the Antarctic region to preserve and protect these sensitive and vital ocean habitats forever. Based in Sydney, Australia.

http://antarcticocean.org

@Antarcticocean

Facebook: Antarctic Ocean Alliance

Leatherback Trust is dedicated to protecting the leatherback turtle and other species of endangered sea turtles. The group worked to found a national park, Parque Marino Las Baulas, on the Pacific coast of Costa Rica, to protect the leatherback and give them a safe place for nesting.

http://leatherback.org

Facebook: Leatherback Trust

Mission Blue was started by renowned oceanographer Dr. Sylvia Earle to heighten public awareness of how critical oceans are to all planet life. Its goal is to establish Marine Protected Areas called Hope Spots, a network of sanctuaries for our "planet's blue heart." (See the Google+ page for stunning pictures.)

http://mission-blue.org

@SylviaEarle

Facebook: Mission Blue

The U.S. National Oceanic and Atmospheric Administration (NOAA) runs the Coral Reef Conservation Program, which funds and equips reef conservation efforts to combat climate change, fishing, and land-base sources of pollution in seven U.S. states and jurisdictions and in international sites in the Pacific Freely Associated States. Contact them for volunteer opportunities.

http://coralreef.noaa.gov

Try ReefsatRisk

Facebook: NOAA Coral Reef Conservation

NOAA's National Marine Sanctuaries include fourteen marine protected areas in the United States, amounting to over 170,000 square miles. That's all of our ocean coastlines (including Hawaii and American Samoa) as well as the U.S. Great Lakes. These sanctuaries are dedicated to the preservation of our ocean treasures, areas as our nation's lands.

http://sanctuaries.noaa.gov
@sanctuaries
Facebook: NOAA Office of National Marine Sanctuaries

NOAA Ocean is an online portal that enables people to learn about and virtually explore the vast undersea expanses of our planet.
http://oceanexplorer.noaa.gov
@oceanexplorer
Facebook: NOAA Office of Ocean Exploration and Research

Oceana teaches you about all things saltwatery. It's the largest international organization focused solely on ocean conservation. Its team members focus on winning "specific and concrete policy changes to reduce pollution and to prevent the irreversible collapse of fish populations, marine mammals, and other sea life."
http://oceana.org/act
@oceana
Facebook: Oceana

Ocean Conservancy brings people together as a voice for the ocean. They are dedicated to keeping the ocean healthy, addressing the needs of people whose livelihood depends on the ocean, and working toward finding solutions to the ocean's problems.
http://oceanconservancy.org
@OurOcean
Facebook: Ocean Conservancy

Offset your CO2

The choice of such greens as the Dixie Chicks and Pearl Jam, **Conservation International** works like most such organizations, investing your contributions in worthy CO_2-reducing projects like preserving carbon-capturing rain forests, teaching agroforestry and biodiversity, and providing incentives to farmers to leave native forests intact.
www.conservation.org
@ConservationOrg
Facebook: Conservation International

TerraPass shows you how to calculate your carbon footprint, then let you buy offsets from a portfolio (from clean energy, farm power, and landfill gas capture) that you can build yourself.

http://terrapass.com
@TerraPass
Facebook: TerraPass

Repurposing and Design

Inhabitat. The design of the future now. Inhabitat works toward sustainable up-cycling and down-cycling, including Pop Up Hotels, ways to turn empty office space into temporary tourist digs.

http://inhabitat.com
@inhabitat
Facebook: Inhabitat

Jill Angelo shows you how to rearrange, repurpose, and redecorate your home to turn it into a sanctuary of sacred space at little or no cost.

http://jillangelo.com
@JillCreates
Facebook: Jill Angelo

Seed Saving and Activism

Native Seeds Search is a Southwestern seed conservation nonprofit and seed bank based in Tucson, Arizona. It promotes seed conservation, crop diversity, and the gathering, safeguarding and distribution of seeds to farming and gardening communities (they'll also show you how to build a straw-bale cottage).

http://nativeseeds.org
@NativeSeedsSRCH
Facebook: Native Seeds/SEARCH

Seed Matters is an initiative started by the Clif energy bar folks. Click on the seed on their home page to take a journey that explains why seed matters and how seed sharing started, as well as the state of our current seed stores. It gives you the lowdown on all sorts of things about seeds, from why we need organic seed (yes, it's way more productive than conventional or GM seed) and why today only about 10 percent of seed is saved in the United States.

www.seedmatters.org
@Seed_Matters
Facebook: Seed Matters

Seeds of Change promotes biodiversity by making certified organic seeds available to gardener and farmers and helping to preserve heirloom varieties in danger of extinction from modern agricultural techniques.

www.seedsofchange.com
@SeedsofChange
Facebook: Seeds of Change

Seed Savers Exchange specializes in saving, sharing, and selling heirloom and open-pollinated (non-GMO) seeds. Based in Decorah, Iowa.

www.seedsavers.org
@Seedsaversx
Facebook: Seed Savers Exchange

Territorial Seed Company is an Oregon-based, family-owned business. They sell vegetable, flower, and herb seeds and are signers of the Safe Seed Pledge. They are "100% non-GMO" and sell organic and biodynamic varieties for year-round growing (they make their own compost and plant teas).

www.territorialseed.com
@TerritorialSeed
Facebook: Territorial Seed Company

Tree Advocacy Groups

Arbor Day Foundation is a terrific guide to everything about trees and is an advocate for replanting our national forests. It gives everyone a way to join in this venture by planting their own trees. "We inspire people to plant, nurture, and celebrate trees."

www.arborday.org
@arborday
Facebook: Arbor Day Foundation

Global Trees Campaign works to save the eight thousand tree species (and their habitats) most threatened by woodland and forest destruction.

http://globaltrees.org
@globaltrees
Facebook: The Global Trees Campaign

Plant a Billion Trees is an initiative begun by the Nature Conservancy to reforest Brazil's Atlantic Forest, restoring one million acres of land (and removing four million tons of CO_2 from the atmosphere each year). A $1 donation plants one tree.

http://plantabillion.org
@nature_org
Facebook: The Nature Conservancy

Trees for Life is a conservation charity working to restore the UK's Caledonian Forest and all its species (now only 1 percent of its original size) to a 1,000-square-mile contiguous area in the Highlands of Scotland. Offers volunteering opportunities.

www.treesforlife.org.uk
@treesforlifeuk
Facebook: Trees For Life

The Act Part of Action

If you've ever seen "The Story of Stuff" on YouTube, you've only scratched the surface of what the website (http://storyof-stuff.org) has to offer. Besides providing some really funny and ingenious short videos that explain issues like cap and trade, how our economy went broke, and why bottled water is a bad idea (among others), it's also a terrific resource (Citizen Muscle Boot Camp) for how to address many of the issues outlined in this book, such as petitions, letters to the editor, boycotts, banner drops, and more. Podcasts follow projects begun by school-age children that deal with "extended corporate responsibility," that helps kids learn how to identify issues and make change happen.

Civil Disobedience: Putting Skin in the Game

In December 2008, a twenty-seven-year-old climate-justice activist named Tim DeChristopher walked into an auction of oil and gas drilling rights being run by the Department of the Interior on 150,000 acres of publicly owned Utah wilderness. He signed up, received a paddle, and began to bid. By the time the auction was over, he had been awarded a dozen leases worth 1.8 million dollars (and had run the usual price per acre into the stratosphere). The auction was eventually made null, because the Bureau of Land Management had not completed the appropriate environmental impact study. A legal battle ensued, and DeChristopher was found guilty of criminal fraud and sentenced to two years in federal prison. DeChristopher engaged in civil disobedience, willingly violating a law in the name of social justice. In an interview with Bill Moyers, he said, "Not everyone has to go to prison. But I think everyone has to feel empowered to take strong actions. If we look at social movement history, the ones that have been most successful and most powerful are the ones that have used a variety of tactics and a variety of strategies."

Increasingly, movements are taking to the streets; some offer nonviolence training and counsel participants how to endure arrest. (Bill McKibben used DeChristopher's arrest to inspire climate activists to action against the proposed Keystone XL Tar Sands pipeline in the summer of 2011. A total of 1,253 people were arrested over a two-week period in Washington, DC, for peacefully gathering in front of the White House.) After his sentencing, DeChristopher told a packed courtroom, "At this point of unimaginable threats on the horizon, this is what hope looks like. In these times of a morally bankrupt government that has sold out its principles, this is what patriotism looks like. With countless lives on the line, this is what love looks like, and it will only grow."[10] Shortly after his release from prison, a documentary about him, called *Bidder 70*, was released. DeChristopher plans to become a Unitarian minister after completing study at the Harvard School of Divinity.

People are not isolated individuals; they're connected to something much bigger than themselves.
—Tim DeChristopher

Climate Activism

350.org was founded by environmental activist Bill McKibben in 2008 in response to NASA climatologist James Hansen's proposition that we need to limit the amount of carbon dioxide in earth's atmosphere to 350 ppm. It has evolved into an activist organization that has inspired a new global movement that's rising to the challenge of the climate change crisis. The organization helps plan nonviolent actions against issues such as tar sands, fracking, and the building of massive coal transports in the Northwest, to name a few.

http://350.org

@350

Facebook: 350.org

Bold Nebraska is an advocacy organization founded in 2009 by Jane Fleming Kleeb, a leading anti-tar sands activist. It's an online destination for progressive and moderate Nebraska politics. In 2011, Kleeb was instrumental in getting the Keystone XL Pipeline's path changed so that it had less impact on the environmentally sensitive Nebraska Sand Hills. The site's focus is on helping to create change both online and on the ground.

http://boldnebraska.org

@BoldNebraska

Facebook: Bold Nebraska

DeSmogBlog is a leading source for sorting out climate change deniers with its "disinformation database." It's the go-to site for many mainstream media outlets for facts on global warming and climate change. The goal is to "clear the PR pollution that cloud climate science." *Time* magazine voted them one of the Top 25 blogs of 2011.

http://desmogblog.com/about

@DeSmogBlog

Facebook: DeSmogBlog

Idle No More lists the contention of Canada's First Nations that the taking of resources by corporate and political interests is—despite treaty promises—leaving the land and waters poisoned. "We must repair these violations, live the spirit and intent of the treaty relationship, work towards justice in action, and protect Mother Earth."

www.idlenomore.ca

@IdleNoMore4

Facebook: Idle No More—In Solidarity

Marcellus Protest is an anti-fracking alliance of Pennsylvania groups and individuals focused on the Marcellus Shale gas region, which spans five

states. Their mission is the eradication of fracking through organized protest and education. They also lend support to other communities affected
by fracking.

www.marcellusprotest.org
@marcellus_SWPA
Facebook: Marcellus Protest

Peaceful Uprising is committed to climate justice. Cofounded by activist
Tim DeChristopher, its motto is "Defending a Livable Future through
Empowering Nonviolent Action." A companion website offers training
for nonviolent activists through its PeaceUp Bold School.

www.peacefuluprising.org
http://corr.peacefuluprising.org
@Peace_UP_
Facebook: Peaceful Uprising

Stop the Frack Attack began as a national network of people affected by
hydraulic fracturing across the nation. It's evolved into a action group aimed
at protecting communities from the detrimental impacts of fracking. Their
ultimate goal is a global transition to a renewable, clean, energy future.

www.stopthefrackattack.org
@stopfrackattack
Facebook: Stop the Frack Attack

Tar Sands Action is made up primarily of Americans and Canadians from
all walks of life who take part in sustained civil disobedience to protest the
expansion of the Keystone XL Pipeline.

www.tarsandsaction.org
@TarSandsAction
Facebook: Tar Sands Action

Tar Sands Blockade is made up of affected residents and climate-
justice organizers using nonviolent direct action to stop the progress of the Keystone XL pipeline.

www.tarsandsblockade.org
@KXLBlockade
Facebook: Tar Sands Blockade

Utah Tar Sands Resistance was created to protest the mining of the only
site for tar sands in the United States, in eastern Utah.

www.tarsandsresist.org
@tarsandsresist
Facebook: Utah Tar Sands Resistance

Courage is contagious.
—Billy Graham

Everything Breathes Together

As earth stewards and climate change activists, what each of us is trying to do is fulfill a role that no governmental agency is willing to accept. We cannot count on our governments to act on our behalf; they will simply enact timid legislation that will offend no one and get us exactly nowhere. We have to be the ones to inspire our leaders and demand their vigor. They cannot do it alone. They must be accountable, and so must we—and they must be able to count on us standing with them.

The way we start this process of rebooting human consciousness and connecting with our heart's ease is by educating ourselves to what's going on around us, by waking up to our own history—our heroic good hearts, genius imaginations, and compassionate natures, as well as our shadowy greed and denial. We start by creating a daily practice that each of us can believe in—and commit to—and we learn by listening to the wisdom that begins to rise from that practice, pointing the way for us.

As Richard Tarnas says, "What we do not know hurts us. Don't fall into spiritual sloth. Instead, fall into spiritual heroism. Do all you can as long as you can."[11] Learn to listen. Trust your gut. Don't despair. Get involved. Open your heart and spirit. Individual acts heal the whole of us. Your earth and your fellow beings need your courage, stamina, sweat, wisdom, passion, and good intentions.

As Tarnas notes, we of the modern era have lost so much connection with our universe that we no longer understand its mystery, and we don't trust it. By objectifying it, we can more easily exploit it on all levels, numbing ourselves to the results that surround us.

In the end, reconnecting to the earth—finding our own Earth Calling—gives us back our cosmic birthright: to love the earth and acknowledge our place in the cosmos, to realize it's not us at the center of it all, but something deep and mysterious and wonderful that is waiting to welcome us home.

Bibliography

Books Referenced

Abram, David. *The Spell of the Sensuous: Perception and Language in a More-than-Human World.* New York: Vintage, 1996.

Altman, Nathaniel. *Sacred Trees: Spirituality, Wisdom and Well-Being.* New York: Sterling, 2000.

Barber, Charles. *Comfortably Numb: How Psychiatry Is Medicating a Nation.* New York: Pantheon, 2008.

Bartholomew, Mel. *Square Foot Gardening.* Franklin, TN: Cool Springs Press, 2006.

Benyus, Janine. *Biomimicry: Innovation Inspired by Nature.* New York: Harper Collins, 1997.

Berry, Thomas. *The Dream of the Earth.* San Francisco: Sierra Club Books, 1988.

Berry, Wendell. *Bringing It to the Table: On Farming and Food.* Berkeley: Counterpoint Press, 2009.

———. *The Gift of Good Land.* San Francisco: North Point Press, 1983.

———. *The Unsettling of America: Culture and Agriculture.* San Francisco: Sierra Club Books, 1981.

Bird, Christopher, and Peter Tompkins. *The Secret Life of Plants.* New York: Harper and Row, 1973.

Brinkley, Douglas. *The Great Deluge.* New York: William Morris/Harper Collins, 2005.

Brown, Lester. *Plan B, 2.0: Rescuing a Planet under Stress and a Civilization in Trouble.* New York: W.W. Norton, 2006.

———. *Plan B, 3.0: Mobilizing to Save Civilization.* New York: W.W. Norton, 2008.

———. *Plan B, 4.0: Mobilizing to Save Civilization.* New York: W.W. Norton, 2009.

Campbell, Joseph, and Bill Moyers. *The Power of Myth.* New York: Random House, 1991.

Carroll, John, Paul Brockelman, and Mary Westfall, eds. *The Greening of Faith: God, the*

Environment, and the Good Life. Hanover, NH: University Press of New England, 1997.

Carson, Rachel. *Silent Spring.* Boston: Houghton Mifflin, 1962.

Cavnar, Bob. *Disaster on the Horizon: High Stakes, High Risks, and the Story behind the Deepwater Well Blowout.* White River Junction, VT: Chelsea Green, 2010.

Cowan, Eliot. *Plant Spirit Medicine: The Healing Power of Plants.* Mill Spring: Swan Raven, 1995.

Davies, Pete. *American Road: The Story of an Epic Transcontinental Journey at the Dawn of the Motor Age.* New York: Henry Holt, 2002.

Davis, Devra Lee. *When Smoke Ran Like Water: Tales of Environmental Deception and the Battle against Pollution.* New York: Basic Books, 2002.

Devereux, Paul. *Re-Visioning the Earth: A Guide to Opening the Healing Channels Between Mind and Nature.* New York: Simon and Schuster, 1996.

Diamond, Jared. *Collapse: How Societies Choose to Fail or Succeed.* New York: Penguin Books, 2005.

Doyle, Jack. *Altered Harvest.* New York: Viking, 1985.

Duncan, Dayton, and Ken Burns. *America's First Road Trip.* New York: Alfred A. Knopf, 2003.

Dyson, Michael. *Come Hell or High Water: Hurricane Katrina and the Color of Disaster.* New York: Perseus Books, 2006.

Elgin, Duane. *The Living Universe: Where Are We? Who Are We? Where Are We Going?* San Francisco: Berrett-Koehler, 2009.

Findhorn Community. *The Findhorn Garden: Pioneering a New Vision of Man and Nature in Cooperation.* New York: Harper and Row, 1975.

———. *The Findhorn Garden Story.* Findhorn: Findhorn Press, 2008.

Foer, Jonathan Safran. *Eating Animals.* New York: Little Brown, 2009.

Fowler, Cary, and Pat Mooney. *Shattering: Food, Politics and the Loss of Genetic Diversity.* Tucson: University of Arizona Press, 1990.

Friedman, Thomas. *Hot, Flat, and Crowded.* New York: Farrar, Straus and Giroux, 2008.

Garrison, Jim. *America as Empire: Global Leader or Rogue Power?* San Francisco: Berrett-Koehler, 2004.

Gladwell, Malcolm. *Blink: The Power of Thinking Without Thinking.* New York: Little, Brown, 2005.

Gore, Al. *Earth in the Balance: Ecology and the Human Spirit.* Boston: Houghton Mifflin, 1992.

Hartmann, Thom. *The Last Hours of Ancient Sunlight.* New York: Three Rivers Press, 2004.

Harvey, Andrew. *Teachings of the Christian Mystics.* Boston: Shambhala, 1998.

———. *The Hope: A Guide to Sacred Activism.* New York: Hay House, 2009.

Hauter, Wenonah. *Foodopoly.* New York: The New Press, 2012.

Hawken, Paul. *Blessed Unrest: How the Largest Social Movement in History Is Restoring Grace, Justice, and Beauty to the World.* New York: Viking, 2007.

———. *The Ecology of Commerce: A Declaration of Sustainability.* New York: HarperCollins, 1993.

Hawken, Paul, Amory Lovins, and L. Hunter Lovins. *Natural Capitalism: Creating the Next Industrial Revolution.* New York: Little, Brown, 1999.

Heinberg, Richard. *Peak Everything: Waking Up to the Century of Declines.* Gabriola Island, BC: New Society, 2007.

Helminski, Camille, ed. *The Book of Nature. A Sourcebook of Spiritual Perspectives on Nature and the Environment.* Watsonville, CA: The Book Foundation, 2006.

Hemenway, Toby. *Gaia's Garden: A Guide to Home-Scale Permaculture.* White River Junction, VT: Chelsea Green, 2000.

Hill, Julia Butterfly. *The Legacy of Luna: The Story of a Tree, a Woman and a Struggle to Save the Redwoods.* New York: Harper Collins, 2000.

Hinton, David, trans. *Mencius.* Washington, DC: Counterpoint, 1998.

Horne, Jed. *Breach of Faith: Hurricane Katrina and the Near Death of a Great American City.* New York: Random House, 2006.

Isaacson, Walter. *Einstein.* New York: Simon and Schuster, 2007.

Jensen, Derrick. *Listening to the Land: Conversations about Nature, Culture, and Eros.* White River Junction, VT: Chelsea Green, 2004.

Kempton, William, James S. Boster, and Jennifer A. Hartley. *Environmental Values in American Culture.* Cambridge, MA: MIT Press, 1995.

Kessel, Anthony. *Air, the Environment, and Public Health.* New York: Cambridge University Press, 2006.

Kidd, Sue Monk. *When the Heart Waits: Spiritual Direction for Life's Sacred Questions.* San Francisco: Harper, 1990.

Kimbrell, Andrew. *Fatal Harvest.* Sausalito, CA: Foundation for Deep Ecology, 2002.

———, ed. *Your Right to Know: Genetic Engineering and the Secret Changes in Your Food.* San Rafael, CA: Earth Aware, 2007.

Kingsolver, Barbara, Stephen L. Hopp, and Camille Kingsolver. *Animal, Vegetable, Mineral: A Year of Food Life.* New York: Harper Perennial, 2007.

Klare, Michael T. *Blood and Oil: The Dangers and Consequences of America's Growing Dependency on Imported Petroleum.* New York: Metropolitan Books, 2004.

Lachman, Gary. *Rudolf Steiner: An Introduction to His Life and Work.* New York: Tarcher (Penguin), 2007.

Lambrecht, Bill. *Dinner at the New Gene Café: How Genetic Engineering Is Changing What We Eat, How We Live, and the Global Politics of Food.* New York: Thomas Dunne, 2001.

Laszlo, Ervin. *The Chaos Point: The World at the Crossroads.* Charlottesville: Hampton Roads, 2006.

Leopold, Aldo. *A Sand County Almanac.* London: Random House, 1966.

Louv, Richard. *Last Child in the Woods.* Chapel Hill, NC: Algonquin Books, 2005.

———. *The Nature Principle: Human Restoration and the End of Nature.* Chapel Hill, NC: Algonquin Books, 2013.

Lynas, Mark. *Six Degrees: Our Future on a Hotter Planet.* Washington, DC: National Geographic, 2008.

Mcgaa, Ed. *Mother Earth Spirituality: Native American Paths to Healing Ourselves and Our World.* New York: HarperCollins, 1990.

McKibben, Bill. *Eaarth: Making a Life on a Tough New Planet.* New York: St. Martin's Griffin, 2011.
———. *The End of Nature.* New York: Random House, 2006.
Mufson, Stephen. *Keystone XL: Down the Line.* TED Books, 2013.
Myss, Caroline. *Anatomy of the Spirit: The Seven Stages of Power and Healing.* New York: Random House, 1996.
———. *Defy Gravity: Healing Beyond the Bounds of Reason.* Carlsbad, CA: Hay House, 2009.
———. *Entering the Castle: An Inner Path to God and Your Soul.* New York: Simon and Schuster, 2007.
———. *Sacred Contracts: Awakening Your Divine Potential.* New York: Random House, 2001.
Nhat Hanh, Thich. *The Long Road Turns to Joy: A Guide to Walking Meditation.* Berkeley: Parallax Press, 1996.
Nepo, Mark. *The Book of Awakening: Having the Life You Want by Being Present to the Life You Have.* Berkeley, CA: Conari Press, 2000.
Nestle, Marion. *Food Politics: How the Food Industry Influences Nutrition and Health.* Berkeley: University of California Press, 2007.
Niman, Nicolette Hahn. *Righteous Porkchop: Finding a Life and Good Food beyond Factory Farms.* New York: Harper Collins, 2009.
Orr, David. *Down to the Wire: Confronting Climate Collapse.* New York: Oxford University Press, 2009.
Pearce, Joseph Chilton. *The Biology of Transcendence: A Blueprint of the Human Spirit.* Rochester, VT: Park Street Press, 2004.
Pfeiffer, David Allen. *Eating Fossil Fuels.* Gabriola Island, BC: New Society, 2006.
Pollan, Michael. *Food Rules: An Eater's Manual.* New York: Penguin, 2009.
———. *In Defense of Food: An Eater's Manifesto.* New York: Penguin, 2008.
———. *Omnivore's Dilemma: A Natural History of Four Meals.* New York: Penguin, 2006.
———. *The Omnivore's Dilemma: The Secrets Behind What You Eat.* Young readers edition. New York: Penguin, 2009.
Ray, Paul H., and Sherry Ruth Anderson. *The Cultural Creatives: How 50 Million People Are Changing the World.* New York: Three Rivers Press, 2000.
Rifkin, Jeremy. *The Hydrogen Economy.* New York: Tarcher, 2002.
Roberts, Paul. *The End of Oil: On the Edge of a Perilous New World.* New York: Mariner Books, 2005.
Rohr, Richard. *Everything Belongs: The Gift of Contemplative Prayer.* New York: Crossroad Publishing, 2003.
———. *The Naked Now: Learning to See as the Mystics See.* New York: Crossroad Publishing, 2009.
Shea, John. *Stories of God: An Unauthorized Biography.* Chicago: Thomas More, 1978.
Shiva, Vandana. *Manifestos on the Future of Food and Seed.* Cambridge, MA: South End Press, 2007.
———. *Stolen Harvest: The Hijacking of the Global Food Supply.* Cambridge, MA: South End Press, 2000.

Smith, Huston. *A Seat at the Table: Huston Smith in Conversation with Native Americans on Religious Freedom.* Berkeley: University of California Press, 2006.

Smith, Jeffrey. *Seeds of Deception: Exposing Industry and Government Lies about the Safety of the Genetically Engineered Foods You're Eating.* Fairfield, IA: Yes! Books, 2003.

Stamets, Paul. *Mycelium Running: How Mushrooms Can Help Save the World.* Berkeley: Ten Speed Press, 2005.

Steffen, Alex, ed. *WorldChanging: A User's Guide for the 21st Century.* New York: Harry A. Abrams, 2006.

Steiner, Rudolf. *Agriculture Course: The Birth of the Bio-Dynamic Method.* London: Rudolf Steiner Press, 1958.

Suzuki, David. *Everything under the Sun: Toward a Brighter Future on a Small Blue Planet.* Vancouver: Greystone Books. 2012.

———. *The Legacy: An Elder's Vision for Our Sustainable Future.* Vancouver: Greystone Books. 2011.

———. *The Sacred Balance: Rediscovering Our Place in Nature.* Vancouver: Greystone Books. 2007

Suzuki, David, and Kathy Vanderlinden. *You Are the Earth: Know Your World So You Can Help Make It Better.* Vancouver: Greystone Books, 2010.

Swimme, Brian, and Thomas Berry. *The Universe Story: From the Primordial Flaring Forth to the Ecozoic Era, A Celebration of the Unfolding of the Cosmos.* San Francisco: Harper, 2004.

Taleb, Nassim. *The Black Swan: The Impact of the Highly Improbable.* New York: Random House, 2007.

Tarnas, Richard. *Cosmos and Psyche: Intimations of a New World View.* New York: Penguin, 2006.

Taylor, Jill Bolte. *My Stroke of Insight: A Brain Scientist's Personal Journey.* New York: Viking, 2008.

Thompson, William Irvin. Foreword to *The Findhorn Garden: Pioneering a New Vision of Man and Nature in Cooperation.* By the Findhorn Community. New York: Harper Collins, 1975.

Tompkins, Peter, and Christopher Bird. *The Secret Life of Plants.* New York: Harper and Row, 1973.

Tucker, Mary Evelyn. *Worldly Wonder: Religions Enter Their Ecological Phase.* Peru, IL: Carus Publishing, 2003.

Ward, Barbara, René Dubos, Thor Heyerdahl, Gunnar Myrdal, Carmen Miró, Lord Zuckerman, and Aurelio Peccei. *Who Speaks for Earth?* New York: W.W. Norton, 1973.

Weber, Karl, ed. *Food, Inc.: A Participant Guide: How Industrial Food Is Making Us Sicker, Fatter and Poorer, and What You Can Do About It.* New York: Perseus, 2009.

Weisman, Alan. *The World Without Us.* New York: Picador, 2007.

Wilson, E. O. *The Social Conquest of Earth.* New York: Liveright, 2012.

WPA Writers Program in State of Texas. *Texas: A Guide to the Lone Star State.* New York: Hastings House, 1940.

Yergin, Daniel. *The Prize: The Epic Quest for Oil, Money, and Power.* New York: Simon and
    Schuster, 2009.

Articles and Blogs

Adams, David. "Ice-free Arctic Could Be Here in 23 Years." *Guardian,* September 5,
    2007, updated January 14, 2008.
Baker, Billy. "Saving 'God's Creation' Unites Scientist, Evangelical Leader." *Boston Globe,*
    May 1, 2008.
Barrett, Paul M. "It's Global Warming, Stupid." *Bloomberg Businessweek,* November 01,
    2012.
Broder, John M. "Many Goals Remain Unmet in 5 Nations' Climate Deal." *New York
    Times,* December 18, 2009.
Chandler, Lynn. "Africa's Lake Chad Shrinks by 20 Times Due to Irrigation Demands,
    Climate Change." GSFC press release (Greenbelt, Maryland: NASA, Goddard
    Space Flight Center, February 27, 2001).
Fischetti, Mark. "Drowning New Orleans." *Scientific American,* October 2001.
Ford, Richard. "A City Beyond the Reach of Empathy." *New York Times,* September 4,
    2005.
Gertner, Jon. "The Future is Drying Up." *New York Times Magazine,* October 21, 2007.
Goldenberg, Suzanne. "Al Gore says Obama must veto 'atrocity' of Keystone XL tar
    sands pipeline." *Guardian,* June 15, 2013.
Goodman, Brenda. "Drought-Stricken South Facing Tough Choices." *New York Times,*
    October 16, 2007.
———. "Georgia Loses Federal Case in a Dispute About Water." *New York Times,*
    February 6, 2008.
Griffith, Kate. "This Too Shall Passacantando." *Grist,* December 29, 2008.
Higgs, Steven. "Surrounded by Factory Farms: Indiana Environment Revisited."
    Bloomington Alternative, March 9, 2008.
Jensen, Derrick. "Taking Shorter Showers Doesn't Cut It: Why Personal Change Does
    Not Equal Political Change." *Orion Magazine,* July 13, 2009.
Jervis, Rick. "New Orleans Population May Have Hit Plateau." *USA Today,* August 4,
    2008.
King, Neil, Jr. "A Past President's Advice to Obama: Act with Haste." *Wall Street Journal,*
    December 11, 2008.
Kluger, Jeffrey. "Global Warming: The Culprit?" *Time,* September 24, 2005.
Kristof, Nicholas. "Food for the Soul." *New York Times,* August 22, 2009.
Marshall, Bob. "Levee Leaks Reported to S&WB a Year Ago." *New Orleans Times-
    Picayune,* November 18, 2005.
Martel, Brett. "45 Bodies Found at New Orleans Hospital." *Associated Press,* September
    12, 2005.
McKibben, Bill. "Civilization's Last Chance." Op-Ed, *L.A. Times,* May 11, 2008.
———. "Global Warming's Terrifying New Math." *Rolling Stone,* July 12, 2012. www
    .rollingstone.com/politics/news/global-warmings-terrifying-new-math-20120719.

McQuaid, John, and Mark Schleifson. "In Harm's Way." Part of the five-part series "Washing Away." *New Orleans Times-Picayune,* June 23–27, 2002.

Meinshausen, Malte, et al. "Greenhouse-Gas Emission Targets for Limiting Global Warming to 2C." *Nature,* April 30, 2009. www.nature.com/nature/journal/v458/n7242/abs/nature08017.html.

Pollan, Michael. "Farmer in Chief." *New York Times Magazine,* October 9, 2008.

———. "Playing God in the Garden." *New York Times Magazine,* October 25, 1998.

Ripley, Amanda. "How Did This Happen?" *Time,* September 4, 2005.

Rosenthal, Elisabeth. "U.S. to Be World's Top Oil Producer in 5 Years, Report Says." *New York Times,* November 12, 2012.

Running, Steven W. "Is Global Warming Causing More, Larger Wildfires?" *Science,* August 18, 2006.

Seabrook, John. "Sowing for Apocalypse: The quest for a global seed bank." *New Yorker,* August 27, 2007.

Shane, Scott, and Eric Lipton. "Federal Response: Government Saw Flood Risk but Not Levee Failure." *New York Times,* September 2, 2005.

Smith, Daniel B. "Is There an Ecological Unconscious?" *New York Times,* January 27, 2010.

"Speaker Hastert Calls for End of European Union's Protectionist, Discriminatory Trade Policies." *U.S. Newswire,* March 26, 2003.

Suzuki, David. "Teach Your Children—By Example—How to Be Healthy." David Suzuki Foundation (blog), February 16, 2011, www.davidsuzuki.org/blogs/science-matters/2011/02/teach-your-children---by-example---how-to-be-healthy.

Szaniszlo, Marie. "Fishing for Compliance: Genetically Engineered Salmon Co. Raises Concerns." *Boston Herald,* January 2, 2013.

Vega, Cecilia M. "As Bodies Recovered, Reporters told, 'No Photos, No Stories.'" *San Francisco Chronicle,* September 13, 2005.

Walsh, Bryan. "The Secret Life of Trees." *Time,* December 14, 2007.

Williams, Carol J. "Drought Yields Lake's Treasures and Trash." *The Nation,* July 19, 2007.

Young, Samantha. "Schwarzenegger Asks Obama for More Auto Emissions Rules." Associated Press, January 22, 2009.

Yovich, Daniel. "Ike's Remnants Blamed for Midwest Deaths, Blackouts." Associated Press, September 15, 2008.

Yue, Pan. Interview from Chinese Ministry of the Environment. "The Chinese Miracle Will End Soon." *Der Spiegel,* March 7, 2005.

———. "China's Green Debt." *Daily Times (Pakistan),* December 1, 2006.

Zito, Kelly, and Matthew Yi. "Governor Declares Drought in California." *San Francisco Chronicle,* June 5, 2008.

Online Articles, Interviews and Speeches

ACS Chemical Neuroscience 2012, Report. "The Top Prescription Drugs of 2011 in the United States: Antipsychotics and Antidepressants Once Again Lead CNS Therapeutics," pubs.acs.org/doi/pdfplus/10.1021/cn3000923.

Adam, David. "Warning over Threatened Wild Food Crops." *Guardian,* September 8, 2006. www.guardian.co.uk/environment/2006/sep/08/food.food.

Alok, Jha. "Deep in Permafrost—A Seedbank to Save the World" *Guardian,* June 20, 2006. www.guardian.co.uk/science/2006/jun/20/food.frontpagenews.

Armstrong, Jennifer. "Genetically Modified Foods." American Academy of Environmental Medicine, May 8, 2009. aaemonline.org/gmopost.html.

BBC News, August 3, 2006. "China Hit by Rising Air Pollution." news.bbc.co.uk/2/hi /asia-pacific/5241844.stm.

Bagley, Katherine. "The Most Influential Climate Science Paper Today Remains Unknown to Most People." *Inside Climate News,* February 14, 2013. insideclimate news.org/news/20140213/climate-change-science-carbon-hbudget-nature-global -warming-2-degrees-bill-mckibben-fossil-fuels-keystone-xl-oil?page=show.

Barber, David and Sheila Watt-Cloutier interviews in "The Big Melt: The Arctic Ice Cap." http://video.on.nytimes.com/?fr_story=aa9ac8c8b71dbc3e2c55b7e6d51020c2 9c0cd8e.

Behar, Michael. "Fracking's Latest Scandal? Earthquake Swarms." *Mother Jones,* MarchApril 2013. motherjones.com/environment/2013/03/ does-fracking-cause-earthquakes-wastewater-dewatering.

Biello, David. "Fertilizer Runoff Overwhelms Streams and Rivers—Creating Vast 'Dead Zones.' " *Scientific American,* March 14, 2008. www.sciam.com/articloe. cfm?id=fertilizer_runoff-overwhelms-streams.

Bishop, Ronald E. "Fracking the Future—The Dangers of Gas Drilling." February 23, 2011. http://desmogblog.com/fracking-the-future/danger.html.

Bureau of Ocean Energy Management, Regulation and Enforcement Press Releases. "BOEMRE Approves Deepwater Drilling Permit for New Well Included in First Approved Exploration Plan." March 30, 2011. www.boem.gov/BOEM-Newsroom /Press-Releases/2011/Press_Release_Catalog_2011.aspx.

"BOEMRE Approves First Deepwater Drilling Permit to Meet Important New Safety Standards in Gulf of Mexico." February 28, 2011. www.boem.gov/BOEM -Newsroom/Press-Releases/2011/Press_Release_Catalog_2011.aspx.

Campbell, Charlie. "Chinese Urged to Put Down Their Chopsticks to Save Trees." *Time,* March 13, 2013. http://newsfeed.time.com/2013/03/13 /chinese-urged-to-put-down-their-chopsticks-to-save-trees.

Canfield, Sabrina. "Transocean Turns on BP with Scorching Oil-Spill Document." Courthouse News Service, March 4, 2013. www.courthousenews. com/2013/03/04/55381.htm

Cardinale, Matthew. "More Aging U.S. Coal Plants Hit the Chopping Block." *Inter Press Service,* January 11, 2013. http://truth-out.org/news/item/13854-more-aging-us -coal-plants-hit-the-chopping-block.

Cathles, Lawrence M., III, et al. "A Commentary on 'The Greenhouse-Gas Footprint of Natural Gas in Shale Formations' by R. W. Howarth, R. Santoro, and Anthony Ingraffea." *Springer,* July 2012. http://link.springer.com/article/10.1007%2 Fs10584–011–0333–0.

China Statistical Yearbook: National Bureau of Statistics: www.stats.gov.cn/english;
www.chinability.com/Population.htm; and http://indexmundi.com/china
.population.html.

Cummins, Ronnie. "In 2013, Our Fight against GMO Food Continues." *Common
Dreams,* January 3, 2013. www.commondreams.org/view/2013/01/03-9.

Cummins, Ronnie, and Katherine Paul. "Did Monsanto Win Prop 37? Round One in
the Food Fight of Our Lives." *Alternet,* November 9, 2012. www.alternet.org/food
/did-monsanto-win-prop-37-round-one-food-fight-our-lives?paging=off.

Dawson, Jonathon quotation. *Findhorn Now.* By the Findhorn Foundation, 2008.
www.findhorn.org/video.

Dean, Amy, D.O. "Genetically Modified Foods." American Academy of Environmental
Medicine, May 8, 2009. www.aaemonline.org/gmopost.html.

Doyle, Alister. "World seed banks get funds to tackle climate, other threats."
Reuters, January 30, 2013. www.reuters.com/article/2013/01/31/
us-climate-crops-idUSBRE90U00020130131.

Dunn, Collin. "Vermicomposting and Vermiculture: Worms, Bins and How to Get
Started." *Treehugger,* August 2, 2007. www.treehugger.com/green-food
/vermicomposting-and-vermiculture-worms-bins-and-how-to-get-started.html.

Earle, Sylvia. "The Sweet Spot in Time: Why the Ocean Matters to Everyone
Everywhere." *Virginia Quarterly Review,* Fall 2012. www.vqronline.org/
articles/2012/fall/earle-oceans.

Environmental Defense Fund, 2007, Report. "Blown Away, How Global Warming Is
Eroding the Availability of Insurance Coverage in America's Coastal States."
www.edf.org/documents/7301_BlownAway_insurancereport.pdf.

Etter, Lauren. "Farmers Wonder if Boom in Grain Prices Is a Bubble." *Wall Street Journal
Online,* January 31, 2008. http://online.wsj.com/public/article
/SB120174466624943059580VjileKfXzheSxhrmkWufQ_Y5s_20080301.
html?mod=tff_main_tff_top.

Everley, Stephen. "On Shaky Ground (Update IV)." Energy in Depth, March 28, 2013.
http://energyindepth.org/national/on-shaky-ground-2.

Farenhold, David A. "Documents Indicate Heavy Use of Dispersants in Gulf Oil Spill."
Washington Post, August 1, 2010. www.washingtonpost.com/wp-dyn/content
/article/2010/07/31/AR2010073102381.html.

Fernia, Will. "Oil industry's best: paper towels." *Maddow Blog,* April 8, 2013.
http://maddowblog.msnbc.com/_news/2013/04/08/17660683-oil-industrys-best
-paper-towels?lite.

Freedman, Andrew. "2012 Has Been Warmest Year in U.S. to Date, Third Hottest
Summer." *Huffington Post,* September 10, 2012. www.huffingtonpost.com
/2012/09/10/2012-warmest-year-summer-record-breaking_n_1871216.html.

Friends of the Earth. "Major U.S. Supermarkets to Boycott GE Salmon." *Ecowatch,*
March 21, 2013. http://ecowatch.com/2013/supermarkets-boycott-ge-salmon.

Gipson, Terry. "Fracking. First Hand." *Senator Terry Gipson* (website), 2011.
www.terrygipsonny.com/fracking.

Goldenberg, Suzanne. "Al Gore says Obama Must Veto 'Atrocity' of Keystone XL Tar
    Sands Pipeline." *Guardian,* June 15, 2013. www.guardian.co.uk/environment/2013
    /jun/15/al-gore-obama-keystone-pipeline?CMP=twt_gu.
Gore, Al. Text of Speech on challenge of converting to alternative energy forms by 2020:
    www.npr.org/templates/story/story.php?storyId=92638501 or http://blog.algore.com
    /2008/07/a_generational_challenge_to_re.html.
———. Opening Comments at Training for New Climate Leaders. Hyatt Regency
    Hotel, August 29, 2012, Burlingame, California.
Green America. "Solving the Diaper Dilemma, *Green America,* January/February 2003.
    www.greenamerica.org/livinggreen/diapers.cfm.
Hammer, Rebecca. "In Fracking's Wake: New Rules Are Needed to Protect Our Health
    and Environment from Contaminated Wastewater." NRDC, May 2012. www.nrdc
    .org/energy/files/Fracking-Wastewater-FullReport.pdf.
Hansen, James E. "Climate change is here—and worse than we thought." *Washington
    Post,* August 3, 2012. www.washingtonpost.com/opinions/climate-change-is
    -here—and-worse-than-we-thought/2012/08/03/6ae604c2-dd90–11e1–8e43–4a3c
    4375504a_story.html.
Howarth, Robert W., Santoro, R. and Ingraffea, Anthony. "Methane and the
    Greenhouse-Gas Footprint of Natural Gas from Shale Formations." *Springer,* 2011.
    eeb.cornell.edu/howarth/Howarth%20et%20al%20%202011.pdf.
———. "Venting and Leaking of Methane from Shale Gas Development: Response to
    Cathles et al." *Springer,* 2011. www.eeb.cornell.edu/howarth/publications
    /Howarthetal2012_Final.pdf.
Hughes, Melissa L. quoted in "Enhancing Coexistence: A Report of the AC21 to the
    Secretary of Agriculture." USDA Advisory Committee on Biotechnology and 21st
    Century Agriculture (AC21), November 19, 2012. www.usda.gov/documents
    /ac21_report-enhancing-coexistence.pdf.
Kimbrell, Andrew. "High-tech Piracy." *Utne Reader,* March-April, 1996. www.utne.
    com/1996–03–01/high-tech-piracy.aspx.
Konigsberg, Eric. "Kuwait on the Prairie." *The New Yorker,* April 25, 2011. www.new
    yorker.com/reporting/2011/04/25/110425fa_fact_konigsberg?currentPage=all.
Mackenzie, Debora. "Billions at Risk from Wheat Super-Blight." *New Scientist,* April 3,
    2008. http://environment.newscientist.com/earth/mg19425983.700-billions-at
    -risk-from-wheat-superblight.html.
Market Watch. "America's Top 5 Oil-Producing States," *Wall Street
    Journal,* December 12, 2012. www.marketwatch.com/story/
    americas-top-5-oil-producing-states-2012–12–12.
Mathai, Wangari. "The Linkage between Patenting of Life Forms, Genetic Engineering,
    and Food Insecurity." October 11, 2004. http://lists.iatp.org/listarchive/archive.
    cfm?id+97248.
Mazza, Patrick. "Adventures in the Smart Grid, No. 1: Why the Smart Grid Is
    Important." *Grist,* June 10, 2007. www.grist.org/article/adventures-in-the-smart
    -grid-no-1.

Mendelsohn, Robert. "Environmental Accounting for Pollution in the United States Economy." *American Economic Review, 2011.* www.aeaweb.org/articles .php?doi=10.1257/aer.101.5.1649.

Mieszkowski, Katherine. "Superbug to the Rescue." Salon, August 28, 2003. www.salon .com/tech//feature/2003/08/28/bioremediation

Moyers, Bill. "Remarks at the 5th Annual Ron Ridenhour Prizes." *Huffington Post*, April 7, 2008. www.huffingtonpost.com/bill-moyers/on-journalism_b_95444.html.

Mufson, Stephen. "Documents Indicate Heavy Use of Dispersants in Gulf Oil Spill." *Washington Post,* August 1, 2010. www.washingtonpost.com/wp-dyn/content /article/2010/07/31/AR2010073102381.html.

Muller, Nicholas Z. "Environmental Accounting for Pollution in the United States Economy." *American Economic Review, 2011.* www.aeaweb.org/articles .php?doi=10.1257/aer.101.5.1649.

Munich Re Press. "North America Most Affected by Increase in Weather-Related Natural Catastrophes." Munich RE, October 17, 2012. www.munichre.com/en /media_relations/press_releases/2012/2012_10_17_press_release.aspx.

National Ocean Service, "The Gulf of Mexico at a Glance: A Second Glance." Washington, DC: U.S. Department of Commerce, 2011. http://stateofthecoast .noaa.gov/NOAAs_Gulf_of_Mexico_at_a_Glance_report.pdf.

National Resources Defense Council. "Dirty Coal Is Hazardous to Your Health." www.nrdc.org/health/effects.coal.index.asp.

Nordhaus, William. "Environmental Accounting for Pollution in the United States Economy." *American Economic Review, 2011.* www.aeaweb.org/articles .php?doi=10.1257/acr.101.5.1649.

Nunez, Joe. "History and Lessons of Potato Late Blight." December 21, 2000. http://cekern.ucdavis.edu/Custom_Program573/History_and_Lessons_of_Potato _Late_Blight.htm.

O'Hara, Doug. "The World's Best Seeds Head for Arctic Vault." www.farnorthscience .com/2008/01/25.

Oliver, Rachel. "All About Food and Fossil Fuels." CNN, March 17, 2008. http://edition .cnn.com/2008/WORLD/asiapcf/03/16/eco.food.miles.

Ott, Riki. "At What Cost? BP Spill Responders Told to Forgo Precautionary Health Measures in Cleanup." *Huffington Post*, May 17, 2010. www.huffingtonpost.com /riki-ott/at-what-cost-bp-spill-res_b_578784.html.

Paik, Analiese. "Connecticut's GE Foods Bill Eviscerated by Lawyers." *Fairfield Green Food Guide*, May 5, 2012. http://fairfieldgreenfoodguide.com/2012/05/05 /connecticuts-ge-foods-bill.

Perpetua, Sonya. "Arkansas residents seek millions after Exxon crude oil spill." NBC News, April, 7, 2013. www.nbcnews.com/business/arkansas-residents -seek-millions-after-exxon-crude-oil-spill-1C9254722.

Philpott, Tom. "A Reflection on the Lasting Legacy of 1970s USDA Secretary Earl Butz." *Grist*, February 7, 2008. www.grist.org/article/the-butz-stops-here.

Pollack, Andrew. "Modified Wheat Is Discovered in Oregon." *New York Times,* May 29,

2013. www.nytimes.com/2013/05/30/business/energy-environment/genetically
-engineered-wheat-found-in-oregon-field.html?_r=0.

Pope, C. T. "Vanishing Lake Chad—A Water Crisis in Central Africa."
Circle of Blue. www.circleofblue.org/waternews/2008/world/
vanishing-lake-chad-a-water-crisis-in-central-africa.

Pribyl, Louis J. "Biotechnology Draft Documents 2/27/92." March 6, 1992. www.bio
integrity.com.org.

Quinlan, Paul. "Less Toxic Dispersants Lose Out in BP Oil Spill Cleanup." *New York
Times,* May 13, 2010. www.nytimes.com/2010/05/13/business/energy
-environment/13greenwire-less-toxic-dispersants-lose-out-in-bp-oil-spil-81183
.html?_r=0.

Raloff, Janet. "Afghanistan's Seed Banks Destroyed." *Science News*, September 11, 2002.
www.sciencenews.org/articles/20020914/food.asp.

Rohr, Richard. "What Is the Emerging Church?" Webcast of November 8, 2008.
www.cac.org.

Rosenthal, Elisabeth. "U.S. to Be World's Top Oil Producer in 5 Years, Report Says."
New York Times, November 12, 2012. www.nytimes.com/2012/11/13/business
/energy-environment/report-sees-us-as-top-oil-producer-in-5-years.html?_r=1&.

Rosner, Hillary. "Seeds to Save a Species." *Popular Science,* January 4, 2008. www.popsci
.com/scitech/article/2008–01/seeds-save-species.

Rulis, Alan, M. "Biotechnology Consultation Agency Response Letter BNF No. 000034
to Dr. Kent Croon, Monsanto from FDA." September 25, 1996. www.fda.gov/Food
/FoodScienceResearch/Biotechnology/Submissions/ucm161107.htm

Sachs, Jeffrey. "Paths to Sustainable Power." Project Syndicate website, March 28, 2013.
www.project-syndicate.org/commentary/building-a-twenty-first-century-global
-energy-system-by-jeffrey-d—sachsms8SGqeiuddGi3pF.99.

Sadamori, Keisuke. "Medium-Term Coal Market Report 2012." International
Energy Agency, December 18, 2012. www.iea.org/newsroomandevents/
speeches/121218MCMR2012_presentation_KSK.pdf.

Sanchez, Pedro. "The Climate Change-Soil Fertility Nexus," http://ifpri.org/2020
conference/PDF/summary_sanchez.pdf.

Schiffman, Richard. "Grassroots Campaigns Can Stop Fracking One Town at a Time."
Guardian, May 13, 2013. www.guardian.co.uk/commentisfree/2013/may/13
/fracking-new-york-grassroots-campaign-to-stop.

Schmeiser, Percy interview. www.percyschmeiser.com/AcresUSAstory.pdf.

Shapley, Dan. "Doomsday Seed Bank Opens This Week." *The Daily Green,* February 26,
2008. www.thedailygreen.com/environmental-news/latest
/doomsday-seeds-47022403.

Shaw, Susan. "Swimming Through the Spill," *New York Times,* May 29 2010.
www.nytimes.com/2010/05/30/opinion/30shaw.html?_r=0.

Shay, Nick. "Gulf Warm-Water Eddies Intensify Hurricane Changes." Press release.
www.nsf.gov/news/news_summ.jsp?cntn_id=104483.

Shiva, Vandana. "Ecologists Should Worry about the Dunkel Draft." September 23,
1993. www.sunsonline.org/trade/areas/environm/09230193.htm.

Snow, Nick. "Salazar Finalizes Oil Shale Plan; BLM Proposes Revisions." *Oil and Gas Journal,* April 1, 2013. www.ogj.com/articles/print/volume-111/issue-4/general -interest/salazar-finalized-oil-shale-plan-blm-proposes.html.

Strom, Stephanie. "Seeking Food Ingredients That Aren't Gene-Altered." *New York Times,* May 26, 2013. www.nytimes.com/2013/05/27/business/food companies -seeking-ingredients-that-arent-gene-altered.html?smid=fb-share&_r=0.

Tarnas, Richard. Lecture given in Chicago, Illinois, 2009.

Taylor, Jill Bolte. Full video and transcript at www.ted.com/talks/lang/eng/jill_bolte _taylor_s_powerful_stroke_of_insight.html.

Thill, Scott. "Frankenfoods' Giant Monsanto Plays Bully over Consumer Labeling." March 6, 2008. www.alternet.org/workplace/78860.

Union of Concerned Scientists. "How It Works: Water for Natural Gas." Union of Concerned Scientists. 2011. Available at http://www.ucsusa.org/clean_energy/our -energy-choices/energy-and-water-use/water-energy-electricity-natural-gas.html.

Urbina, Ian. "U.S. Said to Allow Drilling Without Needed Permits." *New York Times,* May 13, 2010. www.nytimes.com/2010/05/14/us/14agency. html?pagewanted=1&_r=2&.

———. "Pressure Limits Efforts to Police Drilling for Gas," *New York Times,* March 3, 2011. www.nytimes.com/2011/03/04/us/04gas.html?pagewanted=1&_r=3&.

U.S. Department of the Interior press release, "Bakken Formation Oil Assessment in North Dakota, Montana will be updated by U.S. Geological Survey," May 19, 2011. www.doi.gov/news/pressreleases/Bakken-Formation-Oil-Assessment-in-North- Dakota-Montana-will-be-updated-by-US-Geological-Survey.cfm.

VanBriesen, Jeanne. "In Fracking's Wake: New Rules are Needed to Protect Our Health and Environment from Contaminated Wastewater." NRDC, May, 2012. www.nrdc.org/energy/files/Fracking-Wastewater-FullReport.pdf.

Walsh, Bryan. "The Scariest Environmental Fact in the World." *Time,* January 29, 2013. http://science.time.com/2013/01/29/the-scariest-environmental-fact-in-the-world.

Weiss, Rick. "USDA Backs Production of Rice with Human Genes." *Washington Post,* March 2, 2007. www.washingtonpost.com/wp-dyn/content/article/2007/03/01 /AR2007030101495.html.

White, Jim. "Carol Browner Says 75% of Spilled BP Oil is Gone, Georgia Sea Grant Scientists 70–79% Remains in Gulf." *Firedoglake,* August 17, 2010. http:// my.firedoglake.com/jimwhite/2010/08/17/carol-browner-says-75-of-spilled-bp-oil -is-gone-georgia-sea-grant-scientists-say-70–79-remains-in-gulf.

Wood, Ruth, et al. "Shale Gas: A Provisional Assessment of Climate Change and Environmental Impacts." Tyndall Centre Manchester, January 2011. tyndall.ac.uk /sites/default/files/coop_shale_gas_report_final_200111.pdf.

Woynillowicz, Dan. "Tar Sands Fever." *WorldWatch Magazine,* September/October 2007. www.worldwatch.org/node/5287.

Yue, Pan. "The Chinese Miracle Will End Soon." *Der Spiegel,* March 7, 2005.

Documentary Films and CDs

The 11th Hour. Produced by Leonardo DiCaprio. Directed by Nadia Connors and Leila Connors Peterson. Warner Brothers, 2007.

Bad Seed: The Truth about Our Food. Directed and produced by Timo Nadudari and Adam Curry, Scared Crow Productions, 2006.

Bag It: Is Your Life Too Plastic? Directed by Suzan Beraza, Reelthing Films, 2010.

Bidder 70. Directed by Beth and George Gage, written by Beth Gage. Gage & Gage Productions, 2013

Blue Gold: World Water Wars. Directed and narrated by Sam Bozzo. Based on the book by Maude Barlow, Purple Turtle Films, 2008.

Breaking Fuel from the Rock. Illustrations by Stephen Roundtree, design by Stefan Estrada, National Geographic. news.nationalgeographic.com/news/2010/10/101022-breaking-fuel-from-the-rock.

Chasing Ice. Directed by Jeff Orlowski, written by Mark Monroe, Exposure Productions in association with Diamond Docs, 2012.

A Chemical Reaction. Written and directed by Brett Plymale and Paul Tukey, a Pfzmedia production, 2009.

The Clean Bin Project. Directed by Grant Baldwin. Peg Leg Films, 2010.

The Corporation. Produced by Mark Achbar and Bart Simpson. Directed by Mark Achbar and Jennifer Abbott. Zeitgeist Films, 2005.

DIRT! The Movie. Produced and Directed by Bill Benenson and Gene Roscow. Common Ground Media, 2009.

End of Suburbia. Produced by Gregory Green, directed by Barrie Zwicker. Electric Wallpaper Production, 2004.

Fierce Light. Written and directed by Velcrow Ripper. Alive Mind Productions, 2008.

Flow: For Love of Water. Directed by Irena Salina, Group Entertainment/Stephen Starr Productions, 2008.

Food, Inc. Produced and directed by Robert Kenner and Eric Schlosser. Magnolia Pictures Production, 2008.

Frankensteer. Directed by Marrin Canell and Ted Remerowski, written and narrated by Ted Remerowski. Paradigm Productions, 2005.

The Future of Food. Produced by Catherine Lynn Butler. Directed by Deborah Koons Garcia. Lily Films Production, 2004.

Garbage—The Revolution Begins at Home. Written and directed by Andrew Nisker. Garbageman Productions, 2008. www.garbagerevolution.com.

The Garden. Written and directed by Scott Hamilton Kennedy, Black Valley Films, 2008.

Gasland. Written and directed by Josh Fox. HBO Documentary Films, 2010

Gasland part II. Written and directed by Josh Fox. HBO Documentary Films, International Wow Company, 2013.

The GMO Trilogy. Three disk set. Produced by Jeffrey Smith. *(Unnatural Selection* by Bertram Verhaag and Gabriele Krober, produced by Bertram Verhaag and Michel Morales, a DENKmal and Haifisch Films Production, 2004.)

Idle Threat. Written and directed by George Pakenham. Verdant Vigilante, 2012.

Ingredients. Directed by Robert Bates. Optic Nerve Productions, 2009.

Into Great Silence: Inside the Famed Carthusian Monastery. Written and directed by Philip Groning, produced by Philip Groning, Andres Pfaffli and others. Zeitgeist Films, 2008.

King Korn. Produced by Curt Ellis, Ian Cheney, and Aaron Wolf. Directed by Aaron Wolf. Mosaic Films and ITVS Production, 2007.

The Last Reef. Written and directed by Luke Creswell and Steve McNicholas. Giant Screen Films, Liquid Pictures, and Yes/No Productions, 2012.

Symphony of the Soil. Written and directed by Deborah Koons. Lily Films, 2012.

Tapped. Directed by Stephanie Soechtig and Jason Lindsey. Written by Josh David, Jason Lindsey, and Stephanie Soechtig. Atlas Films, 2009.

The Water Front: Directed by Liz Miller. Red Lizard Media, 2008.

You're Eating What? Audio CD by Jeffrey Smith. http://SeedsofDeception.com.

YouTube Videos

Earle, Sylvia. "How to Protect the Oceans." 2009 TED Prize winner. http://blog.ted.com/2009/02/19/sylvia_earles_t.

Finegold, Seth. "When We Grow, This Is What We Can Do." 2011. www.youtube.com/watch?v=PSKJrgGqx_E.

Howarth, Bob and others. "Marcellus Shale Gas and Global Warming." March 31, 2011. www.shaleshockmedia.org/2011/03/31/marcellus-shale-gas-and-global-warming.

Ingraffea, Anthony. "The Intersection Between Hydraulic Fracturing and Climate Change." www.youtube.com/watch?v=o78j77I7XUw.

United States Department of Agriculture. "Hemp for Victory." 1942. www.youtube.com/watch?v=jokV8xlJTNE.

Radio Programs

"Morning Edition Interview." National Public Radio. May 25, 2005.

"Residents Say Levee Leaked Months Before Katrina." National Public Radio. November 22, 2005.

"Saving Kids from 'Nature Deficit Disorder.' " National Public Radio. May 25, 2005.

Television Broadcasts

Horatio's Drive. Directed by Ken Burns, co-produced by Dayton Duncan and Ken Burns, produced by Florentine Films, 2005.

"Kuwait Still Recovering from Gulf War Fires." Directed by Ryan Chilcote, CNN, January 3, 2003.

The Journey of the Corps of Discovery. Directed by Ken Burns, produced by Florentine Films and WETA, 1997.

Lewis and Clark: The Journey of the Corps of Discovery. Directed by Ken Burns, produced by Florentine Films and WETA, 1997.

"Melissa Harris-Perry." *MSNBC,* May 27, 2013.

The National Parks: America's Best Idea. Directed by Ken Burns, produced by Florentine Films and WETA, 2009.

"The Rachel Maddow Show." *MSNBC,* March 24, 2011.

"The Silent Spring of Rachel Carson." *CBS Reports,* 1963.

General Websites Referenced

www.aoml.noaa.gov (Atlantic Oceanographic and Meteorological Laboratory/National Oceanic and Atmospheric Administration)

www.agmrc.org/NR/rdonlyres/6D092BD1–481D43D195CDB8F1821E2F19/0/AIC_FBIB_3organic.pdf (Organic Trade Association's 2006 Manufacturer Survey)

http://fire.ca.gov/index_incidents_overview.php (California wildfire information)

www.ca.gov (Oil and Gas Production History in California)

www.climateprogress.org (Climate Progress)

http://co2now.org (Earth's CO2 homepage)

www.doi.gov/ (U.S. Department of the Interior)

www.edf.org (Environmental Defense Fund)

www.eia.doe.gov/emeu/aer/txt/ptb1105.html (U.S. Department of Energy)

www.foodandwaterwatch.org/water/bottled/ (Food and Water Watch)

www.gmfreeireland.org (GM-Free Ireland)

http://hubblesite.org/ (Hubble telescope)

http://hydrogenroadtour08.dot.gov. ("Hydrogen Road Tour "08")

www.isec.org.ul/toolkit/ustoolkit/html (ISEC Local Toolkit Factsheet)

www.kilgorechamber.com (Kilgore, Texas)

www.nasa.gov/centers/goddard/news/topstory/2003/0321kuwaitfire.html (Kuwaiti oil field fires aftermath)

www.nationalgeographic.com/ (National Geographic)

www.nrdc.org/ (National Resources Defense Council)

www.nytimes.com/interactive/2007/10/01/science/20071002_ ARCTIC_GRAPHIC.html (Animated photos of disappearing ice masses)

www.noaanews.noaa.gov/stories2006/s2656.htm (Hurricane Katrina danger bulletin)

www.nps.gov/yell/naturescience/wildlandfire.htm (Twentieth year anniversary of 1988 fire in Yellowstone)

www.peopleandplanet.net/doc.php?id=2848 (People and Diversity website)

http://maddowblog.msnbc.com (Blog for the Rachel Maddow Show)

www.marketwatch.com (The Wall Street Journal)

http://storyofstuff.org (Also see The Story of Stuff Project's Story of Bottled Water at storyofstuff.org/movies/story-of-bottled-water)

http://links.svalbard.com/index.php?PHPSESSID=j39ghqfbdbhhsfq17rj8892012 (The Svalbard Pages)

Governmental Publications Referenced and Available Online

www.chinability.com/Population.htm (Latest news and statistics on China's economy
and business climate)

http://indexmundi.com/china/population.html (China Population according to CIA
Factbook)

China Statistical Yearbook; National Bureau of Statistics web site: www.stats.gov.cn
/english/ and www.pecad.fas.usda.gov/highlights/2012/03/china%20wheat/

Dooley, Alan. "Sandboils 101: Corps Has Experience Dealing with Common Flood
Danger." http://hq.usace.army.mil/pubs/jun06/story8.htm

www.aoml.noaa.gov (Atlantic Oceanographic and Meteorological Laboratory website)

www.blancogovernor.com/index.cfm/?md=newsroom&tmp=detail&articleID=1523&
("Response to U.S. Senate Committee on Homeland Security and Government
Affairs and Information Request Dated October 7, 2005, and to the House of
Representatives Select Committee to Investigate the Preparation for the Response
to Hurricane Katrina." December 2, 2005.)

www.earth-policy.org/Updates/Update29.htm (Environmental Policy Institute Bulletin)

http://earthobservatory.nasa.gov/Features/GlobalWarming/ (Facts about and latest
updates on global warming)

epa.gov/ghgreporting/documents/pdf/2010/Subpart-W_TSD.pdf (Environmental
Protection Agency report: Greenhouse Gas Emissions Reporting From Petroleum
and Natural Gas Industry)

www.gulflink.osd.mil/owf_ii_tabc.htm (Gulflink, Office of the Special Assistant for the
Gulf War Illness)

www.ipcc.ch/ (Report from Intergovernmental Panel on Climate Change, November
2007. Available as a pdf)

www.nass.usda.gov (Annual U.S. crop statistics, including production reports)

U. S. House of Representatives Committee on Energy and Commerce. (Rep. Waxman
Statement on HHS Report Finding Significant Affordable Care Act Savings
for Consumers, 2011.) http://democrats.energycommerce.house.gov/index.
php?q=news%2Fwaxman-markey-and-degette-investigation-finds-continued-use
-of-diesel-in-hydraulic-fracturing-f

Sources for Journaling and Spiritual Autobiography

Boswell, James, Samuel Johnson, with an introduction by Peter Levi. *The Journey to
the Western Islands of Scotland* and *The Journal of a Tour to the Hebrides.* New York:
Penguin, *1984.*

Cameron, Julia. *The Artist's Way.* New York: Tarcher/Putnam, 2002.

Dillard, Annie. *The Writing Life.* New York: Harper, 1990.

Dowrick, Stephanie. *Journal Writing: the Art and Heart of Reflection.* New York: Tarcher
/Penguin, 2009.

Frank, Anne. *The Diary of Anne Frank.* New York: Doubleday, 1967.

Goldberg, Natalie. *Writing Down the Bones: Freeing the Writer Within.* Boston: Shambhala, 2005.

Lamott, Anne. *Bird by Bird: Some Instructions on Writing and Life.* New York: Anchor /Random House, 1995.

Least Heat-Moon, William. *Blue Highways: A Journey into America.* New York: Little Brown, 1982.

Occhiogrosso, Peter. Classes on Sacred Journaling at his website: www.joyofsects.com /class.shtml and select Sacred Journaling.

Powell, Julie. *The Julie/Julia Project:* http://blogs.salon.com/0001399/2002/08/25.html or http://juliepowell.blogspot.com/ and *Julie and Julia: 365 Days, 524 Recipes, 1 Tiny Apartment,* New York: Little Brown, 2005.

Steinbeck, John. *Travels with Charley in Search of America.* New York: Bantam, 1963.

Thoreau, Henry David. *Walden; or, A Life in the Woods.* Mineola: Dover Publications, 1995.

Wakefield, Dan. *The Story of Your Life: Writing a Spiritual Autobiography.* Boston: Beacon Press, 1990.

A Few Green-Oriented Websites

Note: In addition to the many websites mentioned in chapter 6, there are thousands of green websites, with more coming online every day.

Some farms and ranches have CSAs devoted exclusively to animal-based foods. Search CSAs nationally at http://eatwellguide.org and http://localharvest.org/cas (also check out the Green Fork blog at http://blog.eatwellguide.org—and join it on Facebook if you want instant updates)

www.foodnews.org to find out how to buy organic and what and how to substitute when organic food products are not available.

www.soulofthegarden.com is an amazing website of spiritual and nature sensibilities updated by an Austin native.

www.TED.com features speakers from all arenas of life, from politics, philosophy, and science to the wonders of new inventions; this website is all about what's next and features a diversity of visionaries from all over the world who share their ideas in short, engaging talks.

www.thedailygreen.com provides hits on all things green going on. Short but to the point.

www.treehugger.com is a good general clearinghouse of information about the environment.

http://truefoodnow.org is the Center for Food Safety's True Food Network website advocating healthy food activism.

unitedplantsavers.org is the site for the 360-acre botanical garden that grows endangered indigenous and healing plants that are being threatened in North America.

worldchanging.com is the website for the award-winning book on sustainability and a multiplicity of resources, *WorldChanging*.

www.youtube.com has many videos that can help you go green in endless ways. You can get tips on gardening, composting, seed saving, creating hybrids, permaculture, and biodynamics. There are even previews of the latest documentaries tracking the health of our food, the changes happening to the planet, and the growing cast of characters who are adding their voices to the daily news. It could be called the personal journal gone global. If you have some green wisdom to share, post it yourself.

Biodynamics

For more information about biodynamics, contact the Josephine Porter Institute for detailed listings that show the best calendar times for working the soil, applying the various biodynamic preparations and working with plants in general (jpibiodynamics.org). Also see the Pfeiffer Institute (pfeiffercenter.org) for information about training in biodynamic agriculture.

Notes

Introduction

1. Richard Louv, interview by Steve Inskeep, "Saving Kids from 'Nature Deficit Disorder,'" Morning Edition, NPR, May 25, 2005.
2. "The Top Prescription Drugs of 2011 in the United States: Antipsychotics and Antidepressants Once Again Lead CNS Therapeutics," ACS Chemical Neuroscience, August 15, 2012, website at http://pubs.acs.org/doi/pdfplus/10.1021/cn3000923.
3. Charles Barber, *Comfortably Numb, How Psychiatry Is Medicating a Nation* (New York: Pantheon, 2008), xvi.
4. Thomas Berry, *The Dream of the Earth* (San Francisco: Sierra Club Books, 2006), 12.
5. Bill Moyers, "On Journalism," April 7, 2008, www.huffingtonpost.com/bill-moyers/on-journalism_b_95444.html.
6. Increasingly the two terms are being used interchangeably. In general, global warming refers to the idea that humanity is largely responsible for the measurable increase in the warming of average global temperatures since the Industrial Revolution, due to the rise of greenhouse gases (primarily CO_2) in the atmosphere. Climate change is the condition directly affected by the warming of the globe and the effect probably most recognizable by people as sea levels rise, storms become bigger and more intense and destructive, and other long-term effects—like floods, droughts, desertification of land masses, and increased wildfires—become the new norm instead of once-in-a-lifetime events.
7. From an interview in the 2007 documentary, *The 11th Hour,* produced by Leonardo DiCaprio and Warner Brothers Films.
8. Billy Baker, "Saving 'God's Creation' Unites Scientist, Evangelical Leader," *Boston Globe,* May 1, 2008.
9. Edward O. Wilson, *The Social Conquest of Earth* (New York: Norton, 2012), 7.

Chapter 1: Understanding What We're Made Of

1. The full video and transcript of Dr. Jill Bolte Taylor's story is (http://www.ted.com /talks/jill_bolte_taylor_s_powerful_stroke_of_insight.html); it is also described in her book, *My Stroke of Insight* (New York: Viking, 2006).
2. Paul Hawken, *Blessed Unrest: How the Largest Social Movement in History Is Restoring Grace, Justice, and Beauty to the World* (New York: Viking, 2007), 143.
3. Ibid., 170.
4. Caroline Myss, *Anatomy of the Spirit, The Seven Stages of Power and Healing* (New York: Random House, 1996), xiii.
5. Caroline Myss, *Sacred Contracts, Awakening Your Divine Potential* (New York: Random House, 2001), 165.
6. Information about the chakras and details in the chakra table was compiled from books by Caroline Myss, including *Anatomy of the Spirit, Sacred Contracts,* and *Entering the Castle* (New York: Simon and Schuster, 2008), as well as lectures at her educational institute, CMED.
7. Myss, *Anatomy of the Spirit,* 73.
8. Paul Devereux, *Re-visioning the Earth: A Guide to Reopening the Healing Channels Between Mind and Nature* (New York: Simon and Schuster, 1996), 44.
9. Wendell Berry, *The Unsettling of America: Culture and Agriculture* (Berkeley: Sierra Club Books, 1996), 35.
10. Hawken, *Blessed Unrest,* 145.
11. Ibid., 144.
12. Devereux, *Re-visioning the Earth,* 14.
13. From a lecture at a Caroline Myss workshop at the Hyatt Regency Hotel, Oak Brook, IL, 2003.
14. "The Silent Spring of Rachel Carson," *CBS Reports* documentary, 1963.
15. Hawken, *Blessed Unrest,* 171.
16. Richard Louv, *Last Child in the Woods* (Chapel Hill, NC: Algonquin Books, 2005), 296.
17. Devereux, *Re-visioning the Earth,* 15.
18. William Kempton, James S. Boster, and Jennifer A. Hartley, *Environmental Values in American Culture* (Cambridge, MA: MIT Press, 1997), chap. 1.
19. Quotes from Rabbi Lerner and Imam Rauf from *The 11th Hour,* produced by Leonardo DiCaprio, directed by Nadia Connors and Leila Connors Peterson, Warner Bros., Los Angeles, CA, 2007.
20. Berry, *The Unsettling of America,* 23.

Chapter 2: The Bed We Have Made

1. "Residents Say Levee Leaked Months Before Katrina," *Morning Edition,* National Public Radio, November 22, 2005.
2. Bob Marshall, "Levee Leaks Reported to S&WB a Year Ago," *New Orleans Times-Picayune,* November 18, 2005.

3. Ibid.
4. Alan Dooley, *Sandboils 101: Corps Has Experience Dealing with Common Flood Danger,* http://archive.is/FFbPG.
5. Michael Dyson, *Come Hell or High Water: Hurricane Katrina and the Color of Disaster* (New York: Basic Civitas Books, 2006).
6. Marshall, "Levee Leaks Reported to S&WB a Year Ago."
7. Douglas Brinkley, *The Great Deluge* (New York: Harper, 2005), 7.
8. A recent exception was Hurricane Ike's category 2 winds that struck in September of 2008, defying even this protection when its winds sent water surging over the wall, inundating the town. Natural gas explosions set off fires, but buildings were left to burn because the water was too deep for fire trucks to reach them. From there, Ike moved on to Houston where, in scenes reminiscent of Katrina, residents clung to rooftops begging rescue. At one point, ninety-nine percent of the city's energy provider Centergy's 2.25 million area customers were without any type of power. The company had to bring in 10,000 linemen from across the country to handle debris and repair work. The giant storm ran northeasterly from Texas, up through the entire Ohio Valley. Flash floods and deaths were reported from Texas to Chicago, where the water damage was so sudden and extensive, the Illinois governor had to declare the state a disaster area. One of Ike's deadliest characteristics was its size and slow movement. The storm lasted two full weeks from its days as a baby depression in the central south Atlantic. As it made landfall rolling over Galveston, it stretched nearly six hundred miles, covering up much of the northern Gulf of Mexico, before blowing inland, wreaking havoc in a band that included the northern tier of states, eventually exiting to the North Atlantic via Canada. See Daniel Yovich, "Ike's Remnants Blamed for Midwest Deaths, Blackouts," *Associated Press,* September 15, 2008.
9. "Labor Day Hurricane of 1935: Heavy Life Loss Feared among Keys," September 3, 1935, *SunSentinel* (From the archives of the *Fort Lauderdale Daily News*), www.sun-sentinel.com/news/local/southflorida/sfl-9.12.1935hurricane1,0,6600953.story.
10. A millibar (mbar) is a meteorological way to metrically measure the air pressure of a storm. The lower the pressure, the higher the winds and stronger the storms. Air pressure in a hurricane decreases as the storm's power increases, so the lower the millibars, the worse the storm.
11. John McQuaid and Mark Schleifstein, "In Harm's Way," part of the five-part series, "Washing Away," *New Orleans Times-Picayune,* June 23–27, 2002.
12. "Inventory of Debris Flows and Floods in the Lovingston and Horseshoe Mountain, VA, 7.5' Quadrangles, from the August 19/20, 1969 Storm in Nelson County, Virginia," U.S. Geological Survey, http://pubs.usgs.gov/of/1999/ofr-99-0518/ofr-99-0518.html.
13. "NOAA Issues Service Assessment Report on Hurricane Katrina," www.noaanews.noaa.gov/stories2006/s2656.htm.
14. Brinkley, *The Great Deluge,* xiv–xv.
15. "Anatomy of a Disaster," *U.S. News and World Report,* September 26, 2005.

16. Report from the Intergovernmental Panel on Climate Change, November 2007, www.ipcc.ch.
17. As dire as its warnings are, evidence suggests that even these statements were watered down and edited versions of what the scientists' findings reported. The Copenhagen Climate Conference held in December 2009 was historic in that it brought together dignitaries from 193 nations for the first time to discuss the severity of the issues surrounding climate change and global warming, but at its conclusion, it generated little more than political, nonbinding statements. John M. Broder, "Many Goals Remain Unmet in 5 Nations' Climate Deal," *New York Times*, December 18, 2009.
18. Hawken, *Blessed Unrest*, 15.
19. Jon Gertner, "The Future is Drying Up," *New York Times Magazine*, October 21, 2007.
20. Lynn Chandler, "Africa's Lake Chad Shrinks by 20 Times Due to Irrigation Demands, Climate Change," GSFC press release (Greenbelt, MD: NASA, Goddard Space Flight Center, February 27, 2001).
21. C. T. Pope, "Vanishing Lake Chad—A Water Crisis in Central Africa," www.circleofblue.org/waternews/world/vanishing-lake-chad-a-water-crisis-in-central-africa.
22. Carol J. Williams, "Drought Yields Lake's Treasures and Trash," *The Nation*, July 19, 2007.
23. Andy Reed, "Lake Okeechobee Level Drops; Pumps Will Keep Water Flowing," *Sun-Sentinel*, May 8, 2009.
24. Alexandra Zavis, "DWP Offers Cash Incentives for Water-saving Landscapes," *Los Angeles Times*, June 2, 2009.
25. Brenda Goodman, "Drought-Stricken South Facing Tough Choices," *New York Times*, October 16, 2007.
26. Brenda Goodman, "Georgia Loses Federal Case in a Dispute about Water," *New York Times*, February 6, 2008.
27. James E. Hansen, "Climate Change Is Here—And Worse than We Thought," *Washington Post*, August 3, 2012, www.washingtonpost.com/opinions/climate-change-is-here—and-worse-than-we-thought/2012/08/03/6ae604c2-dd90-11e1-8e43-4a3c4375504a_story.html.
28. Brown, *Plan B 2.0*, 52.
29. Report on Research on the Reasons for Anguli Lake's Shrinkage and Drying Up Using Satellite Remote Sensing, from the International Archives of the Photogrammetry, Remote Sensing and Spatial Information Sciences, volume 37, part B7. Beijing 2008. www.isprs.org/proceedings/XXXVII/congress/7_pdf/11_SS-7/02.pdf.
30. NOAA National Climatic Data Center National Overview, March 2012: www.ncdc.noaa.gov/sotc/national/2012/3.
31. Andrew Freedman, "2012 Has Been Warmest Year in U.S. to Date, Third Hottest Summer," *Huffington Post*, September 10, 2012. www.huffingtonpost.com/2012/09/10/2012-warmest-year-summer-record-breaking_n_1871216.html.

32. Brown, *Plan B 2.0*, 42.

33. Ibid., 55.

34. China Statistical Yearbook; National Bureau of Statistics website: www.stats.gov.cn /english/ and www.pecad.fas.usda.gov/highlights/2012/03/china%20wheat.

35. www.chinability.com/Population.htm and http://indexmundi.com/china /population.html.

36. Brown, *Plan B 3.0*, 97.

37. Ibid., 96.

38. Ibid., 92.

39. Ibid., 70–71.

40. Source: NASA Goddard Institute for Space Studies website: www.giss.nasa.gov. This animation shows how this trend has been heating up since the 1880s: www.giss.nasa.gov/research/news/20130115.

41. The revised 2006 number is significantly higher than originally reported in 2003. Lester R. Brown, Earth Policy Institute, *Plan B 2.0* (New York: Norton, 2005), 251, and www.earth-policy.org/plan_b_updates/2006/update56.

42. Environmental Policy Institute bulletin, www.earthpolicy.org/Updates/Update29. htm.

43. Patrick Mazza, "Adventures in the Smart Grid, No. 1: Why the SmartGrid Is Important." *Grist*, June 10, 2007, http://grist.org/article/ adventures-in-the-smart-grid-no-1.

44. Steven W. Running, "Is Global Warming Causing More, Larger Wildfires?" *Science*, August 18, 2006.

45. Ibid.

46. Pedro Sanchez, "The Climate Change—Soil Fertility—Food Security Nexus," presented September 4–6, 2001, at Sustainable Food Security for all by 2020. www.ifpri.org/2020conference/PDF/summary_sanchez.pdf.

47. Brown, *Plan B*, 3.0, 53.

48. "Sea Ice in Retreat," *New York Times*, October 1, 2007, www.nytimes.com /interactive/2007/10/01/science/20071002_ARCTIC_GRAPHIC.html.

49. David Adams, "Ice-free Arctic Could Be Here in 23 Years," *Guardian*, September 5, 2007, updated January 14, 2008.

50. Andrew Freedman, "Large Fractures Spotted in Vulnerable Arctic Sea Ice," Climate Central, March 13, 2013, www.climatecentral.org/news/large-fractures-spotted -in-arctic-sea-ice-15728.

51. "The Arctic's Record Breaking Ice Melt," NOAAVisualizations, www.youtube.com /watch?v=UaKqhRTqSlg.

52. Brown, *Plan B 2.0*, 67.

53. David Barber interview in "The Big Melt: The Arctic Ice Cap," *New York Times*, video, November 29, 2005, www.nytimes.com/video/science/1194816481964/ the-big-melt-the-arctic-ice-cap.html?playlistId=1194811622279.

54. Ibid.

55. Ibid.

56. Sylvia Earle, "How to Protect the Oceans," TED, http:/blog.ted.com/2009/02/19 /sylvia_earles_t. The 2009 TED prizewinner.

57. Email to Ellen Gunter from Nancy Knowlton, coral reef biologist and Sant Chair for Marine Science at the Smithsonian's National Museum of Natural History, November 17, 2013.

58. Sylvia Earle, "The Sweet Spot in Time: Why the Ocean Matters to Everyone Everywhere," *Virginia Quarterly Review,* Fall 2012, www.vqronline.org/ articles/2012/fall/earle-oceans.

59. Seth Borenstein, "Climate Change: Arctic Passes 400 Parts per Million Milestone," *Associated Press*, May 31, 2012, www.csmonitor.com/Science/2012/0531/Climate -change-Arctic-passes-400-parts-per-million-milestone; and Justin Gillis, "Heat-Trapping Gas Passes Milestone, Raising Fears," *New York Times*, May 10, 2013, www.nytimes.com/2013/05/11/science/earth/carbon-dioxide-level-passes-long -feared-milestone.html?_r=0.

60. Kelly Zito and Matthew Yi, "Governor Declares Drought in California," *San Francisco Chronicle,* June 5, 2008.

61. "Threat of Wildfires in California Eases," *New York Times*, July 13, 2008, www. nytimes.com/2008/07/13/world/americas/13iht-12wildfire.14456554.html?_r=0.

62. Brinkley, *The Great Deluge,* 575–76.

63. http://www.ipccinfo.com/west.php.

64. Running, "Is Global Warming Causing More, Larger Wildfires?"

65. Ibid.

66. The text of Al Gore's speech can be found at www.npr.org/tem-plates/story/story.php?storyId=92638501 or at http://blog.algore. com/2008/07/a_generational_challenge_to_re.html.

67. Climate Change Indicators in the United States, Environmental Protection Agency report, p. 1. Updated August 2013. www.epa.gov/climatechange/science/indicators/ weather-climate/temperature.html.

68. Justin Gillis, "Not Even Close: 2012 Was Hottest Ever in U.S.," *New York Times,* January 8, 2013, www.nytimes.com/2013/01/09/science/earth/2012-was-hottest -year-ever-in-us.html.

69. Sheryl Canter, "Insurance Coverage Crumbles in Coastal States," Environmental Defense Fund blog, November 2, 2007, http://blogs.edf.org/ climate411/2007/11/02/insurance_industry/.

70. Brinkley, *The Great Deluge,* 84.

71. Jeffrey Kluger, "Global Warming: The Culprit?" *Time,* September 24, 2005.

72. Brinkley, *The Great Deluge,* 7.

73. Environmental Defense Fund, *Blown Away.*

74. "State Farm Cancels Thousands in Fla.," NBC, February 3, 2010. www.msnbc.msn .com/id/35220269/ns/business-personal_finance.

75. Ibid.

76. Environmental Defense Fund, *Blown Away.*

77. Because the buoy registers averages, the actual height was even greater. Sandy's peak energy was 2.7 times higher than Katrina's.

78. Paul M. Barrett, "It's Global Warming, Stupid," *Bloomberg BusinessWeek,* November 1, 2012.

79. "Causes of Sea Level Rise: Rapidly Rising Seas: What the Science Tells Us," Union of Concerned Scientists Report, April 2013, www.ucsusa.org/assets/documents /global_warming/Causes-of-Sea-Level-Rise.pdf.

80. "Comparing the Winds of Sandy and Katrina," Earth Observatory, November 6, 2012, http://earthobservatory.nasa.gov/IOTD/view.php?id=79626

81. "North America Most Affected by Increase in Weather-Related Natural Catastrophes," Munich Re, October 17, 2012, from its publication "Severe Weather in North America," www.munichre.com/en/media_relations/press_releases /2012/2012_10_17_press_release.aspx.

82. Statement by Nick Shay, a meteorologist and physical oceanographer from the University of Miami Rosenstiel School of Marine and Atmospheric Science. "Gulf Warm-Water Eddies Intensify Hurricane Changes," National Science Foundation, October 3, 2005, www.nsf.gov/news/news_summ.jsp?cntn_id=104483.

83. Brinkley, *The Great Deluge,* 76.

84. Ibid., 629.

85. Ibid., 157.

86. Ibid., 169.

87. Jed Horne, *Breach of Faith: Hurricane Katrina and the Near Death of a Great American City* (New York: Random House, 2006).

88. Ibid., 261.

89. Cecilia M. Vega, "As Bodies Recovered, Reporters Told, 'No Photos, No Stories,'" *San Francisco Chronicle,* September 13, 2005.

90. Brett Martel, "45 Bodies Found at New Orleans Hospital," *Associated Press,* September 12, 2005 and Brinkley, *The Great Deluge,* 605–610.

91. Brinkley, *The Great Deluge,* 261.

92. Information on vacant lots and displaced population during Katrina from Rick Jervis, "New Orleans Population May Have Hit Plateau," *USA Today,* August 4, 2008. New Orleans population figures pre- and post-Katrina are from U.S. Census data. The 2012 total is based on information from Gordon Russell, "St. Bernard, Orleans among Nation's Fastest-growing Counties, Census Bureau Says," *Times-Picayune,* April 5, 2012, www.nola.com/politics/index.ssf/2012/04/orleans_st _bernard_among_natio.html.

93. Amanda Ripley, "How Did This Happen?" *Time,* September 4, 2005.

94. Ibid.

95. Scott Shane and Eric Lipton, "Federal Response: Government Saw Flood Risk but Not Levee Failure," *New York Times,* September 2, 2005.

96. Louisiana Coastal Wetlands: A Resource at Risk, USGS Fact Sheet, U.S. Geological Survey, http://pubs.usgs.gov/fs/la-wetlands.

97. Brinkley, *The Great Deluge,* 13.

98. Ibid., 9.

99. "U.S. Crude Oil, Natural Gas, and Natural Gas Liquids Reserves, 2005 Annual

Report, U.S. Department of Energy, November 2006, www.eia.gov/pub/oil_gas /natural_gas/data_publications/crude_oil_natural_gas_reserves/historical/2005/pdf /arr.pdf.

100. Brinkley, *The Great Deluge*, 15.
101. Mark Fischetti, "Drowning New Orleans," *Scientific American*, October 2001.
102. Ripley, "How Did This Happen?"
103. Fishehetti, "Drowning New Orleans."
104. Richard Ford, "A City Beyond the Reach of Empathy," *New York Times*, September 4, 2005.
105. PBS, *The Journey of the Corps of Discovery*, directed by Ken Burns, 1997.
106. "The melting north." *The Economist*, June 16, 2012. Special report: *The Arctic: Cold Comfort* www.economist.com/node/21556798
107. Myss, *Anatomy of the Spirit*, chapter 2.

Chapter 3: Oil is One

1. World Resources Institute 2003 report: *The Environment: Another Casualty of War?* www.sdearthtimes.com/et0103/et0103s8.html; Daniel Yergin, *The Prize, the Epic Quest for Oil, Money and Power*, (New York: Simon and Schuster, 2008, 758–59); NASA Goddard Space Flight photos: www.nasa.gov/centers/goddard/news /topstory/2003/0321kuwaitfire.html; "Fighting the Oil Well Fires," Gulflink, Office of the Special Assistant for Gulf War Illness: www.gulflink.osd.mil/owf_ii/owf_ii _tabc.htm; Ryan Chilcote, "Kuwait Still Recovering from Gulf War Fires," CNN, January 3, 2003.
2. Yergin, *The Prize*, 762.
3. Thom Hartmann, *The Last Hours of Ancient Sunlight: The Fate of the World and What We Can Do Before It's Too Late* (New York: Three Rivers Press, 2004), 271.
4. "Oil and Gas Production History in California," ftp://ftp.consrv.ca.gov/pub/oil /history/History_of_Calif.pdf.
5. Neil King, Jr., "A Past President's Advice to Obama: Act with Haste." *Wall Street Journal*, Dec. 11, 2008.
6. Jeremy Rifkin, *The Hydrogen Economy* (New York: The Penguin Group, 2002), 64.
7. Pollan, *Omnivore's Dilemma*, 83–84.
8. Rachel Oliver, "All About Food and Fossil Fuels." March 17, 2008. CNN online: http://edition.cnn.com/2008/WORLD/asiapcf/03/16/eco.food.miles
9. Amory B. Lovins, E. Kyle Datta, Odd-Even Bustnes, Jonathan B. Koomey, and Nathan J. Glasgow, *Winning the Oil Endgame, Innovation for Profits, Jobs and Security* (Snowmass, Colorado: Rocky Mountain Institute, 2005), ix.
10. *Texas: A Guide to the Lone Star State, Compiled by Workers of the Writers Program of the Works Project Administration in the State of Texas* (New York: Hastings House, 1940), 196.
11. "Horatio's Drive," PBS. A Film by Ken Burns, from a book by Dayton Duncan, 2003.
12. Hartmann, *The Last Hours of Ancient Sunlight*, 163.

13. Pete Davies, *American Road: The Story of an Epic Transcontinental Journey at the Dawn of the Motor Age* (New York: Henry Holt, 2002).
14. Yergin, *The Prize*, 4–12.
15. Ibid., 15.
16. Ibid., 70.
17. Kilgore Chamber of Commerce website: www.kilgorechamber.com
18. Yergin, *The Prize*, 178.
19. Rifkin, *The Hydrogen Economy*, 72.
20. Paul Roberts, *The End of Oil* (New York: Houghton Mifflin, 2004), 36.
21. Yergin, *The Prize*, 114–15.
22. Ibid., 152–154 [taxi armada ref].
23. Ibid., 311–314 [synthetic fuel].
24. Ibid., 344–345 [oil disparity U.S. vs Japan].
25. Ibid., 332. [Speer and oxen pulling trucks].
26. Ibid. [Hitler's body burned].
27. Aramco's original partners were SoCal (today's Chevron) and Texaco (descended from Spindletop).
28. Williamson and Andreano, *The American Petroleum Institute,* 2:805.
29. Roberts, *The End of Oil,* 41.
30. Ibid., 40.
31. The Annual Energy Review 2012, U.S. Energy Information Administration, September 27, 2012, www.eia.doe.gov/emeu/aer/txt/ptb1105.html; earlier reviews available there.
32. Roberts, *The End of Oil,* 42.
33. Thomas Friedman, *Hot, Flat, and Crowded: Why We Need a Green Revolution—and How It Can Renew America* (New York: Farrar, Straus and Giroux, 2008), 109.
34. Between 1978 and 1985 CAFÉ standards for cars went from 18 mpg to 27.5 mpg where they stayed until 2007 when President Bush signed a new law designed to raise car and truck standards to 35 mpg by 2020. (Fuel standards for light trucks went from 17.5 mpg in 1979 to 22.2 mpg in 2007.) In May of 2009, President Obama improved on the 2020 requirement by raising the standard to a combined 35.5 mpg by 2016 (42 mpg for cars, 26 mpg for trucks); he raised them again in 2012 to 54.5 mpg for cars and light-duty trucks by Model Year 2025.
35. In 1986 the percentage began to rise again. In 2009, the amount of our total imports was close to 70 percent (although U.S. consumption in general had begun to slow slightly). By 2012 our dependency on oil had dropped to less than 50 percent—and trends indicate that will continue largely because of slowed demand, increased domestic production of fracked oil and natural gas alternatives, and higher automobile efficiency standards—but in 2014 the United States is still the world's leading oil importer.
36. In the fall of 2002, the National Park Service installed three solar power systems on the White House grounds, on both a maintenance building to provide electricity and hot water for personnel and on the roof of the presidential cabana to heat water for the pool and spa.

37. Friedman, *Hot, Flat, and Crowded*, 16.
38. Brown, *Plan B, 3.0*, 27.
39. Siddhartha P. Saikia, "Indian Oil Companies Fear Price Volatility," My Digital Financial Chronicle, December 29, 2009, www.mydigitalfc.com/petroleum/indian-oil-companies-fear-price-volatility-837; and "World Oil Production Peaked in 2008," *The Oil Drum*, March 17, 2009, www.theoildrum.com/node/5177.
40. Index mundi, "World Crude Oil Consumption by Year," www.indexmundi.com/energy.aspx.
41. "Running Dry: Oil Production Fails to Keep Up with Demand," *The Economist*, June 9, 2011, www.economist.com/blogs/dailychart/2011/06/oil-production-and-consumption.
42. Friedman, *Hot, Flat, and Crowded*, 39.
43. Ibid.
44. Elisabeth Rosenthal, "U.S. to Be World's Top Oil Producer in 5 Years, Report Says," *New York Times*, November 12, 2012, www.nytimes.com/2012/11/13/business/energy-environment/report-sees-us-as-top-oil-producer-in-5-years.html?_r=0.
45. Siobhan Hughes, "U.S. Interior Dept. Offers Deepwater Drilling Details," *Dow Jones Newswires*, May 31, 2010, www.rigzone.com/news/article.asp?a_id=93919.
46. National Ocean Service, NOAA, *The Gulf of Mexico at a Glance: A Second Glance* (Washington, DC: U.S. Department of Commerce, 2011). http://stateofthecoast.noaa.gov/NOAAs_Gulf_of_Mexico_at_a_Glance_report.pdf.
47. "Review: Oil rig inspections fell short of guidelines," *Associated Press*, May 16, 2010, http://www.timesnews.net/article/9023118/review-oil-rig-inspections-fell-short-of-guidelines.
48. Bob Cavnar, *Disaster on the Horizon: High Stakes, High Risks, and the Story Behind the Deepwater Well Blowout* (White River Junction, VT: Chelsea Green Publishing, 2010), 81.
49. Ibid., 92.
50. Riki Ott, "At What Cost? BP Spill Responders Told to Forgo Precautionary Health Measures in Cleanup," *Huffington Post*, May 17, 2010, www.huffingtonpost.com/riki-ott/at-what-cost-bp-spill-res_b_578784.html.
51. Cavnar, *Disaster on the Horizon*, 125.
52. Sabrina Canfield, "Transocean Turns on BP with Scorching Oil-Spill Document," Courthouse News Service, March 4, 2013, www.courthousenews.com/2013/03/04/55381.htm.
53. Paul Quinlan, "Less Toxic Dispersants Lose Out in BP Oil Spill Cleanup," *New York Times*, May 13, 2010, www.nytimes.com/2010/05/13/business/energy-environment/13greenwire-less-toxic-dispersants-lose-out-in-bp-oil-spil-81183.html?_r=0.
54. Susan Shaw, "Swimming through the Spill," *New York Times*, May 29, 2010, www.nytimes.com/2010/05/30/opinion/30shaw.html?_r=0.
55. David A. Fahrenthold and Steven Mufson, "Documents Indicate Heavy Use of Dispersants in Gulf Oil Spill," *Washington Post*, August 1, 2010. www.washingtonpost.com/wp-dyn/content/article/2010/07/31/AR2010073102381.html.

56. Jim White, "Carol Browner Says 75% of Spilled BP Oil is Gone, Georgia Sea Grant Scientists 70–79% Remains in Gulf," August 17, 2010, Firedoglake blog: http://my.firedoglake.com/jimwhite/2010/08/17/carol-browner-says-75-of-spilled-bp-oil-is-gone-georgia-sea-grant-scientists-say-70-79-remains-in-gulf/

57. Cavnar, *Disaster on the Horizon*, 157.

58. Bob Cavnar, interview by Rachel Maddow, *The Rachel Maddow Show*, MSNBC, March 24, 2011, www.nbcnews.com/id/42273067/ns/msnbc-rachel_maddow_show/t/rachel-maddow-show-thursday-march-th/.UVWxdr9z0X4

59. Cavnar, *Disaster on the Horizon*, 169.

60. "BOEMRE Approves Deepwater Drilling Permit for New Well included in First Approved Exploration Plan," March 30, 2011. Press Release from The Bureau of Ocean Energy Management, Regulation and Enforcement. www.boem.gov/BOEM-Newsroom/Press-Releases/2011/Press_Release_Catalog_2011.aspx

61. Peter LaFontaine, "Maddow Tears Apart Drilling Plan Safety Claims," March 28, 2011, National Wildlife Federation blog, http://blog.nwf.org/2011/03/maddow-tears-apart-drilling-safety-claims.

62. "AP Impact, Inspections of Oil Rig Fall Short of Fed's Own Policy, Result in Few Violations," May 16, 2010, *Associated Press*, www.foxnews.com/us/2010/05/16/ap-impact-inspections-oil-rig-fall-short-feds-policy-result-violations.

63. Ian Urbina, "U.S. Said to Allow Drilling Without Needed Permits," *New York Times*, May 13, 2010, www.nytimes.com/2010/05/14/us/14agency.html.

64. Bob Cavnar, *The Rachel Maddow Show*, March 24, 2011.

65. Dan Woynillowicz, "Tar Sands Fever." *WorldWatch Magazine*, September/October 2007, www.worldwatch.org/node/5287.

66. Greenpeace report, "Tar Sands and Climate Change," April 2010. www.greenpeace.org/canada/Global/canada/report/2010/4/ClimateChange_FS_Footnotes_rev_4.pdf.

67. Sophia Perpetua, "Arkansas Residents Seek Millions after Exxon Crude Oil Spill." NBC News, April, 7, 2013, www.nbcnews.com/business/arkansas-residents-seek-millions-after-exxon-crude-oil-spill-1C9254722.

68. Will Femia, "Oil Industry's Best: Paper Towels." April 8, 2013. http://www.msnbc.com/rachel-maddow-show/oil-industrys-best-paper-towels.

69. Woynillowicz, "Tar Sands Fever."

70. U.S. Department of Transportation Corrective Action Order to TransCanada, June 3, 2011, http://blog.nwf.org/wildlifepromise/files/2011/06/320115006H_CAO_06032011.pdf.

71. Check out today's CO_2 here: http://co2now.org.

72. Edwin Dobb, "The New Oil Landscape: The Fracking Frenzy in North Dakota Has Boosted the U.S. Fuel Supply—But at What Cost?" *National Geographic*, March 2013, http://ngm.nationalgeographic.com/2013/03/bakken-shale-oil/dobb-textclose-modal. To view graphics and a brief video that explains fracking, see "America Strikes Oil," National Infographic, February 20, 2013, http://juanvelasco blog.com/2013/02/20/america-strikes-oil.

73. U.S. Department of the Interior, "Bakken Formation Oil Assessment in North Dakota, Montana will be updated by U.S. Geological Survey," May 19, 2011. www.doi.gov/news/pressreleases/Bakken-Formation-Oil-Assessment-in-North-Dakota-Montana-will-be-updated-by-US-Geological-Survey.cfm.

74. Eric Konigsberg, "Kuwait on the Prairie," *The New Yorker,* April 25, 2011. www.newyorker.com/reporting/2011/04/25/110425fa_fact_konigsberg?currentPage=all.

75. Market Watch, "America's Top 5 Oil-producing States," *Wall Street Journal,* December 12, 2012, www.marketwatch.com/story/americas-top-5-oil-producing-states-2012-12-12.

76. Steve Mufson, *Keystone XL: Down the Line,* ebook, location 558, www.amazon.com/Keystone-XL-Kindle-Single-Books-ebook/dp/B00C0YZKHC.

77. You can see how the process works here: an interactive video on fracking from *National Geographic,* news.nationalgeographic.com/news/2010/10/101022-breaking-fuel-from-the-rock.

78. Anthony Ingraffea lecture on "The Intersection between Hydraulic Fracturing and Climate Change," Published April 9, 2013. PSE Healthy Energy (Physicians, Scientists, and Engineers for Healthy Energy). 6:42 minutes. www.youtube.com/watch?v=o78j77I7XUw.

79. Robert W. Howarth, Renee Santoro, and Anthony Ingraffea, "Methane and the greenhouse-gas footprint of natural gas from shale formations," Cornell University, November 12, 2010. www.eeb.cornell.edu/howarth/Howarth%20et%20al%20%20 2011.pdf.

80. Robert Howarth, Renee Santoro, and Tony Ingraffea, "Marcellus Shale Gas and Global Warming." shaleshockmedia.org/2011/03/31/marcellus-shale-gas-and-global-warming. According to the report, the fourth author, Milton Taam, is from the private sector. Although Howarth's team's conclusions were quickly challenged by other studies, including one by three Cornell colleagues, Howarth's follow-up response included absolute fealty to his original conclusions. See Lawrence M. Cathles III, Larry Brown, Milton Taam, and Andrew Hunter, "A Commentary on 'The Greenhouse-Gas Footprint of Natural Gas in Shale Formations,' by R. W. Howarth, R. Santoro, and Anthony Ingraffea," *Climatic Change,* vol. 113 (2012), no. 2, 525–35, http://link.springer.com/article/10.1007%2Fs10584-011-0333-0.

81. Climate Change Division, U.S. Environmental Protection Agency, "Greenhouse Gas Emissions Reporting from the Petroleum and Natural Gas Industry," 2010. www.epa.gov/ghgreporting/documents/pdf/2010/Subpart-W_TSD.pdf. To see how the EPA calculates leaks, see theenergycollective.com/david-lewis/48209/epa-confirms-high-natural-gas-leakage-rates.

82. Ruth Wood, Paul Gilbert, Maria Sharmina, and Kevin Anderson. "Shale Gas: A Provisional Assessment of Climate Change and Environmental Impacts," Tyndall Centre for Climate Change Research, January 2011, 69, http://tyndall.ac.uk/sites/default/files/coop_shale_gas_report_final_200111.pdf.

83. Union of Concerned Scientists, "How it Works: Water for Natural Gas," October 5, 2010, www.ucsusa.org/clean_energy/our-energy-choices/energy-and-water-use/water-energy-electricity-natural-gas.html.

84. Carol Linnitt, "The Dangers of Gas Drilling," in "Fracking the Future," *DeSmogBlog*, February 23, 2011, http://desmogblog.com/fracking-the-future /danger.html.

85. Rebecca Hammer and Jeanne VanBriesen, "In Fracking's Wake: New Rules Are Needed to Protect Our Health and Environment from Contaminated Wastewater," NRDC, May 2012, www.nrdc.org/energy/files/Fracking-Wastewater-FullReport .pdf.

86. Ian Urbina, "Pressure Limits Efforts to Police Drilling for Gas," *New York Times,* March 3, 2011, www.nytimes.com/2011/03/04/us/04gas. html?pagewanted=1&_r=3&.

87. Ibid.

88. Linnitt, "The Dangers of Gas Drilling."

89. Google "PA_DEP2009GasETCmigrationINTERNALREPORT.pdf" and choose a download tool.

90. Committee on Energy and Commerce, "Waxman, Markey, and DeGette Investigation Finds Continued Use of Diesel in Hydraulic Fracturing Fluids," U.S. House of Representatives, January 31, 2011, http://democrats.energycommerce. house.gov/index. php?q=news/waxman-markey-and-degette-investigation-finds -continued-use-of-diesel-in-hydraulic-fracturing-f.

91. Linnitt, "The Dangers of Gas Drilling."

92. Michael Behar, "Fracking's Latest Scandal? Earthquake Swarms," *Mother Jones,* March/April 2013, www.motherjones.com/environment/2013/03/ does-fracking-cause-earthquakes-wastewater-dewatering.

93. Ibid. The *Mother Jones* article contains an animated .gif that demonstrates how the high-pressure injection of wastewater contributes to the seismic shifts that cause earthquakes.

94. Steve Everley, "Update VI On Shaky Ground," *Energy in Depth*, March 28, 2013, http://energyindepth.org/on-shaky-ground.

95. Richard Schiffman, "Grassroots Campaigns Can Stop Fracking One Town at a Time," *Guardian,* May 13, 2013, www.guardian.co.uk/commentisfree/2013/may/13 /fracking-new-york-grassroots-campaign-to-stop.

96. New York State Senator Terry Gipson's website, "Fracking. First hand," www.terry gipsonny.com/fracking.

97. To see the latest map of shale gas and shale oil wells in the United States go here: www.postcarbon.org/drill-baby-drill/map.

98. Nick Snow, "Salazar finalizes oil shale plan; BLM proposes revisions." April 1, 2013, *Oil and Gas Journal,* www.ogj.com/articles/print/volume-111/issue-4/general -interest/salazar-finalized-oil-shale-plan-blm-proposes.html.

99. National Resources Defense Council, "Dirty Coal is Hazardous to Your Health," October 2007, www.nrdc.org/health/effects/coal/coalhealth.pdf .

100. Nicholas Z. Muller, Robert Mendelsohn, and William Nordhaus, "Environmental Accounting for Pollution in the United States Economy," *American Economic Review* 101, no. 2 (2011), www.aeaweb.org/articles.php?doi=10.1257/aer .101.5.1649.

101. Matthew Cardinale, "More Aging US Coal Plants Hit the Chopping Block," *Inter Press Service*, January 10, 2013, www.ipsnews.net/2013/01/more-aging-u-s-coal-plants-hit-the-chopping-block.

102. Bryan Walsh, "The Scariest Environmental Fact in the World," *Time*, January 29, 2013, http://science.time.com/2013/01/29/the-scariest-environmental-fact-in-the-world.

103. "The Chinese Miracle Will End Soon," interview with Pan Yue, from China's ministry of the environment. *Der Spiegel*, March 7, 2005.

104. Keisuke Sadamori, "Medium-term Coal Market Report 2012," International Energy Agency, December 18, 2012, www.iea.org/newsroomandevents/speeches/121218MCMR2012_presentation_KSK.pdf.

105. "China Hit by Rising Air Pollution," BBC News, August 3, 2006. http://news.bbc.co.uk/2/hi/asia-pacific/5241844.stm.

106. Devra Lee Davis, *When Smoke Ran Like Water* (New York: Basic Books, 2003), 43.
106. Anthony Kessel, *Air, the Environment and Public Health* (New York: Cambridge University Press, 2006), 85.

107. Anthony Kessel, *Air, the Environment and Public Health* (New York: Cambridge University Press, 2006), 85.

108. Bryan Walsh, "The Secret Life of Trees." *Time*, December 14, 2007.

109. Friedman, *Hot, Flat, and Crowded*, 149.

110. Walsh, "The Secret Life of Trees."

111. Friedman, *Hot, Flat, and Crowded*, 141.

112. Ibid., 142.

113. Ibid.

114. Hartmann, *The Last Hours of Ancient Sunlight*, 190.

115. Matthew Knight, "Air Pollution Kills over Two Million People Each Year, Study Says," CNN, July 16, 2013. www.cnn.com/2013/07/16/world/air-pollution-killing-study.

116. Jennifer Chu, "Study: Air Pollution Causes 200,000 Early Deaths Each Year in the U.S.," MIT News Office, August 28, 2013, web.mit.edu/newsoffice/2013/study-air-pollution-causes-200000-early-deaths-each-year-in-the-us-0829.html.

117. U.S. Department of Transportation, "Early Estimate of Motor Vehicle Traffic Fatalities in 2012," May 2013, www-nrd.nhtsa.dot.gov/Pubs/811741.pdf.

118. Sourced from Lester Brown: Sarah Janssen, Gina Solomon, and Ted Schettler, *Chemical Contaminants and Human Disease: A Summary of Evidence* (Boston: Alliance for a Healthy Tomorrow, 2004); Geoffrey Lean, "US Study Links More than 200 Diseases to Pollution," *Independent News* (London), November 14, 2004.

119. Brown, Plan B 3.0, 113.

120. Ibid., 113–14.

121. Ibid., 114.

122. Ibid.

123. Ibid.

124. Ibid, 6.

125. Ibid.
126. Ibid., 13.
127. Pan Yue, "China's Green Debt." *Daily Times* (Pakistan), December 1, 2006.
128. *Der Spiegel* "The Chinese Miracle Will End Soon."
129. Charlie Campbell, "Chinese Urged to Put Down Their Chopsticks to Save Trees," *Time,* March 13, 2013. http://newsfeed.time.com/2013/03/13/chinese-urged -to-put-down-their-chopsticks-to-save-trees.
130. Brown, *Plan B 3.0,* xii.
131. Barbara Ward et al., *Who Speaks for Earth?* (New York: W.W. Norton & Company, 1973), 31. Originally a Distinguished Lecture Series given to the United Nations in 1972.
132. Dale Allen Pfeiffer, *Eating Fossil Fuels: Oil, Food and the Coming Agriculture Crisis* (Gabriola Island, BC: New Society Publishers, 2006), 21.
133. Rifkin, *The Hydrogen Economy,* 244.
134. Roberts, *The End of Oil,* 261.
135. Friedman, *Hot, Flat, and Crowded,* 188.
136. Bill McKibben, "Global Warming's Terrifying New Math," *Rolling Stone,* July 12, 2012. www.rollingstone.com/politics/news/ global-warmings-terrifying-new-math-20120719.
137. Malte Meinshausen et al., "Greenhouse-Gas Emission Targets for Limiting Global Warming to 2°C," *Nature.* April 30, 2009, www.nature.com/nature/journal/v458 /n7242/abs/nature08017.html.
138. McKibben, "Global Warming's Terrifying New Math."
139. Katherine Bagley, "The Most Influential Climate Science Paper Today Remains Unknown to Most People." *Inside Climate News,* February 14, 2013, http://inside climatenews.org/news/20140213/climate-change-science-carbon-budget-nature -global-warming-2-degrees-bill-mckibben-fossil-fuels-keystone-xl-oil?page=show.
140. Ibid.
141. Ibid.
142. Ibid.
143. These are cumulative figures; 82 percent of greenhouse gases come from burning fossil fuels used to generate electricity and power our cars, buses, trucks, and commercial airplanes. As yet, there are no reliable figures that include calculations that include the additional forty to fifty million tons of methane greenhouse gas being added the atmosphere daily because of the rising loss of permafrost in places like Siberia, due to global warming.
144. Barbara Kingsolver, *Animal, Vegetable, Miracle: A Year of Food Life* (New York: Harper Collins, 2007), 345–46.

Chapter 4: Seeds of Discontent

1. Al Gore, *Earth in the Balance* (New York: Houghton Mifflin, 1992), 281–82.
2. Ibid.
3. Hawken, *Blessed Unrest,* 31.
4. In 2010 a plan to plow up the institute's fields to allow developers to create luxury

homes was put on hold after widespread protests forced the government to reevaluate the proposed construction.

5. Fred Pearce, "Saving the Seeds of the Next Green Revolution," *Yale Environment 360*, September 22, 2008, http://e360.yale.edu/feature/saving_the_seeds_of_the_next_green_revolution/2065.

6. Elisabeth Rosenthal, "Near Arctic, Seed Vault Is a Fort Knox of Food," *New York Times*, February 29, 2008, www.nytimes.com/2008/02/29/world/europe/29seeds.html?pagewanted=all&_r=0.

7. See the Svalbard Pages, http://links.svalbard.com/index.php?show=pop.

8. Dan Shapley, "Doomsday Seed Bank Opens This Week," *The Daily Green*, February 26, 2008, www.thedailygreen.com/environmental-news/latest/doomsday-seeds-47022403.

9. "Rice," Thomas Jefferson's Monticello, www.monticello.org/site/house-and-gardens/rice.

10. Janet Raloff, "Afghanistan's Seed Banks Destroyed," *Science News*, September 11, 2002, www.sciencenews.org/articles/20020914/food.asp.

11. Claire Hope Cummings, *Uncertain Peril: Genetic Engineering and the Future of Seeds* (Boston: Beacon Press, 2008), 21.

12. Alister Doyle, "World Seed Banks Get Funds to Tackle Climate, Other Threats," Reuters, January 30, 2013, www.reuters.com/article/2013/01/31/us-climate-crops-idUSBRE90U00020130131.

13. Rosner, "Seeds to Save a Species."

14. Bill Lambrecht, *Dinner at the New Gene Cafe: How Genetic Engineering Is Changing What We Eat, How We Live, and the Global Politics of Food* (New York: St. Martin's Press, 2001), 285.

15. John Seabrook, "Sowing for Apocalypse: The Quest for a Global Seed Bank," *New Yorker*, August 27, 2007.

16. Rachel Carson, *Silent Spring* (New York: Houghton Mifflin, 1962), 10.

17. David Adam, "Warning over Threatened Wild Food Crops," *Guardian*, September 8, 2006, www.guardian.co.uk/environment/2006/sep/08/food.food.

18. Alok Jha, "Deep in Permafrost—A Seed Bank to Save the World," *Guardian*, June 19, 2006, www.guardian.co.uk/science/2006/jun/20/food.frontpagenews

19. *The Future of Food*, a documentary film by Deborah Koons Garcia, director, and Catherine Lynn Butler, producer, a Lily Films production, 2004.

20. For apples, see Andrew Kimbrell, ed., *Fatal Harvest* (Sausalito: The Foundation for Deep Ecology, 2002), 24; for broccoli, see Michael Pollan, *In Defense of Food: An Eater's Manifesto* (New York: Penguin, 2008), 116.

21. Doug O'Harra, "The World's Best Seeds Head for Arctic Vault," *Far North Science*, January 25, 2008, www.farnorthscience.com/2008/01/25.

22. Debora Mackenzie, "Billions at Risk from Wheat Super-blight," *New Scientist*, April 3, 2007, http://environment.newscientist.com/channel/earth/mg19425983.700-billions-at-risk-from-wheat-superblight.html.

23. Joe Nunez, "History and Lessons of Potato Late Blight," University of California Cooperative Extension, December 21, 2000, http://archive.is/cn0Dl.

24. More detailed descriptions were given in two fine books, Jack Doyle, *Altered Harvest* (New York: Viking, 1985), and Cary Fowler and Pat Mooney, *Shattering: Food, Politics and the Loss of Genetic Diversity* (Tucson: University of Arizona Press, 1990).

25. Fowler and Mooney, *Shattering,* x–xi.

26. Tom Philpott, "A Reflection on the Lasting Legacy of 1970s USDA Secretary Earl Butz," *Grist,* February 7, 2008, http://grist.org/article/the-butz-stops-here.

27. Lauren Etter, "Farmers Wonder if Boom in Grain Prices Is a Bubble," *Wall Street Journal,* January 31, 2008, http://online.wsj.com/news/articles/SB1201744 66249430595.

28. Fowler and Mooney, *Shattering,* 8.

29. Rosner, "Seeds to Save a Species."

30. Fowler and Mooney, *Shattering,* 116.

31. Vandana Shiva, *Stolen Harvest: The Hijacking of the Global Food Supply,* Cambridge: South End Press, 2000, 80.

32. Hawken, *Blessed Unrest,* 25.

33. Katharine Mieszkowski, "Superbug to the Rescue!" August 28, 2003, *Salon,* www.salon.com/tech/feature/2003/08/28/bioremediation.

34. Andrew Kimbrell, "High-Tech Piracy," *Utne Reader,* March-April 1996, www.utne .com/environment/high-tech-piracy-andrew-kimbrell.aspxaxzz2mpZzFP9P.

35. Vandana Shiva, "Ecologists Should Worry about the Dunkel Draft," Sept. 23, 1993, from the SUNS website, www.sunsonline.org/trade/areas/environm/09230193.htm.

36. Ibid.

37. Wangari Mathai, "The Linkage between Patenting of Life Forms, Genetic Engineering and Food Insecurity," October 11, 2004, www.newfarm.org /international/gleanings/nov04/patent_debate.shtml.

38. Jeffrey Smith, *Seeds of Deception: Exposing Industry and Government Lies about the Safety of the Genetically Engineered Foods You're Eating* (Fairfield, IA: Yes! Books, 2003), 50.

39. Exceptions include any food that is certified organic. *Farm-raised, cage-free, free range, hormone-free, natural,* and other such designations by themselves do not guarantee that a food is GM free. Likewise, milk that indicates it is "rBGH free" or "rBST free" lacks the bovine growth hormone, but unless it is labeled "organic," it may still come from dairy cows that eat GM grain. Ask your grocer to be sure.

40. Pioneer hi-Bred, Syngenta, Dow AgroSciences, and Bayer CropScience also sell varieties of genetically modified seeds.

41. *The Future of Food.*

42. As quoted in Michael Pollan, "Playing God in the Garden," *New York Times Magazine,* October 25, 1998.

43. In November 2013, a Washington state initiative (522) to label GMOs also failed to pass.

44. Ronnie Cummins and Katherine Paul, "Did Monsanto Win Prop 37? Round One in the Food Fight of Our Lives," November 9, 2012, *AlterNet.* www.alternet.org /food/did-monsanto-win-prop-37-round-one-food-fight-our-lives?paging=off.

45. Ronnie Cummins, "In 2013, Our Fight Against GMO Food Continues," *Common Dreams*, January 3, 2013, www.commondreams.org/view/2013/01/03-9.

46. Analiese Paik, "Connecticut's GE Foods Bill Eviscerated by Lawyers," May 5, 2012, *Fairfield Green Food Guide*. http://fairfieldgreenfoodguide.com/2012/05/05 /connecticuts-ge-foods-bill.

47. John Upton, "GMO Labeling Becomes Law in Connecticut," *Grist*, December 16, 2013, http://grist.org/news/gmo-labeling-becomes-law-in-connecticut.

48. Dan Flynn, "Letter From The Editor: A GM Food labeling Win," *Food Safety News*, May 12, 2013, www.foodsafetynews.com/2013/05/letter-from-the-editor-a-gm-food-labeling-win/.UZKaCZW-xvY.

49. Carson, *Silent Spring*, 188.

50. Smith, *Seeds of Deception*, 145.

51. Dr. L. R. B. Mann Dr. D. Straton, and W. E. Crist, "The Thalidomide of Genetic 'Engineering,'" Third World Network, revised in April 2001 from the GE issue of *Soil & Health* (NZ), August 1999, www.connectotel.com/gmfood/trypto.html.

52. Smith, *Seeds of Deception;* condensed from chapter 4, "Deadly Epidemic."

53. Ibid., 162.

54. *Bad Seed: The Truth About Our Food,* a documentary film by Tim Nadudvari and Adam Curry, codirectors and coproducers, Bad Seed Productions, 2006.

55. Smith, *Seeds of Deception*, 176.

56. Rafaat M. Elsanhoty, A. I. Al-Turky and Mohamed Fawzy Ramadan, "Prevalence of Genetically Modified Rice, Maize, and Soy in Saudi Food Products," *Applied Biochemistry and Biotechnology*, August 1, 2013, abstract available at www.greenmedinfo.com/article/ prevalence-genetically-modified-rice-maize-and-soy-saudi-food-products.

57. Smith, *Seeds of Deception*, 153–55.

58. Andrew Pollack, "Modified Wheat Is Discovered in Oregon," *New York Times*, May 29, 2013.

59. From the documentary film, *David vs Monsanto*, directed by Bertram Verhaag, Syndicado Studio, 2011.

60. Kimbrell, *Your Right to Know*, 38.

61. Marie Szaniszlo, "Fishing For Compliance: Genetically Engineered Salmon Co. Raises Concerns," January 2, 2013, *Boston Herald.*

62. Friends of the Earth, "Major U.S. Supermarkets to Boycott GE Salmon," March 21, 2013. http://ecowatch.com/2013/supermarkets-boycott-ge-salmon/; for a current list of retailers declining to carry GM fish, see the Center for Food Safety's Guide to Avoiding GE Fish, www.centerforfoodsafety.org/files/ge_fish_guide_may_46822 .pdf.

63. Pollan, *In Defense of Food*, 116–17.

64. Pollan, *Omnivore's Dilemma*, 91.

65. A. Aris and S. Leblanc, "Maternal and fetal exposure to pesticides associ- ated to genetically modified foods in Eastern Townships of Quebec, Canada," *Reproductive Toxicology*, January 2012, www.uclm.es/Actividades/repositorio/pdf/ doc_3721_4666.pdf.

66. Melissa L. Hughes, quoted in "Enhancing Coexistence: A Report of the AC21 to the Secretary of Agriculture," by the USDA Advisory Committee on Biotechnology and 21st Century Agriculture (AC21), p. 44, November 19, 2012. www.usda.gov /documents/ac21_report-enhancing-coexistence.pdf.

67. Biotechnology Consultation Agency Response Letter BNF No. 000034 to Dr. Kent Croon, Monsanto, from Alan M. Rulis, FDA. September 25, 1996. www.fda.gov /Food/FoodScienceResearch/Biotechnology/Submissions/ucm161107.htm

68. Genna Reed, "GE French Fries, Coming to a Fast Food Restaurant Near You," *Food and Water Watch*, June 12, 2013. www.foodandwaterwatch.org/blogs/ge-french -fries-coming-to-a-fast-food-restaurant-near-you.

69. John Vidal, "The GM Tree Plantations Bred to Satisfy the World's Energy Needs," *Guardian*, November 15, 2012, www.guardian.co.uk/environment/2012/nov/15 /gm-trees-bred-world-energy.

70. "Into the wildwood: A GM species may soon be liberated deliberately," *Economist*, May 2, 2013, www.economist.com/news/science-and-technology/21577033-gm -species-may-soon-be-liberated-deliberately-wildwood.

71. Court papers on Civil Action No. 11–1457, Center for Food Safety, et al, Plaintiffs, v. Ken Salazar, et al., Defendants, James E. Boasberg, U.S. District Judge, October 23, 2012. www.peer.org/assets/docs/nwr/10_24_12_Southeast_GE_decision.pdf

72. Rick Weiss, "USDA Backs Production of Rice with Human Genes, March 2, 2007," *Washington Post*, www.washingtonpost.com/wp-dyn/content/article/2007/03/01 /AR2007030101495.html

73. You can see the growing list of new GMO candidate crops at the USDA website: www.aphis.usda.gov/biotechnology/news.shtml.

74. Kimbrell etal., *Fatal Harvest*, 6.

75. Interview with Melissa Harris-Perry on MSNBC, May 27, 2013.

76. Editor, "Sustainable Farming Can Double Food Production in 10 Years According to UN Report," January 22, 2012, *Living Green Magazine*. http://livinggreenmag. com/2012/01/22/people-solutions/sustainable-farming-can-double-food -production-in-10-years-according-to-un-report/

77. Charles M. Benbrook, "Impacts of Genetically Engineered Crops on Pesticide Use in the U.S.—The First Sixteen Years," *Environmental Sciences Europe* 24, no. 24 (2012). www.enveurope.com/content/pdf/2190-4715-24-24.pdf. See also Dr. Charles Benbrook, "GE Crop Risk Assessment Challenges: An Overview," *Food Safety News*, May 6, 2013, www.foodsafetynews.com/2013/05/ge-crop-risk -assessment-challenges-an-overview/.UaFNJ5W-xii

78. Laura Tagliani, Regulatory Leader, "Petition for Determination of Nonregulated Status for Herbicide Tolerant DAS-40278-9 Corn," August 19, 2009, last revised April 12, 2011 by Dow AgroSciences, www.aphis.usda.gov/brs/aphisdocs /09_23301p.pdf.

79. Pollan, *Omnivore's Dilemma*, 95.

80. Stephanie Strom, "Seeking Food Ingredients that Aren't Gene-Altered," *New York Times*, May 26, 2013, www.nytimes.com/2013/05/27/business/

food-companies-seeking-ingredients-that-arent-gene-altered.html?smid
=fb-share&_r=0.

81. Pollan, *In Defense of Food*, 123.

82. Christina DeMartino, "2013 OTA Industry Survey Data Show Fresh Organic
Produce Continues to Lead the Category," August 30, 2013, www.producenews
.com/index.php/news-dep-menu/test-featured/11151-2013-ota-industry-survey
-data-show-fresh-organic-produce-continues-to-lead-the-category. Also see
Organic Trade Association's 2006 Manufacturer Survey (from printout),
www.agmrc.org/NR/rdonlyres/6D092BD1-481D-43D1-95CD-B8F1821E2
F19/0/AIC_FBIB_3organic.pdf.

83. Culled from the GM-Free Ireland website: www.gmfreeireland.org.

84. Interview with attorney Steven Druker in *The Future of Food*, a documentary film by
Deborah Koons Garcia, director, and Catherine Lynn Butler, producer, a Lily Films
production, 2004.

85. Smith, *Seeds of Deception*, 131.

86. Document showing comments from Dr. Linda Kahl, FDA compliance officer, to
Dr. James Maryanski, FDA Biotechnology Coordinator, about the Federal Register
document "Statement of Policy: Foods from Genetically Modified Plants," January
8, 1992. These and other documents were obtained by Steven Druker as part of discovery resulting from a lawsuit his organization filed to challenge the FDA's claim
that most of its scientists approved of the introduction of genetically modified foods
into the American marketplace without testing them. This document and others are
www.biointegrity.org/list.html

87. Louis J. Pribyl, "Biotechnology Draft Document, 2/27/92," March 6, 1992,
www.biointegrity.org/FDAdocs/04/view1.html.

88. "Speaker Hastert calls for End of European Union's Protectionist, Discriminatory
Trade Policies," *U.S. Newswire*, March 26, 2003.

89. Kimble was acting Assistant U.S. Secretary of State for Oceans and International
and Environmental Scientific Affairs in 1999. Reference is from *Dinner at the New
Gene Café*, 322.

90. Organic Consumers Association, "Information on rBGH or rBST—aka Posilac—
Eli Lilly's Genetically Engineered Bovine Growth Hormone," www.organic
consumers.org/rbghlink.cfm; and Organic Consumers Association, "Despite
Industry Propaganda Monsanto's Bovine Growth Hormone Still Threatens Public
Health," www.organicconsumers.org/rBGH/milkismilk20405.cfm.

91. Andrew Pollack, "Modified Wheat Is Discovered in Oregon," *New York Times*, May
29, 2013. www.nytimes.com/2013/05/30/business/energy-environment/genetically
-engineered-wheat-found-in-oregon-field.html?_r=0.

92. Katherine Goldstein and Gazelle Emami, "Monsanto's GMO Corn Linked to
Organ Failure, Study Reveals," *Huffington Post*, updated May 25, 2011, www.huffing
tonpost.com/2010/01/12/monsantos-gmo-corn-linked_n_420365.html.

93. "Enhancing Coexistence: A Report of the AC21 to the Secretary of Agriculture," by
the USDA Advisory Committee on Biotechnology and 21st Century Agriculture

(AC21), November 19, 2012. www.usda.gov/documents/ac21_report-enhancing
-coexistence.pdf.

94. Wendell Berry, *The Unsettling of America: Culture and Agriculture,* Berkeley: Sierra
Club Books, 1996, 87.

95. Dr. Jill Bolte Taylor lecture, "My Stroke of Insight," posted March 2008, www.ted
.com/index.php/talks/view/id/229.

96. Carson, *Silent Spring,* 56.

97. Ibid., 53.

98. David Biello, "Fertilizer Runoff Overwhelms Streams and Rivers—Creating Vast
'Dead Zones,'" *Scientific American,* March 14, 2008, www.sciam.com/article
.cfm?id=fertilizer-runoff-overwhelms-streams.

99. ISEC Local Food Toolkit Factsheet, www.isec.org.uk/toolkit/ustoolkit.html.

100. Berry, *The Unsettling of America,* 7.

101. Shiva, *Stolen Harvest,* 8.

102. Berry, *The Unsettling of America,* 60.

103. Pollan, *In Defense of Food,* 133.

104. Ibid., 14.

105. Larry B. Woodward, "Ronald McDonald Fallout: What Role Does Advertising
Have in Childhood Obesity?" ABC News, April 7, 2010, http://abcnews.go.com
/Business/ronald-mcdonald-fallout-role-advertising-childhood-obesity
/story?id=10298693.

106. Adam Voiland and Angela Haupt, "10 Things the Food Industry
Doesn't Want You to Know," *U.S. News and World Report,* March 30,
2012, http://health.usnews.com/health-news/articles/2012/03/30/
things-the-food-industry-doesnt-want-you-to-know.

107. Pollan, *In Defense of Food,* 100.

108. www.cia.gov/library/publications/the-world-factbook/geos/us.html.

109. Pollan, *In Defense of Food,* 73.

110. Ibid., 120–21.

111. From the documentary film, *Ingredients,* directed by Robert Bates. Optic Nerve
Productions, 2009.

112. Carson, *Silent Spring,* 12.

Chapter 5: Reconnecting to the Earth

1. Duane Elgin, *The Living Universe: Where Are We? Who Are We? Where Are We Going?*
(San Francisco: Berrett-Koehler Publishers, 2009), 148–49.

2. Some journals and their authors:

Walden, by Henry David Thoreau
The Diary of Anne Frank, by Anne Frank
Travels with Charlie, by John Steinbeck
A Journey to the Western Islands of Scotland, James Boswell and Samuel Johnson

Some good how-to books and writers:

Bird by Bird, by Anne Lamott
The Artist's Way, by Julia Cameron
Writing Down the Bones, by Natalie Goldberg
The Writing Life, by Annie Dillard
Journal Writing: the art and heart of reflection, by Stephanie Dowrick
The Story of Your Life: Writing a Spiritual Autobiography, by Dan Wakefield.

3. Derrick Jensen, *Listening to the Land: Conversations about Nature, Culture and Eros* (White River Junction: Chelsea Green Publishing, 2004), 198–200.
4. Ibid.
5. Jane Poynter's 16-minute talk, "Life in Biosphere 2," can be viewed online at TED. com: www.ted.com/talks/jane_poynter_life_in_biosphere_2.html.
6. Mary Evelyn Tucker, *Worldly Wonder: Religions Enter Their Ecological Phase* (Peru, IL: Carus Publishing, 2003), 108.
7. Richard Louv, *The Nature Principle: Human Restoration and the End of Nature* (Chapel Hill: Algonquin Books, 2013), 9 (Kindle edition).
8. Sue Monk Kidd, *When the Heart Waits, Spiritual Direction for Life's Sacred Question* (San Francisco: Harper and Row, 1990).
9. John Shea, *Stories of God: An Unauthorized Biography* (Chicago: Thomas More Press, 1978), quoted in Kidd, *When the Heart Waits.*
10. Nicholas Kristof, "Food for the Soul," *New York Times,* August 22, 2009.
11. From the foreword by Dr. Ehrenfried Pfeiffer to Rudolf Steiner, *Agriculture Course: The Birth of the Bio-Dynamic Method* (London: Rudolf Steiner Press, 1958, reprinted 2004).
12. Wendell Berry, *The Gift of Good Land* (San Francisco: North Point Press, 1981), 281.
13. Aldo Leopold, *A Sand County Almanac: With Essays on Conservation from Round River* (New York: Random House, 1966), 189–90.
14. The Findhorn Community, *The Findhorn Garden: Pioneering a New Vision of Man and Nature in Cooperation* (New York: Harper and Row, 1975), 2–3.
15. Peter Tompkins, *The Secret Life of Plants,* "Findhorn and the Garden of Eden," 361–73.
16. The Findhorn Community, *The Findhorn Garden,* 13.
17. The Findhorn Community, *The Findhorn Garden Story* (Findhorn, United Kingdom: Findhorn Press, 2008), 23.
18. Quote from Jonathan Dawson, Global Ecovillage Network in *Findhorn Now,* video by the Findhorn Foundation, 2008: www.findhorn.org/aboutus/video/findhorn -now/.UmsCUCSrvmE.
19. William Irvin Thompson, from the foreword to *The Findhorn Garden.*
20. Opening comments at training for new Climate Leaders by The Climate Reality Project founder and leader, Al Gore, Hyatt Regency Hotel, August 29, 2012, Burlingame, California.
21. Suzuki, *The Sacred Balance,* 209.
22. Jensen, *Listening to the Land,* 76.

Chapter 6: The Alchemy of Action

1. David Suzuki, *The Sacred Balance: Rediscovering Our Place in Nature* (New York: Prometheus Books, 1998), 76.

2. Toby Hemenway, *Gaia's Garden: A Guide to Home-Scale Permaculture* (White River Junction, VT: Chelsea Green, 2000), 5.

3. Peter Tompkins and Christopher Bird, *The Secret Life of Plants* (New York: Harper and Row, 1973), xiii.

4. Andrew Kimbrell, *Your Right to Know: Genetic Engineering and the Secret Changes in Your Food* (San Rafael, CA: Earth Aware Books, 2007).

5. Collin Dunn, "Vermicomposting and Vermiculture: Worms, Bins and How to Get Started," *Treehugger,* August 2, 2007. www.treehugger.com/green-food /vermicomposting-and-vermiculture-worms-bins-and-how-to-get-started.html.

6. "Solving the Diaper Dilemma," *Green America,* January/February 2003. www.greenamerica.org/livinggreen/diapers.cfm.

7. For more information, see www.storyofbottledwater.org and www.foodandwater watch.org/water/bottled.

8. *Hemp for Victory:* www.youtube.com/watch?v=jokV8xlJTNE&feature=player _embedded; and *When We Grow, This Is What We Can Do:* www.youtube.com /watch?v=PSKJrgGqx_E.

9. Suzanne Goldenberg, "Al Gore says Obama must veto 'atrocity' of Keystone XL tar sands pipeline," *Guardian,* June 15, 2013. www.guardian.co.uk/environment/2013 /jun/15/al-gore-obama-keystone-pipeline?CMP=twt_gu.

10. From Tim DeChristopher's speech at his sentencing, www.peacefuluprising.org /tims-official-statement-at-his-sentencing-hearing-20110726.

11. From a lecture Richard Tarnas gave in Chicago, Illinois, October 3, 2009.

Index

Acknowledgments

At the end of the day, so much of what gets any book out the door is the support and love that comes from others. In that spirit, we have a lot of people to thank, both together and separately. Our deepest love and gratitude go to John and Miles Gunter and Gregory Bembry. These were dark and difficult issues to wrestle with day in and day out for more than six years, but the love and patience with which they sustained us kept this book breathing and moving forward.

Our dear friend Caroline Myss gave selflessly of her time as *Earth Calling* progressed from an evolving idea to the book you hold in your hands. Her friendship, wisdom, and patience were steadfast through even the most challenging times. This book owes much of its life to her encouragement and generosity of spirit. Her foreword is one of her many gifts to us.

Our mutual friend Andrew Harvey read every chapter and directed us toward a wide body of literature that supported our claims about earth stewardship in both Eastern and Western religious traditions. Thank you, Andrew, for that and for your generosity in making our book part of your Sacred Activism series.

Endless gratitude to Julie and Patrick Flaherty, who midwifed

Earth Calling's very birth; there's a bit of you on every page. To Jan and Jim Gunter, family Katrina survivors, many thanks for reviewing the chapter about Hurricane Katrina.

Much gratitude to CMED's co-founder, David Smith, for his encouragement and support, and to the wise Lench Archuleta, who has taught us so much about the earth. Thanks to the dozens of our wonderful CMED friends and classmates for their encouraging words and deeds through the years.

A huge thanks to the fantastic editing team at North Atlantic: Louis Swaim, Emily Boyd, and Jennifer Eastman, who expertly combed every page, providing careful and cogent changes and saving us from many cringe-worthy moments. And to the wonderful eyes and energy of friends who gave this effort one last shove: Jill Angelo, Cheryl Rogers and Ina Warren.

Ellen's personal thanks: A special thanks goes to my spiritual director, Jim Curtan, who helped inspire me to write this book through the deep and revealing work I did with him. There's no one like you, Jim. For Harriet Salinger, my dear friend and classmate in spiritual direction training in Los Angeles, thanks for your patient wisdom and validation.

Much love to my family for their support, love, and appreciation over the years: my brothers, John and David Sylvester, sisters, Deb Sylvester and Suzanne Alexander, and cousins, Jeannie Schultz, Bev House, and Victoria Davenport.

Thank you to long-time Texas friends for being patient as I "went dark" for so long, the many sisters and brothers of my heart and soul: Susan Clark, Cecilia Galbraith, Julia Callaway, Margaret Ryan, Margie Bowles, John Clark, Joe Madden, Jay Setliff, Charlie and Marcia Smith, Ted Debosier, Dennis Luczycki, Dotty Umphress and Diane Tucker.

Thanks as well to the dozens of people from the Climate Reality Project I've met, trained, and mentored with. Their depth of knowledge and commitment to teaching others about what's happening to our planet have stunned, nourished, and inspired me. They have no equal. Thanks also to 350.org and Tar Sands Action for teaching me the impact of simple action during the late summer of 2011, when hundreds of us were arrested protesting the Keystone XL pipeline.

Eternal gratitude to precious friends who stood by me when my beloved husband John died unexpectedly near the end of 2013, especially Bronwyn Boyle, Tracy Barrett, Terrie Crowley, Lorena Williams, Caroline Myss and Uwe and Linda Hirschberg, for their loving, generous hearts. And to my son Miles, who became my rock, no words suffice.

Lastly, I want to thank my partner in this endeavor, Ted Carter. His steadfastness, unquestioning support, quiet patience, and uncanny sense of how the invisible world of nature works was an essential lifeline for me. We encountered endless sobering truths, but we also found wonders together and so many good-hearted, courageous souls who love this planet we live on and live without judging those who do not yet have the capacity to see with their clarity.

Ted's personal thanks: The people and experiences in our lives change us forever. The bravery and achievements of my daughter, Valeria, has always amazed me. Living and working in a war-torn foreign land is not an easy task, but she does all of it with style and grace. Gregory, my life partner, continually gives me the love and support one needs to succeed in this world. I have never met a kinder, more caring, and loving person. We disagree on many issues, but he helps me see more than just one side of a given situation. My siblings—Abby, Mike, and Doug—and their spouses and wonderful children continue to amaze and delight me. Special thanks to my parents, Julie and Bob Carter, for the gift of being allowed to be myself. During my summers as a child I remember a large dump-truck load of sand being delivered to our back yard, followed two hours later by a load of bricks. I played with my brother Mike and neighborhood friends creating entire neighborhoods with streets and landscaped yards. We happily hand-sculpted brick houses, walkways, and driveways into the sand. Twigs and broken branches placed upright in the sand became the village trees. With a garden hose, we made lakes and streams. It fascinated me to see the sand move and shift as water poured through our villages, undermining our brick structures. Houses were always giving way to the endless cycle of destruction and rebirth. This was how I began to see the earth from different perspectives.

Many years later I was gazing down from thirty-five thousand feet on the earth below on a flight to California, on my way to a three-day workshop with Caroline Myss. I sat marveling at the ancient, wrinkled whorls below me, at how a stretch of land could remind me of the thick, crinkly hide of an elephant. As I watched, I became aware of a subtle shift in my perception, as if time stood still. The Earth spoke to me—not with words, but rather a sense of connection, like an open channel. She was bereft. "I am so tired," she said. "No one hears me anymore, no one understands me."

I found myself weeping for the loss of our sacred connection with her and how we have grown numb to her pain. At some point I snapped back into my seat and wiped my face in utter embarrassment, hoping no one had seen me. The seats around me were nearly empty, but a young Native American woman across the aisle was looking at me, smiling.

"Were you speaking to the earth?" she asked. Struck speechless with surprise, I could only nod. She added, "She hears you." As we began to talk, it turned out that she, too, had experienced such dialogues with the earth. We parted in the airport in Oakland, California, and I have never seen her since, but the experience haunted me. That flight was the beginning of the weekend that marked my first time seeing Caroline teach and my initiation into learning about dimensions of the human spirit that had been completely out of my vocabulary. I could never have guessed then that I would attend years of classes at her institute and travel to distant, sacred places with her and fellow classmates, or how the people I met during those years would shape and change my life forever.

One of those people was Ellen Gunter. My dear friend Jim Curtan said to me one time, "Ted, there are people in this lifetime that you climb hills with, and then there are people you climb mountains with—Ellen climbs mountains." I never doubted this for a minute. Ellen worked tirelessly for six years as we pulled this book together. She is a gifted writer with amazing foresight and vision. It has been a privilege and an honor to work by her side.

About the Authors

ELLEN GUNTER is a journalist, spiritual director, and climate, activist who lectures and writes about the connections between spirituality, the environment, and climate change. She also delivers the updated slideshow from *An Inconvenient Truth* for Al Gore's Climate Reality Project.

Blog: ellengunter.com
Twitter: @ellengunter
Facebook: Ellen Gunter and Earth Calling

TED CARTER has been designing earth-centric landscapes along the northeast coast for more than thirty years. His award-winning work has been featured in local and national publications.

Website: TedCarterLandscapes.com
Twitter: @TedBCarter
Facebook: Ted Carter and TedCarterLandscapes
LinkedIn: Ted Carter

Heart in Action

Sacred Activism Series Titles

When the joy of compassionate service is combined with the pragmatic drive to transform all existing economic, social, and political institutions, a radical divine force is born: Sacred Activism. The Sacred Activism Series, published by North Atlantic Books, presents leading voices that embody the tenets of Sacred Activism—compassion, service, and sacred consciousness—while addressing the crucial issues of our time and inspiring radical action.

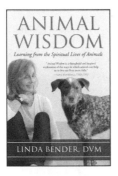

Animal Wisdom
Linda Bender, DVM

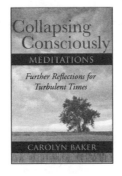

Collapsing Consciously Meditations
Carolyn Baker

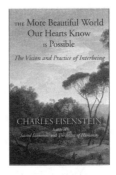

The More Beautiful World Our Hearts Know Is Possible
Charles Eisenstein

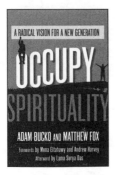

Occupy Spirituality
Adam Bucko and Matthew Fox

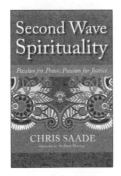

Second Wave Spirituality
Chris Saade

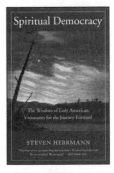

Spiritual Democracy
Steven Herrmann
OCTOBER, 2014

For more information about the Sacred Activism series, go to:
www.nabcommunities.com/sacredactivism

North Atlantic Books
Berkeley, California

Personal, spiritual, and planetary transformation

North Atlantic Books, a nonprofit publisher established in 1974, is dedicated to fostering community, education, and constructive dialogue. NABCommunities.com is a meeting place for an ever-growing membership of readers and authors to engage in the discussion of books and topics from North Atlantic's core publishing categories.

NAB Communities offer interactive social networks in these genres:

NOURISH: Raw Foods, Healthy Eating and Nutrition, All-Natural Recipes

WELLNESS: Holistic Health, Bodywork, Healing Therapies

WISDOM: New Consciousness, Spirituality, Self-Improvement

CULTURE: Literary Arts, Social Sciences, Lifestyle

BLUE SNAKE: Martial Arts History, Fighting Philosophy, Technique

Your free membership gives you access to:

Advance notice about new titles and exclusive giveaways

Podcasts, webinars, and events

Discussion forums

Polls, quizzes, and more!

Go to www.NABCommunities.com and join today.